The Merrymount Press
1893–1949

NOTES

On the Merrymount Press & its Work

By Daniel Berkeley Updike

With a Bibliographical List of Books
printed at the Press
1893–1933
By Julian Pearce Smith

to which has been added

A Supplementary Bibliography of Books
printed at the Press
1934–1949
By Daniel Berkeley Bianchi

With Views of the Press at Various Periods
Specimens of Types alluded to
&c. &c. &c.

San Francisco
Alan Wofsy Fine Arts
1975

ISBN No. 0-915346-10-9
Library of Congress No. 75-28553

This edition, limited to five hundred copies,
has been published in 1975 by

ALAN WOFSY FINE ARTS
150 Green Street
San Francisco, CA 94111

The major portion of this volume entitled
"Notes on the Merrymount Press & its Work
by Daniel Berkeley Updike with a Bibliographical List of Books printed at the Press
1893–1933 by Julian Pearce Smith" was originally published by Harvard University Press.

Preface

*This book owes its existence to Mr. Julian Pearce Smith,
of New York, who some years ago undertook to catalogue
the numerous Merrymount Press imprints in his collection. At first he intended it to be merely a check-list of
his own books, but as, if a list was to be made at all, it
appeared desirable to have it as complete as possible, we
filled in titles of volumes that Mr. Smith did not own
from "file copies" in the library of the Press—this work
being done by Mr. Lester Frey, one of our own force.
When completed, further bibliographical details seemed to
be desirable, and so every book printed here was compared
anew by Mr. D. B. Bianchi. Many of the books listed are
of very slight merit or interest typographically—though
they must be judged by the standards of their period—
but as the object was to make the list complete, all have
been included. Thus Mr. Smith's brief check-list has grown
into the present catalogue, and what was never originally
contemplated in the end came to pass.*

*It was not at first planned to print anything more than
the bibliography; but when this was finished it appeared
to call for some description of the more notable books enu-
merated therein. This in turn seemed to involve some ex-
planation of how the Press came into being; and as (un-
happily for me) I knew more about that than anyone else,
the Notes introducing the bibliography were added—an
example of the saying that prefatory matter is always*

Preface

the last thing to be written! So this volume, like many things in life—in fact, like the Press itself—is the result of a series of accidental compulsions. As no friends have "urged me" to print this book, I have not "reluctantly consented"; so I am happily enabled to avoid what Saint-Simon calls "le jargon de préface."

D. B. U.

Note to the Supplementary Bibliography
1934–1949

The Supplementary Bibliography which has been added to this volume spans the period beginning with 1934 and ending in February 1949 when the operation of the Press ceased. Until December 31, 1941, the work was produced through the joint efforts of Mr. Updike and John Bianchi. Following Mr. Updike's death on that date, it was solely the product of Mr. Bianchi's hand.

The supplementary list is intended to complete the record of the output of the Press for students of printing and others. The major work of compilation was undertaken just prior to the closing of the Press. Since that time little has been done to apply the final touches until retirement from active work permitted an opportunity to devote the required attention to various details.

In arrangement, the Supplement follows the style of the Smith Bibliography. Some departure in type face has been necessitated by the unavailability of the hand-set Stempel Janson used in the earlier volume. Monotype Janson has been employed for the Supplement and special preliminary pages as well as for the added Annual Keepsakes, as being the best presently available substitute. For the earlier volume, all type was specially cast by the Press.

The list is complete, so far as I know, except for the following omissions which I have been unable to locate:

1941   The Book of Remembrance for the Church of the Advent, Boston. One copy printed for the late Lawrence Coolidge

1942   The Woodland Book. Composition and presswork

Note

only by the Press. Printed in two colors. Work done
for Howell Soskin, New York

1946   St. Peter's Church, Albany, N.Y. Book of Memorials.
One copy printed for The Reverend Erville B.
Maynard

The Chrysanthemum and the Sword by Ruth Benedict.
Composition and plates only by the Press. Work done
for The Riverside Press

The Merry Adventures of Robin Hood by Howard
Pyle. Composition and plates only by the Press. Work
done for Charles Scribner's Sons

*I have added hitherto unpublished photographs of the Messrs.
Updike and Bianchi at the front in the hope that these may add
some further interest to a final bit of history of the Press.*

*I am indebted to Miss Selma Ordewer for invaluable as-
sistance in the preparation of the manuscript for composition,
for help in reading proof and in preparing the final copy
for camera.*

D.B.B.

Bridgewater, Connecticut
July 1975

[viii]

Contents

D. B. UPDIKE IN HIS MID-TWENTIES

JOHN BIANCHI IN HIS EARLY THIRTIES

List of Views of the Press

Notes on the Press
&
its Work

Notes on the Press and its Work

BY DANIEL BERKELEY UPDIKE

PRINTING became the occupation of my life by pure accident. Books, as literature, have been familiar to me as long as I can remember, for my mother, a woman of very remarkable intellectual powers who knew thoroughly both English and French literature, trained my taste in reading; but I knew nothing about how books were printed or put together. However, an experience that occurred after my father's death in 1878 familiarized me with the outside and inside of many volumes I should never have known about otherwise. This was a winter passed as an assistant at the Providence Athenaeum, when the librarian, being invalided, asked me to relieve him by taking some hours of duty there each day. I had access also to the interesting but then crowded library of Brown University; and when in Newport I spent many hours among the books at the Redwood Library. All this was done without any particular aim. How the books were made never interested me; least of all did it occur to me that I should ever make books myself. But this substratum of familiarity with books of all sorts, their appearance, titles, contents, stood me later in good stead. My mother, who was a thorough student, was impatient at my miscellaneous and ineffective browsings. "You are not a scholar," she used to say. "You do not love to learn as I do." Nor did I love to learn. I was unhappy at school, and as I look back upon it I had reason to be. The only thing I ever got there was a deepened religious sense, for the master, an Episcopal clergyman of real "Evangelical" piety, in the short daily morning talks before lessons began, made an impression that I have never forgotten. Eagerness for knowledge about things I wanted to know was not lack-

The Merrymount Press

ing, but most of the knowledge imparted did not concern the things I wanted to know about. One scar inflicted on me has never been effaced—nor forgiven. On the last Friday of each month a torturing hour was devoted to an exercise called "declamation." I was paralyzed by the necessity of speaking in public, not so much because I feared to speak as because I could put nothing into the dreary selected "pieces" I was set to declaim. Such was my dread of these occasions that by the time the fateful Friday arrived I was ill with apprehension. I trace to these oratorical forced marches a lifelong inability to address with ease any assemblage large enough to be considered an audience. By inheritance I ought to have had some capacity in this direction, for my father and my grandfather were both effective speakers. The latter constantly spoke on public questions and was for many years a factor to be reckoned with in the General Assembly, and my father was presiding officer of the Rhode Island House of Representatives during the first two years of the Civil War.

The temporary employment at the Providence Athenaeum of which I have spoken became more regular on the death of the librarian, and I held for a few months the place of assistant to the librarian *pro tempore* until the election of a new librarian-in-chief. Then came the question: what next was I to do? Some members of my family proposed a position in a bank, being ignorant or forgetful of the fact that I could not then (nor now) readily add a simple column of figures. Having made this "gesture," and having met with a refusal—which may be numbered among the few wise decisions of a long life—they washed their hands of the matter and me. College was impossible in the state of our affairs and although I ostensibly regretted this, my previous experience of education was so little alluring that I privately counted necessity a virtue.

Notes on its Work

But in the spring of 1880 this lull was broken by a telegram from a cousin* in Boston: "A place is open for you with Houghton, Mifflin & Company." I replied that I would take the position, and the next day I left Providence for the city where I have lived ever since. The place I was given was that of errand boy—I was told that everyone began there in that way, and I certainly did. The firm had been driven by a fire from its quarters in Park Street and occupied some dreary temporary offices in Franklin Street, near Hawley. The installation was provisional, and as uncomfortable and inconvenient as provisional installations generally are. The *personnel* of the office was unattractive, the hours were long, the duties new and wearisome. Later a return was made to Park Street. But by summer I was so tired that at the end of a two weeks' holiday, after much searching of heart, I gave up the place. Four days later a letter arrived. The firm was so pleased with my efforts and saw in me (God knows why!) so much promise that I could return on shorter time. That was enough to arouse an already uneasy conscience.

The Park Street offices to which I returned were in a pleasant old house formerly belonging to the Quincy family, fronting the Common, with back windows giving on the Granary Burying-ground. Park Street was still residential, and this situation was an improvement over the Franklin Street quarters. At first my work was much the same. After a time, however, my occupations became a bit more congenial. I began to help the advertising manager in small ways, and was deputed to look through the endless newspapers that came to the firm for notices of its books. It does not seem as if

---

*Miss Elizabeth Bigelow Greene, a pupil of William Hunt, and still remembered by the older generation of Bostonians as an able flower painter, as well as for her unusual and charming personality. For many years she shared a studio in Mt. Vernon Street with a lifelong friend, Miss Elizabeth Bartol.

[5]

The Merrymount Press

this occupation could have any bearing on my future work as a printer, but it did; for my eye became so trained to the kinds of types employed in the press of the country that I was able to tell at sight from what paper an extract had been cut. My next step was to prepare "copy" for advertisements and, after a while, to direct how it was to be set up; and this led to making up material for catalogues and revising those already made, and trying to put into them some uniformity of arrangement and harmony of style. The havoc that I created for the compositors and the expense I caused the firm did not occur to me, for since I had never seen type and did not know how it was set (no one thinking it worth while to instruct me), I treated it as if it were made of india-rubber. What those extra corrections must have cost the establishment I have never cared to contemplate.

My expensive performances in this direction arose chiefly from a love of order. The only event I recall that had any effect upon my typographic efforts was an exhibition of early books and manuscripts held by Quaritch of London at the old Tremont House. I visited this exhibition several times and in my work for the firm tried to imitate in a modern way some of the early printing displayed, and, as I look back upon it, anticipated by some years the essays of people who had a definite objective and really knew what they were about. In those days knowledge now commonplace enough was not available, nor were axioms current on unity of style and "rhythm, balance, and colour"—terms which I yet but dimly understand, but evidences of which (I am told by those who know) are often artlessly exhibited in my own work.

I was in the employ of Houghton, Mifflin & Company for twelve years, broken by one short and one long and delightful stay abroad. My interest in typography was even then so slight that I troubled myself little to see fine books when in

[6]

Notes on its Work

great centres, or to visit places where good books could be seen. My aim seems to have been *not* to know about printing, but to forget a work that had been so full of drudgery. On my return from my second journey, which lasted a year, and the most interesting parts of which my mother and I passed in Morocco, Spain, and Italy, I began to be treated as a person who had taste in typographical arrangement—a fact which never would have been discovered if after my departure the work I had been accustomed to do had not shown a sudden slump. Instead, however, of making better terms before returning, I went back to Park Street at my inadequate salary and received compliments instead of the dollars I so much needed. But the return was depressing.

And yet the experience of those years—too long drawn out though they were—was not fruitless. I made in Park Street some lasting friends: Mr. Francis Garrison, with whose opinions I wholly disagreed and whose character I as wholeheartedly admired; Miss Susan Francis, assistant editor of *The Atlantic Monthly*, upon whose efforts a succession of often indolent editors depended for the impeccable scholarship of the magazine; Dr. Abner Post, of the *Medical and Surgical Journal*, which was published there; and many other interesting people—Mr. Howells, Miss Sarah Orne Jewett, Mrs. Fields, Mrs. Bell, Mrs. Whitman, and Mr. Aldrich. In my position I naturally met Dr. Holmes, Mr. Lowell, Mr. Longfellow, Mrs. Stowe; and I remember Miss Ellen Emerson conducting her father to a desk whereon lay a visitors' book in which the old man tremulously signed his name. Aldrich, then editor of *The Atlantic Monthly*, had an office next to mine. His talk was a constant firework of witticisms. I remember how he confused the man on the Common who, for a consideration, permitted one to peep through his telescope, by asking him seriously: "Is Venus naked to the visible eye?"

[7]

The Merrymount Press

Mr. Houghton and Mr. Mifflin both had a sincere desire for excellence in book-making. Mr. Houghton, the senior partner, was a Vermont man, and his character had in it much of "the strength of the hills," though I did not perceive it then. His taste typographically was of the sixties, and it was a sound taste of its kind. He had travelled abroad and had met printers like-minded with himself — I remember a line in one of his letters: "The people of Holland are industrious and happy," which was received by the stay-at-homes with derisive smiles. To me his manner appeared somewhat hectoring, and perhaps I had, unconsciously, the power of irritating him. But a gruff and sometimes rasping speech concealed a tender heart for those in trouble, especially if they were old associates or former workpeople. I have seen tears in his eyes as he parted from some old friend less fortunate in life than himself who had come to ask aid, and who was never sent empty away. Mr. Mifflin, of a different outlook on the world, was equally earnest in his wish that the firm publish good and well-made books. To both men a new publication was an event, and they could talk of nothing else until the next publication day with its new books arrived. In particular I remember Mr. Houghton's pride in a new issue of Webster's Dictionary. Everyone who came to Park Street was told of the Dictionary, shown the Dictionary, and — if possible — made to praise the Dictionary. One day Mr. Edwin Whipple arrived. Mr. Houghton showed him the volume, and gently leading the conversation in the direction of further commendation, asked: "Mr. Whipple, when you don't know the meaning of a word, what do you do?" "Well," said Mr. Whipple meditatively, "I generally use another word."

It was a tradition of the establishment that no one — unless for grave cause — was ever dismissed. Accordingly, when persons were not agreeable to those in authority, the tactic

[8]

Notes on its Work

of Louis XIV was adopted whereby it was signified to un-
congenial courtiers or those who would not "court" that retirement to a distance from Versailles would be appreciated.
There in retirement they languished. Something like that
happened to me, though for a quite different reason. The work
I was beginning to do with efficiency I could do better under
Mr. Mifflin's eye at the Riverside Press than in Boston, and so
it was thought best that I should be sent to Cambridge. I was
sent there, and I, personally, languished to such an extent that
after two years of it I decided it was not worth while to lan-
guish more. Meanwhile I had, in an inadequate and half-
hearted fashion, learned to set type or, more accurately, learned
how it was set. And I then also learned how much time and
money I had wasted by not knowing this earlier.

In the summer of 1892, while still at the Riverside Press,
I was asked by the rector of Grace Church, New York, the
Rev. William Huntington, to help him and some colleagues
out of a difficulty. The 1892 revision of the Book of Common
Prayer had just been completed, and a "standard copy" on
vellum and an edition on paper had been handsomely printed
by Theodore De Vinne in his chilly but workmanlike style.
The idea unfortunately occurred to Dr. Huntington, Dr.
Doane, Bishop of Albany, and some others that a reissue might
be made of this Prayer Book from the existing plates, with
margins adorned with symbolic decorative borders. With
more haste than discretion they launched the scheme before
completing the arrangements for it; and a relative of a member of the committee was chosen to make designs "because
he could draw," without much consideration as to whether
he could draw what was wanted. When I saw the designs
submitted, I also saw the committee's dilemma. The offer of
a very decent sum was made if I would plan some general
scheme of decoration and select a competent designer. I de-

[9]

The Merrymount Press

clined. The offer was doubled. I reluctantly accepted it, and chose Bertram Goodhue to make a series of borders based on the *Benedicite omnia opera*, for which I picked out appropriate texts. In these decorations Goodhue's line was very far from De Vinne's typography, and I fancy it was a painful task for the latter to reprint his uninspired but dignified book with the *appliques* so continuously, unremittingly (and sometimes unwillingly), supplied by Goodhue and myself. I remember that we begged those in authority to be allowed to omit borders on the Gospel for Good Friday; but this could not be. The borders were to go on *every* page — so the committee had promised — and on every page they accordingly went. The best things about the book were the cover and charming end-papers which Goodhue designed for it. Sad to relate, the edition had an immediate and astounding success! We were congratulated, and we blushed. Our shame was taken for modesty and we were congratulated more! While the book is indeed a strange one, it is by no means so strange as the designs originally made for it. These I preserved until lately as *pièces justificatives* for a performance about which Goodhue and I often exchanged "the augur's wink."

The time spent at the Riverside Press had convinced me that I must do something on my own lines, and through a commission to print an Altar Book, which my old friend the late Harold Brown of Rhode Island stood ready to finance, the opportunity was offered.* Had I not had this definite work

---

* This book I describe on a later page. Mr. Brown and I had already co-operated in the production of a book entitled: *On the Dedications of American Churches. An Enquiry into the Naming of Churches in the United States, some Account of English Dedications, and Suggestions for future Dedications in the American Church. Compiled by Two Laymen of the Diocese of Rhode Island.* This was printed under my direction at the Riverside Press in 1891 while I was still employed there. Neither Mr. Brown nor I had much in common with American Protestantism, and his position theologically was Tractarian or, as it would now be called, Anglo-Catholic, as mine has continued to be.

Notes on its Work

to do I should not have had the courage to leave my position there. Although I did not then know it, I was starting at a fortunate moment. The repercussion of Mr. Morris's work at the Kelmscott Press was greatly felt in New England. The printing of forty years ago, is, to quote a friend's words, "just old enough to awaken reminiscences." "What days those were," he adds, "when we first began to realize that beauty could become, even in New England, an integral part of life. What names rush to our minds: Bertram Goodhue, Will Bradley, Carl Heintzemann, Copeland & Day, and dozens of other brave companions from the time when to be young was very heaven, and we all were young!"* With all these men I was acquainted, but Goodhue was the only one I knew well. The best and most consistent printing of that time was done at the instance of Mr. F. H. Day and his partner Herbert Copeland. What they printed was little to my taste, for there was about their performances a certain conscious pose of the kind that made Lord Minto say at the soulful house party: "I hate clever people—they're so damned silly." But their books were the best of that period.

When I left the Riverside Press in 1893, Mr. Mifflin, who liked my work and had come to trust my judgment, was considerably disappointed, and did not conceal his impatience with my projects; but later our happy relations were resumed, and I always saw him once or twice a year as long as he lived. On these occasions he always said the same words, meant as a compliment. "You know," he would exclaim, "I can only

* Mr. David Pottinger, of the Harvard University Press, in an article in the *Boston Transcript*, March 14, 1931. Of the many articles about the Merrymount Press perhaps the most notable are those in the *London Times*, Printing Number of 1912; in Volume III of *The Fleuron*, London, 1924, by Mr. W. A. Dwiggins; Mr. G. P. Winship's notice in the volume entitled *The Merrymount Press of Boston*, published by Herbert Reichner, Vienna, in 1929; and the paper above quoted by Mr. Pottinger. There is also a very good account of its work in the Encyclopaedia Britannica, under "Books."

The Merrymount Press

say that I think your success *Perfectly Remarkable!* " He was probably right. As I look back upon it, the venture must have seemed to my elders and betters a desperately silly enterprise, and they were quite correct in estimating my valour as ignorance. I required capital and had little; comprehension of my own trade, of which I had less; and business experience, of which I had none at all. I had no equipment whatever when I began work on my own account. My innocence was such that I thought I could obtain orders and have other printers undertake the composition and press-work at my direction; and to differentiate myself from wiser colleagues, I announced — for a short time — that I undertook "decorative printing." The result was that though other printers did my work they charged the prices ordinarily charged to a customer and I had to make what profit I could over and above that. Thus my prices were higher than those of other printers, and higher than was warranted by any betterment I could give the work; and when my results appeared an improvement on current typography, the printers whom I employed copied the feeble thing they called my "style" with varying degrees of success. So I was forced to invest, most unwillingly, in a small amount of type and ornaments, and by this tortuous path I arrived where most printers begin! Perhaps the reason that I survived, in spite of mistakes, was that a simple idea had got hold of me — to make work better for its purpose than was commonly thought worth while, and by having one's own establishment to be free to do so.

The first quarters occupied by the Press consisted of two connecting rooms on the upper floor of a building at the corner of Beacon Street and Tremont Place. These rooms, which were lofty of stud, had been formerly occupied by an architect, who had installed a tasteful wooden mantel-piece and a hearth on which it was possible to light a fire. The narrow

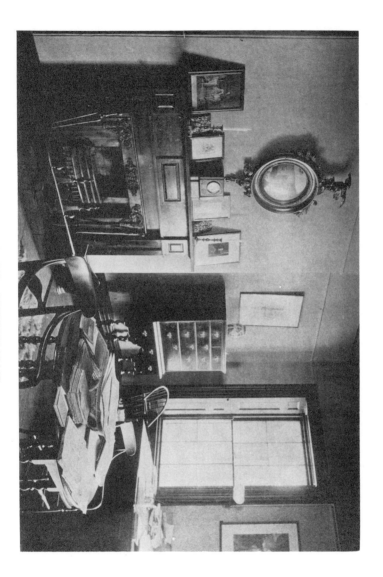

GENERAL OFFICE, 7 TREMONT PLACE

Notes on its Work

windows, lofty ceilings, and hardwood floor made a good background for some pieces of old furniture, which presented a much better effect than the office equipment of that day. The back room, looking out on an angle of the Boston Athenaeum, was occupied by Mr. J. E. Hill, who did much of the designing of ornament which I required, as well as work on his own account.

The first book printed under my supervision was a volume of selections for each day in the year, compiled by Lucy Bradlee Stone, under the title *Vexilla Regis Quotidie*. The Riverside Press was responsible for the composition and presswork, but the arrangement of the little volume was mine. Originally privately printed, it became by the printing of a second edition in 1895 the first book bearing my name as publisher. It was set in a "modernized old style" type.

Several other books were printed while the Altar Book was being planned and produced, and before any varied stock of type was acquired. Perhaps the best one was *The Hazard Family of Rhode Island, 1635–1894*, a genealogical book by Caroline Robinson, the expense of production of which was borne by her sister, Sarah Rodman Woodward. This book, issued in 1895, was very carefully schemed and was set up by that conscientious and thorough craftsman, the late Carl Heintzemann of Boston. Its decorations were redrawn from the fine series used by the eighteenth-century London printer Boywer — ornaments among the best of their kind, and splendidly used in some of his folios. These embellishments, with strips of Caslon "flowers," were combined in a quarto book set in various sizes of Caslon type.

After a stock of type was acquired, the first volume set up by us was *The Governor's Garden*, by George R. R. Rivers, a romance based on the life of Governor Hutchinson and his house at Milton. I was familiar with this place, which be-

The Merrymount Press

longed to the author's aunt, Miss Rose Russell, and the garden with its arbours and pleached alleys remained much as the Governor had left it. It occurred to me to illustrate the book with a series of fictitious silhouettes representing the characters of the story. The headpieces, each one different but all made up of combinations of but two Caslon "units," were the clever arrangement of Mr. John Bianchi, then foreman of our composing-room. What I remember chiefly, however, is the small amount of type I had with which to print, and the patience of the author under the consequent delay. The "period business" is perhaps a bit overdone for the reader's comfort, but its format attracted considerable attention when the book came out in 1896.

The same year saw the second of my few publishing ventures, in Hans Andersen's *The Nightingale*, cleverly illustrated by Mary Newill of the then popular Birmingham Guild of Handicraft, for whose short-lived magazine *The Quest* we also were agents. My old friend the late Edward Hort New of Oxford contributed some charming illustrations to that periodical, as did Gere, Gaskin, Miss Newill, and others. And in the same year the Altar Book appeared.

It was largely the dissatisfaction felt with the "decorated" Prayer Book that suggested the publication of this volume, and Mr. Brown, who was of my way of thinking in such matters, stood ready to back the undertaking. His stipulations were that the book should be as fine a piece of work as I could make it, and that while strictly conforming to the text of those parts of the Book of Common Prayer containing the altar services, it should yet fall in line with missals of an older period. When musical notation is introduced, the canon law of the Episcopal Church allows a departure from the uniformity required for all service books without music. Accordingly a few notes of plain-song were placed before the col-

Notes on its Work

lect for the First Sunday in Advent, with which the book opened. Thus the book was strictly canonical, and having received the authorization of the Rev. Samuel Hart, the registrar of the Book of Common Prayer, we were able to place " By Authority" on the title-page. Dr. Huntington, when he saw the volume (which he did not much like), exclaimed: "'By Authority'! We must look into that!" But as when he looked he found nothing to see, we heard no more about it.

To enumerate the difficulties met with at that period in obtaining what is now easily available would take longer to tell than is here desirable. It is enough to say that after various essays a type was designed for the book by Bertram Goodhue, who also drew the borders and initials — no two of the latter exactly alike — the illustrations being by Anning Bell. The amount of work the undertaking involved was increased by the difficulty in obtaining hand-made paper, in cutting the type, and by various troublesome details. And when the type was designed and cast a separate workshop had to be found where it and a hand-press could be installed and a proof-reader could work. For this purpose an office at the corner of Aldine Street and Estes Place, near the South Station, was rented, and there, through a hot summer, the work was carried on. The press-work was placed with DeVinne, who turned out a magnificent piece of work, although he was frankly out of sympathy with the style of the volume. Begun in 1893, the book was finished at Easter, 1896.

Whatever satisfaction I might have taken in its completion was destroyed by my mother's sudden illness and death, which seemed to deprive me of any incentive to continue along the path on which I had set out. Probably I should not have gone on if I had not already had the nucleus of a tiny organization. When at the Riverside Press I had made the acquaintance of Mr. Anselmo Bianchi, and when I started for

[15]

The Merrymount Press

myself I asked him to join me. This he could not do, since he was bound by an indenture for a certain period of service there, but he suggested his brother as a man suitable for the place. It thus came to pass that John Bianchi came to the Press. He was later joined by his brother Anselmo, who remained with us for several years, finally returning to the Riverside Press in a position which he has developed into an important one. Miss Ellen Powers, also a former employee of Houghton, Mifflin & Company, was acting as proof-reader and accountant at that time. To the loyalty, patience, and confidence of these three, and to friends who supplied work to do, the Press owes its existence in those early and difficult years. In looking back one realizes the truth of Emerson's phrase: "Every man's task is his life preserver."

The following summer I passed abroad. In London I visited Kelmscott House, where I was kindly received by Mr. Cockerell. This was shortly after Mr. Morris's death, and the London Society of Arts and Crafts was at the moment holding an exhibition where the Kelmscott books were magnificently displayed. I remember making some rather ineffective researches at the British Museum, and there meeting Mr. Alfred Pollard; our first contact with the Caslon house was also made at this time. Between this date and 1914 I made several other foreign journeys, but as I travelled chiefly in Spain and places somewhat remote from printing interests these have little to do with this narrative. I did, however, go to Parma on one of these journeys and saw the splendid collection of Bodoni's books preserved in the library there, and I also went to Mainz and Leipzig. And on my last foreign journey I visited the Plantin Museum at Antwerp, partly because I was so tired of saying "No" when anyone asked if I had seen it. I doubt if visits to homes of great and good printing amount to much except from the sentimental point of view. To my mind, a

PRIVATE OFFICE, 104 CHESTNUT STREET

Notes on its Work

printer can learn more from a few visits to such an exhibition of printed books as is shown in the King's Library of the British Museum than by desultory wanderings to less well arranged and more distant collections.

Owing to the demolition of the Beacon Street building in 1896, the Press, so called, had to go elsewhere, and rooms were secured in a building round the corner, at 7 Tremont Place, in a house formerly, I believe, occupied by the Winthrop family. The ground floor was used by our landlords, Messrs. Ginn & Company, as a shop or shops, and we occupied the next floor, or "noble storey," consisting of two drawing-rooms connected by folding doors and a small side room occupied as a private office. The front room on Tremont Place covered the width of the house, and here a composing-room was installed; the back room, which commanded pleasant glimpses of the Granary Burying-ground, was the general office.

It was while occupying these quarters that I first met Mr. Bruce Rogers. I was already familiar with a book in which he had had a hand—*Notes on the Walters Collection*—so he needed no introduction. The splendid results of his eighteen years' work at the Riverside Press are known of all men. At that early period we saw much of each other, both in town and in country, for in summer I had a country house at Harvard, Massachusetts, where he, Cleland, and others were often visitors.

The further story of the Press, from this time on, is chiefly the history of such outstanding books as it has printed year by year, save for those years—and they were not uncommon—when nothing interesting is to be chronicled. A connection with the house of T. Y. Crowell & Co. of New York that lasted for a long period was inaugurated in 1897 by the appearance of a book, set in Clarendon type, called *What is*

The Merrymount Press

Worth While?, which in my absence abroad was planned by
Mr. John Bianchi. This book showed the influence of Mr.
Morris's ideas upon commercial work, and the long series of
similar 16mo volumes printed for this house followed the
general style of the first one, though with varying degrees of
success. The covers — rather tasteless affairs — were usually
supplied by the publishers, though this first book and *Ships and
Havens* had the advantage of a binding designed by Bertram
Goodhue. Our first use of Scotch-face type was made in
the same year for Messrs. Crowell & Co. in a little book by
Richard Le Gallienne entitled *If I were God*.

We remained at 7 Tremont Place only two years, for in
1898 another move became necessary when the whole row
of old houses had to make way for an office building. The
next situation for the Press was 104 Chestnut Street — commonly called (since those were the days of stables in that
neighbourhood) "Horse Chestnut Street." This house was
three storeys high, and had two large and two small rooms
to a floor. The composing-room was placed on the first floor,
the main office on the second at the back, my own office on
the same floor at the front, and a proof-readers' room in a
hall bedroom. Two views in this book show the library in
this modest Victorian dwelling-house. The third storey I at
first occupied as an apartment. Later on, in 1903, we utilized
the third storey as a proof-readers' room and added No. 102
Chestnut Street to No. 104, connecting the lower floors of
both houses and using them as a composing-room. The two
upper floors of No. 102 I moved into, this apartment being
completely separated from the Press.

In 1899 appeared under my imprint a book that had a family
interest, namely, a diary kept by my great-great-uncle, James
MacSparran, D.D., between the years 1743 and 1751. MacSparran was an Anglican missionary sent to Rhode Island from

ANOTHER VIEW OF PRIVATE OFFICE
CHESTNUT STREET

Notes on its Work

London by the Venerable Society for the Propagation of the Gospel in Foreign Parts. There he became rector of St. Paul's Church, Narragansett. His diary is a quaint affair recording the daily life of an American Parson Woodforde. In printing it I conformed to his manuscript—superior letters, odd spelling, and all. This volume was edited by the Rev. Daniel Goodwin, a former rector of the same church.

The Press has been fortunate in its friends, but never more so than in the friendship of Mrs. Wharton. I had known her before she wrote *The Greater Inclination*, her first book of short stories, and when the volume came to be published, in 1899, she stipulated with the Scribners, who issued it, that I should be employed to print it. In this and in all her later books that we printed, we employed a Scotch-face type that, common enough in England then and in America now, had not before been used for fiction in this country. To Mrs. Wharton's thoughtful act the Press owed not merely the prestige of printing her books, but also the printing of many other volumes for Scribner's—indeed we were constantly employed by the firm until it set up a press of its own. Nothing could have helped the Press more, just then, than the Scribner connection, for it showed we were not amateurs but could hold our own with larger printing houses; and this was all due to the friend who used her influence as generously, intelligently, and effectively then, as many times before and since, for persons or causes that she thought deserved a "lift." Besides the volume mentioned the following books written by Mrs. Wharton were printed here: *The Touchstone* (1900); *Crucial Instances* (1901); *The Valley of Decision* (1902); *Sanctuary* (1903); *Madame de Treymes* (1907).

The most ambitious book of 1900 was printed for Mrs. J. V. L. Pruyn—a description of a pastoral staff given by her to the Diocese of Albany. The pictures of the staff were repro-

The Merrymount Press

duced in photogravure, which made an odd alliance with a text set throughout in black-letter type. Goodhue designed the elaborate frameworks of the opening pages and, in fact, all the decorations and the binding. The book is an exhibition of his cleverness as a draughtsman rather than of any skill of mine.

In the same year a little book that had a great success was printed for Scribner's, set in Scotch-face type. This was Stevenson's *Christmas Sermon*, bound in boards, with a green cloth back and paper sides of that gloomy shade of blue known to my childhood in Seidlitz powders. This was reprinted several times, and was followed by a number of short essays in the same format. A genealogical book of importance typographically, set throughout in Caslon, was *Mumford Memoirs*, by my old friend the late Dr. James Gregory Mumford. Another genealogy was printed for the late Josiah Henry Benton, the first of a series of books brought out by him. The best of these volumes were the catalogue, set in Mountjoye and Oxford types, of his splendid collection of English and American Prayer Books now in the Boston Public Library; and a memoir of Baskerville, read by Mr. Benton before the Society of Printers and printed later in amplified form—a book now rare and much sought after. For the latter we used a Caslon type of the period when Caslon's founts showed the influence of Baskerville, and its title-page is a good bit of "period" printing. Between Mr. Benton's wife and my mother's family there was an ancient friendship, though I became aware of this only after our first meeting. Mr. Benton, under a brusque manner, concealed great sensitiveness and a warm heart; but these were not always apparent. On my first visit to him at his office in the Ames Building accompanied by Mr. Bianchi, Benton, expecting to see one person and seeing two, exclaimed: "Who's that?—plumber's helper?"

Notes on its Work

Possibly the most ambitious "period" book in the so-called colonial style that we ever attempted was an edition in quarto of Irving's *Knickerbocker's History of New York*, printed for R. H. Russell in 1900. The arrangement of its complicated and voluminous preliminary matter I am proud of, and the book "hangs together" in spite of Maxfield Parrish's eight illustrations (then the vogue), which are only pseudo-"colonial." This volume was set up at the Press, though it was printed outside it. A catalogue of Doubleday, Page & Co.'s books also deserves attention for its use of Clarendon type—one of the few times I have used it to my own satisfaction.

Mr. Charles Goodspeed first became a customer in 1901 by commissioning me to print Sanborn's *Personality of Thoreau*. For this slim volume, printed in a limited edition, Scotch-face type, much leaded, was used, printed on a highly calendered paper, with some copies on Japan paper. The result was a somewhat attenuated elegance, but it found favour and was followed by more books in the same style. A more sympathetic piece of work was a little volume printed for Miss Sarah Cooper Hewitt called *Some Old Letters & Bits of History*, a paper written by her aunt, Margaret Adelia Cooper. Its cover of Empire paper, with white label, yellow edges, and endpapers printed from wood-blocks in green and pink, and the Bewickian decorations accord with its leisurely well-bred text. The book-marker in blue and pink was much consulted about, and Miss Hewitt—very much *la maîtresse-femme*—adjured me that under no possible pretence should like endpapers and ribbons adorn the books of any other living being! Only two hundred copies were printed, to be used as gifts.

Two French *batarde* types that I acquired in Paris were first used in a tiny rubricated volume printed for Edwin S. Gorham of New York, *The Form of Solemnization of Matrimony*,

[21]

The Merrymount Press

issued in 1901. We later used the same type in a circular, *Merrymount: Being a few Words on the Derivation of the Name of The Merrymount Press*, brought out after our removal to Summer Street. Of these two interesting founts, the larger is a true *batarde*, the smaller a *lettre de somme*. The same year brought to the Press the service for the consecration of a life-long friend, the late Charles Brent, as Bishop of the Philippines; several of Brent's books we afterwards printed. This service was one of a long series of similar services for consecrations of bishops and of churches, the institution of rectors, and the like, that have been printed here. As these ceremonies usually included a celebration of the Eucharist, we began the composition by first printing the two pages containing the prayer of consecration facing each other and worked back from that point, so there should be no noise of turning leaves at the most solemn moment of the service. All "turn-overs" were planned as far as possible to occur at liturgical points when they would not disturb the congregation: for three thousand people turning a leaf at once gives the effect of the sudden flight of a flock of pigeons.

The year 1902 was marked by my publication of *Four Addresses*, by Henry Lee Higginson. Its cover, as were those of several other books printed at the Press, was designed by Mrs. Henry Whitman, a figure in the artistic circles of Boston, who for many years designed the best of the covers for Houghton, Mifflin & Company's books. She was a woman of taste and charm, though the personal impression she produced was perhaps greater than any definite accomplishment. Somewhat fantastic in phrase and manner, she dealt with us, to use her own words, "very handsomely." I remember at the first exhibition of the Society of Arts and Crafts, in 1897, on seeing a folio leaf of our Latin Tacitus set in Goodhue's Merrymount type, she cried: "Phoebus, what a page!" This year saw also

[22]

RECEPTION ROOM, 232 SUMMER STREET

Notes on its Work

the beginning of a set of octavo books finished in 1903 —*The Life and Works of Charles Lamb*—printed in Scotch-face type and issued in twelve volumes for the Pafraets Book Company of Troy, New York.

The Poet Gray as a Naturalist, edited by Charles Eliot Norton, is an essay based on a copy of a book in Mr. Norton's library—the *Systema Naturae* of Linnaeus, interleaved for annotation and illustration by Thomas Gray. From the text pages and those interleaved a few of the most interesting drawings were chosen for reproduction, and selections from Gray's manuscript notes were also printed. These facsimiles are extraordinary pieces of reproduction. The book was published by Goodspeed in an edition of five hundred copies in November, 1903—or so the colophon says—though as I recall it, it was early in December and much too late for the Christmas trade. As I look back I am impressed with the casual manner in which I then regarded practical affairs.

Mr. Norton was from the beginning of our work most sympathetic and helpful. We were brought together more particularly because of some projects for an endowed University Press at Cambridge. He gave my own Press one or two books to print, presented it with proofs of interesting types and ornaments, and placed at our disposal any books in his library at Shady Hill. He was a great aid in these early years, before other people had found me out or—what was more important—I had "found" myself. But about the business end of the Press he was always a bit nervous, fearing that it might be diverted from the Service of Beauty to the Worship of Mammon; and he grieved at my "defection," as he considered it, when we abandoned the amateur atmosphere of Chestnut Street for the commercial air of Summer. In vain I pointed out that the presses would go through the floor if we had to install them in Chestnut Street. I had, he thought, gone

The Merrymount Press

over to the "enemy," though what particular enemy he was loath to specify. For as work increased it was obvious that however much we enlarged the Chestnut Street quarters we could not go on without printing-presses, since without our own machines our press-work was uneven and expensive. The construction of the Chestnut Street houses would not bear much weight, and if a press-room were built out over the small back-yard this would consume capital and obstruct light. Wandering about in the neighbourhood of the South Station one Sunday afternoon, I found a building just completed on Summer Street, and the top floor, although only a well-built loft, seemed to have possibilities. After much cogitation this floor was taken. Some old glass Directoire doors* I had found in East Cambridge, which formerly figured in the Tremont Street façade of the old Boston Museum, were fitted into "compo board" partitions, arranged as nearly as possible on an axis in a building in which nothing was symmetrical. To the old furniture we had, more pieces were added — notably some fine chairs, the gift of two well-disposed friends; and a collection of framed engravings pertinent to printing was begun. All this gave the rooms a certain effect. Three presses were installed and a decent composing-room was arranged. The offices consisted of an ante-room, a reception room, a counting-room, and a library. It was from this locale that we issued the first of a series of illustrated pamphlets describing the Press. All our work was done here for twenty-eight years. It is amusing to remember with how much perturbation of spirit we made

* Of these doors there must have been thirty or more. I purchased three, and Miss Amy Lowell, whom I told about them, bought, characteristically, *all* the rest. Two, possibly four, she placed in her house at Brookline; a few more she gave to her architect, who used them in one or two houses on the water side of Beacon Street, where they can still be seen. The rest Miss Lowell stored in her garage with some idea of ultimately making an *"orangerie"* of them. But this did not come to pass, for through a fire the garage, the doors, and the project went up in smoke together.

[24]

LIBRARY, SUMMER STREET

Notes on its Work

each move, only to regret that it was not made long before.

No particularly interesting book was produced in 1903 except the two-volume set of the poems of Dante Gabriel Rossetti — the Cheyne Walk edition — edited by Herbert Copeland, of Copeland & Day, and with a decorative design on the title-page by T. M. Cleland, who also designed the cover. Set in Caslon throughout, the book somewhat reflects the aesthetic movement of which Rossetti was patron saint. Cleland had been living in Boston a little before this time and occupied a small studio, or office, in Cornhill, which was then more of an old-world locality than now, the picturesque effect of its low brick buildings on the curve of the street being then unspoilt by modern erections. Besides designing, Cleland produced several little books at what he called the Cornhill Press, which, like my own, was a press only because we chose to call it so. Our friendship—and I may add my admiration of his talents and his work — dates from those remote days. He was an idealist—quite impractical — often in difficulties; but he produced delightful things then, as in maturity he has continued to do. Perhaps none of us at that period were very sensible or businesslike, and if we had been would never have been heard of more.

Of the long series of music-books turned out for Messrs. Oliver Ditson Company under the title *The Musicians Library*, the major part consisted of lithographic music, all we contributed being the title-pages and introductory matter. For this reason these are not included in the list of work. In this connection sheet-music covers should be mentioned. These were executed chiefly for Schirmer of Boston and New York, the larger number being printed for the New York house. For these titles little money was available, and most of them had to be produced in a hurry. How to vary them attractively without expense was the problem. Some could be

[25]

The Merrymount Press

printed solely from type and type ornaments, but for those requiring decoration we reproduced designs from the engraved ornamentation of the seventeenth and eighteenth centuries. A collection of such engraved work belonged to the Press, and we drew from these plates and procured others for the purpose. Many of the most successful designs were reproduced from the elaborate and often beautiful *cartouches* on old maps. Others were taken from the *Chinoiseries* of Pillement, designs by the Du Cerceau and other *maîtres ornemanistes*, Pompeian wall-paintings, German silhouettes—everything conceivable was pressed into service. We continued to turn out this work until 1914.

Music programmes also were brought to the Press to be printed. Among the earliest friends of my undertaking was the late Montgomery Sears, whose house during his lifetime and since has been known for the *musicales* at which famous artists have assisted. The programmes for these concerts Mr. Sears always brought personally to the Press to be printed, and these leaflets brought that class of our work into notice, leading to more commissions from other quarters. As I look back on the small beginnings of my establishment, I am grateful for the sympathetic interest in its work that my friends have all along shown. I like to record here in addition to those mentioned in connection with the books I am describing the names of others—and these are by no means all—who in ways great and small have been as friendly as Mr. Sears was in those early days: Bishop Brent; Mrs. John Carter Brown; Mrs. Harold Brown; Mr. and Mrs. John Nicholas Brown, Sr.; Mr. John Nicholas Brown, Jr.; Mrs. William Gammell; Mr. John Chipman Gray; Miss Eleanor Burges Green; Miss Belle da Costa Greene; Mr. Rowland Hazard; Miss Caroline Hazard; Mrs. Cadwalader Jones; Mr. William Vail Kellen; Mr. Henry W. Kent; Miss Amy Lowell; Mr. John Pierpont Morgan, Sr.;

Notes on its Work

Mr. John Pierpont Morgan, Jr.; Dr. Charles L. Nichols; Miss Elizabeth Norton; Mrs. J. M. Sears; Mr. Edward Perry Warren; Professor Barrett Wendell; Mrs. Henry Whitman.

The year 1904 was to us notable for the launching of a type designed for the Press by Herbert Horne of London, whose essays in typography in *The Hobby Horse* had already attracted attention. The type was a roman letter of fourteen-point size modelled on early Florentine founts, named Montallegro as an Italian equivalent of "Merrymount." Horne stipulated that the first volume printed in it should be designed by him, and for the text he employed his own translation of Ascanio Condivi's life of Michael Angelo, or, as Horne preferred to call him, Michelagnolo Buonarroti. He chose as a format for the book a small square quarto resembling early Florentine woodcut books, with type closely and solidly set; and he also designed the title-page and initials. This type was afterwards employed in volumes of *The Humanists' Library*, where it had a more open and, I think, more agreeable treatment. Horne afterwards designed for other firms two similar types, the Florence and the Riccardi, all three being cut by E. P. Prince, who executed the types used by Morris and Cobden-Sanderson. I have never considered Montallegro a complete success—there is about it a rigidity which makes one conscious of the type instead of the text. The same year Bertram Goodhue's Merrymount type, hitherto used only in the Altar Book was utilized for a large folio edition of the *Opera Minora* of Tacitus, a text suggested by Mr. Norton and edited by the late Professor Morris Morgan of Harvard University. Only one hundred copies were printed of this volume, which was designed to display the Merrymount type—a fount solely adapted to an enormous page. I sent specimen pages of the book abroad, and our choice of this text suggested its use to the Doves Press, whose first book, the *Agricola*, appeared

[27]

The Merrymount Press

in 1901. Another book which attracted attention for its type was Thackeray's *Letters to an American Family*, printed for the Century Company, New York. Here we employed a Mountjoye (or, as it would now be called, "Bell") fount, and although this was not its first use by us, it was our first use of it in a book of popular appeal. This Mountjoye type was much the same, if not the same, as some founts existing at the Riverside Press known in my time as "copper-face," but afterwards called "Brimmer" because they were first used in an address by Martin Brimmer, delivered at Wellesley College at the opening of the Farnsworth Art School. This address was published in October, 1891, and its format and typography were designed by Mrs. Henry Whitman, who was a great friend of Mr. Brimmer's. Mrs. Whitman also arranged the more ambitious volume by Mr. Brimmer, entitled *Egypt*, which was printed in the same type and published at the Riverside Press in December, 1891.

For the Mountjoye type I traced the history of the fount until I found what British type-foundry owned the matrices and then obtained strikes of them for our own casting. As I write, this fount (discovered by Mr. Stanley Morison to be the production of John Bell of London, 1745–1831) has just been placed on the market—twenty-nine years after its first use by the Press in a little volume of sketches by Frances Dabney entitled *Saudades*, privately printed in 1903 for Miss Amy Lowell. This same type was also used in 1904 for the text of a fourteen-volume set of the Bible printed in several editions on various papers for the R. H. Hinkley Company of Boston. With the commonplace illustrations we had nothing to do—except to deplore their use; and of the various bindings only those in cloth were ours.

One more book must be mentioned under 1904: *The Letters of Three Dutiful & Affectionate Rhode Island Children to*

COMPOSING–ROOM, SUMMER STREET

Notes on its Work

their Honoured Parents—the children being Master Nicholas, Miss Hope, and Miss Joanna Brown, whose letters were written between 1779 and 1781. This and two succeeding volumes, *The Course of True Love in Colonial Times*, issued in the next year, and *James Browne—His Writings In Prose and Verse*, printed in 1917, seem to me as good "colonial" typography as the Press has ever put out. But few persons have ever seen these books, for the limited numbers printed were chiefly for family distribution.

A volume devoted to the dedication of the John Carter Brown Library in 1903, issued in 1905, was the beginning of a long connection that still continues with this library, of which I am a member of the board of management. In the following year use was made of the Mountjoye type in *The Life of Benvenuto Cellini*, for Brentano's, New York. The title-page of this edition was designed by Cleland. The edition was a great success, but the early issues are the only ones in which the press-work was executed here. Later editions showed an unfortunate declension in this feature.

In the next year the first volume in *The Humanists' Library* was published. This series was under the general editorship of Lewis Einstein, and Maurice Baring translated for its initial issue Leonardo da Vinci's *Thoughts on Art and Life*. These books employed, as I have said, Horne's Montallegro type, and for them Horne designed the initials and title-pages of the first series, which consisted of four volumes in editions of 303 copies. The other three volumes of the first series were *Erasmus Against War*, edited by J. W. Mackail, brought out in 1907; *Petrarch and the Ancient World*, by Pierre de Nolhac, issued in 1907; and Sidney's *Defence of Poesie*, edited by George Edward Woodberry, issued in 1908.

In January, 1906, we printed a handbook of an exhibition, *The Development of Printing as an Art*, arranged in honour

The Merrymount Press

of the bicentenary of Benjamin Franklin by the Society of Printers of Boston. This modest organization—of which I was at one time president—still exists, largely because, having no definite programme, it has done such necessary work as occasion has presented. Their show was held at the Boston Public Library, and I had a hand in the preparation of the text of its catalogue as well as charge of its typography. Many of the specimens exhibited came from our library. A somewhat elaborate volume was also issued in 1906 for the Club of Odd Volumes, Harold Murdock's *Historie of the Life and Death of Sir William Kirkaldy of Grange, Knight*. The decorations and initials for this edition of 114 copies were cut on wood, and although great pains were taken with the entire production, I have never thought the book as successful as it should have been. It was printed from a late Caslon fount.

I must mention Mrs. John Lowell Gardner as another good friend to the Press. The pamphlet guide for visitors to her house, Fenway Court, we printed for many years. On each revision I spent a morning there, and Mrs. Gardner and I, acting as "visitors," made a tour of the house, guide-book in hand. In this way we were able to test the convenience of arrangement in each succeeding issue. These mornings were always enlivened by Mrs. Gardner's talk about her acquisitions and the way in which she came to possess them. One of our dealings was, however, less fortunate. Mrs. Gardner had endeavoured to have prepared for her a catalogue of her books, and, failing to find the desired co-operation in several quarters, she decided to compile it herself, entitling it *A Choice of Books from the Library of Isabella Stewart Gardner, Fenway Court*. Now the compilation of catalogues, like the keeping of hotels, appears within the powers of most Yankees until they try it; and Mrs. Gardner's cataloguing was no better nor worse than the work of most amateurs. When the manuscript

PRESS–ROOM, SUMMER STREET

Notes on its Work

was in type I detected so many errors that I was sure there were more, and so I told her. But she was positive that all was right, and in spite of my begging that some competent person might revise the work, she held to her opinion. We accordingly printed the catalogue as it stood, but omitted the imprint of the Press. When the volume was distributed— it was privately printed in 1906—numberless errors were found, and the omission of the imprint was (I hoped) thereby accounted for. No one was very happy about the matter, least of all Mrs. Gardner, who corrected in pencil such errors as she caught and sent the book out, its blunders naturally being attributed to our carelessness. Some of my friends (who perhaps did not know Mrs. Gardner) said I should not have "permitted" her to make such mistakes. Mr. Norton in particular was severely critical and declared one evening at Shady Hill, in the presence of a number of people, that I should have insisted that some competent person look over the final proofs. "But I did suggest a very competent person," said I, "and it was not well received." "Whom did you suggest?" asked Mr. Norton. "You, sir," I replied. Everybody laughed, and the point was not laboured—nor I belaboured further. For some time after this my friendship with Mrs. Gardner, as Horace Walpole said of his with Lady Lucan, "rather waned than improved." But before long the difficulty was forgotten—indeed, we printed in 1922 a companion volume, *A Choice of Manuscripts and Bookbindings from the Library of Isabella Stewart Gardner, Fenway Court.* Mrs. Gardner was then ill and the consultations about the book were held in her motor, in which, rain or shine, she punctually kept any appointment she had made. "You must hurry, hurry," she said one day with a humorous expression. "I am dying, and if we don't make haste I shall die first." She had an indomitable spirit—never more finely shown than in those last years.

[31]

The Merrymount Press

The chief work of 1907 was the issue, in three volumes, of a second edition of Wilkins Updike's *History of the Episcopal Church in Narragansett, Rhode Island.* This book, by my grandfather, first published in 1847 in a very casual manner, I had long intended to reissue, and had collected a mass of material to that end. But when I had assembled it I had neither the time nor the ability to arrange it, and the project lay dormant. As luck would have it, a later rector of this ancient cure, the Rev. Daniel Goodwin (editor of the *MacSparran Diary* already mentioned), was greatly interested in the church's history and was free to edit the work, using the material gathered by me; and no man was better fitted for the work or could have done it better. The book is much more than a history of a country parish. It is the history of the whole countryside, and gives especially a picture of social life and manners in eighteenth-century southern Rhode Island that has been the basis of everything written on the subject from that day to this. Fortunately, too, a distant kinsman of mine, Mr. Moses Goddard of Providence, also much attached to Rhode Island traditions, stood ready to help me out, his only stipulation being that the editor should annotate the work to his heart's content. When the manuscript was complete the amount of text had been enormously increased — fourteen hundred printed pages as against four hundred in the first edition! Encouraged by Dr. McVickar, then Bishop of Rhode Island, I cast about for means of publishing the manuscript, which was effected by the aid of several Rhode Island friends: Mr. George Gordon King; Mr. William H. Potter; Mr. George Peabody Wetmore; Mr. William Watts Sherman; and Mr. Goddard, who took the largest share in the production of a book which, alas, he did not live to see completed. A feature of the work is its fifty illustrations, chiefly from portraits hitherto unpublished.

Notes on its Work

On the publication of the original work in 1847 its author received an honorary degree from Brown University, and the completion of the second edition was signalized by degrees given by Brown University to Dr. Goodwin and to me. The German ambassador Bernstorff received a degree on the same day, and I was deputed by our host at a luncheon afterwards to look after him, since he was not familiar with the intricacies of Providence streets. As we walked along he said to me: "You know, I have to give an address before the alumni of the University this afternoon. I have given twenty such addresses in thirty days. None of them amounted to anything. If I say anything worth hearing I am called to account by Berlin. So my speeches give no pleasure to me nor to anyone else."

The connection of this Press with Brown University began in 1905. The printing of its catalogues set a style somewhat new in college publications—a style widely copied all over this country. Ever since, a large part of the University's "academic" printing has been done here, and also books such as Bronson's *History of Brown University* and ephemera for special occasions, such as the Sesquicentennial of the college, requiring programmes, tickets, orders of service, and the like.

I am often asked if it is not uninteresting to undertake the printing of catalogues and similar material. As a matter of fact, such work is often both interesting and difficult, for in no class of printing is it so necessary to preserve clearness and simplicity. Refractory tabulation has to be so managed as to conceal its refractoriness; type arrangements that will be suitable to all the varying classes of instruction have to be schemed; and that a college catalogue is a book of reference has to be kept clearly in view. To the printer such work appears interesting, to the layman dull. For at the risk of digression I may add that the attitudes of mind of a professional

The Merrymount Press

and of an amateur about printing—as in most forms of creative endeavour—are quite different. The onlooker supposes the printer to enjoy doing what he enjoys seeing and to be bored by what bores him; and he also believes that the feeling of a man who does a piece of work successfully is "joy," when it is mostly relief. The *problem* is what interests all but beginners in typography. Its solution may be, and often is, moderately exciting; although if the problem is successfully solved no one perceives it has existed. Because all persons who work realize this, it is easier for one worker to talk to another, however dissimilar their occupations may be, than it is to talk with (or to be talked to by) an admirer of one's own class of work—whose likes or dislikes are often based on quite the wrong reasons.

A great mass of work for schools, colleges, and institutions followed in the wake of the academic work for Brown University. Even more important than the printing for Brown has been a long connection with the Carnegie Foundation for the Advancement of Teaching. This printing requires ingenuity in its arrangement and in the co-ordination of material, and accuracy as absolute as can be attained. The Foundation has shown the Press much consideration; the Press in turn has given the best it has. Begun in 1909, the work continues today, and will, it is hoped, *ad multos annos*.

A volume of Oakes Ames's *Orchidaceae*—one of a series the Press has since turned out—which showed what could be done typographically with a learned botanical work, and the *Catalogue of a Memorial Exhibition of the Works of Augustus Saint-Gaudens*, printed for the Metropolitan Museum of New York, were the two pieces of work most notable in 1908. The inscriptions in the Saint-Gaudens catalogue presented a problem that was interesting to solve.

An important work printed in six volumes in 1911, at the

Notes on its Work

expense of the late Mr. J. Pierpont Morgan, was the *Archives of the General Convention*, devoted to the correspondence of John Henry Hobart. It was intended to issue more volumes, but the Hobart correspondence was so interminably strung out by the editor and the prospect of arriving at the end of the series became so remote that the project was given up. These severely plain volumes were set in Mountjoye type combined with those Oxford founts which accord well with it. Another book set in Mountjoye type that was thought successful is the "period" volume, *Letters of Bulwer-Lytton to Macready*, printed for the Carteret Book Club of Newark.

The second series of *The Humanists' Library*, set like the first series in Horne's Montallegro type, was begun in 1912. These volumes we thought great improvements over those of Series I in two respects: (1) by the adoption of a more ample paper-page, and (2) by a reduction of price. The first idea was a good one, the second was not; for collectors, a skittish race unaccustomed to good books at low prices, were thereby scared off, fighting shy of the very feature intended to attract them! And the general public was not interested in such books at all. Both series of *The Humanists' Library* have, however, long been out of print, and so the project justified itself financially. The four volumes in the second series were: *The Correspondence of Philip Sidney and Hubert Languet*, Albrecht Dürer's *Records of Journeys to Venice and the Low Countries*, Pico Della Mirandola's *Platonick Discourse upon Love*, and Della Casa's *Galateo of Manners & Behaviours*, edited, respectively, by W. A. Bradley, Roger Fry, Edmund G. Gardner, and J. E. Spingarn. Of the title-pages, two were by Cleland and two by W. A. Dwiggins, and plain initials were substituted for the decorated series by Horne used in the first four volumes.

As will be seen, the number of types used by the Press shows little variety. For most books, Caslon, Scotch-face, or

The Merrymount Press

the Mountjoye-Oxford combination of founts is the best, and a departure is desirable only when a new type performs the task to be done better than these types can. But new material—borders, initial letters, and type ornaments with which to vary the effect of the types used—was all along acquired, some of it during my several journeys abroad. And here, in parenthesis, I may say that one's attitude towards new movements in typography, and to new types produced under their influence, may be summed up in a comment on literary criticism,* which I adapt to printing: "The new should be welcome, the old not forgotten. What one misses in most contemporary work is a sense of proportion. Men do not remember what has been produced in the past, and do not distinguish between the briefly novel and the permanently valid"—between which one cannot too carefully differentiate. When one sees some ancient type horror revived as new one remembers the words of Marie Antoinette's milliner: "There is nothing new except what is forgotten."

The Club of Odd Volumes began to commission the Press to do work as early as 1904. Good examples of the printing for this organization are *A Catalogue of an Exhibition of Waltoniana* (May, 1912) and the more important volume by the late Dr. Charles Lemuel Nichols of Worcester, *Isaiah Thomas, Printer, Writer & Collector*. Both pieces of work were set in Oxford type, and *Isaiah Thomas* is as satisfactory a book in that fount as we have ever printed. The most important books of 1913 were the *Ordinary and Canon of the Mass*, printed in Goodhue's Merrymount type, set in double column and rubricated; and Mr. F. B. Crowninshield's *Story of George Crowninshield's Yacht, Cleopatra's Barge*, in quarto, set in Scotch-face type, somewhat in the style of the period. The amusing "ship" end-papers of this volume were designed by Mr. Dwiggins.

* Sir John Squire.

LIBRARY, BEACON STREET

Notes on its Work

In 1915 Mr. John Bianchi was made a partner as some recognition of effective work in carrying out the aims of the Press and his steadiness and patience in tiding over times of my indifferent health and discouragement at the slow pace of advance. Addressing himself to the problem from a different angle than mine, and bringing to the undertaking thorough knowledge of the processes of production and sound financial judgment, he has always been at one with me in objective. Furthermore, his taste in typography and an instinctive Italian sense of order and proportion have made his collaboration, when planning work or producing it, invaluable.

The *Jonny-Cake Papers of "Shepherd Tom"* ("Shepherd Tom" being Thomas Robinson Hazard) was, like the edition of the *Narragansett Church*, a reprint of a Rhode Island book. It is chiefly notable for its illustrations from pen-and-ink sketches by my old friend Rudolph Ruzicka. It was issued in 1915 and was followed in the next year by another book illustrated by Ruzicka commemorating the fiftieth anniversary of the opening of Vassar College—views of the college buildings enhanced by the introduction of colour. But Ruzicka's best-known work for the Press is the series of Annual Keepsakes he has designed and engraved since 1912. These are listed on a later page.

The *Catalogue of the Collection of Prints from the Liber Studiorum of Joseph Mallord William Turner, formed by the late Francis Bullard . . . and bequeathed by him to the Museum of Fine Arts* was printed as a memorial to Mr. Bullard for Mr. Grenville Winthrop, in an edition of three hundred copies for private distribution. It was brought out in 1916. The reproduction of the prints was attended with difficulty, for the originals could not be taken from the Museum, and so trial proofs of each of our plates had to be brought there, compared, and corrected. I have spoken of problems in printing which,

[37]

The Merrymount Press

if surmounted, should be invisible. There was such a problem in this book. Many of the pictures were not uniform in depth, so that if they were to occupy the same relative position from the top margin of the book throughout, the distance between them and the first line of type, which also had to be invariable in position, differed. We overcame this difficulty by never allowing two pictures to face each other, so that in turning the page the eye did not catch the discrepancy.

The War brought a number of books to the Press in the shape of memorials to single individuals or to groups of men. The most ambitious of these publications is *The Book of the Homeless*, edited by Edith Wharton. Besides the articles in prose and verse contributed by "eminent hands," the illustrations were to be reproductions from a number of original paintings and drawings. To unify all this material was a considerable undertaking, and, when unified, to select the various *media* which would do justice to the originals was a further task. Accordingly, while the title-page and half-titles were printed from blocks engraved by Ruzicka, the illustrations were reproduced by photogravure and in coloured half-tone. The latter were printed here. Besides the regular edition, a special issue of 175 copies was printed in a large format with some extra features. The book was sold for the benefit of the American hostels for refugees, and other war charities.

Apropos of Ruzicka's work, in 1917 we printed for the Carteret Book Club of Newark a book illustrated entirely by him. The volume, which was entitled *Newark*, was by Mr. Walter Pritchard Eaton, and the text illustrations were printed at the Press, but the five delightful full-page coloured plates Ruzicka printed himself. Another volume brought out in the same year was Percival Merritt's monograph *The Parochial Library of the Eighteenth Century in Christ Church, Boston*, printed to accord with the subject, which made a pretty little

Notes on its Work

"eighteenth-century" volume. Also in 1917 we printed for Brentano's the two-volume edition of Madame Campan's *Memoirs* (in a sense a companion set to the *Cellini* made for the same house), a handsome book set in Mountjoye type. The title-page is a reproduction of an old French engraved title-page; and the cover reproduces a binding said to have been executed by Derôme for Marie Antoinette, called *De Présent*, its design covering uninterruptedly the whole back, the old-fashioned "ribs" being done away with. The bindings of many books printed at the Press have been arranged here. Some of them are simple affairs with cloth backs and marbled cloth or paper sides; others adaptations of old designs which, while not always remarkable, have the advantage of being "on good terms" with the printing inside the cover — which is saying a good deal.

In 1919 we finished the *List of Books Privately Printed by William K. Bixby and those Privately Printed by Book Clubs from Manuscripts in his Collection*. This recalls Mr. Bixby's various brochures printed at this Press, such as *Two Letters of Charles Lamb* and *Martha Washington's Letter*, issued in 1922, which both include facsimiles of the letters themselves. The cover of the Washington letter is an adaptation by Ruzicka of the design of a *toile de Jouy*—an Indian introducing Liberty to the French Monarchy; and this same design was used, though with a different combination of colours, on a reproduction of letters from Wayne and Washington (1922). The most interesting of these books, of which there were a good many, is *Benjamin Franklin on Balloons*. I had chosen for the title-page a reproduction of an old engraving of Franklin's house at Passy, with a Montgolfier balloon riding the sky, and as luck would have it I received at just the right moment a visit from the representative of the French paper-makers Canson and Montgolfier. Finding that the Montgolfier of this

The Merrymount Press

firm was a descendant of the famous aeronaut, I procured from him the paper for the booklet, water-marked with a balloon—for the Montgolfier balloon was made of paper from this same mill. For the cover paper an amusing "balloon" design used by Oberkampff for a printed chintz was chosen, being redrawn for our purpose by Mr. Dwiggins. A quotation on the title-page from Franklin's prophetic letter about the future of air warfare is not the least interesting feature of the book.

In the same year (1919) we printed Part I of the first volume of the Catalogue of the John Carter Brown Library's magnificent collection of Americana—a series still in process. The typographic requirements of this work in diacritical marks, symbols, superior letters, and the like, and the careful proof-reading needful for entries in Latin, Italian, German, Dutch, and other languages make the production one requiring constant care. Three volumes have so far been published, the first two in two parts each, and the third in one.

A Grolier Club edition of Washington Irving's *Notes and Journal of Travel in Europe, 1804–1805* is specially to be remarked for Ruzicka's three illustrations and title-pages, executed in aquatint with details heightened in water-colour. This was issued in three volumes in 1921.

The Wedding Journey of Charles and Martha Babcock Amory was a journal kept by Mrs. Amory during her travels in France, Italy, Switzerland, Holland, and Germany in 1833 and 1834 and afterwards copied by her into a finely bound blank-book, the tooling of which was reproduced on the binding of the printed volumes. To set up this book seemed an easy task, but as Mrs. Amory's "fine Italian hand" looked legible and wasn't, and as the journey was taken by carriage, the proper names of the less known towns and villages through which the carriage passed—or sometimes broke

Notes on its Work

down—had to be verified by road-maps of the period. The titles of pictures, statues, and the like, had to be verified from guide-books of that period, for modern guide-books described galleries wholly rearranged since 1830. The preparation of the manuscript, therefore, proved an almost endless piece of work, and was a triumph of patience and ingenuity. The *résumé* of the contents of chapters, as well as the preface, I wrote myself. The book was issued in two small quarto volumes, and but one hundred copies were printed.

Mrs. Gordon Dexter, for whom the book was printed — great-granddaughter of Copley, grand-niece of Lord Lyndhurst, and daughter of the diarist—was one of the most remarkable figures of the society of her period, and had the most original and distinguished personality I have ever known. Whimsical, unreasoning, autocratic, she belonged to the eighteenth century, and might in appearance have stepped out of one of the many Copley portraits that hung on the walls of her splendid house. Underneath an extremely sophisticated exterior she had the simplicity of a child, and went straight to the heart of matters much as a child does, and sometimes with the same devastating results. She retained her charm to the day of her death. Through all the vicissitudes of life, one trait never varied—Mrs. Dexter's devotion to her mother. These volumes were one of many testimonies to that devotion.

The production, in 1922, of my own book, *Printing Types*, which was printed here though published by the Harvard University Press, came about through an invitation to give some lectures (or, as I preferred to call them, "talks") on printing in the School of Business Administration at Harvard University. As I have said, I have always been tongue-tied when obliged to address an audience, and it was with something akin to panic that I found myself in Cambridge, one late autumn afternoon, to open the course. The subject as-

The Merrymount Press

signed me was "type and composition," and to veil my inability to speak fluently *ex tempore* I wrote out what I had to expound in as colloquial a style as I could manage, so that I might run for shelter to the manuscript when too confused to remember what I wanted to say next. To my surprise, my efforts appeared to those in authority a success; the lectures were extended to some sixteen sessions, and continued up to the entrance of this country into the War. It was then proposed that these discourses should be made into a book, but since a successful spoken style is by no means satisfactory as a written style, my elaborate informalities had to be transmuted into a more chastened text before they could be printed. This was a terrible job, and would never have been completed except for the help of one of our own force, William Smallfield.* He it was who hunted up references, verified dates, corrected my grammar, and did the thousand and one odd jobs inherent in the preparation of a work full of names, dates, titles, and like matter requiring accurate transcription.

---

*William H. Smallfield, Jr., was born at Renfrew, Ontario, in 1893, and died at Guelph, Ontario, in 1928. He was of English descent, and of the third generation of a printing family. His grandfather, Albert Smallfield, originally in the employ of the old London firm of Waterlow & Company, became on his removal to Canada the founder of the *Mercury* of Renfrew, Ontario; and his son, William Smallfield, a man of ability, conducted the paper for nearly fifty years, until its sale in 1919. After a breakdown caused by overwork in assisting his father, the son took a place with us, first as pressman, afterwards as compositor, and, later, when we began to realize his scholarship, as proof-reader and secretary. Sensitive and retiring, a born student, a great reader with a sound taste in literature, he was invaluable to me in the completion of the *Wedding Journey* for Mrs. Gordon Dexter and of my own *Printing Types*. He left us because he thought family duties called him home, but with the hope that he might again take up the position that was always open for him. It was not to be, and after a year or two of invalidism and frustration he died. I like to place beside Smallfield's name the names of two other men sometime of our force: Frank Callan and Walter Vincent Smith. To those who know their histories, these names call up memories of faithfulness, generosity, and fortitude under circumstances in which tragedy had its part. *Lux perpetua luceat eis.*

ENTRANCE TO LIBRARY FROM COMPOSING ROOM
BEACON STREET

Notes on its Work

In those last days the "sunny solidity of the *pax Victoriana*" was coming to an end. The lengthening shadows of war darkened too many lives to make the shape of a letter or the characteristics of a fount of type seem of importance, and indeed much of the task was in such "hours of gloom fulfilled" that I doubted whether there need be any book at all.

When the text was in final shape, Mr. Bianchi suggested that it would be far more interesting if illustrated. I had not much faith that what I had written would interest anyone, so I saw the value of his suggestion with dismay; for this new plan involved more delay and difficulty. Some of the illustrations I could easily lay my hand on in the library of the Press, but there were many gaps to be filled from books outside it. The Harvard College Library, largely through the kindness and influence of the late Archibald Coolidge, let me take rare books from the Library and photograph the required pages; and the Boston Athenaeum and the Pierpont Morgan Library in New York also gave me valuable special privileges. But the Boston Public Library was bound by law to keep certain books in its possession. To meet this requirement a small Irish boy was deputed to represent the Library. Wherever I went he had to go. Thus we passed interminable hours that summer in the hot, stifling lofts of photo-engravers, the boy dangling his legs from a bench while I examined negatives of the illustrations. Day after day, I and my unwilling twin left the Library in the morning with books, and wearily returned with them at night. Finally, after infinite labour, the illustrations, the little boy, and I were all "done" together, and the book was printed. By that time I was so convinced that no one would ever read it that I left for a month in the country without seeing the finished volumes. The book has, by those who know, been called a monumental work, and came, so far as I was concerned, fatally near being so. For

The Merrymount Press

it I received the medal of the American Institute of Graphic Arts.* The issue of three successive editions was no doubt instrumental in bringing me in later years a master's degree from Harvard University and membership in the Massachusetts Historical Society, as well as in the Harvard chapter of the Phi Beta Kappa Society; of this society I am also an honorary member at Brown University. Later on, a paper which originally had been a part of the course of lectures but which was not included in *Printing Types* was combined with two others and issued under the title *In the Day's Work* by the Harvard University Press.

The year 1922 also saw the production of *The Felicities of Sixty*, by I. K. Lionberger, printed for the Club of Odd Volumes in an edition of one hundred copies. For this book we used a fount of Dutch type somewhat on the lines of the Fell type, cut by Janson in the seventeenth century, which has long been in our possession. This type we have employed in many of our subsequent books.

Another journal written by a member of the Amory family was produced in the next year, in printing which, as in the former book, expense was not spared. This was *The Journal of Mrs. John Amory, 1775–1777*, issued in an edition of one hundred copies. It was illustrated with some delightful portraits and other material, and was susceptible of interesting treatment typographically. The arrangement of the first page of text is satisfactory, but the title-page would have been improved by making the panel of ornament smaller—reversing the arrangement shown on page one. The cover reproduces

* Many books described in the bibliography have been among those chosen for "Fifty Books of the Year," an annual exhibition of the outstanding bookmaking for each twelvemonth arranged by this organization. In the ten years since the first exhibition in 1923, this Press has contributed fifty-six books, an average of over five a year—more than have been designed and printed by any one press in this country, and more than enough to fill a year's exhibit.

Notes on its Work

a very fine English binding. That same year Mrs. Meyer's *Chinese Painting as Reflected in the Thought and Art of Li Lung-Mier, 1070–1106* appeared. This volume gave the establishment a reputation for scholarly printing not wholly deserved, for the insertion of lines of Chinese characters had an impressive effect—if one did not know each one was supplied in written form for reproduction by photography and had to be carefully marked "This side up" before we dared place it in the text!

That eccentric English amateur of printing, Edward Rowe Mores, wrote a paper entitled "Of English Founders and Founderies." This was published after his death in 1777, in a very small edition, by John Nichols, who gave it the title by which it has since been commonly known: *A Dissertation upon English Typographical Founders and Founderies.* The book is very queer—its author was even queerer—but it contains a mass of curious information on the subject. I had always been interested in this work, and, after some correspondence, induced the Grolier Club of New York to publish it. The issue of the volume depended, however, on finding someone to write a short introduction. This I offered to do, as our library contained some material for it. The result was that the short introduction became a long one, and the most careful literary performance I have ever attempted, though I have never met more than one or two persons who have taken the trouble to read it. The format of the book was determined by that of Mores's original essay. The decorations, made up from varying combinations of two or three typographical flowers, are worth looking at.

Two books issued in 1925—more interesting to print or to look at than to read—fell into the category of printing problems. The first was *The Record of Those who Gave to an Endowment Fund collected by The National Society of Colonial*

The Merrymount Press

Dames of America for the Maintenance of Sulgrave Manor, the Home of the Ancestors of George Washington — a title which sufficiently describes what the book is about, and also suggests that it is scarcely more exciting to the reader than a telephone directory. Our problem was to make "something" out of it, and the result was a great folio volume of considerable typographical splendour enhanced by a beautiful heraldic design by Ruzicka. Forty-eight copies were all that were needed to supply one copy for Sulgrave Manor and copies for branches of the Society of Colonial Dames throughout the country, which subscribed at ten dollars each; and even then there were a few to spare. A college library purchased the last example of this unreadable and unread volume for a sum that would supply a very decent representation of the "world's best books."

The second volume, printed for the Boston Latin School Association also in 1925 and entitled *The Public Latin School of Boston in the World War, 1914–1918. A Roll of Honor,* shows the part played in the war by masters and students of this ancient school. The book at first sight seems easy to print, but the proviso that it was to be kept in a glass case and a page turned every day involved the presentation of entries which must be complete on each two facing pages. The pages dedicated to men who died in war were rubricated and each inscription had a page to itself; but for men still living the inscription had — in printer's language — to be "run in." Further stipulations were (1) that the names should be arranged in strictly alphabetical order, and (2) that there could be no omissions in each record. To see how these difficulties were overcome and the rules complied with, one must see the book. It was set entirely in Poliphilus and Blado types. The pages were surrounded by emblematic borders, in which the arms of the United States, eagles bearing olive branches, and heads

COMPOSING-ROOM, BEACON STREET

Notes on its Work

of Liberty figure in white on black backgrounds—one of the earliest "native" American type ornaments, produced just after the War of 1812. I have had quite enough of books "with borders on every page," but bordered pages were adopted here since no more than two pages were to be shown at once.

The Lutetia type designed by J. Van Krimpen we first used in 1927, in a little book entitled *The Higher Citizenship*, by Alfred L. Baker, and we also employed it for some specimen pages for a folio Book of Common Prayer that were discarded in favour of pages set in Janson type. We also prepared for the Enschedé Foundry of Haarlem, which brought out the Lutetia series, some Latin pages that displayed some of the sizes of this type. In the same year appeared the only book printed at this Press ever placed under a ban: Adam H. Dickey's *Memoirs of Mary Baker Eddy*, set in Mountjoye. The Christian Science authorities suppressed this volume, and as many copies were recalled as possible. To those outside the fold it appears innocuous—and a "collectors' item."

The completion of thirty-five years of the work of the Press was signified by an exhibition of Merrymount books in New York under the auspices of the American Institute of Graphic Arts, one book being selected from the output of each year from 1894 to 1928. I was not present at the opening, on the principle that one would rather have it asked why one was not, than why one was, there. But I sent this letter to the president of the Institute, Mr. Frederic Melcher:

When you kindly suggested an exhibition of the work of the Merrymount Press to inaugurate the use of your new room at the Art Centre, I was only too glad to fall in with the plan; though when it was pointed out that 1928 rounded out thirty-five years in the life of the Press, it caused some searchings of heart. Furthermore, the proposal that the exhibition should be a chronological display of its books presented some very disconcerting possibilities, and reminded me of the proverb that "Old sins have long

The Merrymount Press

shadows." In looking back over what (I now realize) is more than
a third of a century, instead of having a sense of orderly progres-
sion in one's work, these years appear to have been nothing more
than (as the late Barrett Wendell said of life) "a confused getting
ready to begin." So perhaps my feelings about this thirty-fifth
birthday are best expressed by a phrase often used by a great-
grandfather of mine, an unworldly man, who kept silk worms
that produced no silk, and wrote a poem called "The Sabbath"
that none but his family ever read. When children came to see
him on their birthdays, he had, when told their age, an invariable saying which serves me very well now. And this saying was:
"What! So old and no better?"

Three books of typographical interest: *Notes By Lady Louisa
Stuart on "George Selwyn and His Contemporaries," By John
Heneage Jesse*, an edition of Walton's *Angler*, and *The Form
of Consecration of St. George's Chapel* appeared in 1928. In the
Stuart book, printed for the Oxford University Press, New
York, a complicated problem was presented, for the original
passages in Jesse's *Selwyn* had first to be given, then Lady
Louisa's notes upon them, and finally the editor's notes on
her annotations. Only a printer can realize the difficulties of
getting all these notes on one page—successfully—and yet
making a readable volume. The *Angler*, in a small 16mo format, is chiefly remarkable for the delightful *en-têtes* by Mr.
Dwiggins, printed in colour, and for its cover, also designed
by him. The typography was kept simple that it might be
subordinate to the illustrative decoration. The St. George's
Chapel service is a piece of liturgical printing set in one of
Janson's seventeenth-century founts. Except for rubrication
(which is always decorative), it has no ornamentation at all.
The cover we designed. Apart from its use, the book had a
great success as a piece of typography, and copies have since
sold at an absurdly high price.

For the Harvard University Press we printed in 1930 a

selection of David Garrick's letters, somewhat whimsically entitled *Pineapples of Finest Flavour*. This also was set in Janson type, and preserves with fidelity the spelling, abbreviations, and peculiarities of the original. It also contains some successful facsimiles of letters. The same year produced an edition of La Fontaine's *Fables*, illustrated with designs engraved on copper by Ruzicka, whose delicate line required a cool and restrained employ of the Janson founts used. Another book of this period was Caspar Whitney's life of his father-in-law, Charles Adelbert Canfield, in quarto, the first book printed at this Press in Bodoni type—perhaps rather too elegant a letter for Mr. Canfield's rugged personality, but chosen by Mr. Whitney.

The chief accomplishment of 1930 was the completion of an edition of the revised Book of Common Prayer for which I and three other printers were asked to prepare specimen pages, and for which our pages seemed to the Commission on Revision the most practical. It was an enormous task, and one which taxed our resources in many different directions, but in which what knowledge I had of the history of a Church to which my family have been for nearly three hundred years adherents and of the liturgical requirements and practical use of the Prayer Book stood me in good stead. The proofs were read not only by our own proof-readers and by those members of the Commission in charge of the work, but also by the readers of the Harvard University Press and of the Riverside Press, Cambridge. The planning of the book was complicated by the fact that from the beginning of Morning Prayer to the end of the Psalter this edition set the pace for all Prayer Books in small format, which by canon law must conform in pagination thereto. Then again, some new features were introduced for which previous books supplied no liturgical precedent, and finally, some solecisms in the typog-

The Merrymount Press

raphy of the Standard Book of 1892 had to be corrected. The various tables preceding Morning Prayer were the most difficult portion of the book to arrange. In the edition of 1892 these were "boxed" in rules. These rules we did away with, spacing and leading being depended on to separate the figures in the tables from one another. We also induced the Committee to permit the rubrics to be set in roman type printed in red, these directions previously having been set in italic and then rubricated—an unfortunate piece of typographic redundancy. Besides the copies printed on paper, five examples were printed on vellum, and one of these became the "Standard" Book of Common Prayer, which was presented with considerable ceremony to the Convention of the Episcopal Church, sitting at Denver in the autumn of 1931. The expense of the whole undertaking was borne by Mr. J. Pierpont Morgan, who thus repeated his father's generous gift to the Church of the Standard Prayer Book of 1892. Copies were given to the members of the Commission on Revision, to all dioceses and missionary jurisdictions and their cathedral churches, and to dignitaries of Churches in communion with the American Church throughout the world. The book was begun in 1928 and was finished in the autumn of 1930.

Mr. Lawrence C. Wroth, librarian of the John Carter Brown Library, is the author of a scholarly book entitled *The Colonial Printer*, published by the Grolier Club, New York, and printed by us in 1931. This very straightforward piece of work was executed in Mountjoye type, our intention being to make its typography wholly subservient to Mr. Wroth's text. Like most Grolier Club publications, this book was issued in a limited edition at a fairly high price, though it is a pity that a work so valuable to students is restricted to a class of readers who seldom have occasion to make practical use of it. In contrast one may mention the illustrated *Catalogue of the Ex-*

PRESS-ROOM, BEACON STREET

Notes on its Work

hibited Paintings and Drawings of the Isabella Stewart Gardner Museum, Boston, a volume in which much is to be had at a small price, and (to digress a little) the kind of book that it is interesting to arrange. There are in this country few well-printed books at moderate prices, and it is much more of a feat to produce one than it is to print limited editions at unlimited expense. If this particular catalogue is successful it is because there were limitations and these limitations were fairly well surmounted, and yet the cost of the book was kept at a moderate sum. Compare it with the thirty-dollars-a-copy limited edition of *Ellen Terry and Bernard Shaw: A Correspondence,* also printed here, and my meaning is obvious.

The outstanding book printed in 1931 was the Latin and English version of Pope Pius XI's Encyclical Letter on Christian marriage, *Casti Connubii.* This was printed from Bodoni type, with the Latin text on left-hand pages and the English version facing it on right-hand pages. The problem here was to keep the two versions parallel, this being difficult because Latin is so much more concise than English. It was solved by beginning a new page at each section of the Pope's letter and by setting the English translation in italic—a more condensed letter than roman—and leading it less than the Latin page. The volume is a very Italian affair and was purposely made as Roman as the Prayer Book is Anglican in effect.

The production of the Prayer Book was hampered by a lack of space in which to do the work conveniently, and before the book was finished this was so evident that a change of location, which we had for some time been considering, became a definite necessity. The Press had occupied its Summer Street quarters for some twenty-eight years. When we first moved into them they were considerably beyond our needs. Later we had use for all the space we had; then it became a tight fit; finally, hopelessly congested. We added half

[51]

The Merrymount Press

a floor to our quarters, but to little purpose, and year by year the workrooms became more crowded and inconvenient. Our workpeople complained of cramped quarters and poor light in exact ratio to the increasing praise of visitors as to the "atmosphere"—attributable chiefly (it may as well be confessed) to the smoke and grime from the South Station directly opposite. But the dirtier the place got the *more* it reminded the romanticist of "the craftsman of the Middle Ages," and the amateur of printing of "some delightful old-world workshop." Finally, after an infinite amount of wearisome search for places that would "do" and of inspection of places that would not, we found at 712 Beacon Street better and larger quarters, and the Press returned to the same street at the other end of which, more than thirty years earlier, it first started out.

Among the things I have learned from conducting a press is the importance of efficient co-operation which in industrial establishments is often hampered by a kind of hierarchy. There can be, and often is, in workshops, a table of precedence—with the result that the office snubs the proof-readers, and the proof-readers the compositors, and the compositors the pressmen, and the pressmen the shippers, and these last insult the office boy, who maltreats the cat because it is the only thing left to which he can be nasty! And, too, when an error is discovered in one department, hours are spent to show that another department is responsible—a game of industrial tag to prove who is "it." In this Press I have remedied this, or think I have done so.

I have also learned the importance of having the office of a press and its workrooms together. Offices in town and workrooms elsewhere usually beget perpetual controversy, and points which could be easily solved by conference are relegated to correspondence. An enormous amount of time is wasted by lack of the personal contact which promotes speed in turning out work and good feeling between the workrooms and the office. The tone of a letter or of even a telephone conversation may be very different in its effect from a face-to-face talk. Often what appears to be the fault of a worker is the result of inadequate instructions from the office or some difficulty the office has not realized that can be explained in three minutes by the workman.

For this reason and others it becomes evident that it is best to know personally the people in one's employ. I have been told that this cannot be done in large establishments; but even there this acquaintance can be extended more widely than is believed. If a man has a thousand employees he perhaps cannot know them all, but he can know some of them, and it is better to know a hundred than none. One reason for this lack of contact is that usually too much power is given to the different foremen, who dismiss and employ on their own initiative and are responsible only to the employer, with whom the workpeople have no direct contact and, in some cases, seldom even see. With us the arrangement has been modified; neither in press-room nor in composing-room may the foreman engage help without the applicant's having been seen by Mr. Bianchi or by me, nor dismiss help without first consulting us and stating a good reason for doing so. The result of such an arrangement is that the establishment is much more of a unit than when the foremen have unlimited power to engage or dismiss.

It is often as difficult for an employer to enter into the attitude of the worker as it is for the latter to enter into the employer's state of mind. But if, as is sometimes the case, an employer is better educated and has a wider outlook than the man he employs, it is discouraging to discover that when an indus-

The Merrymount Press

trial difficulty arises, and an employee states his position some-what tactlessly, the employer—forgetting his advantages—becomes as unreasonable as his subordinate. If as a result a matter that might be adjusted ends in a state of unnecessary irritation on both sides, the employer is more at fault than the employee. But my experience has shown me that if a situation is calmly, clearly, simply, and patiently stated, the working-man—when he understands the matter—usually is entirely reasonable.

The difficulties inherent in large establishments can be rem-edied very simply—by having small ones. And the advantage of that is that the work then shows definite characteristics because the output is controlled by one guiding hand. A good many years ago the late Horace Hart of the Clarendon Press, Oxford, came to see the Press, and looking it over said, "Very interesting, but it will never be very big." To which I replied, "Please God, no." In current typography, the printing one likes for its individuality usually comes from small plants, in which the ideas of the proprietor have not been swamped by the size of his establishment. Small shops do not pay great dividends, but, to quote a distinguished colleague, "It is the wages of life and not the wages of the trade that reward us."

Besides learning something about printing by practising it, I have also come to perceive that even a modest success brings its penalties. One of these is the incursion of youth-ful applicants for positions in which they expect to learn how to help us make beautiful books, although admitting complete ignorance of the simplest operations in any de-partment of book-making. Some of them naïvely confess an ultimate intention—after having absorbed whatever we could teach—to set up printing offices of their own. Others, loving literature, suppose that the making of books (which may or may not contain it) leads to delightful literary associa-

Notes on its Work

tions, and an opportunity to enjoy a book while reading its proofs. As far as I can judge, the unconfessed wish of these young persons is shortly to occupy, in this or some other establishment, the places that Mr. Bianchi and I modestly strive to fill; believing, it would seem, that by a kind of benign contagion they can speedily catch the trick of designing well-made books without knowing how.

Another penalty for a slight proficiency in one's trade is that people become apologetic in presenting little jobs; and by word of mouth and by letter one is asked if one would be "willing to undertake" or "sufficiently interested to do" this or that. Now what a Press needs and wants is work, and there is no reason to appear condescending in accepting it. Over and over we have said that all kinds of work are done here and that no piece of printing, however small, is neglected—much less despised. But this is all to no purpose. "I thought that you only did beautiful work," says the applicant, thereby showing that he thinks beautiful work must look "beautiful" to him, and also incidentally suggesting that standards are being let down in his behalf! The reiterated statement that labels for biscuit boxes would be a welcome job is supposed to be the amusingly exaggerated but unconvincing product of a whimsical mind.

As these days of labour have lengthened into years and decades it has become increasingly clear that the beauty of any piece of printing is almost always the by-product of its adaptation to its purpose, that its beauty must be a structural beauty and that ornament, if ornament there be, is only ornamental when allied to its use. In other words, the charm of good printing is something thrown off from its harmonious working. In the visible world we may find an analogy to this if we recognize that, in the charming phrase of Mozley, "all the colours of the landscape, the tints of spring and autumn,

[55]

The Merrymount Press

the hues of twilight and of dawn—all that might seem the
superfluities of Nature, are only her most necessary operations
under another view: her ornament is but another aspect of her
work: and in the very act of labouring as a machine, she also
sleeps as a picture."

. . . .

This is the story of the Merrymount Press, and of that seg-
ment of my life pertaining thereto. The Press took its name
from the fancy that one could work hard and have a good
time—which was not true at its beginning, although it has
sometimes been since. In no exact sense was the Press ever
founded—it only began; and as to its progress—it merely
continued. After any venture enjoys for a sufficient number
of years a sufficient degree of success, perspective as to its
beginnings is gradually lost. What was merely a venture as-
sumes the dignity of a foundation, and its continuance appears
to have been a confidently charted course. Far from being
conceived at the outset with a sort of "vision," the Press was
begun because of the lack of opportunity in a previous like
employment, where the writer was not master but man. Had
the difficulties been foreseen, and the likelihood of founder-
ing, rather than of founding, been realized, the project might
never have been undertaken at all.

The reason that it has had a measure of success is that it
had a sound programme which was patiently pursued, i.e. to
do the ordinary work of its day well and suitably for the purpose for which it is intended. I have never seen anything amiss
with this programme, though I have often seen much the
matter with the way it was carried out. Nevertheless the effort
to get printing "right" led me to collect types and to study
them, and to study the history of printing, and finally I began
to know something about it, or (as the man said about
horses) to "know more than I did." Nearly fourteen thou-

[56]

Notes on its Work

sand pieces of printing of all sorts have been turned out here, and each one of them has had the personal supervision of my partner or myself; and not one but every page of each book has come under our inspection. This means labour, and constant labour; and to such effort—which is within the power of any man—the success of the Press is chiefly due. Add to this a love of order, a wish to make good, and, as a by-product, the desire to demonstrate that a trade can be profitably practised in the spirit of a profession, and one has the whole story. None of these characteristics or desires has, necessarily, a connection with printing; each is as applicable to other occupations. In this case, through force of circumstances I happened to apply them to printing, for which I had little taste when I began, nor ever the kind of fervour that is stated (in improving books) to be essential to success. "*Dans toutes les carrières, il existe un conscience du métier,*" said Balzac; and if this conscience is of the New England variety, the result may easily be mistaken for an enthusiastic love of one's calling.

Here my experiences as a printer and my record of the Merrymount Press come to an end together. As I cannot know when the inevitable *Finis* will be written against it—or me—instead of saying "The End," I prefer to hope that both are "To be continued." But in looking back over all these years, I still must say with John Clare, "If Life had a second edition, how I would correct the proofs!"

Bibliographical List
1893–1933

This record contains the titles of all books printed at the Press so far as is known, arranged chronologically under years and numbered consecutively. Following the titles for each year, a small selection of minor printing—catalogues, reports, and the like—is appended. It should be noted that in this minor work if no place of issue is mentioned Boston is to be understood.

Bibliographical List

1893

[1]

Vexilla Regis | Quotidie | L. B. S. [*Lucy Bradlee Stone*] | [*cut*] | Boston | Privately printed | MDCCCXCIII.

On reverse of title: One hundred copies printed for the compiler at the Riverside Press, Cambridge, under the supervision of D. B. Updike, Six Beacon Street, Boston. The Selections from Longfellow, Lowell, Whittier, and Emerson are used by permission of Messrs. Houghton, Mifflin & Co. Collation: [i–vi], 1–168, [169]. Leaf, 4¼ × 6⅞. Binding, boards. Rubricated title. Type, Modernized Old Style.

[2]

Rari Nantes | Being Verses and a Song | By M. A. De Wolfe Howe, Jr. | [*floret*] | Privately Printed | Boston, MDCCCXCIII.

Colophon: Eighty copies printed for the author at the Riverside Press, Cambridge, from designs of D. B. Updike, Six Beacon Street, Boston. The Verses from *Harper's Weekly* and *Monthly* are included by permission. Collation: [1–16]. Leaf, 4⅜ × 6⅞. Binding, paper. Type, Modernized Old Style.

1894

[3]

[*within border*] A Memorial Tribute | to our Beloved Directress | Sister Mary Loretto King | of the Order of the Visitation | of the Blessed Virgin Mary | [*inscription between florets*] | Convent of the Visitation George-|town, in the District of Columbia | June xx, Anno Domini MDCCCXCIIII.

Colophon: Printed from Designs of D. B. Updike, at 6 Beacon St., Boston. Collation: [1–20]. Leaf, 5⅜ × 7⅞. Binding, paper. Type, Caslon.
Title-page design, headpiece, and tailpiece by J. E. Hill.

[4]

[*within rules*] The Year Book of | American Authors | Written and Compiled by | Ida Scott Taylor and Il-|lustrated in colours by | C. Klein | [*florets*] | New York | Raphael Tuck and Sons | Company, Limited | MDCCCXCIIII.

[61]

The Merrymount Press

Colophon: Printed under the supervision of D. B. Updike, 6 Beacon Street, at the Norwood Press, Boston. Collation: 1–371,[372–373]. Leaf, 4½ × 6⅞. Binding, cloth. With 12 illustrations. Type, Modernized Old Style.

[5]

[*within rules*] The History | of the | Class of 'Sixty-nine | Amherst College | 1889–1894 | [*motto*] | [*cut*] | Printed for the Class | 1894.

Colophon: Printed for the Class of 'Sixty-nine, Amherst, under the supervision of D. B. Updike, 6 Beacon Street, Boston, Massachusetts. One hundred and fifty copies printed. Copy No. —. Collation: [i–ii], 1–77, [78–79]. Leaf, 4½ × 7. Binding, paper. With 57 portraits. Type, Modernized Old Style.

[6]

[*within rules*] The Year Book of | English Authors | Written and Compiled by | Ida Scott Taylor and Il-|lustrated in colours by | Frederic Hines | [*florets*] | New York | Raphael Tuck and Sons | Company, Limited | MDCCCXCIIII.

Colophon: Printed under the supervision of D. B. Updike, 6 Beacon Street, at the Norwood Press, Boston. Collation: 1–371,[372–373]. Leaf, 4½ × 6⅞. Binding, cloth. With 12 illustrations. Type, Modernized Old Style.

[7]

[*within rules*] The | Rules | of The | Tavern Club | of | Boston. | With a list of the | Officers & Members | [*cut*] | [*quotation*] | Boston: | Printed for The Tavern Club, and to be had | at the Sign of the Bear, 4, Boylston Place. | MDCCCXCIV.

Colophon: Printed, with decorations drawn by F. G. Attwood, from designs of D. B. Updike, 6 Beacon Street, Boston, at the University Press, Cambridge, March thirteenth MDCCCXCIV. Collation: 1–30, [31]. Leaf, 4¼ × 6⅝. Binding, cloth. Type, Modernized Old Style.

[8]

A Memorial of | Caldwell Hart Colt | 1858–1894 | [*cut*] | Hartford | A. D. MDCCCXCIIII.

Colophon: Printed under the charge of D. B. Updike, Six Beacon Street, Boston. Collation: [i–ii], 1–52, [53–56]. Leaf, 6 × 8⅝. Binding, paper. With 4 illustrations. Type, Modernized Old Style.

Bibliography

[9]

The Importance of Musical | Knowledge to the Priest-|hood of the Church | [*floret*] | by The Reverend | James Nevett Steele | Mus.Doc.,S.T.B. | [*cut*] | [*quotation*] | New York | James Pott and Co. | MDCCCXCIIII.

Colophon: Printed under the supervision of D. B. Updike, 6 Beacon Street, Boston. Collation: [i–vi], 1–21, [22–24]. Leaf, 7½ × 10⅛. Binding, paper. Rubricated title. Type, Caslon.

Minor Printing

Order of Service, S. Mark's Church, Minneapolis, for Easter Day, Minneapolis; for the Christmas Festival of the Sunday-School of Trinity Church, in the City of Boston; for the Christmas Festival of the Sunday-School of Emmanuel Church; for the Fortieth Anniversary of the Consecration of Rt. Rev. Thomas March Clark, D.D., LL.D., Bishop of Rhode Island, Providence.

Year Book of the Church of Our Saviour, Longwood, Brookline.

Appeal in Aid of the Memorial to the late Rt. Rev. Samuel S. Harris, Second Bishop of Michigan: by the Rt. Rev. Thomas F. Davies, Detroit.

1895

[10]

A Year of Sacred Song | With Selections in Prose | from Sources Old and New | By Martha Capps Oliver | and with Illustrations from | Water-colour Sketches by | C. Klein | [*cut and quotation*] | New York | Raphael Tuck and Sons | Company, Limited | MDCCCXCV.

Colophon: Printed under the supervision of D. B. Updike, 6 Beacon Street, Boston, at the Norwood Press. Collation: i–vi, 1–366, [367]. Leaf, 4⅝ × 7⅛. Binding, cloth. With 12 illustrations. Type, Modernized Old Style.

[11]

[*within border*] A Year's Good Wishes | in Prose and Poetry | Compiled by Martha C. | Oliver. With XII Illus-|trations by F. C. Price | [*inscription*] | Raphael Tuck and Sons Co. | Limited, New York, MDCCCXCV.

The Merrymount Press

Colophon: Printed under the supervision of D. B. Updike, 6 Beacon Street, Boston, at the Norwood Press. Collation: i–vi, 1–367, [368]. Leaf, 4½ × 6⅞. Binding, cloth. With 12 illustrations in colours and with decorative title, headpieces, etc. Type, Modernized Old Style.

[12]
Vexilla Regis | Quotidie | L. B. S. [*Lucy Bradlee Stone*] | [*cut*] | Boston | Berkeley Updike | MDCCCXCV.

Collation: [i–vii], 1–168, [169–171]. Leaf, 4⅜ × 6¾. Binding, cloth. *Reissue of No. 1.*

[13]
[*within border*] Bill Pratt | The Saw-Buck | Philosopher | [*floret*] | An Appreciation of the | Life, Public Services, and | Speeches of One who for | over half a Century | ministered to the En-|tertainment and Edifi-|cation of the Students | of Williams College. By | John Sheridan Zelie of | the Class of 'Eighty-|seven, and Carroll Perry | of the Class of 'Ninety. | [*florets*] | Williamstown, MDCCCXCV.

Colophon: Printed under the supervision of D. B. Updike, Six Beacon Street, Boston, Massachusetts. Collation: i–x, 1–121, [122–123]. Leaf, 5⅝ × 7⅝. Binding, boards. With frontispiece. Type, Caslon.

[14]
[*within rules*] In Memoriam | Ellen Hampson | Horne | [*cut*] | A.D. MDCCCXCV.

Colophon: Printed under the supervision of D. B. Updike, six Beacon Street, Boston, Massachusetts. Collation: [1–11]. Leaf, 5 × 6⅝. Binding, paper. Type, Caslon.

[15]
[*within rules*] The | Hazard Family | of | Rhode Island | 1635–1894 | Being a Genealogy and History of the Descendants | of Thomas Hazard, with Sketches of the Worthies | of this Family, and Anecdotes Illustrative of their | Traits and also of the Times in which they Lived | Embellish'd with Por-traits and Fac-Similes, and with Map and Index | By | Caro-

[64]

Bibliography

line E. Robinson | [*arms*] | Boston | Printed for the Author |
MDCCCXCV.

Colophon: Printed under the supervision of D. B. Updike, 7 Tremont Place, Boston, Massachusetts. Collation: i–viii, 1–293, [294]. Leaf, 8⅜ × 11. Binding, boards. With 15 illustrations. Type, Caslon.

The fine headpieces, tailpieces, etc., were redrawn from one of Bowyer's folios or set from Caslon ornaments of the period. The composition and press-work were by Carl Heintzemann, Boston. The book was printed at the expense of Mrs. William Woodward (Sarah Rodman), sister of Mrs. Robinson. Though the title-page bears 1895 as date of issue, the volume did not appear until 1896.

Minor Printing

Catalogue of the Episcopal Theological School at Cambridge, Massachusetts, for 1895–1896.

Order of Service for the Christmas Festival of the Sunday-School of Saint Andrew's Church, Boston; for the Easter Festival of the Sunday-School of Emmanuel Church.

Year Book of the Church of Our Saviour, Longwood, Brookline.

Massachusetts Churchmanship, A Paper read at a Meeting of the Clerical Association in Boston, by George Hodges, Cambridge.

The Missionary Work of the Diocese of Massachusetts.

1896

[16]

[*within rules*] In Memory | of | Martin Brimmer | A Sermon preached in | Trinity Church | in the | City of Boston | Sunday, January 26, 1896 | by | Rev. E. Winchester Donald | Printed by Request of the | Wardens and Vestry | 1896.

Colophon: D. B. Updike, The Merrymount Press, 6 Beacon Street, Boston. Collation: [i–ii], 1–17, [18–19]. Leaf, 4¾ × 7⅜. Binding, paper. Type, Caslon.

[17]

[*within border*] The | Governor's | Garden | A Relation of Some Passages in the Life of | His Excellency Thomas Hutch-

The Merrymount Press

inson, sometime | Captain-General and Governor-in-Chief of | His Majesty's Province of Massachusetts Bay. | By George R. R. Rivers | [cut] | Printed at Boston, in New England, for | the Publishers, Joseph Knight Company | in the Year of Our Lord MDCCCXCVI.

Colophon: This Book was set up and printed for the Joseph Knight Company by D. B. Updike, The Merrymount Press, 7 Tremont Place, Beacon Street, Boston, Massachusetts, New England. Collation: [i–viii], 1–259, [260–261]. Leaf, 5 × 7¾. Binding, boards. With 6 illustrations. Type, Caslon.

The first book actually set at the Merrymount Press. The varied headpieces and tailpieces were arranged by Mr. John Bianchi.

[18]

Thanksgivings | after the Communion | of the Body and Blood | of Christ | Compiled from Ancient and | Modern Sources by a Layman | of the American Church | With an Introduction by Rev. | George McClellan Fiske, D.D. | [cross] | Privately printed at The Merrymount Press | Boston, Anno Domini, MDCCCXCVI.

Colophon: D. B. Updike, The Merrymount Press, 7 Tremont Place, Beacon St., Boston. Collation: [i–viii], [1–79]. Leaf, 4⅜ × 7⅝. Binding, red parchment. Type, Clarendon.

Also issued in decorated paper covers. The compiler was Stuart A. Coats.

[19]

[*within design*] The Nightingale | By Hans Andersen | Boston: | Berkeley Updike, The Merrymount Press | MDCCCXCVI.

Colophon: The Merrymount Press, Boston, MDCCCXCVI. Collation: [i–iv], 1–16, [17–19]. Leaf, 6⅝ × 8⅝. Binding, boards. Printed Japanese-fold. Type, Caslon.

Title-page design and 4 drawings by Mary J. Newill.

[20]

The Altar Book: Containing the Order for the | Celebration of the Holy Eucharist according | to the use of the American Church: MDCCCXCII | [*engraved plate and inscription*] | By Authority.

Bibliography

Colophon: In Gloriam Trinitatis Sanctissimae et Indivisae, Dei Unius Bene-dicti in Saecula: Alleluia. The making of this Altar Book was begun about the feast of the Nativity of Saint John Baptist, A. D. MDCCCXCIII, and fin-ished at Easter, A. D. MDCCCXCVI, by Daniel Berkeley Updike and Harold Brown, laymen of the Diocese of Rhode Island. The plain-song is arranged by Sir John Stainer, Mus.Doc.Oxon.; the plates are designed by Robert Anning Bell; the borders, initials, type and cover by Bertram Grosvenor Goodhue; and the colophons are engraved by Charles Sherborn. The type for this volume was set at The Merrymount Press, Boston, and three hun-dred and fifty copies of the book were printed at The De Vinne Press, New York. [*engraved arms of Brown and Updike families*] Published by Daniel Berkeley Updike, The Merrymount Press, Boston, Massachusetts, in the Year of our Lord MDCCCXCVI. Collation: [i–vi], [1–195]. Leaf, 11¼ × 15. Binding, pigskin. Rubricated throughout. Type, Merrymount.

The late Harold Brown of Newport, Rhode Island, was associated with Mr. Updike in this undertaking. Eight pages of the plain-song were printed as a sep-arate leaflet.

[21]
[*within border*] In the Old Days | A Fragment | by | Elisa-beth Bigelow Updike | The Merrymount Press | Boston, A. D. MDCCCXCVI.

Collation: [1–13]. Leaf, 4¾ × 7⅜. Binding, boards. With portrait. Type, Caslon.

The first chapter of a volume of reminiscences by Mrs. C. A. Updike which was never completed. It was printed for private distribution only.

Minor Printing

Order of Service for the Easter Festival of the Sunday-School of Trinity Church in the City of Boston; for the Closing Day of Miss Hersey's School.

Year Books: Church of Our Saviour, Longwood, Brookline; Trin-ity Church in the City of Boston.

Exhibition of Pictures for Schools and Hospitals, Allston Hall, Clarendon Street.

The Birth and Death of Pain: A Poem by S. Weir Mitchell, M.D.

Dedham Pottery, Dedham, Massachusetts.

Seventeenth Annual Exhibition of the Boston Art Students' Asso-ciation.

The Merrymount Press
1897

[22]

What is Worth While? | by Anna Robertson Brown | [*cut*] | Thomas Y. Crowell & Company | New York & Boston. [n.d.]

Colophon: This book was printed from original designs supplied by D. B. Updike, The Merrymount Press, 7 Tremont Place, Beacon Street, Boston, for Thomas Y. Crowell and Company. Collation: [i–iv], [1–37]. Leaf, 5 × 7⅜. Binding, boards. Rubricated throughout. Type, Clarendon.

The first of a series of similar books printed for these publishers. Cover and title-page designs by Bertram Goodhue.

[23]

[*within rules*] Mark Antony DeWolfe Howe | 1808–1895 | A Brief Record of a Long Life | by E. W. H. | [*floret*] | Privately Printed | 1897.

Colophon: D. B. Updike, The Merrymount Press, Boston. Collation: [i–ii], 1–45, [46–49]. Leaf, 6⅛ × 9⅛. Binding, boards. With 3 illustrations. Type, Caslon.

[24]

If I were God | By Richard Le Gallienne | Author of "The Religion of a Literary Man," | "Prose Fancies," "The Book-Bills of Narcissus," etc. | [*quotation*] | [*floret*] | T. Y. Crowell & Company | Publishers, New York and Boston. [n. d.]

Colophon: Printed for Thomas Y. Crowell and Company, by D. B. Updike, The Merrymount Press, 104 Chestnut Street, Boston. Collation: 1–36, [37–39]. Leaf, 4¼ × 6¾. Binding, boards. Rubricated throughout. Type, Scotch-face.

The first use of Scotch-face type by the Press.

[25]

[*within rules*] General Grant's | Letters | to a Friend | 1861–1880 | With Introduction and Notes by | James Grant Wilson | Author of "Life of Grant," | "Sketches of Illustrious Soldiers," | "Bryant and his Friends," etc. | [*cut*] | T. Y. Crowell & Company | New York and Boston | MDCCCXCVII.

Colophon: Printed for Thomas Y. Crowell and Company, by D. B. Updike, The Merrymount Press, 104 Chestnut Street, Boston. Collation: i–x, 1–132, [133]. Leaf, 4¾ × 7. Binding, cloth. With portrait. Type, Caslon.

Bibliography

Minor Printing

Catalogues: Exhibition of Pictures for Schools and Hospitals, Public Library; Loan Exhibition of One Hundred Masterpieces, Copley Hall; Loan Collection of Water Colours and Pastels accompanying the Exhibition of One Hundred Masterpieces, in Allston Hall.

Order of Service for the Christmas Festival of the Sunday-School of Trinity Church, in the City of Boston.

Trinity Church in the City of Boston, Year Book.

Annual Circular of Miss Heloise E. Hersey's School for Girls.

Dartmouth Commencement, 1897, Hanover; *also* Class Day Exercises.

1898

[26]

[*within rules*] Memorial | Book for the | Endowment Fund | of Christ Church | Cathedral, Louisville, Kentucky | [*inscription*] | All Saints' Day, A. D. MDCCCXCVII | Being the Year of the Seventy-fifth Anniversary | of the Formation of the Parish of Christ Church.

Colophon: This Book was made at the Merrymount Press, Boston, being begun in October, Anno Domini, MDCCCXCVII and finished at Michaelmas, MDCCCXCVIII[*inscription*]. Collation: [i–viii], 1–177,[178–211].Leaf,11 × 15⅜. Binding, pigskin and iron. Rubricated throughout. Type, Black-letter.

1 copy printed. Cover design by G. E. Barton.

[27]

Men and Movements | in | the English Church | By | Arthur Rogers | [*publisher's mark*] | New York | Longmans, Green, and Co. | London and Bombay | 1898.

Colophon: D. B. Updike, The Merrymount Press, 104 Chestnut St., Boston. Collation: i–xii, 1–374, [375–377]. Leaf, 4¾ × 7¼. Binding, cloth. With 4 portraits. Type, Scotch-face.

[28]

The Shadows | of the Trees | and other Poems | By Robert Burns | Wilson | [*cut*] | New York | R. H. Russell | MDCCCXCVIII.

The Merrymount Press

Colophon: D. B. Updike, The Merrymount Press, 104 Chestnut St., Boston. Collation: i–viii, 1–158, [159–160]. Leaf, 5¼ × 7⅜. Binding, cloth. Title in black and green. With 12 illustrations. Type, Scotch-face.

Composition and electrotype plates only by the Press. Plates also employed in printing a large-paper edition on hand-made paper.

[29]

Shapes | and | Shadows | Poems by Madison Cawein | [*cut*] | New York: R. H. Russell | MDCCCXCVIII.

Colophon: Arranged in types by D. B. Updike, The Merrymount Press, Boston, U. S. A. Printed from plates by Redfield Bros., 411 Pearl St., New York. Collation: [i–x], 1–77, [78]. Leaf, 5⅛ × 7¼. Binding, boards. Rubricated title. Type, Caslon.

[30]

Alice | in Wonderland | A Play | Compiled from Lewis Carroll's Stories | Alice in Wonderland and Through the Looking-Glass, and | What Alice Found There | By | Emily Prime Delafield | Originally presented, for the benefit of The Society of | Decorative Art, at The Waldorf, New York, March | thirteenth, 1897, and now for the first time printed | [*florets*] | New York | Dodd, Mead & Company | 1898.

Colophon: Printed by D. B. Updike, The Merrymount Press, Boston, 1898. Collation: i–xii, 1–89, [90–91]. Leaf, 5⅛ × 7⅞. Binding, decorated boards. Rubricated title. With 4 illustrations. Type, Caslon, chiefly.

Cover design, illustrations, and end-papers by Bertram Goodhue.

[31]

[*within border*] Songs and Sonnets | By | William Shakespeare | [*quotation*] | Edited by | F. T. Palgrave | T. Y. Crowell & Company | New York and Boston. [n. d.]

Colophon: D. B. Updike, The Merrymount Press, 104 Chestnut Street, Boston. Collation: [i–vi], 1–271, [272–273]. Leaf, 4⅜ × 6½. Binding, cloth. Type, Scotch-face.

[32]

[*within border*] Worldly | Ways | & | Byways | By | Eliot Gregory | "An Idler" | [*cut*] | New York | Charles Scribner's Sons | MDCCCXCVIII.

Bibliography

Collation: i–xi, 1–281. Leaf, 4⅞ × 7½. Binding, cloth. Rubricated title. No imprint. Type, Caslon.

Composition and electrotype plates only by the Press. An English edition, printed by the Press was issued in 1900 with the imprint of John Lane.

[33]
The | Queen's | Garland | Being Chosen Lyrics of the Reign of | Q. Elizabeth. Selected & | arranged by FitzRoy Carrington | [*publisher's mark*] | Printed for R. H. Russell | New York | 1898.

Collation: i–xvi, 1–105. Leaf, 4¼ × 6⅝. Binding, parchment. With 11 portraits. No imprint. Type, "XVII Century" Old Style.

Composition and electrotype plates only by the Press.

[34]
The Society of the | Resurrection. [n. d.]

Collation: [i–iv], 1–26. Leaf, 3⅛ × 4⅛. Binding, cloth. No imprint. Type, Scotch-face.

Printed for the clergy of St. Stephen's Church, Florence Street, Boston.

[35]
Ships and Havens | By Henry Van Dyke | [*cut and inscription*] | T. Y. Crowell and Company | New York and Boston. [n. d.]

Colophon: Arranged and printed by D. B. Updike, The Merrymount Press, 104 Chestnut Street, Boston. Collation: [i–iv], 1–42. Leaf, 5 × 7½. Binding, boards. Rubricated throughout. Type, Clarendon.

Cover and title-page designs by Bertram Goodhue. A number of copies were bound in cloth.

[36]
The War Horses | A Sermon by Rev. Roland Cotton | Smith, preached at the Church of | S. Saviour, Bar Harbor, Maine, | on Sunday, the Sixth of August, | Eighteen hundred and ninety-eight | Printed by request. [n. d.]

On fourth page of cover: The Merrymount Press, Boston. Collation: 1–15. Leaf, 4¾ × 7⅜. Binding, paper. No title. Type, Caslon.

[37]
Prosperity | A Sermon preached by Leighton Parks in Em-

The Merrymount Press

manuel Church, | Boston, on Sunday morning, January ninth, 1898, and stenograph-|ically reported. [n. d.]

On third page of cover: The Merrymount Press, 104 Chestnut Street, Boston. Collation: 1–12, [13–17]. Leaf, 7⅞ × 10½. Binding, paper. With 2 illustrations. Type, Scotch-face.

Minor Printing

Order of Service for the Christmas Festival for the Sunday-School of Trinity Church, in the City of Boston; for the Easter Festival of the Sunday-School of St. Andrew's Church.

Trinity Church in the City of Boston, Year Book.

Notes for Meditation on St. Mark's Account of the Passion of Our Lord, by the Rt. Rev. A. C. A. Hall, D.D., New York.

The Parish Library, Saint Stephen's Parish House.

An Exhibition & Competition of Colonial Pictures under the Auspices of the Colonial Dames of Massachusetts.

1898, Boston Children's Aid Society, Mid-Summer Calendar, 1899.

The Cecilia, B. J. Lang, Conductor, Boston Music Hall.

Comments of D. Appleton & Co. upon the World's Great Books, in six little books devoted to a description of one hundred and twenty great ones. Number One, New York.

1899

[38]

[*within rules*] A | Letter Book | and | Abstract of Out Services | Written during the Years 1743–1751 | By the | Revd. James MacSparran | Doctor in Divinity, and sometime Rector of | Saint Paul's Church, Narragansett, Rhode Island | Edited, with Sketch of the Author & numerous Notes, | by the Reverend Daniel Goodwin, Ph.D. | lately Rector of the Same Parish | With Portraits | Printed & Published by D. B. Updike, The Merry-|mount Press, Chestnut Street, Boston, A.D. 1899.

Colophon: Printed by D. B. Updike, The Merrymount Press, At the Sign of the Maypole, 104 Chestnut St., Boston, U. S. A., November 11, 1899.

Bibliography

Collation: [i–ii], i–xlvi, [i–ii], 1–197, [198–199]. Leaf, 5½ × 8⅝. Binding, boards. With 2 portraits. Type, Caslon.

Dr. MacSparran was connected with the Updike family, being great-great-uncle to the publisher.

[39]

Rosamund, | Queen of the Lombards | A Tragedy | By Algernon Charles Swinburne | [*ornament*] | New York | Dodd, Mead & Company, 1899.

On reverse of title: D. B. Updike, The Merrymount Press, Boston. Collation: [i–vi], 1–81. Leaf, 5¼ × 8⅛. Binding, boards. Rubricated title. Type, Scotch-face.

[40]

[*within rules*] Snow on the | Headlight | A story of the great | Burlington Strike | By Cy Warman | Author of the Story of the Railroad, The | Express Messenger, Tales of an Engineer, | Frontier Stories, etc. | [*florets*] | New York | D. Appleton and Company MDCCCXCIX.

Colophon: D. B. Updike, The Merrymount Press, 104 Chestnut St., Boston. Collation: [i–viii], 1–248, [249–255]. Leaf, 4⅞ × 7⅜. Binding, cloth. Type, Scotch-face.

[41]

[*within border*] The Art of | Living | By | Robert Grant | [*printer's ornament*] | New York | Charles Scribner's Sons | MDCCCXCIX.

Colophon: D. B. Updike, The Merrymount Press, 104 Chestnut Street, Boston. Collation: i–vi, 1–317, [318–319]. Leaf, 4⅞ × 7½. Binding, boards. Rubricated title. Type, Caslon.

[42]

[*within border*] Search-Light | Letters | By | Robert Grant | [*printer's ornament*] | New York | Charles Scribner's Sons | MDCCCXCIX.

Colophon: D. B. Updike, The Merrymount Press, 104 Chestnut Street, Boston. Collation: [i–vi], 1–233, [234–235]. Leaf, 4⅞ × 7½. Binding, boards. Rubricated title. Type, Caslon.

The Merrymount Press

[43]

Lamb and Hazlitt | Further Letters and Records | Hitherto Unpublished | Edited by | William Carew Hazlitt | [*floret*] | New York | Dodd, Mead and Company | MDCCCXCIX.

On reverse of title: Typography by D. B. Updike, The Merrymount Press, Boston. Presswork by The University Press, Cambridge, U. S. A. Collation: i–liv, [i–ii], 1–161. Leaf, 5⅛ × 7½. Binding, cloth. Type, Scotch-face.

[44]

[*within border*] Salámán | and Absál | an Allegory trans-|lated from the | Persian of Jámi: | together with a | bird's-eye view of | Faríd-Uddin Attar's | Bird-Parliament. By | Edward Fitzgerald | Edited by Nathan | Haskell Dole | Trinity Edition | Boston: L. C. Page | and Company | Incorporated. | 1899.

Colophon: This edition of Salámán & Absál was specially designed and printed for Messrs. L. C. Page and Company and finished in November, 1899. Collation: i–vi, [i–ii], 1–187, [188–189]. Leaf, 4¼ × 6¾. Binding, cloth. Decorated title, half-titles, etc., rubricated. With portrait and illustrations. No imprint. Type, Caslon.

The decorations are from old prints after designs by Du Cerceau.

[45]

[*within border*] Rubáiyát | of Omar Khayyám | Rendered into Eng-|lish Quatrains by | Edward Fitzgerald | A reprint in full of the first | edition, 1859, of the second edi-|tion, 1868, and of the fifth edi-|tion, 1889, | together with notes | indicating the minor variants | [found in the third, 1872, and | in the fourth edition, 1879]. | Ed-|ited by Nathan Haskell Dole | Boston: L. C. Page | and Company | Incorporated. | 1899.

Colophon: This edition of Omar Khayyám was designed and printed by D. B. Updike, The Merrymount Press, 104 Chestnut Street, Boston, in September, 1899. Collation: 1–159, [160–161]. Leaf, 4¼ × 6¾. Binding, cloth. Decorated title, half-titles, etc., rubricated. With portrait. Type, Caslon.

Uniform with "Salámán and Absál."

[46]

Santa Claus's | Partner | By | Thomas Nelson Page | Illustrated by W. Glackens | [*cut*] | New York | Charles Scribner's Sons | 1899 | Copyright, 1899, by Charles Scribner's Sons.

Bibliography

Colophon: D. B. Updike, The Merrymount Press, Chestnut St., Boston. Collation: [i–viii], 1–176, [177–179]. Leaf, 5⅛ × 7¼. Binding, cloth. With title and 7 illustrations in colours. Type, Scotch-face.

[47]
[*within border*] Nathan Hale | A Play | In Four Acts | By | Clyde Fitch | [*cut*] | New York | R. H. Russell, MDCCCXCIX.

Collation: [i–x], [i–ii], 1–100. Leaf, 5⅜ × 8. Binding, boards. Rubricated title. With 12 illustrations. No imprint. Type, Caslon.

[48]
The Reminiscences | of a Very Old Man | 1808–1897, By John Sartain | Academican of the Pennsylvania | Academy of Fine Arts, Cava-|liere of the Royal Equestrian | Order of the Crown of Italy, etc. | [*publisher's mark*] | D. Appleton and Company | Publishers, New York, MDCCCXCIX.

Colophon: D. B. Updike, The Merrymount Press, 104 Chestnut St., Boston. Collation: i–xii, [i–ii], 1–297, [298–299]. Leaf, 6 × 8⅞. Binding, cloth. Rubricated title. With 20 illustrations. Type, Caslon.

[49]
The Greater | Inclination | By Edith Wharton | [*cut*] | Charles Scribner's | Sons, New York, 1899.

Colophon: D. B. Updike, The Merrymount Press, Boston. Collation: [i–vi], [i–ii], 1–254, [255]. Leaf, 4⅞ × 7½. Binding, boards. Rubricated title. Type, Scotch-face.
The first of Mrs. Wharton's books, printed for Charles Scribner's Sons.

[50]
Cupid and Coronet | Drawings by Malcolm A. Strauss | [*publisher's mark*] | New York | R. H. Russell, Publisher | MDCCCXCIX.

On reverse of title: D. B. Updike, The Merrymount Press, Boston. Collation: [i–iv], [1–47]. Leaf, 8⅝ × 11¾. Binding, boards. Rubricated title. With 25 illustrations. Type, Caslon.

[51]
[*within rules*] Bob | The Story of Our | Mocking-Bird. By | Sidney Lanier. With Six-|teen Illustrations in Color | Charles Scribner's Sons | New York, MDCCCXCIX.

The Merrymount Press

Colophon: D. B. Updike, The Merrymount Press, 104 Chestnut Street, Boston. Collation: [i–x], [i–ii], 1–64, [65–71]. Leaf, 5¾ × 8½. Binding, boards. Printed in green and black throughout. With 16 illustrations. Type, Modern-face, italic.

[52]

[*within rules*] The | Great Piano Virtuosos | of Our Time | from Personal Acquaintance | [*floret*] | Liszt, Chopin, Tausig, | Henselt | By | W. Von Lenz | Author of "Beethoven et ses trois Styles," and "Beethoven, | eine Kunststudie." | Translated from the German by | Madeleine R. Baker | New York | G. Schirmer | MDCCCXCIX.

Colophon: D. B. Updike, The Merrymount Press, 104 Chestnut St., Boston. Collation: [i–viii], [i–ii], 1–169, [170–171]. Leaf, 5 × 7½. Binding, cloth. Rubricated title. Type, Scotch-face.

[53]

[*within border*] The Rime of the | Ancient Mariner | in Seven Parts | By | S. T. Coleridge. | [*cut*] | New York | Thomas Y. Crowell & Co. | Publishers. [n. d.]

Collation: [i–iv], 1–28. Leaf, 4½ × 7. Binding, limp leather. No imprint. Type, Caslon.

Composition and electrotype plates only by the Press.

[54]

With God | in the World | A Series of Papers | By | Charles H. Brent | of St. Stephen's Church | Boston | [*publisher's mark*] | New York | Longmans, Green, & Co. | London and Bombay | 1899.

Colophon: Electrotype plates by D. B. Updike, The Merrymount Press, Boston. Presswork by Trow Directory Printing & Bookbinding Company, New York. Collation: [i–x], 1–143, [144–147]. Leaf, 4⅝ × 6⅝. Binding, cloth. Type, Caslon.

Cover design by Bertram Goodhue.

[55]

The | Kings' | Lyrics | Lyrical Poems of the Reigns of | King James I. and | King Charles I. | Together with the Ballad

Bibliography

of Agincourt writ-|ten by Michael Drayton. Selected & arranged | by FitzRoy Carrington | [*quotation*] | [*publisher's mark*] | Printed for R. H. Russell | New York | 1899.

Colophon: Printed for R. H. Russell by D. B. Updike, The Merrymount Press, at the Sign of the Maypole, 104 Chestnut Street, Boston. Collation: i–xiv, 1–127, [128–129]. Leaf, 3⅞ × 6⅜. Binding, boards. With 15 portraits. Type, "XVII Century" Old Style.

[56]
A Poem | Written on the Occasion of | The Centenary | of | Georgetown Convent of the Visitation | by | Harriet Monroe | [*cut*] | Read before The Alumnae on Wednesday, May the | thirty-first, in the Year of Our Lord MDCCCXCIX.

On fourth page of cover: D. B. Updike, The Merrymount Press, 104 Chestnut Street, Boston. Collation: 1–8. Leaf, 7½ × 10½. Binding, paper. Type, Caslon.

[57]
Rubáiyát | of | Omar Khayyám | Rendered into English Quatrains by | Edward FitzGerald | A Reprint in full of the first edition, 1859, of the | second edition, 1868, and of the fifth edition, 1889, | together with notes indicating the minor variants | [found in the third, 1872, and in the fourth, 1879]. | Printed under the editing of Nathan Haskell Dole | Illustrated with twelve photo-|etchings from drawings by Gilbert | James and Edmund H. Garrett and | with portrait of Edward FitzGerald | Boston | L. C. Page and Company | Incorporated | 1899.

Colophon: Composition and Electrotype Plates by D. B. Updike, The Merrymount Press, 104 Chestnut Street, Boston. Presswork by C. H. Simonds & Co., The Colonial Press, Boston. Collation: 1–282, [283]. Leaf, 4⅞ × 7¼. Binding, cloth. Extra title in colours. Type, Scotch-face.

[58]
[*within cut*] The | Book | of | Common | Prayer | The | Three Hundred and | Fiftieth Anniversary | of Its Publication in | English | James Pott and Co. | New York | 1899.

The Merrymount Press

Colophon: D. B. Updike, The Merrymount Press, 104 Chestnut St., Boston. Collation: 1–29, [30–36]. Leaf, 5¾ × 8⅞. Binding, paper. With 2 illustrations. Rubricated throughout. Type, Caslon.

Pagination includes cover.

Minor Printing

School Catalogues: Berwick Academy, South Berwick, Maine; Pupils of the Georgetown Convent of the Visitation of the Blessed Virgin Mary, Georgetown, D. C.; *also* Centenary.

Catalogue of Paintings and Sketches by John S. Sargent exhibited at Copley Hall.

Order of the Service on February Twenty-second A. D. 1899 in commemoration of the birth of George Washington; for the Easter Festival of the Sunday-School of Trinity Church in the City of Boston.

Trinity Church in the City of Boston, Year Book.

The Society of the Resurrection, Prayers.

Record of the Class of 'Ninety-Nine, Ogontz School.

The Revival of the Romantic. By Heloise E. Hersey.

1900

[59]

A Description of the Pastoral Staff given to the Diocese of | Albany, New York, Anno Domini MDCCCXCVII: with Rep-| resentations of the chief Parts of the Staff.

Colophon: This Book was arranged and printed by D. B. Updike, the Merrymount Press, Boston, and was finished at All Saints, A. D. MDCCCC. Of the one hundred and fifty copies issued this is Number —. Collation: [1–31]. Leaf, 12⅛ × 17¼. Binding, half leather. Rubricated throughout. With 27 photogravures and 1 line-cut. Type, Caslon black-letter.

Line-cut, decorations, and binding by Bertram Goodhue. The book was printed for Mrs. J. V. L. Pruyn, of Albany, donor of the staff.

[60]

The Touchstone | By Edith Wharton | Author of The | Greater Inclination | [*cut*] | Charles Scribner's | Sons, New York: 1900.

Bibliography

Colophon: D. B. Updike, The Merrymount Press, Boston. Collation: [i–iv], 1–155, [156–159]. Leaf, 4⅞ × 7½. Binding, boards. Rubricated title. Type, Scotch-face.

[61]

[*ornament*] | The Monk | and | The Dancer | By | Arthur Coslett Smith | New York: Charles Scribner's Sons | [*ornament*] | 1900.

Colophon: D. B. Updike, The Merrymount Press, Boston. Collation: [i–viii], [i–ii], 1–241, [242–243]. Leaf, 4⅞ × 7⅝. Binding, boards. Type, Caslon.

[62]

The Old Gentleman | of the | Black Stock | By | Thomas Nelson Page | Illustrated by | Howard Chandler Christy | [*cut*] | New York | Charles Scribner's Sons | 1900 | Copyright, 1897, 1900, by Charles Scribner's Sons.

Colophon: D. B. Updike, The Merrymount Press, Boston. Collation: i–xii, 1–169, [170–171]. Leaf, 5⅛ × 7⅛. Binding, cloth. Title and 7 illustrations in colours. Type, Scotch-face.

[63]

A | Christmas | Sermon | By | Robert Louis Stevenson | [*cut*] | New York | Charles Scribner's Sons | 1900.

On reverse of title: D. B. Updike, The Merrymount Press, Boston. Collation: [i–iv], 1–23, [24–25]. Leaf, 4¼ × 7⅜. Binding, boards. Type, Scotch-face.

A number of copies were bound in parchment.

[64]

The Poetry of | the Psalms | for Readers | of the English | Bible | by Henry Van Dyke, LL.D. | Professor of Literature in | Princeton University | T. Y. Crowell and Company | Publishers, New York MDCCCC.

Colophon: Designed and printed by D. B. Updike, The Merrymount Press, Boston. Collation: [i–iv], 1–24, [25–27]. Leaf, 5 × 7⅜. Binding, cloth. Rubricated throughout. Type, Clarendon.

[65]

Olde Love and Lavender | & | Other Verses | By Roy L. McCardell | [*cut*] | New York | Godfrey A. S. Wieners | 1900.

The Merrymount Press

On reverse of title: D. B. Updike, The Merrymount Press, Boston. Collation: i–x, [i–ii], 1–93, [94–97]. Leaf, 5⅜ × 7¼. Binding, boards. Rubricated title and half-titles. Type, Caslon.

[66]
The Prince Who did not Exist | By Edward Perry Warren | With Pictures by Arthur J. Gaskin.

Colophon: Three hundred and fifty copies of this Book, of which three hundred are for sale, are printed by D. B. Updike, The Merrymount Press, Boston, U. S. A., and are published by Messrs. Charles Scribner's Sons, New York and London. MCM. Number —. Collation: [i–vi], [1–19]. Leaf, 4⅝ × 7⅛. Binding, boards. With 3 illustrations. Printed Japanese-fold. Type, Caslon black-letter.

[67]
Ward Family | Papers | Collected and Written | by Samuel Gray Ward | Privately Printed: MDCCCC.

Colophon: Twelve copies of this book were printed at The Merrymount Press, Boston, in the month of December, 1900. This is No. —. Collation: i–xii, [i–ii], 1–209, [210–215]. Leaf, 5⅝ × 8⅞. Binding, full leather. With 13 illustrations. Type, Caslon.

Printed sheets only supplied by the Press.

[68]
The Ways of | Men | By | Eliot Gregory | "An Idler" | Author of "Worldly Ways and Byways" | [cut] | New York | Charles Scribner's Sons | MCM.

Colophon: D. B. Updike, The Merrymount Press, Boston. Collation: i–vi, [i–ii], 1–282, [283–287]. Leaf, 4⅞ × 7½. Binding, cloth. Rubricated title. Type, Caslon.

[69]
The Golden Gate | of Prayer | Devotional Studies on | The Lord's Prayer | By | J. R. Miller, D.D. | Author of "Silent Times," "Making the | Most of Life," "Strength and Beauty," etc. | [quotation] | New York | Thomas Y. Crowell & Co. | Publishers. [n. d.]

On reverse of title: D. B. Updike, The Merrymount Press, Boston. Collation: [i–x], [i–ii], 1–218, [219]. Leaf, 4⅜ × 6⅝. Binding, boards. Title and chapter-heads rubricated. Type, Scotch-face.

Bibliography

[70]

The Beginner's Shakespeare. | The Comedy of | The Tempest |
Abridged and edited by | Sarah Willard Hiestand | With
Illustrations after | Drawings by F. A. M. Retzsch | Boston,
U. S. A. | D. C. Heath & Co., Publishers | 1900.

Collation: [i–ii], i–x, 1–98. Leaf, 4⅞ × 7¼. Binding, cloth. With 10 illustrations. No imprint. Type, Scotch-face.

Also issued in paper covers.

[71]

Anglo-Saxons & Others | By | Aline Gorren | New York |
Charles Scribner's Sons | 1900.

Colophon: D. B. Updike, The Merrymount Press, Boston. Collation: [i–vi],
1–158, [159]. Leaf, 5⅛ × 7⅝. Binding, boards. Rubricated title. Type,
Caslon.

[72]

Songs of Two | By | Arthur Sherburne Hardy | New York |
Charles Scribner's Sons | MDCCCC.

Colophon: D. B. Updike, The Merrymount Press, Boston. Collation: [i–iv],
[i–ii], 1–36, [37–39]. Leaf, 5 × 7½. Binding, cloth. Type, Scotch-face.

[73]

The Beginner's Shakespeare | A | Midsummer-Night's | Dream |
Abridged and edited by | Sarah Willard Hiestand | With Il-
lustrations after | Drawings by R. Smirke | Boston, U. S. A. |
D. C. Heath & Co., Publishers | 1900.

Collation: [i–ii], i–x, 1–102. Leaf, 5 × 7½. Binding, paper. With 9 illustrations. No imprint. Type, Scotch-face.

[74]

Mumford | Memoirs | Being the Story of the New | England
Mumfords from the | Year 1655 to the Present Time | By |
James Gregory Mumford, M.D. | [*florets*] | Privately printed
by D. B. Updike, | The Merrymount Press, Boston, 1900.

Collation: i–xxx, [i–ii], 1–248. Leaf, 6¼ × 9⅝. Binding, cloth. Rubricated
title. With genealogical table. Type, Caslon.

[81]

The Merrymount Press

[75]
Andrew Benton | 1620–1683 | A Sketch | By | Josiah Henry
Benton, Jr. | [*printer's ornament*] | Privately printed | The
Merrymount Press | Boston | 1900.

On reverse of title: Two hundred and fifty copies printed. Collation: [i–vi],
1–30. Leaf, 6¼ × 9½. Binding, paper. With illustrations. Type, Caslon.

[76]
Smith College Stories | Ten Stories by | Josephine Dodge
Daskam | [*cut*] | New York | Charles Scribner's Sons | MCM.

On reverse of title: D. B. Updike, The Merrymount Press, Boston. Collation: [i–x], [i–ii], 1–343, [344–348]. Leaf, 5⅛ × 7½. Binding, cloth. Title
and half-titles printed in black and green. Type, Caslon.

Binding designed by Mrs. Henry Whitman.

[77]
A | History | of | New York | from | The Beginning of the
World | to | the End of the Dutch Dynasty | Containing,
among many Surprising and Curious Matters, the | Unutter-
able Ponderings of Walter the Doubter, the Disastrous Pro-
jects of Wil-|liam the Testy, and the Chivalric Achievements
of Peter the Headstrong— | the Three Dutch Governors of
New Amsterdam; Being the Only Authen-|tic History of the
Times that Ever Hath Been or Ever Will be Published. |
By Diedrich Knickerbocker | [*quotation*] | The Whole Em-
bellished by Eight Pictures from the Hand of | Maxfield Par-
rish, Esqre | New York: Published by R. H. Russell | Anno
Domini, MCM.

On reverse of title: D. B. Updike, The Merrymount Press, Boston. Collation: i–xxxii, [i–ii], 1–298, [299]. Leaf, 8⅞ × 12½. Binding, decorated
boards. Rubricated title. With 8 illustrations. Type, Caslon.

[78]
A | Catalogue | of Books | Published by | Doubleday, Page |
and Company | 34 Union Square | New York | 1900–1901.

On fourth page of cover: Composition and electrotype plates by The Merrymount Press, Boston. Collation: [i–ii], 1–154. Leaf, 4¼ × 6¾. Binding,
paper. Type, Clarendon.

A number of copies were bound in cloth, retaining their paper covers.

Bibliography

[79]
An Office of Prayer | for Missions | with Selected Psalms | and Hymns | [*cut*] | New York | Published by the Domestic & Foreign Missionary | Society of the Protestant Episcopal Church in | the United States of America, at the Church | Missions House, 281 Fourth Avenue. [n. d.]

On fourth page of cover: D. B. Updike, The Merrymount Press, Boston. Collation: [i–ii], 1–45. Leaf, 4⅝ × 7½. Binding, paper. Type, Caslon.

[80]
The Physician. [n. d.]

Colophon: Sixty copies printed at the Merrymount Press, Boston. Collation: [i–ii]. 1–7, [8–9]. Leaf, 7 × 9⅞. Binding, paper. Type, Caslon.

By S. Weir Mitchell. Read before the Congress of American Physicians and Surgeons, May 3, 1900.

[81]
The Influence of | Anaesthesia on the | Surgery of the Nine-| teenth Century: | By J.Collins Warren, M.D., LL.D., | F.R.C.S., Being the Address of the | President before the American | Surgical Association, MDCCCXCVII | Boston: Privately printed, MCM.

Colophon: One hundred copies of this Address were printed at the Merrymount Press, Boston, in December, MCM. Collation: [i–vi], 1–30, [31–33]. Leaf, 6 × 9½. Binding, paper. With 6 illustrations. Type, Caslon.

[82]
Jacob Crowninshield Rogers | Born at Salem, October 7, 1828 | Died at Boston, January 2, 1900.

Colophon: Privately printed at the Merrymount Press, Boston, in February, 1900. Collation: [1–7]. Leaf, 5⅛ × 7⅞. Binding, paper. Type, Caslon.

[83]
Prayer and Praise | for the Officers of | the Church Army | in the Diocese of | Pittsburgh | [*cut*] | A.D. MDCCCC.

On fourth page of cover: The Merrymount Press, Boston. Collation: [i–ii], 1–14. Leaf, 3⅜ × 4⅞. Binding, paper. Type, Scotch-face.

The Merrymount Press

Minor Printing

Order of Service on December 21, 1900, in Commemoration of the Landing of the Pilgrims; for the Christmas Festival of the Sunday-School of Trinity Church, in the City of Boston; for the Easter Festival of the Sunday-School of Saint Andrew's Church, Boston.

Trinity Church in the City of Boston, Year Book.

Constitution of the Vincent Club.

Thursday Morning Musical Club, Rules and Regulations.

Thursday Morning Musical Club, MDCCCC.

Katherine Jewell Everts: Announcement.

Exhibition of Pictures for Schools and Hospitals at the Public Library.

The Church and the Nation, Messages from the Front, New York.

Announcing the Opening of Seton Inn, Lakewood, New Jersey.

Broadside: Public Statutes of Massachusetts, Chapt. 59: Sections 35 and 36.

1901

[84]

Mistress Nell | A Merry Tale of a | Merry Time | (Twixt Fact and Fancy) | By George C. Hazelton, Jr. | Author of the Play | [*quotation*] | New York: Charles Scribner's Sons | 1901.

On reverse of title: D. B. Updike, The Merrymount Press, Boston. Collation: i–viii, [i–ii], 1–311, [312–313]. Leaf, 4⅞ × 7⅝. Binding, cloth. With frontispiece. Type, Caslon.

[85]

Harvard College | The Class of 1876 | Seventh Report of the Secretary | covering the Class History for | Twenty-five Years to MDCCCCI | Printed for the use of the Class | The Merrymount Press, Boston, 1901.

Collation: i–xx, [i–ii], 1–157, [158]. Leaf, 5⅞ × 9⅛. Binding, cloth. Type, Caslon.

Bibliography

[86]

Religion in | Literature | and Religion | in Life. Being | Two
Papers | written by | Stopford A. | Brooke, M.A. | LL.D. | Thomas
Y. Crowell & Company | New York. Anno Domini MDCCCCI.

On reverse of title: D. B. Updike, The Merrymount Press, Boston. Collation: [i–iv], [i–ii], 1–58, [59]. Leaf, 5 × 7½. Binding, boards. Rubricated
title and chapter-heads. Type, Clarendon.

[87]

In Whom was no Guile | A Sermon preached in Memory of |
Henry Martyn Torbert, Minister | of Saint Stephen's Church,
Boston | Massachusetts, by Reverend C. H. | Brent, his asso-
ciate in work, on | Sunday, October sixth, MDCCCCI | [cut] |
Boston: Privately Printed at | The Merrymount Press: MDCCCCI.

Colophon: D. B. Updike, The Merrymount Press, Boston. Collation: [i–ii],
1–17, [18–20]. Leaf, 5¼ × 8¼. Binding, paper. Type, Caslon.

[88]

French Art | Classic and Contemporary | Painting and Sculp-
ture | By W. C. Brownell | New and enlarged edition | with
forty-eight | illustrations | New York | Charles Scribner's Sons |
1901.

On reverse of title: D. B. Updike, The Merrymount Press, Boston. Collation: [i–xvi], 1–228. Leaf, 7⅛ × 9⅞. Binding, boards. Rubricated title.
With 48 illustrations. Type, Scotch-face.

[89]

Samuel Slade Benton | His Ancestors and | Descendants | By |
Josiah Henry Benton, Jr. | 1620 [cut] 1901 | Privately Printed |
The Merrymount Press | Boston | 1901.

Colophon: Two hundred and fifty copies of this book were printed in the
month of March, 1901, by D. B. Updike, The Merrymount Press, Boston.
Collation: i–x, [i–ii], 1–354, [355]. Leaf, 6⅛ × 9⅝. Binding, cloth. With
25 illustrations, facsimiles, coats of arms (in colour), etc. Type, Caslon.

A number of copies were bound in cloth and boards.

[90]

Gyges' Ring | A Dramatic Monologue | By | Rupert Hughes |
[cut] | R. H. Russell | New York | MDCCCCI.

The Merrymount Press

Collation: [i–viii], 1–47, [48]. Leaf, 5½ × 8¼. Binding, boards. With frontispiece. No imprint. Type, Scotch-face.

[91]

A Memoir of the Life of | John Codman Ropes, LL.D., | with the Proceedings of | various Societies | Addresses, Papers, and Resolutions | in Commemoration | of him | [*floret*] | Boston: Privately printed | MDCCCCI.

Colophon: Five hundred copies of this book were printed by D. B. Updike, at The Merrymount Press, Boston, in April, 1901. Collation: [i–vi], [i–ii], 1–114, [115–117]. Leaf, 6½ × 10¼. Binding, cloth. With portrait. Type, Scotch-face.

[92]

Forty | Modern Fables | By | George Ade | [*cut*] | New York | R. H. Russell | 1901.

On reverse of title: D. B. Updike, The Merrymount Press, Boston. Collation: i–viii, 1–303. Leaf, 5⅛ × 7½. Binding, boards. Type, Scotch-face.

[93]

The Personality of | Thoreau | By F. B. Sanborn | [*publisher's mark*] | Boston | Charles E. Goodspeed | 1901.

Colophon: A Limited Edition of five hundred copies of this book was printed on French hand-made paper, and fifteen copies on Japan paper, by D. B. Updike, The Merrymount Press, Boston, in December, 1901. This copy is No.—. Collation: [i–vi], 1–70, [71–73]. Leaf, 5⅞ × 9⅝. Binding, boards. With illustrations and 2 facsimiles. Type, Scotch-face.

The Japan-paper copies had parchment backs.

[94]

Amos Judd | By | J. A. Mitchell | Illustrated by A. I. Keller | [*cut*] | New York | Charles Scribner's Sons | 1901 | Copyright, 1895, 1901, by Charles Scribner's Sons.

On last page of text: D. B. Updike, The Merrymount Press, Boston. Collation: [i–vi], 1–251, [252]. Leaf, 5⅛ × 7⅛. Binding, cloth. Title and 8 illustrations in colour. Type, Scotch-face.

[95]

The Ruling Passion | Tales of Nature and | Human Nature |

Bibliography

By | Henry Van Dyke | With Illustrations | by W. Appleton Clark | [*cut*] | New York | Charles Scribner's Sons | MDCCCCI.

On reverse of title: D. B. Updike, The Merrymount Press, Boston. Collation: i–xiv, 1–295, [296]. Leaf, 4⅞ × 7⅝. Binding, cloth. Rubricated title. With 8 illustrations. Type, Scotch-face.

[96]

Stevenson's Attitude | to Life: with Read-|ings from his Essays | and Letters. By John | Franklin Genung | Thomas Y. Crowell and Company | Publishers: New York: MDCCCCI.

On reverse of title: D. B. Updike, The Merrymount Press, Boston. Collation: [i–vi], 1–43, [44]. Leaf, 5 × 7⅜. Binding, cloth. Rubricated throughout. Type, Clarendon.

[97]

Aes | Triplex | By | Robert Louis Stevenson | [*cut*] | New York | Charles Scribner's Sons | 1901.

On reverse of title: D. B. Updike, The Merrymount Press, Boston. Collation: [i–iv], 1–25, [26]. Leaf, 4⅜ × 7⅛. Binding, boards. Type, Scotch-face.

[98]

The Marching | Morrows | [*quotation*] | The Merrymount Press | Boston, MDCCCCI | [*inscription within decorative border*].

Collation: [i–vi], [1–189]. Leaf, 5½ × 7⅝. Binding, boards. Type, Caslon.

[99]

The Story of Cupid and Psyche | done into English from the | Latin of Lucius Apuleius | By Walter Pater | Illustrated with Drawings | by Raphael | [*cut*] | New York R. H. Russell MDCCCCI.

On reverse of title: Typography and presswork by The Merrymount Press, Boston. Collation: 1–43, [44–48]. Leaf, 8 × 12⅛. Binding, boards. With 31 illustrations and initials printed in brown. Type, Caslon italic.

[100]

The Unfolding Life | Passages from the Diaries, Note-|books and Letters of Howard | Munro Longyear, and from the | Letters he received from his | Parents and Friends. Arranged |

The Merrymount Press

and edited by Henry D. Nunn | [*cut*] | Privately printed by D. B. Updike | The Merrymount Press, Boston, in | the Year of our Lord MDCCCCI.

Colophon: Printed at The Merrymount Press, Boston, in April, 1901. Collation: i–xviii, [i–ii], 1–191, [192–193]. Leaf, 5⅞×9⅛. Binding, boards. With 13 illustrations. Type, Caslon.

Title-page design by Mary J. Newill. 20 copies on Japan paper were printed in November, 1902.

[101]

Some Old Letters | & | Bits of History | By | Margaret Adelia Cooper | [*cut*] | Privately printed | New York | 1901.

Colophon: Two Hundred Copies of this book were printed at the Merrymount Press, Boston, in June, 1901. Collation: i–xii, 1–54, [55–57]. Leaf, 4⅞×7¾. Binding, boards. Type, Scotch-face.

Printed for Miss Sarah Cooper Hewitt.

[102]

Harvest-Tide | A Book of Verses | By Sir Lewis Morris, Knt., M.A. | [*cut*] | New York | T. Y. Crowell & Company | 1901.

On reverse of title: Composition and electrotype plates by D. B. Updike, The Merrymount Press, Boston. Collation: i–x, 1–163. Leaf, 5×7½. Binding, cloth. Rubricated title. Type, Scotch-face.

[103]

New Practical | Speller | By | James H. Penniman | Master in the DeLancey School, and author of "Common | Words Difficult to Spell," "The School Poetry Book," etc. | Boston, U. S. A. | D. C. Heath & Co., Publishers | 1901.

Collation: i–vi, 1–154. Leaf, 5×7¼. Binding, cloth. No imprint. Type, Scotch-face.

Composition and electrotype plates only by the Press.

[104]

The | Delectable | Mountains | By | Arthur Colton | [*cut*] | New York | Charles Scribner's Sons | 1901.

On reverse of title: D. B. Updike, The Merrymount Press, Boston. Collation: [i–x], [i–ii], 1–236, [237]. Leaf, 4⅞×7⅝. Binding, boards. Type, Scotch-face.

[88]

Bibliography

Selections | Katharine Coolidge | [*cut*] | Boston: Privately printed at | The Merrymount Press 1901.

Collation: [i–viii], 1–117. Leaf, 5⅛ × 8¾. Binding, boards. With portrait. Title in blue and black. Type, Caslon.

[106]

In Memoriam Alexander Williams | Born at Boston, August 24, A.D. 1818 | Died at Boston, January 11, A.D. 1900.

Colophon: Reprinted, by the courtesy of the New-England Historic Genealogical Society, at the Merrymount Press, Boston, April, 1901. Collation: [1–13]. Leaf, 6 × 9⅝. Binding, paper. With portrait. Type, Caslon.

[107]

[*within cut*] Crucial | Instances | by Edith Wharton | Author of | The Touchstone | The Greater | Inclination | Charles Scribner's | Sons, New York, 1901.

On reverse of title: D. B. Updike, The Merrymount Press, Boston. Collation: [i–viii], [i–ii], 1–241, [242]. Leaf, 4⅞ × 7½. Binding, boards. Rubricated title. Type, Scotch-face.

[108]

Christopher | in his | Sporting Jacket | By | John Wilson | [Christopher North] | Illustrated | [*cut*] | New York | McClure, Phillips & Co. | 1901.

On reverse of title: This Edition of Christopher in his Sporting Jacket is limited to twenty-five hundred copies, for distribution in England and America. Collation: i–xx, [i–ii], 1–132, [133]. Leaf, 5½ × 8¼. Binding, boards. With 8 hand-coloured illustrations. No imprint. Type, Scotch-face.

[109]

The Form of Solemnization | of Matrimony: Together with | a Certificate of Marriage | New York: Edwin S. Gorham | Fourth Avenue and XXII Street. [n. d.]

Colophon: Printed by D. B. Updike at The Merrymount Press, Chestnut St., Boston. Collation: [i–iv], [i–ii], i–xi, [xii–xxv]. Leaf, 4 × 5¾. Binding, cloth. Rubricated throughout. Type, Batarde.

[110]

The Beginner's Shakespeare | The Comedy of | The Winter's Tale | Abridged and edited by | Sarah Willard Hiestand | With

The Merrymount Press

Illustrations after Drawings | By Hamilton, Opie, Wheatley | and Wright | Boston, U. S. A. | D. C. Heath & Co., Publishers | 1901.

Collation: [i–ii], i–x, 1–132. Leaf, 5 × 7⅜. Binding, paper. No imprint. Type, Scotch-face.

Composition and electrotype plates only by the Press.

[111]

Order of Service | for the Consecration of the | Rev. Charles Henry Brent D.D. as | Bishop of the Philippine Islands | at Emmanuel Church Boston on | Thursday December Nineteenth | [*cut*] | Anno Domini MDCCCCI.

Colophon: The Merrymount Press, 104 Chestnut Street, Boston. Collation: [1–31]. Leaf, 5⅜ × 8¼. Binding, paper. Type, Caslon.

[112]

Harold Brown, Born on The Twen-|ty-Fourth of December, MDCCCLXIII | Died on The Tenth of May MDCCCC.

Colophon: Twenty copies printed at The Merrymount Press, Boston, in September MDCCCCI. Collation: [1–9]. Leaf, 5¾ × 9⅛. Binding, paper. Type, Caslon.

Written by D. B. Updike.

[113]

The | Constitution and By-laws | of the Society of the Oblates | of Mount Calvary [*Baltimore*]. [n. d.]

Colophon: D. B. Updike, The Merrymount Press, Boston. Collation: [i–iv], 1–27, [28]. Leaf, 3⅛ × 5⅛. Binding, cloth. Type, Scotch-face.

[114]

Respice | Sophia Frances Brent: Septem-|ber the Twentieth, MDCCCXXXV: | March the Second, A. D. MDCCCCI. [n. d.]

Collation: [1–9]. Leaf, 5⅜ × 8½. Binding, paper. With portrait. No imprint. Type, Caslon.

[115]

[*within rules*] The | Rules | of The | Tavern Club | of | Boston. | With a list of the | Officers & Members. | [*cut*] | [*quotation*] |

Bibliography

Boston: | Printed for The Tavern Club, and to be had | at the Sign of the Bear, 4, Boylston Place. | MCMI.

Colophon: Printed, with decorations drawn by F. G. Attwood, from designs of D. B. Updike, 6 Beacon Street, Boston, at the University Press, Cambridge. January first MCMI. Collation: 1–31, [32].

Reissue of No. 7.

Minor Printing

The Domestic and Foreign Missionary Society Publications, New York: Mid-Day Intercessions for Missions; The Church and the Nation; Are Foreign Missions Worth While?; Church Schools among the Indians of South Dakota; A Church Calendar for the Year of Our Lord Nineteen Hundred and One.

Order of Service for the Christmas Festival of the Sunday-School of Saint Andrew's Church, Wilmington, Delaware; for the Easter Festival of the Sunday-School of Trinity Church in the City of Boston.

The Variorum and Definitive Edition of the Poetical and Prose Writings of Edward Fitzgerald, arranged by George Bentham, with a preface by Edmund Gosse, New York (*circular*).

Annual Report of St. Paul's College, Tokyo, Japan, MDCCCC, New York.

The Society of Arts and Crafts: Boston, Massachusetts.

1902

[116]
Addresses | By | Henry Lee Higginson | on | the Occasion of Presenting | the Soldiers' Field and the | Harvard Union to Harvard | University | [*cut*] | The Merrymount Press | Boston MDCCCCII.

On reverse of title: D. B. Updike, The Merrymount Press, Boston. Collation: [i–iv], 1–50, [51]. Leaf, 4⅜ × 7. Binding, cloth. With 2 portraits. Type, Scotch-face.

[117]
Four Addresses | By Henry Lee Higginson | The Soldiers' Field: The Harvard | Union I: The Harvard Union II |

The Merrymount Press

Robert Gould Shaw | [*cut*] | D. B. Updike | The Merry-
mount Press | Boston MDCCCCII.

On reverse of title: D. B. Updike, The Merrymount Press, Boston. Collation: [i–vi], 1–106, [107]. Leaf, 4½ × 7¾. Binding, boards. With 2 portraits.
Type, Scotch-face.

Cover design by Mrs. Henry Whitman.

[118]
The Same.

Colophon: A Limited Edition of one hundred and fifty copies of this
book was printed on Japan Vellum, by D. B. Updike, The Merrymount
Press, Boston, in June, 1902. This is copy No. —. Collation: [i–vi], 1–106,
[107–109]. With portraits.

[119]
The Book Lover | A Guide to the Best Reading | By James
Baldwin | Revised Edition with New | List and Additional |
Matter | [*floret*] | [*quotation*] | Chicago | A. C. McClurg &
Company | MDCCCCII.

On reverse of title: D. B. Updike, The Merrymount Press, Boston. Collation: [i–ii], 1–292, [293]. Leaf, 4¼ × 6⅝. Binding, cloth. Rubricated title.
Type, Scotch-face.

[120]
Rabbi Ben Ezra | by Robert Browning | with Supplementary
Illustra-|tive Quotations and an Intro-|duction by William
Adams Slade | [*cut*] | Thomas Y. Crowell & Company | Pub-
lishers, New York, MDCCCCII.

On reverse of title: Composition and electrotype plates by D. B. Updike,
The Merrymount Press, Boston. Collation: [i–vi], 1–50, [51]. Leaf, 5 × 7⅜.
Binding, cloth. Rubricated throughout. Type, Clarendon.

[121]
Of | Gardens | An Essay | By | Francis Bacon | with Intro-
duction by Helen Milman | and Frontispiece and Cover De-
sign by | Edmund H. New | [*printer's ornament*] | John Lane |
London & New York | MDCCCCII.

Bibliography

On reverse of title: D. B. Updike, The Merrymount Press, Boston. Collation: 1–29, [30–41]. Leaf, 4 × 5¾. Binding, cloth. Rubricated title. With frontispiece. Type, Caslon.

[122]

Letters | of | Hugh Earl Percy | from | Boston and New York | 1774–1776 | Edited by | Charles Knowles Bolton | [*printer's ornament*] | Boston | Charles E. Goodspeed | 1902.

On reverse of title: D. B. Updike, The Merrymount Press, Boston. Collation: 1–88. Leaf, 6¾ × 8½. Binding, boards. With portrait. Type, Caslon.

[123]
The Same.

Colophon: Of this book, printed by D. B. Updike, The Merrymount Press, Boston, in May, 1902, twenty-five copies are on Japan paper, of which this is copy No. —. Collation: 1–88, [89]. Binding, boards, parchment back.

[124]
Thoreau | The Poet-Naturalist | with Memorial Verses | By William Ellery Channing | New Edition, Enlarged | Edited by F. B. Sanborn | [*quotation*] | Charles E. Goodspeed | Boston: 1902.

On reverse of title: D. B. Updike, The Merrymount Press, Boston, Mass. Collation: i–xx, 1–396, [397]. Leaf, 5½ × 8¼. Binding, cloth. With portrait. Type, Scotch-face.

[125]
The Same.

Colophon: A limited edition of two hundred and fifty copies of this book, with engravings and etchings by Sidney L. Smith, was printed on French hand-made paper by D. B. Updike, The Merrymount Press, Boston, in November, 1902. This is copy No. —. Collation: i–xx, 1–396, [397–399]. Binding, boards. With publisher's mark following quotation on title, and 6 illustrations.

[126]
The Same.

Colophon: A limited edition of twenty-five copies of this book, with etchings in two states and engravings by Sidney L. Smith, was printed on Japan

The Merrymount Press

paper by D. B. Updike, The Merrymount Press, Boston, in November, 1902. This is copy No. —. Collation: i–xx, 1–396, [397–399]. Binding, boards. With publisher's mark following quotation on title, and 10 illustrations.

[127]

Ralegh in Guiana | Rosamond | and | A Christmas Masque | by | Barrett Wendell | New York | Charles Scribner's Sons | 1902.

On reverse of title: D. B. Updike, The Merrymount Press, Boston. Collation: 1–143. Leaf, 5¼ × 8. Binding, cloth. Type, Scotch-face.

[128]

Our Annual Execution | Preceded by | a Word on the Annuals | by | William Makepeace Thackeray | Philadelphia | H. W. Fisher and Company | MDCCCCII.

On reverse of title: D. B. Updike, The Merrymount Press, Boston. Colophon: Of this edition there have been printed five hundred and fifty copies only for H. W. Fisher and Company of Philadelphia. No. —. Collation: i–x, 1–70, [71]. Leaf, 5⅛ × 8¼. Binding, watered silk. Type, Scotch-face.

[129]

A Paper in Memory | of the Reverend Percy Browne | read before the Boston Clericus | Club on Monday, December Second | MDCCCCI by the Reverend Charles | H. Learoyd: and also a sonnet by | the Reverend John McGraw Foster | Printed for the Clericus at The | Merrymount Press, Boston, MCMII.

On reverse of title: One hundred copies privately printed. Collation: 1–13. Leaf, 5¾ × 9¼. Binding, paper. Type, Caslon.

[130]

Dramatic | Verses by | Trumbull | Stickney | Charles E. | Goodspeed | Boston | MDCCCCII.

Colophon: A limited edition of three hundred & fifty-two copies of this book, of which three hundred and twenty-five copies are for sale, was printed by D. B. Updike, The Merrymount Press, Boston, in October, MDCCCCII. Of the edition this copy is number —. Collation: [i–viii], 1–119, [120–121]. Leaf, 4½ × 7¾. Binding, boards. Rubricated title. Type, Caslon.

Bibliography

[131]

The Land | of the Latins | By | Ashton Rollins Willard | [*publisher's mark*] | Longmans, Green and Co. | 91 and 93 Fifth Avenue, New York | London & Bombay | 1902.

On reverse of title: Composition and electrotype plates by D. B. Updike, The Merrymount Press, Boston. Presswork by The University Press, Cambridge, U. S. A. Collation: [i–viii], 1–255, [256–260]. Leaf, 5¼ × 7¾. Binding, cloth. Rubricated title. With 11 illustrations. Type, Caslon.

[132]

Helpful Thoughts | from the Meditations | of Marcus Aurelius | Antoninus | [*floret*] | Selected | By Walter Lee Brown | [*quotation*] | Chicago | A. C. McClurg & Company | MDCCCCII.

On reverse of title: D. B. Updike, The Merrymount Press, Boston. Collation: 1–127. Leaf, 4¼ × 6⅛. Binding, cloth. Rubricated title. Type, Scotch-face.

[133]

In Argolis | By George Horton | Author of "The Tempting of Father | Anthony," "Like Another Helen," "Mod-|ern Athens." With Introductory Note | by Dr. Eben Alexander, late United | States Minister to Greece. Illustrated | from original photographs | [*cut*] | A. C. McClurg and Company, Chicago | MDCCCCII.

On reverse of title: D. B. Updike, The Merrymount Press, Boston. Collation: i–xiv, 1–225, [226]. Leaf, 5½ × 7½. Binding, boards. Title in black and brown. With 16 illustrations. Type, Caslon.

[134]

The House of | Caesar | and the Imperial Disease | By Seymour Van Santvoord | [*cut*] | Pafraets Book Company | Troy New York MDCCCCII.

On reverse of title: D. B. Updike, The Merrymount Press, Boston. Collation: i–xxvi, 1–397, [398]. Leaf, 6⅜ × 9¾. Binding, cloth. With 103 illustrations. Type, Scotch-face.

[135]

The Elegy of Faith | A Study of Alfred Tennyson's | In Me-

The Merrymount Press

moriam by Walter Rader | [*cut*] | Thomas Y. Crowell and Company | Publishers: New York, MDCCCCII.

On reverse of title: Composition and electrotype plates by D. B. Updike, The Merrymount Press, Boston. Collation: [i–iv], 1–56, [57]. Leaf, 5 × 7½. Binding, cloth. Rubricated throughout. Type, Clarendon.

[136]
Rubáiyát of Omar | Khayyám the As-|tronomer-poet of | Persia, rendered | into English verse | by Edward Fitzger-|ald, the text here | given being that of | the Fifth Recension | with the same done | into Greek by Ernest | Crawley of Bradfield | College, Berkshire | England. Privately | printed for Nathan | Haskell Dole at The | Merrymount Press | Bos-ton, Massachu-|setts, in the United | States of America | Anno Domini MDCCCCII.

On reverse of title: This poem, Rubáiyát of Omar Khayyám, is printed by The Merrymount Press, Boston, and is issued with the authorization of Dr. W. Aldis Wright, the executor of Edward Fitzgerald. The version in Greek elegiacs is the work of Ernest A. Crawley of Bradfield College, Berks, England. Of the present edition are made 150 copies on hand-made paper and 25 copies on Japan. Collation: [i–viii], 1–69. Leaf, 6 × 9½. Binding, paper. Rubricated title. Type, Caslon.

The Japan-paper copies were bound in red vellum.

[137]
The Valley of Decision | A Novel | By | Edith Wharton | Volume I [II] | [*quotation*] | New York | Charles Scribner's Sons | MDCCCCII.

On reverse of title: D. B. Updike, The Merrymount Press, Boston. Collation: Vol. I, [i–viii], 1–342, [343]; Vol. II, [i–vi], 1–311, [312]. Leaf, 4⅞ × 7½. Binding, cloth. Rubricated title. Type, Scotch-face.

[138]
The Service | By Henry David Thoreau | Edited by F. B. Sanborn | [*publisher's mark*] | Boston | Charles E. Good-speed | 1902.

Colophon: A Limited Edition of five hundred copies of this book was printed on French hand-made paper, and twenty copies on Japan paper, by D. B. Updike, The Merrymount Press, Boston, in March, 1902. This is

Bibliography

copy No. —. Collation: i–xii, [i–ii], 1–30, [31–33]. Leaf, 5⅞×9¾. Binding, boards. Type, Scotch-face.

The Japan-paper copies had parchment backs.

[139]
Catalogue | of the Collection of the late Mrs. | S. D. Warren of Boston, Massachusetts | Comprising Oriental & European Por-|celain, China, Glass, Pottery, Bronzes, | Lacquer, Silver, Tapestries, Silks, Em-|broideries, Old Jewellery, Fans, Ivories, | Watches, Miniatures and Furniture | which are to be Sold | at Auction by order of the Executors | on Tuesday, December ninth, 1902, and | the following days at three o'clock | at the Beacon Art Galleries | 31 Beacon Street | Boston | [*floret*] | Beacon Art Galleries, at 31 Beacon St. | Boston, Frank A. Leonard, Auctioneer. [n. d.]

On reverse of title: D. B. Updike, The Merrymount Press, Boston. Collation: 1–118, [119–120]. Leaf, 9×11⅞. Binding, paper. With 58 illustrations. Type, Caslon.

[140]
Catch Words of Cheer | Compiled by | Sara A. Hubbard | [*floret*] | [*quotation*] | [*floret*] | Chicago | A. C. McClurg & Company | MDCCCCII.

On reverse of title: D. B. Updike, The Merrymount Press, Boston. Collation: [i–vi], [1–159]. Leaf, 4¼×6¼. Binding, cloth. Rubricated title. Type, Scotch-face.

[141]
Autobiography of | T. Jefferson Coolidge | Drawn in Great Part from his | Diary and brought down to | the Year MDCCCC | Boston: Privately printed at | The Merrymount Press, MCMII.

Collation: [i–vi], 1–410, [411]. Leaf, 6¼×9⅝. Binding, boards. Rubricated title. Type, Caslon.

[142]
Verba Crucis | A Meditation upon what Jesus | Said on Calvary. By T. Calvin | McClelland, minister of United | Church,

The Merrymount Press

Newport, Rhode Island | [*cut*] | Thomas Y. Crowell and Company | Publishers, New York: MDCCCCII.

On reverse of title: Composition and electrotype plates by D. B. Updike, The Merrymount Press, Boston. Collation: [i–x], 1–79. Leaf, 5 × 7½. Binding, cloth. Rubricated throughout. Type, Clarendon.

[143]

Flowers of Song | from Many Lands | being short Poems and detached Verses | gathered from various Languages and | rendered into English | by | Frederic Rowland Marvin | [*cut*] | Pafraets Book Company | Troy New York. [n. d.]

On reverse of title: This Edition of Flowers of Song from Many Lands consists of one thousand copies, printed at The Merrymount Press, Boston, of which sixty-three contain a portrait of the Author on parchment and are numbered. Collation: [i–ii], 1–137, [138]. Leaf, 6⅞ × 10. Binding, boards. Rubricated title. Type, Scotch-face.

[144]

Henry Wheaton | an Appreciation | being the Address delivered before the | Alumni of Brown University on the Occa-|sion of the Hundredth Anniversary of | his Graduation, June Seventeenth, MDCCCCII | By William Vail Kellen, Ph.D. | Boston | Printed at The Merrymount Press | MDCCCCII.

On reverse of title: D. B. Updike, The Merrymount Press, Boston. Collation: [i–iv], 1–52. Leaf, 5⅞ × 9¼. Binding, boards. With portrait. Type, Scotch-face.

[145]

An Office of Prayer | for Missions | with Selected Psalms | and Hymns | [*cut*] | New York | Published by the Domestic & Foreign Missionary | Society of the Protestant Episcopal Church in | the United States of America, at the Church | Missions House, 281 Fourth Avenue. [n. d.]

Reissue of No. 79.

[146]

Right Reading | Words of Good Counsel | on | the Choice and Use of Books | Selected | from the Writings | of | Ten

Bibliography

Famous | Authors | [*floret*] | Chicago | A. C. McClurg & Company | MDCCCCII.

On reverse of title: D. B. Updike, The Merrymount Press, Boston. Collation: 1–97. Leaf, 4¼ × 6⅛. Binding, cloth. Rubricated title. Type, Scotch-face.

[147]
[*cut*] | Private Devotions | [*quotation*]. [n. d.]

Collation: [i–viii], 1–133, [134–140]. Leaf, 3¾ × 6⅛. Binding, limp leather. No imprint. Type, Scotch-face.

Compiled by Mrs. Francis S. Foster. 10 copies printed.

[148]
[*cut*] | Verse | Read before the University | of Pennsylvania on the Birth-|day of Washington, MDCCCCII | By S. Weir Mitchell, M.D. LL.D. [n. d.]

Colophon: The Merrymount Press, Boston. Collation: [i–ii], i–vii, [viii–ix]. Leaf, 6⅝ × 10⅛. Binding, paper. Type, Caslon.

[149]
[*within border*] Captain Jinks | of | the Horse Marines | a Fantastic Comedy in Three Acts | By Clyde Fitch | New York | Doubleday, Page & Company | 1902.

Collation: [i–x], 1–166, [167]. Leaf, 5¾ × 8¼. Binding, cloth. With 17 illustrations. No imprint. Type, Scotch-face.

Composition and electrotype plates only by the Press.

[150]
The Life and Works | of | Charles Lamb | Pafraets Book Company | Troy New York. [n. d.]

On reverse of title: Of this Library Edition of the Life and Works of Charles Lamb One Thousand Sets have been printed at The Merrymount Press, Boston. 12 vols. Collation: Vol. I, i–xii, 1–251, [252]; Vol. II, i–xxxii, [i–ii], 1–340, [341]; Vol. III, i–xvi, [i–ii], 1–270, [271]; Vol. IV, i–xxvi, [i–ii], 1–394, [395]; Vol. V, i–xxxii, [i–ii], 1–290, [291]; Vol. VI, i–viii, [i–ii], 1–267, [268]; Vol. VII, i–xviii, [i–ii], 1–291, [292]; Vol. VIII, i–x, [i–ii], 1–267, [268]; Vol. IX, i–xl, 1–252, [253]; Vol. X, i–xii, 1–274, [275]; Vol. XI, i–xiv, 1–262, [263]; Vol. XII, i–xiv, 1–293, [294]. Leaf,

[99]

The Merrymount Press

5⅞ × 9⅛. Binding, cloth. Rubricated title. With illustrations. Type, Scotch-face.

Edited with introduction and notes by Alfred Angier. Issued in 1902–03.

[151]

The Same. Edmonton Edition.

On reverse of title: Of this Edmonton Edition Japan Vellum of the Life and Works of Charles Lamb One Hundred Sets have been printed at The Merrymount Press, Boston, of which this is Copy No.—. Leaf, 5⅞ × 9¼. Binding, boards.

Issued in 1902–03.

[152]

A Sermon preached by the | Right Rev. William Croswell Doane | D.D., LL.D., Bishop of Albany, at the | Consecration of the Rev. Frederick | Burgess, D.D., as Bishop of Long Island | in Grace Church, Brooklyn Heights | on Wednesday, January Fifteenth | [cut] | Anno Domini MDCCCCII.

Colophon: D. B. Updike, The Merrymount Press, Boston. Collation: [i–ii], 1–14, [15–17]. Leaf, 5¼ × 8¼. Binding, paper. Type, Caslon.

[153]

Catalogue of Antique | Chinese Porcelains | owned by George B. Warren of Troy | New York. With a Note of Introduc-|tion by Thomas B. Clarke of New York | [cut] | Boston: Privately printed at The | Merrymount Press, A.D. MDCCCCII.

Collation: 1–85, [86–87]. Leaf, 5⅜ × 8⅝. Binding, cloth. Rubricated title. With 18 illustrations. Type, Caslon.

[154]

Order of Service | at the Consecration of the New | Building of Emmanuel Church | Newport, erected to the Greater | Glory of God and in Memory of | John Nicholas Brown | [cut] | Newport Rhode Island | June Third A. D. MDCCCCII.

On fourth page of cover: D. B. Updike, The Merrymount Press, Boston. Collation: [1–36]. Leaf, 5¼ × 8¼. Binding, paper. Rubricated cover. Type, Caslon.

Bibliography

[155]

Order of Service | for the Consecration of the | Rev. Frederick Burgess, D.D., as | Bishop of Long Island at Grace | Church, Brooklyn Heights, on | Wednesday, January Fifteenth | Anno Domini MDCCCCII.

On second page of cover: D. B. Updike, The Merrymount Press, Boston. Collation: [i–iv], 1–14, [15–17]. Leaf, 5¼ × 8¼. Binding, paper. Type, Caslon.

[156]

[*within rules*] The Book of | Remembrance | wherein are recorded the | Divers Gifts made to | the Cathedral Church of | Saint John the Divine | [*seal*] | in the City of New York | Anno Domini, MDCCCCII.

Colophon: This Book was designed and printed by D. B. Updike, The Merrymount Press, Boston, Massachusetts, and was finished in October, Anno Domini, MDCCCCII. Leaf, 9⅜ × 13¼. Binding, full pigskin. Rubricated throughout. Type, Black-letter.

Collation not obtainable. 1 copy printed and bound for the Cathedral.

Minor Printing

The Domestic and Foreign Missionary Society Publications, New York: A Church Calendar for the Year of Our Lord Nineteen Hundred and Two; Programme and Hymnal, the Missionary Council held at Philadelphia; Mid-Day Intercessions for Missions.

Order of Service for the Easter Festival of the Sunday-School of St. Andrew's Church, Wilmington, Delaware; for the Christmas Festival; Third Service of The Society of Mayflower Descendants.

The Annual Report of the Society of Arts & Crafts of Boston, Massachusetts.

Fourteenth Annual Session of the American Pediatric Society at Boston, Massachusetts.

How can I make the Most of Myself, by Harvey S. McLeod, Troy, N. Y.

John Lane's List of Books on the Garden, Nature, Animals & Travel, New York.

The Merrymount Press

1903

[157]

Founders | of Music | Life-Sketches for | Young Readers | By
Hannah Smith, Author of | "Music; How it came to be |
what it is" | [*floret*] | New York: G. Schirmer. [n. d.]

On reverse of title: D. B. Updike, The Merrymount Press, Boston. Collation: [i–x], 1–149, [150–151]. Leaf, 5¼ × 8⅛. Binding, cloth. Rubricated
title. With 13 portraits. Type, Scotch-face.

[158]

Happiness | Essays on the Meaning | of Life by Carl
Hilty | Professor of Constitutional Law | University of Bern.
Translated by | Francis Greenwood Peabody | Professor of
Christian Morals in | Harvard University, Cambridge | [*cut*] |
New York: The Macmillan Co. | London: Macmillan & Co.,
Ltd. 1903.

On reverse of title: D. B. Updike, The Merrymount Press, Boston. Collation: [i–ii], i–x, 1–154, [155–156]. Leaf, 4¾ × 7¼. Binding, cloth. Rubricated title. Type, Caslon.

[159]

Saudades | [*quotation*] | By | Frances S. Dabney | Privately
printed | MDCCCCIII.

Colophon: One hundred copies of this book were printed at The Merrymount Press, Boston, in August 1903. Collation: i–viii, 1–102, [103–105].
Leaf, 4⅞ × 7¾. Binding, boards. Type, Mountjoye.

The first use of Mountjoye type by the Press.

[160]

[*within border*] A Little Booke | of Poets' Parleys | Being a
set of Conversa-|tions between sundry | pairs of poets as-
sent-|ing or anon dissenting | in conveying to one an-|other
their minds on | various subjects | Selected & arranged in |
Dialogue form by Char-|lotte Porter and Helen | A. Clarke
& Accompanied | with Designs by Marion | L. Peabody |
New York: Thomas Y. Crowell | and Company, Publishers,
1903.

Bibliography

On reverse of title: Composition and electrotype plates by D. B. Updike, The Merrymount Press, Boston. Collation: i–x, 1–68, [69]. Leaf, 5⅛ × 6½. Binding, cloth. Printed in black and brown throughout. Type, Clarendon.

[161]
[*within border*] Little | Stories | By | S. Weir Mitchell, M.D. | LL.D. Harvard and Edinburgh | [*cut*] | New York | The Century Co. | MDCCCCIII.

On reverse of title: D. B. Updike, The Merrymount Press, Boston. Collation: [i–vi], 1–109, [110]. Leaf, 4⅜ × 7⅜. Binding, cloth. Title in black and green. Type, Scotch-face.

[162]
Mors et Victoria | [*cut*] | Longmans, Green & Co. | 39 Paternoster Row, London | New York and Bombay | 1903.

On reverse of title: D. B. Updike, The Merrymount Press, Boston. Collation: [i–viii], 1–116, [117]. Leaf, 5¼ × 8⅛. Binding, cloth. Title in brown and black. Type, Caslon.

[163]
The Order | of | Evening Worship | in | the Meeting House on | Star Island | [*cut*] | MDCCCCIII.

On reverse of title: Five hundred copies of this edition have been printed at The Merrymount Press, Boston, of which this is Number —. Collation: [1–16]. Leaf, 5½ × 8¼. Binding, boards. Rubricated throughout. Type, Caslon.

[164]
The Warriors | By Anna Robertson | Brown Lindsay, Ph.D. | Author of, What is | Worth While?, Cul-|ture and Reform, | The Victory of Our Faith, Etc. Etc. | Thomas Y. Crowell and Co. | Publishers, New York, MDCCCCIII.

On reverse of title: D. B. Updike, The Merrymount Press, Boston. Collation: i–viii, 1–217, [218]. Leaf, 5 × 7½. Binding, cloth. Rubricated title and initials. Type, Caslon.

[165]
Alice Freeman Palmer | In Memoriam | MDCCCLV–MDCCCCII | [*seal*] | Association of Collegiate Alumnae | MDCCCCIII.

The Merrymount Press

On reverse of title: D. B. Updike, The Merrymount Press, Boston. Collation: [i–vi], [i–ii], 1–41, [42]. Leaf, 7 × 10¼. Binding, boards. With portrait. Type, Scotch-face.

Also issued in paper covers.

[166]
Parsifal | A Mystical Drama by Richard | Wagner Retold in the Spirit of | the Bayreuth Interpretation by | Oliver Huckel | Thomas Y. Crowell & Co. | Publishers New York MDCCCCIII.

On reverse of title: D. B. Updike, The Merrymount Press, Boston. Collation: i–xviii, 1–70, [71]. Leaf, 5 × 7⅜. Binding, cloth. Rubricated throughout. With 5 illustrations. Type, Clarendon.

[167]
Boston Common | in | Colonial and Provincial Days | By | Mary Farwell Ayer | [*printer's ornament*] | Boston | Privately printed | 1903.

Colophon: One hundred and seventy-five copies of this book were printed for private distribution, by D. B. Updike, The Merrymount Press, Boston, in December, 1903. Collation: [i–x], 1–47, [48–49]. Leaf, 6⅜ × 8¾. Binding, boards. With 7 illustrations. Type, Caslon.

[168]
Optimism | An Essay | By Helen Keller | Author of | "The Story of My Life" | [*cut*] | New York | T. Y. Crowell and Company | MDCCCCIII.

On reverse of title: D. B. Updike, The Merrymount Press, Boston. Collation: [i–viii], 1–75, [76]. Leaf, 5 × 7⅜. Binding, cloth. Rubricated throughout. With portrait. Type, Clarendon.

[169]
In the Dawn of the World. Being | Twenty-five pictures illustrative | of a portion of the Book of Genesis | By Edward Burne-Jones. | Boston: Charles E. Goodspeed: MCMIII.

Colophon: One hundred and eighty-five copies of this Book were printed on hand-made paper, by D. B. Updike, at the Merrymount Press, Boston, in the month of December, 1903. This is Number —. Collation: [1–31]. Leaf, 8½ × 13⅝. Binding, boards. Type, Merrymount.

Bibliography

[170]

The Poet Gray | as a Naturalist | with Selections from his Notes on | the Systema Naturae of Linnaeus and | Facsimiles of some of his Drawings | By Charles Eliot Norton | [*publisher's mark*] | Charles E. Goodspeed | Boston: MDCCCCIII.

Colophon: A Limited Edition of five hundred copies of this book was printed on hand-made paper, by D. B. Updike, The Merrymount Press, Boston, November, 1903. This is copy No.—. Collation: 1–66, [67–69]. Leaf, 5¾ × 8⅝. Binding, boards. With 12 facsimiles. Type, Scotch-face.

[171]

Joy and Power | Three Messages with | One Meaning | By | Henry van Dyke | [*cut*] | New York | T. Y. Crowell and Company | MDCCCCIII.

On reverse of title: D. B. Updike, The Merrymount Press, Boston. Collation: i–x, 1–74, [75]. Leaf, 5 × 7½. Binding, cloth. Rubricated throughout. Type, Clarendon.

[172]

Sanctuary | By | Edith Wharton | With illustrations by | Walter Appleton Clark | [*floret*] | Charles Scribner's Sons | New York: MDCCCCIII.

On reverse of title: The Merrymount Press, Boston. Collation: [i–vi], 1–183, [184]. Leaf, 5½ × 8⅛. Binding, cloth. With 11 illustrations. Type, Scotch-face.

[173]

Poems | By | Josephine Daskam | [*floret*] | New York | Charles Scribner's Sons | MDCCCCIII.

On reverse of title: D. B. Updike, The Merrymount Press, Boston. Collation: i–x, 1–72, [73]. Leaf, 5⅛ × 7⅝. Binding, cloth. Type, Scotch-face.

[174]

The Personality of | Emerson | By F. B. Sanborn | [*publisher's mark*] | Boston | Charles E. Goodspeed | 1903.

Colophon: A Limited Edition of five hundred copies of this book was printed on French hand-made paper, and twenty-five copies on Japan paper, by D. B. Updike, The Merrymount Press, Boston, in March, 1903. This is copy No.—. Collation: [i–vi], [i–ii], 1–133, [134–135]. Leaf,

The Merrymount Press

5⅞ × 9⅝. Binding, boards. With portrait and 2 facsimiles. Type, Scotch-face.

The Japan-paper copies had parchment backs.

[175]
A | New Year's Address | to the Patrons of | The Essex Gazette | 1828 | with a Letter, hitherto unpublished | By | John G. Whittier | [*publisher's mark*] | Boston | Charles E. Goodspeed | 1903.

Colophon: A Limited Edition of Sixty Copies of this book was printed by D. B. Updike, The Merrymount Press, Boston, in September, 1903. This copy is No.—. Collation: [i–vi], 1–10, [11]. Leaf, 5¾ × 8½. Binding, boards. Type, Scotch-face.

[176]
The Turquoise Cup | and | The Desert | By | Arthur Coslett Smith | Illustrated | New York: Charles Scribner's Sons | 1903.

On reverse of title: D. B. Updike, The Merrymount Press, Boston. Collation: [i–viii], 1–208, [209]. Leaf, 4⅞ × 7½. Binding, boards. With 2 illustrations. Type, Caslon.

[177]
The Poems of | Dante Gabriel Rossetti | Volume I | The Blessed Damozel | and Longer Poems [Volume II | The House of Life | and Shorter Poems] | [*cut*] | The Pafraets Book Company | Troy New York. [n. d.]

Colophon: The Cheyne Walk Edition of the Complete Poems of Dante Gabriel Rossetti, consisting of five hundred sets on Arnold hand-made paper, arranged and edited by Herbert Copeland, designed and printed by D. B. Updike at The Merrymount Press, Boston, is published by the Pafraets Book Company at Troy, New York, in the autumn of 1903. This is set No.—. Collation: Vol. I, [i–viii], 1–245, [246–247]; Vol. II, i–xiv, [i–ii], 1–246, [247–249]. Leaf, 5⅞ × 9. Binding, cloth. Rubricated title. With portrait. Type, Caslon.

Cover and title-page designs by T. M. Cleland.

[178]
[*within border*] Poems | of | Tennyson | Chosen and edited

Bibliography

with | an Introduction | By | Henry van Dyke | [*floret*] |
Boston, U. S. A. | Ginn & Company, Publishers | 1903.

On reverse of title: D. B. Updike, The Merrymount Press, Boston. Collation: i–cxxx, 1–342, [343]. Leaf, 4¾ × 7½. Binding, cloth. With 4 illustrations. Type, Scotch-face.

[179]
A Descriptive Catalogue of | Paintings Pastels | and Water-
colors | Collected by | the late Mrs. S. D. Warren | of Bos-
ton | to be sold at absolute Public Sale | by order of the
Executors | Edition de Luxe | The Sale will be conducted
by | Thomas E. Kirby | of the American Art Association,
Managers | New York: 1903.

On reverse of title: This Edition is limited to Two Hundred and fifty
Copies, of which this is Number —. D. B. Updike, The Merrymount
Press, Boston. Collation: i–clxvi, [clxvii–clxix]. Leaf, 8½ × 11⅞. Bind-
ing, boards. Rubricated title. With 66 illustrations. Type, Scotch-face.

[180]
The Same.

On reverse of title: D. B. Updike, The Merrymount Press, Boston. Collation: i–cxxxviii, [cxxxix]. Leaf, 7 × 9⅞. Binding, paper. Without illustrations.

[181]
[*within cut*] Christmas Songs | and Easter Carols | By
Phillips Brooks | New York: E. P. Dutton & Company:
MDCCCCIV.

Colophon: This book was printed by D. B. Updike at the Merrymount
Press, Boston, for E. P. Dutton and Company, in September, 1903. Collation: 1–45, [46–47]. Leaf, 5½ × 8. Binding, cloth. Rubricated title and
half-titles. Type, Caslon.

Though 1904 appears on the title-page, the book was copyrighted in 1903.

[182]
The Same.

Colophon: One hundred and fifty copies of this book on hand-made
paper were printed by D. B. Updike at The Merrymount Press, Boston,
for E. P. Dutton and Company, in September 1903. This is No. —. Leaf,
5⅜ × 8⅛. Binding, boards.

The Merrymount Press

[183]
The Third Catalogue of | The Signet | [*floret*] | The Merry-mount Press | Boston, MDCCCCIII.

Colophon: Twenty copies of this catalogue were printed on Arnold hand-made paper and three hundred and fifty copies on machine-made paper in June, 1903. Collation: i–xxxvi, [i–ii], 1–115, [116–117]. Leaf, 5⅞ × 9¼. Binding, cloth. Type, Caslon.

The hand-made paper copies were bound in boards.

[184]
The Cross | Builders | By T. Calvin McClelland | Author of Verba Crucis | Thomas Y. Crowell and Company | Publishers, New York. [n. d.]

On reverse of title: Composition and electrotype plates by D. B. Updike, The Merrymount Press, Boston. Collation: [i–x], 1–92, [93]. Leaf, 5 × 7½. Binding, cloth. Rubricated title. Type, Clarendon.

[185]
A Sermon | preached by | Rev. Charles H. Williams | at the | Annual Memorial Service | of the | Cambridge Odd Fellows | Sunday June 14 | MDCCCCIII | [*floret*].

On reverse of title: The Merrymount Press, Boston. Collation: [i–ii], 1–13, [14]. Leaf, 4¼ × 6⅝. Binding, paper. Type, Caslon.

Minor Printing

The Domestic and Foreign Missionary Society Publications, New York: A Church Calendar for the Year of Our Lord Nineteen Hundred and Three; Mid-Day Intercessions for Missions; Programme and Hymnal, the Missionary Council, held at Washington; Are Foreign Missions Worth While?; The Spirit of Missions, New York.

The Order of Service for the Easter Festival of the Sunday-School of S. Andrew's Church, Wilmington, Delaware.

Annual Report of the Society of Arts & Crafts of Boston.

Catalogue Fenway Court.

The Constitution of the Vincent Club of Boston.

A List of Books & Engravings published by Charles E. Goodspeed.

Bibliography

1904

[186]

The Collects | for the several | Sundays and Holy Days | throughout the Year | and also in the Occasional | Offices Prescribed | in the | Book of Common Prayer | [*cut*] | New York | E. P. Dutton & Company | MDCCCCIV.

Collation: i–iv, 1–123, [124]. Leaf, 3½ × 5⅞. Binding, cloth. Rubricated title. No imprint. Type, Caslon.

An edition bound in limp leather was rubricated throughout.

[187]

[*within rules*] The | Letters | of | Three Dutiful & Affectionate | Rhode Island | Children | to their | Honoured Parents | Which are here first printed for the In-|struction and Entertainment of Their Chil-|dren of the Third and Fourth Generation | [*quotation and printer's ornament*] | Boston in New England: Printed at the | Merrymount Press in Summer Street in the Year | of our Lord, 1904.

On reverse of title: Twenty-five copies printed. Collation: i–vi, 1–48, [49]. Leaf, 4⅜ × 7¼. Binding, boards. Type, Caslon.

[188]

Old Age & Immortality | an Address | delivered before the Worcester | Fire Society at its Centennial | January 21, 1893 | by | George Frisbie Hoar | [*floret*] | Worcester 1904.

On reverse of title: D. B. Updike, The Merrymount Press, Boston. Collation: [i–vi], 1–27, [28]. Leaf, 4½ × 7⅝. Binding, boards. Type, Mountjoye.

[189]

[*within border*] [*floret*] The | Life of | Michelagnolo | Bvonarroti | Collected | by | Ascanio Condivi | da la Ripa | Transone [*florets*].

Colophon: Here ends the Life of the divine Michel-Agnolo Buonarroti, written in Italian by Ascanio Condivi, and first printed at Rome, on xvi July, MDLIII, by Antonio Blado, printer to the Camera, and now done into English by Herbert P. Horne, and newly printed at Boston in the United States of America, at The Merrymount Press, by Daniel Berkeley Updike,

The Merrymount Press

1 September, MCMIIII, with the types and ornaments designed for him by the Translator. Collation: i–x, 1–85, [86–88]. Leaf, 6¼ × 8. Binding, boards. Type, Montallegro.

Arranged by H. P. Horne, designer of the Montallegro type, of which this was the first use.

[190]

[*within border*] An | Historical Address | delivered at the Celebration of the | Fiftieth Anniversary | of the Incorporation of the | Town of Nahant | July 14, 1903 | by | Henry Cabot Lodge | [*cut*] | Published by | the Town of Nahant | 1904.

Colophon: A Limited Edition of five hundred and fifty copies of this volume was printed by D. B. Updike, The Merrymount Press, Boston, in June, 1904. Collation: [i–iv], 1–22, [23–27]. Leaf, 5⅞ × 9¼. Binding, boards. With map. Type, Scotch-face.

Also issued in paper covers.

[191]

A. E. G. | Whistler's Art Dicta | and | Other Essays | [*floret*] | Boston: Charles E. Goodspeed | London: Elkin Mathews | MDCCCCIIII.

On reverse of title: D. B. Updike, The Merrymount Press, Boston. Collation: [i–viii], 1–46, [47–50]. Leaf, 4¾ × 7¾. Binding, boards. With 5 facsimiles. Type, Mountjoye.

Written by A. E. Gallatin.

[192]

Groton School | Verses | 1886–1903 | [*floret*] | Privately printed. [n. d.]

On reverse of title: D. B. Updike, The Merrymount Press, Boston. Collation: i–x, [i–ii], 1–410, [411–412]. Leaf, 4¾ × 7½. Binding, cloth. Type, Scotch-face.

Written by William Amory Gardner.

[193]

Prayers | written at Vailima | by | Robert Louis Stevenson | with | an Introduction by | Mrs. Stevenson | [*cut*] | New York | Charles Scribner's Sons | MDCCCCIIII.

Bibliography

On reverse of title: D. B. Updike, The Merrymount Press, Boston. Collation: [i–ii], i–xiv, 1–19. Leaf, 4⅜ × 7¼. Binding, boards. Title in blue and black. Type, Mountjoye.

[194]
The Consolations of | the Cross | Addresses on the Seven Words | of the dying Lord | given at S. Stephen's Church | Boston, on Good Friday, 1902 | together with two Sermons | by | Rt. Rev. C. H. Brent, D.D. | Bishop of the Philippine Islands | [*publisher's mark*] | Longmans, Green, and Co. | 91 and 93 Fifth Avenue, New York | London and Bombay | 1904.

On reverse of title: Composition and electrotype plates by D. B. Updike, The Merrymount Press, Boston, Mass. Collation: [i–x], 1–121, [122]. Leaf, 4½ × 7. Binding, cloth. Type, Caslon.

[195]
Sarah Whitman | [*cut and quotation*] | Boston | The Merry-mount Press | MDCCCCIIII.

Collation: [i–viii], 1–27, [28–29]. Leaf, 5¼ × 8⅛. Binding, boards. Type, Mountjoye.

[196]
The Splendor of | the Human Body | A Reparation and | an Appeal | by | The Rt. Rev. C. H. Brent, D.D. | Bishop of the Philippine Islands | [*publisher's mark*] | Longmans, Green, and Co. | 91 and 93 Fifth Avenue, New York | London and Bombay | 1904.

Collation: [i–viii], 1–59, [60–62]. Leaf, 4⅜ × 7. Binding, cloth. No imprint. Type, Scotch-face.

Composition and electrotype plates only by the Press.

[197]
[*within border*] Letters | from | a Portuguese Nun | to an Officer in the | French Army | Being a Reproduction | of | The Edition of 1817 | New York | Brentano's | 1904.

On reverse of title: D. B. Updike, The Merrymount Press, Boston. Collation: [i–vi], i–xvi, 1–133. Leaf, 4 × 6⅜. Binding, boards. With frontispiece. Type, Scotch-face.

[III]

The Merrymount Press

[198]

A | Wintersnight | Tale | [*cut*] | Boston: MDCCCCIIII.

On reverse of title: D. B. Updike, The Merrymount Press, Boston. Collation: [i–vi], 1–21, [22]. Leaf, 5½ × 9. Binding, boards. Type, Mountjoye.

[199]

[*within border*] A Browning | Calendar | Edited by | Constance M. Spender | [*printer's ornament*] | New York | Thomas Y. Crowell & Co. | Publishers. [n. d.]

On reverse of title: D. B. Updike, The Merrymount Press, Boston. Collation: [i–iv], 1–75, [76]. Leaf, 5 × 7⅜. Binding, cloth. Rubricated title. With portrait. Type, Caslon.

[200]

Thackeray's | Letters | to an American Family | with an Introduction by | Lucy D. Baxter | and original Drawings | by Thackeray | [*cut, with caption*] | New York | The Century Co. | 1904.

On reverse of title: D. B. Updike, The Merrymount Press, Boston. Collation: i–viii, [i–ii], 1–193, [194]. Leaf, 5⅜ × 8⅜. Binding, cloth. Title in brown and black. With 19 illustrations. Type, Mountjoye.

[201]

[*within design*] Arcady | in | Troy | The Merrymount Press Boston. [n. d.]

Collation: [i–vi], 1–22, [23–25]. Leaf, 5¼ × 8¾. Binding, boards. Title in green and black. With 2 illustrations. Type, Mountjoye.

Title-page design by T. M. Cleland.

[202]

Cornelii Taciti | De Vita et Moribvs Iulii Agricolae Liber | De Origine Sitv Moribvs ac Popvlis Germanorvm Liber | De Oratoribvs Dialogvs.

Colophon: Huius libri, cui forma est binaria, exempla centum diligenter typis descripsit Magister Daniel Berkeley Vpdike in officina sua quae Hilarimontium dicitur, Bostoniae in Republica Massachusettensi, Martio mense anno Salutis M.D.CCCC.IIII. Collation: [1–49]. Leaf, 12 × 17¼. Binding, boards. Type, Merrymount.

Bibliography

[203]

[*within border*] A Book | of | Beverages | Being Recipes se-
cured from those | Housewives most Notable for their | Skill
in the Preparation of Choice | & Delectable Beverages for
Winter | Nights and Summer Noons | [*quotation*] | [*cut*] |
Worcester, Massachusetts | Printed for the Colonel Timothy |
Bigelow Chapter, Daughters of | the American Revolution,
1904.

On reverse of title: D. B. Updike, The Merrymount Press, Boston. Collation: i–viii, 1–37, [38]. Leaf, 4¼ × 7¼. Binding, boards. Type, Caslon.

[204]

Charter and By-Laws | of the | Episcopal Theological |
School | Cambridge | Massachusetts | [*seal*] | A. D. MDCCCCIIII.

On reverse of title: D. B. Updike, The Merrymount Press, Boston. Collation: [i–iv], 1–15. Leaf, 4½ × 7⅜. Binding, cloth. Rubricated title. Type,
Caslon.

[205]

The | Club of Odd Volumes | of Boston | Constitution and
By-laws with a | List of the Officers and Members |
[*floret*] | April 1904.

Colophon: Two hundred copies of this book were printed for The Club
of Odd Volumes by D. B. Updike, The Merrymount Press, Boston, in
April, 1904. Collation: [i–iv], 1–33, [34–35]. Leaf, 5⅛ × 8¼. Binding,
boards. Type, Caslon.

[206]

[*floret*] A Man of Faith | A Sermon preached in Memory
of | Daniel Fuller Appleton in the | Memorial Church of
the Ascension | Ipswich Masstts by the Reverend | Roland
Cotton Smith on Sunday | July the Twenty-fourth MDCCCCIV |
The Merrymount Press Boston. [n. d.]

Collation: [1–14]. Leaf, 5¾ × 9¼. Binding, paper. No imprint. Type,
Caslon.

[207]

[*within border*] A | Notable Libel Case | The Criminal Prose-
cution of | Theodore Lyman Jr. by Daniel Webster | in

The Merrymount Press

the | Supreme Judicial Court of Massachusetts | November Term 1828 | Josiah H. Benton Jr. | [*cut*] | Boston | Charles E. Goodspeed | 1904.

Colophon: A Limited Edition of four hundred copies of this volume was printed by D. B. Updike, The Merrymount Press, Boston, in June, 1904. This copy is No. —. Collation: [i–vi], 1–117, [118–119]. Leaf, 5⅞ × 9⅜. Binding, boards. With 5 portraits. Type, Scotch-face.

[208]
An Office of Prayer | for Missions | with Selected Psalms | and Hymns | [*cut*] | New York | Published by the Domestic & Foreign Missionary | Society of the Protestant Episcopal Church in | the United States of America; at the Church | Missions House, 281 Fourth Avenue. [n. d.]

Reissue of No. 79.

[209]
The Holy Bible | containing | the Old and New Testaments | and the Apocrypha | [*volume numeral*] | [*books contained in volume*] | [*publisher's mark*] | R. H. Hinkley Company | Boston. [n. d.]

On reverse of title: D. B. Updike, The Merrymount Press, Boston. Collation: Vol. I, i–xiv, 1–285, [286]; Vol. II, i–viii, 1–347, [348]; Vol. III, i–viii, 1–265, [266]; Vol. IV, i–viii, 1–276, [277]; Vol. V, i–viii, 1–293, [294]; Vol. VI, i–viii, 1–338, [339]; Vol. VII, i–viii, 1–316, [317]; Vol. VIII, i–viii, 1–282, [283]; Vol. IX, i–viii, 1–287, [288]; Vol. X, i–viii, 1–318, [319]; Vol. XI, i–viii, 1–299, [300]; Vol. XII, i–viii, 1–261, [262]; Vol. XIII, i–viii, 1–250, [251]; Vol. XIV, i–x, 1–237, [238]. Leaf, 5⅞ × 9½. Various bindings. Rubricated title. With 72 illustrations. Type, Mountjoye.

86 sets were printed on Japan paper, 488 sets on hand-made paper, 1000 sets on laid machine-made paper, and 1000 sets on wove machine-made paper. There is also an edition note which varies according to the kind of paper employed. The illustrations and bindings (except those in cloth) were supplied by the publishers.

Minor Printing

The Domestic and Foreign Missionary Society Publications, New York: Mid-Day Intercessions for Missions; An Office of Prayer for Missions; The Church Calendar for the Year of Our Lord

Bibliography

Nineteen Hundred and Four (*also for 1905*); Committee to arrange an Order of Work for the Tricennial Meeting of the Board of Missions.

The Annual Report of the Society of Arts & Crafts of Boston, Massachusetts; *also* By-Laws of the Society.

Catalogue Fenway Court.

The Choral Art Society of Boston, Fourth Season, First Programme.

Grueby Pottery.

Merrymount: Being a few Words on the Derivation of the Name of the Merrymount Press, Boston.

1905

[210]
[*within rules*] The | Course | of | True Love | in | Colonial Times | Being the Confessions of William Pal-|frey of Boston and the Friendly | Advice of Moses Brown of | Providence Concerning | Polly Olney | [*cut*] | Boston in New England: Printed at | The Merrymount Press in Summer Street, 1905.

On reverse of title: [One Hundred and Twelve Copies]. Collation: i–xii, 1–33, [34]. Leaf, 4⅜ × 7¼. Binding, boards. Type, Caslon.

[211]
Adventure for God | by | The Rt. Rev. Charles H. Brent | Bishop of the Philippine Islands | [*quotation*] | [*publisher's mark*] | Longmans, Green, and Co. | 91 and 93 Fifth Avenue, New York | London and Bombay | 1905.

On reverse of title: D. B. Updike, The Merrymount Press, Boston. Collation: i–xii, 1–158, [159–160]. Leaf, 4⅞ × 7⅜. Binding, cloth. Type, Scotch-face.

[212]
[*within rules*] An | Empty Purse | A Christmas Story | by | Sarah Orne Jewett | [*cut*] | Boston | Privately printed | 1905.

The Merrymount Press

On reverse of title: The Merrymount Press, Boston. Collation: 1–15, [16]. Leaf, 4½ × 7¼. Binding, paper. Type, Scotch-face.

[213]
Chronicles | of a Connecticut Farm | 1769–1905 | Compiled by Mary E. Perkins | author of "Old Houses of the Ancient Town of Norwich" | for Mr. and Mrs. Alfred Mitchell | the present Proprietors of the Mumford | and Woodbridge Homesteads. | With Maps and Portraits | [*floret*] | Boston | Privately printed | 1905.

On reverse of title: D. B. Updike, The Merrymount Press, Boston. Collation: [i–ii], i–x, 1–298, [299]. Leaf, 6¼ × 9¾. Binding, boards. With 25 illustrations and coloured maps. Type, Caslon.

50 copies printed.

[214]
The Little Clay Cart | [Mṛcchakaṭika] | A Hindu Drama | Attributed to King Shūdraka | Translated from the original Sanskrit and Prākrits | into English Prose and Verse | by | Arthur William Ryder, Ph.D. | Instructor in Sanskrit in Harvard University | [*floret*] | Cambridge, Massachusetts | Published by Harvard University | 1905.

On reverse of title: Printed by D. B. Updike at The Merrymount Press, Boston, Massachusetts. Collation: i–xxx, 1–176, [177–178], 1–7, [8]. Leaf, 6¾ × 10. Binding, cloth. Type, Scotch-face.

Harvard Oriental Series, Vol. IX, edited by C. R. Lanman.

[215]
Steadfastness and | Brightness | A Sermon preached in S. John's Church | Wilkinsonville, Massachusetts | on Sunday, May 21, 1905 | at a Memorial Eucharist for | Mrs. James Fletcher Whitin | By | Lucius Waterman, S.T.D. | Rector of S. Thomas's Church | Hanover, New Hampshire | [*cut*] | Privately printed | 1905.

On reverse of title: D. B. Updike, The Merrymount Press, Boston. Collation: [i–vi], 1–26, [27]. Leaf, 4½ × 7⅝. Binding, cloth. With cut on title-page in colour. Type, Mountjoye.

Bibliography

[216]

[*within border*] An Emerson | Calendar | Edited by | Huntington Smith | [*printer's ornament*] | New York | Thomas Y. Crowell & Co. | Publishers. [n. d.]

On reverse of title: D. B. Updike, The Merrymount Press, Boston. Collation: i–vi, 1–117, [118]. Leaf, 5 × 7⅜. Binding, cloth. Rubricated title. With portrait. Type, Caslon.

[217]

The Valiant Woman | A Sermon | preached at the Requiem Eucharist in | S. Stephen's Church, Providence, Rhode Island | on Saturday, December 10, A.D. 1904 | by the Rev. George McClellan Fiske, D.D. | In Memory of | Anne Ives Carrington Dwight Ames | who fell asleep in Jesus | on November 10, A.D. 1904 | [*floret*] | [*quotation*] | The Merrymount Press | MDCCCCV.

Collation: [i–iv], 1–21, [22]. Leaf, 5⅜ × 8⅝. Binding, cloth. Type, Mountjoye.

Also issued in paper covers.

[218]

[*within cut*] The Marching | Morrows | [*quotation*] | [*floret*] | Volume II | Boston | The Women's Educational | and Industrial Union | 1905.

On reverse of title: The Merrymount Press, Boston. Collation: [i–viii], [1–133]. Leaf, 5½ × 7½. Binding, boards. Title in brown and black. Type, Caslon.

[219]

[*within cut*] Old | Fashioned | Flowers | and Other | Out-of-Door | Studies | by | Maurice | Maeterlinck | with | Illustrations by | Charles B. Falls | New York | Dodd, Mead & Co. | 1905.

On reverse of title: Composition and electrotype plates by D. B. Updike, The Merrymount Press, Boston. Collation: [i–viii], 1–105, [106]. Leaf, 4½ × 7½. Binding, cloth. Title and headpieces in green and black. With 6 coloured plates. Type, Mountjoye.

[220]

The Bride | by Samuel Rowlands | Reprinted for the First

[117]

The Merrymount Press

Time from a Copy | of the Original Edition of 1617 in | the Library of Harvard College | With an Introductory Note by | Alfred Claghorn Potter | [*floret*] | Boston | Printed for C. E. Goodspeed | at The Merrymount Press | 1905.

Colophon: A Limited Edition of two hundred and ten copies of this book (of which one hundred and ninety are for sale) was printed on Old Italian hand-made paper, by D. B. Updike, The Merrymount Press, Boston, in February, 1905. This copy is No. —. Collation: [1–45]. Leaf, 6¼ × 8½. Binding, boards. Type, Caslon.

[221]

The | School of Life | by | Henry van Dyke | [*cut*] | New York | Charles Scribner's Sons | 1905.

On reverse of title: D. B. Updike, The Merrymount Press, Boston. Collation: [i–iv], 1–36, [37]. Leaf, 4½ × 7⅛. Binding, boards. Type, Scotch-face.

Also issued in parchment.

[222]

[*within rules*] A Brief Sketch of the Life of | James Read | by his grandson | James Read Chadwick, M.D. | A Paper read before the | Hyde Park Historical Society | April 19, 1905 | [*within cut* 1789 | 1870] | Privately printed | The Merrymount Press, Boston | 1905.

Collation: [i–iv], 1–34. Leaf, 5⅜ × 8⅝. Binding, boards. With 2 illustrations and 2 facsimiles. Type, Scotch-face.

[223]

[*border*] | The | Life that Counts | by | Samuel Valentine Cole | President of Wheaton Seminary | [*cut*] | New York | Thomas Y. Crowell & Co. | Publishers | [*border*]. [n. d.]

On reverse of title: D. B. Updike, The Merrymount Press, Boston. Collation: i–xii, 1–124. Leaf, 5 × 7⅜. Binding, cloth. Rubricated title. Type, Caslon.

[224]

[*within rules*] The Happy Life | by Charles W. Eliot, LL.D. | President of Harvard University | [*cut*] | New York | Thomas Y. Crowell & Co. | Publishers. [n. d.]

Bibliography

On reverse of title: D. B. Updike, The Merrymount Press, Boston. Collation: [i–vi], 1–39, [40]. Leaf, 5 × 7⅜. Binding, cloth. Rubricated throughout. With portrait. Type, Clarendon and Batarde.

[225]
The Success of | Defeat | by | Maltbie D. Babcock, D.D. | [*cut*] | New York | Charles Scribner's Sons | 1905.

On reverse of title: D. B. Updike, The Merrymount Press, Boston. Collation: [i–x], [i–ii], 1–29, [30]. Leaf, 4⅜ × 7¼. Binding, boards. Type, Scotch-face.

[226]
The | Pipe of Desire | and | Other Plays | by | George Edward Barton | [*cut*] | Boston | The Old Corner Book Store, Inc. | 1905.

On reverse of title: D. B. Updike, The Merrymount Press, Boston. Collation: [i–x], 1–80, [81]. Leaf, 4⅝ × 7⅝. Binding, boards. Type, Caslon.

[227]
The Pipe of Desire | An Opera in one Act | [*printer's ornament*] | Text by | George Edward Barton | Music by | Frederick S. Converse | [*cut*] | Boston | The Old Corner Book Store Inc. | 27 & 29 Bromfield Street. [n. d.]

On reverse of title: D. B. Updike, The Merrymount Press, Boston. Collation: [i–vi], 1–19, [20]. Leaf, 4⅝ × 7⅝. Binding, paper. Type, Caslon.

[228]
Lohengrin | Son of Parsifal | A Mystical Drama by Richard | Wagner freely translated in | poetic narrative form by | Oliver Huckel | [*cut*] | Thomas Y. Crowell & Co. | Publishers New York. [n. d.]

On reverse of title: D. B. Updike, The Merrymount Press, Boston. Collation: i–xx, 1–76, [77]. Leaf, 5 × 7⅜. Binding, cloth. Rubricated throughout. With 4 illustrations. Type, Clarendon.

[229]
The John Carter Brown Library | The Dedication of the | Library Building | May the Seventeenth | A.D. MDCCCCIIII |

[119]

The Merrymount Press

with the Addresses by William Vail Kellen LL.D. | and
Frederick Jackson Turner Ph.D. | [*arms*] | Providence Rhode
Island | MDCCCCV.

On reverse of title: The Merrymount Press, Boston. Collation: [i–vi],
1–68, [69]. Leaf, 5⅝ × 9½. Binding, boards. Type, Mountjoye.

[230]
The King's Cup-Bearer | A Sermon in Memory of the |
Rev. E. Winchester Donald D.D. | preached in Trinity
Church | on the Sunday next before Advent | November
20, 1904 | by the | Rev. William Reed Huntington D.D. |
Rector of Grace Church | New York | [*cut*] | Printed for
Trinity Church | in the City of Boston | MDCCCCV.

On reverse of title: D. B. Updike, The Merrymount Press, Boston. Collation: [i–iv], 1–22, [23]. Leaf, 4⅝ × 7⅝. Binding, boards. With portrait.
Type, Mountjoye.

[231]
Glimpses of | Early Roxbury | Compiled by | The "Mary
Warren" Chapter | Daughters of the Revolution | in the
Commonwealth of | Massachusetts | MDCCCCV | [*seal*] | Printed
at | The Merrymount Press | Boston.

Collation: 1–30, [31]. Leaf, 4½ × 7⅝. Binding, boards. Type, Caslon.

[232]
The Society of Printers | for the Study and Advancement of |
the Art of Printing | [*cut*] | Boston Massachusetts | MDCCCCV.

Collation: [1–12]. Leaf, 5¾ × 9. Binding, paper. Rubricated title. No imprint. Type, Caslon.

[233]
The | Melody of God's Love | A New Unfolding of | The
Twenty-third Psalm | By | Oliver Huckel | [*cut*] | New
York | Thomas Y. Crowell & Co. [n. d.]

On reverse of title: D. B. Updike, The Merrymount Press, Boston. Collation: [i–viii], 1–49, [50]. Leaf, 5 × 7⅜. Binding, leather. Rubricated
throughout. With portrait. Type, Clarendon.

Bibliography

[234]

Story Norman Goss | Doctor of Medicine | of Chelsea
Vermont | 1831–1905 | Boston | 1905.

On reverse of title: The Merrymount Press, Boston. Collation: [i–iv],
1–34. Leaf, 4¼ × 7½. Binding, paper. With portrait. Type, Caslon.

[235]

[*within rules*] A Sermon in Memory of | E. Winchester
Donald, D.D., LL.D. | Late Rector of Trinity Church |
Boston | preached in Trinity Church | Sunday Afternoon,
November 20, 1904 | by | Joseph N. Blanchard, D.D. | [*cut*] |
Printed for Trinity Church | in the City of Boston |
MDCCCCV.

Colophon: The Merrymount Press, Boston. Collation: [i–ii], 1–11. Leaf,
5¼ × 8¼. Binding, paper. Type, Caslon.

Minor Printing

Reports: Society of Arts & Crafts of Boston; Workingmen's
Building Association; Report of Progress, Women's Educational
and Industrial Union; Annual Report of the President to the
Corporation of Brown University, Providence.

Catalogue of Brown University, 1905–1906, Providence.

Catalogue Fenway Court.

The Choral Art Society of Boston, Fourth Season, Second Programme; *also* Fifth Season, First Programme *and* Second Programme.

School Civics with Civics of New York State, by Frank David
Boynton, Ginn & Company, New York City.

Subjects Adopted by the Committee on Syllabus Revision to
constitute Group IV History and Social Science, Ginn & Company, New York.

Twelfth Night at Eagleroost, The Century Association, New York.

Grueby Garden Pottery, Grueby Faience Company.

The Constitution of the Vincent Club.

Notes on Saint John's Church [formerly King's Church] in Providence (*by D. B. Updike*).

The Merrymount Press
1906

[236]

[*within border*] The Playhouse Series | Lilies that Fester |
and | Love's Constancy | Arranged by | William Poel | Di-
rector of the Elizabethan | Stage Society | Brentano's New
York. [n. d.]

On reverse of title: D. B. Updike, The Merrymount Press, Boston. Collation: [i–ii], i–viii, [i–iv], 1–109. Leaf, 5⅛ × 7¾. Binding, boards. Type,
Scotch-face.

[237]

[*within rules*] Putting the Most | Into Life | by Booker T.
Washington | Author of "Up from Slavery" | [*cut*] | New
York | Thomas Y. Crowell & Co. | Publishers. [n. d.]

On reverse of title: Composition and electrotype plates by D. B. Updike,
The Merrymount Press, Boston. Collation: [i–viii], 1–35, [36]. Leaf, 5 × 7⅜.
Binding, cloth. Rubricated throughout. With portrait. Type, Clarendon.

[238]

Smith of Bear City | and Other Frontier Sketches | by |
George T. Buffum | [*floret*] | Illustrated with six photo-
gravures | from Original Drawings by | F. T. Wood |
[*publisher's mark*] | New York | The Grafton Press | 1906.

On reverse of title: D. B. Updike, The Merrymount Press, Boston. Collation: i–xiv, 1–248, [249]. Leaf, 5½ × 8⅛. Binding, cloth. With 6 illustrations. Type, Scotch-face.

[239]

[*within decorative design*] The Life of Benvenuto Cellini |
written by himself | Edited and Translated by John Ad-
dington | Symonds with a Biographical Sketch of | Cellini
by the same hand together with | an Introduction to this
edition upon | Benvenuto Cellini, artist and writer, by |
Royal Cortissoz with reproductions | of forty original
portraits and views | illustrating the life | Brentano's New
York. [n. d.]

Bibliography

On reverse of title: D. B. Updike, The Merrymount Press, Boston. 2 vols. Collation: Vol. I, i–xxx, 1–359, [360]; Vol. II, i–viii, 1–386, [387]. Leaf, 5⅞×9⅛. Binding, cloth. Title and illustrations in photogravure. Type, Mountjoye.

Title-page design by T. M. Cleland. Binding from design by Laurence Housman.

[240]
[*within rules*] Great Riches | by Charles W. Eliot, LL.D. | President of Harvard University | [*cut*] | New York | Thomas Y. Crowell & Co. | Publishers. [n. d.]

On reverse of title: Composition and electrotype plates by D. B. Updike, The Merrymount Press, Boston. Collation: [i–vi], 1–37, [38]. Leaf, 5 × 7⅜. Binding, cloth. Rubricated throughout. With portrait. Type, Clarendon.

[241]
[*within rules*] Germelshausen | By Friedrich Gerstäcker | Translated from the German | By Clara M. Lathrop | [*printer's ornament*] | New York | Thomas Y. Crowell & Co. | Publishers. [n. d.]

On reverse of title: D. B. Updike, The Merrymount Press, Boston. Collation: [i–iv], 1–45, [46]. Leaf, 5 × 7⅜. Binding, cloth. Rubricated throughout. With frontispiece. Type, Clarendon.

[242]
[*within rules*] The World's | Christmas Tree | By Charles E. Jefferson | [*cut*] | New York | Thomas Y. Crowell & Co. | Publishers. [n. d.]

On reverse of title: Composition and electrotype plates by D. B. Updike, The Merrymount Press, Boston. Collation: [i–iv], 1–44, [45]. Leaf, 5 × 7⅜. Binding, cloth. Rubricated throughout. Type, Caslon.

[243]
[*within border*] The Soul of the People | A New Year's Sermon | by | William M. Ivins | [*publisher's mark*] | The Century Co. | New York | 1906.

On reverse of title: D. B. Updike, The Merrymount Press, Boston. Collation: [i–ii], 1–68, [69]. Leaf, 4⅜ × 7¼. Binding, boards. Type, Scotch-face.

Also issued in paper covers.

[123]

The Merrymount Press

[244]
Poems | by | Anne Whitney | [*floret*] | Boston | Privately
printed | 1906.

On reverse of title: D. B. Updike, The Merrymount Press, Boston. Collation: i–v, [i–iv], 1–170, [171–173]. Leaf, 5⅛ × 7⅜. Binding, cloth. Type,
Scotch-face.

[245]
A Game at Love | and other Plays | by | George Sylvester
Viereck | [*cut*] | New York | Brentano's | 1906.

Collation: i–x, 1–98, [99]. Leaf, 5 × 7¾. Binding, cloth. No imprint. Type,
Caslon.

[246]
A Record of | the Ceremony and Oration | on the Occa-
sion of the | Unveiling of the Monument Commemorat-
ing | The Great Swamp Fight | December 19, 1675 | in the
Narragansett Country | Rhode Island | Erected by the Socie-
ties of the Colonial Wars | of Rhode Island and Massachu-
setts | October 20, 1906 | [*seal*] | Printed for the | Societies of
Colonial Wars | MDCCCCVI.

On reverse of title: D. B. Updike, The Merrymount Press, Boston. Collation: [i–x], 1–68, [69]. Leaf, 5¾ × 9⅛. Binding, cloth. With 3 illustrations
and 3 maps. Type, Mountjoye.

[247]
[*within border*] Thoughts | on | Art and Life | by | Leonardo
da Vinci | [*floret*] | Translated | by | Maurice Baring | [*floret*] |
Boston | The Merrymount Press | 1906.

Colophon: Of this volume, translated by Maurice Baring and edited by
Lewis Einstein, with types and decorations by Herbert P. Horne, CCCIII
copies were printed [*printer's mark*] by D. B. Updike at The Merrymount
Press, Boston, Massachusetts, in the month of September MCMVI. Collation:
i–xxvi, 1–200, [201–202]. Leaf, 5⅝ × 9½. Binding, boards. Rubricated
throughout. Type, Montallegro.
The Humanists' Library, Vol. I. Title-page design by Herbert P. Horne.

[248]
Liberty | and Other Sermons | by | the Rt. Rev. Charles H.
Brent | Bishop of the Philippine Islands | [*publisher's mark*] |

Bibliography

Longmans, Green, and Co. | 91 and 93 Fifth Avenue, New York | London and Bombay | 1906.

On reverse of title: D. B. Updike, The Merrymount Press, Boston. Collation: [i–x], 1–190, [191–195]. Leaf, 5 × 7⅜. Binding, cloth. Type, Scotch-face.

[249]
The Development | of Printing as an Art | a Handbook | of the Exhibition in honor of | the Bi-centenary of Franklin's birth held at the | Boston Public Library | under the auspices | of the Society | of Printers | [*seal*] | Publications of the Society, Number II | Boston, Massachusetts | January 1 to 29, 1906.

Collation: [i–vi], 1–94. Leaf, 5½ × 8¾. Binding, paper. Rubricated title. No imprint. Type, Caslon.

[250]
A Guide-Book of Boston | for Physicians | Prepared for the | Fifty-seventh Annual Session | of the | American Medical Association | June fifth, sixth, seventh and eighth | 1906 | Edited by | Dr. Walter L. Burrage | [*cut*] | Boston | The Merrymount Press | MDCCCCVI.

On reverse of title: D. B. Updike, The Merrymount Press, Boston. Collation: i–xii, 1–234. Leaf, 5 × 7¾. Binding, paper. Profusely illustrated. Type, Scotch-face.

[251]
The Donald Family | With Notes on Related Families | by | Donald Gordon | [*printer's ornament*] | Boston | 1906.

On reverse of title: D. B. Updike, The Merrymount Press, Boston. Collation: i–xii, 1–78, [79]. Leaf, 5⅜ × 8¾. Binding, boards. With 20 illustrations and map. Type, Caslon.

[252]
[*cross*] The Memory of the Just | A Benediction | A Memorial Sermon delivered by | Rt. Rev. Thomas A. Jaggar, D.D. | Ascension Day A. D. 1906 | on the Occasion of the Placing

The Merrymount Press

of | a Tablet in S. Paul's Church, Boston | to the Memory of | Mrs. William Appleton | [*floret*] | Boston | Privately printed | 1906.

On reverse of title: D. B. Updike, The Merrymount Press, Boston. Collation: [i–vi], 1–13, [14]. Leaf, 4½ × 7⅝. Binding, cloth. Type, Mountjoye.

[253]
The Man | Without a Country | by | Edward Everett Hale | [*printer's ornament*] | New York | Thomas Y. Crowell & Company. [n. d.]

On reverse of title: D. B. Updike, The Merrymount Press, Boston. Collation: [i–iv], 1–51, [52]. Leaf, 5 × 7⅜. Binding, cloth. Rubricated throughout. With frontispiece. Type, Clarendon.

[254]
Tannhäuser | A Dramatic Poem by Richard | Wagner freely translated | in poetic narrative form by | Oliver Huckel | [*floret*] | Thomas Y. Crowell & Co. | Publishers New York. [n. d.]

On reverse of title: Composition and electrotype plates by D. B. Updike, The Merrymount Press, Boston. Collation: i–xviii, 1–68, [69]. Leaf, 5 × 7⅜. Binding, cloth. Rubricated throughout. With 4 illustrations. Type, Clarendon.

[255]
Euripides | and | the Spirit of his Dramas | By | Paul Decharme | Professor of Greek Poetry in the | Faculté des Lettres at Paris | Translated | by James Loeb, A.B. | New York: The Macmillan Co. | London: Macmillan & Co. Ltd. [n. d.]

On reverse of title: D. B. Updike, The Merrymount Press, Boston. Collation: i–xxiv, 1–392. Leaf, 5⅝ × 8¾. Binding, cloth. With frontispiece. Type, Scotch-face.

[256]
George Atherton Spalding | by | C. A. Herter M.D. | Reprinted from the | New York Medical Journal | [*floret*] | MDCCCCVI.

On reverse of title: D. B. Updike, The Merrymount Press, Boston. Collation: [i–iv], 1–6, [7]. Leaf, 4½ × 7⅝. Binding, paper. Type, Mountjoye.

Bibliography

[257]

[*within border*] A Longfellow | Calendar | Edited by | Anna Harris Smith | [*printer's ornament*] | New York | Thomas Y. Crowell & Co. | Publishers. [n. d.]

On reverse of title: Composition and electrotype plates by D. B. Updike, The Merrymount Press, Boston. Collation: [i–iv], 1–136, [137]. Leaf, 5 × 7⅜. Binding, cloth. Rubricated title. With portrait. Type, Caslon.

[258]

Historie of the Life and Death of | Sir William Kirkaldy | of Grange, Knight | Wherein is declared his many Wise Designs and Valiant Ac-|tions, with a True Relation of his Heroic Conduct in the Castle of | Edinburgh which he had the Honour to defend for the Queen of Scots. | Now set forth from Authentic Sources by Harold Murdock. | [*arms*] | Printed for The Club of Odd Volumes at Boston in | New England in the Year of Our Lord, MDCCCCVI.

Colophon: This book is one of an edition of One Hundred and Fourteen copies printed on Arnold hand-made paper, by D. B. Updike at The Merrymount Press, Boston [*arms*]. Printing completed and type distributed in June MDCCCCVI. Collation: i–xii, 1–130, [131]. Leaf, 6½ × 10¼. Binding, boards. With 7 portraits, maps, and facsimiles. Type, Caslon.

[259]

The | Duties | & | Qualifications | of a | Librarian | A Discourse pronounced in | the General Assembly | of the Sorbonne | December 23 | 1780 | by | Jean-Baptiste Cotton | des Houssayes | [*floret*] | Chicago | A. C. McClurg & Co. | MDCCCCVI.

On page facing title: An Edition of two hundred and fifty copies in this form and of twenty-five copies on Large Paper were printed at The Merrymount Press, Boston, in July, 1906. Collation: 1–56. Leaf, 3⅞ × 6⅝. Binding, cloth. Type, Mountjoye.

Literature of Libraries, Vol. I. Literature of Libraries in the Seventeenth and Eighteenth Centuries, edited by John Cotton Dana and Henry W. Kent. 6 vols.: Vols. I to IV (1906) and Vols. V and VI (1907). Each book has an extra decorative title-page to the series in black and brown.

[260]
The Same.

Large-paper edition. On page facing title: Of this Large-Paper Edition

The Merrymount Press

Twenty-five copies were printed at The Merrymount Press, Boston, in July, 1906. Leaf, 4⅝ × 7¾. Binding, boards.

[261]
The | Reformed | Librarie-Keeper | or | Two Copies of Letters | Concerning | the Place and Office of | a Librarie-Keeper | By | John Dury | [*floret*] | Chicago | A. C. McClurg & Co. | MDCCCCVI.
Collation: 1–71. For full description, *see* No. 259.
Literature of Libraries, Vol. II.

[262]
The Same.
Large-paper edition. For description, *see* No. 260.

[263]
The Life of | Sir Thomas Bodley | Written by Himself | Together with | the first Draft of the | Statutes | of the | Public Library | at Oxon | [*floret*] | Chicago | A. C. Mc-Clurg & Co. | MDCCCCVI.
Collation: 1–116. For description, *see* No. 259.
Literature of Libraries, Vol. III. Issued in November.

[264]
The Same.
Large-paper edition. For description, *see* No. 260.
Issued in November.

[265]
Two Tracts on the Founding | and Maintaining of | Parochial Libraries | in | Scotland | By | James Kirkwood | [*floret*] | Chicago | A. C. McClurg & Co. | MDCCCCVI.
Collation: 1–89. For description, *see* No. 259.
Literature of Libraries, Vol. IV. Issued in November.

[266]
The Same.
Large-paper edition. For description, *see* No. 260.
Issued in November.

Bibliography

[267]

The Influence of | Anaesthesia on the | Surgery of the Nine- | teenth Century: | By J. Collins Warren, M.D., LL.D., | F.R.C.S., Being the Address of the | President before the American | Surgical Association, MDCCCXCVII | Boston: Privately printed, MDCCCCVI.

Colophon: One hundred and fifty copies of this address were printed at The Merrymount Press, Boston, in November, MDCCCCVI. A previous edition of one hundred copies was printed at this press in MDCCCC. Leaf, 5½ × 8¾. Binding, boards. With 9 illustrations and facsimiles. *Also issued in paper covers. Reissue of No. 81.*

[268]

[*ornament*] | The | Love Letters | of | Henry VIII | to | Anne Boleyn | With Notes | [*floret*] | John W. Luce & Company | Boston: London | [*ornament*]. [n. d.]

On reverse of title: D. B. Updike, The Merrymount Press, Boston. Collation: [i–vi], [i–ii], i–lix, [lx]. Leaf, 4⅞ × 7¾. Binding, full leather. With illustration. Type, Caslon.

[269]

A Choice of Books | from | the Library of | Isabella Stewart Gardner | Fenway Court | [*cut*] | MDCCCCVI.

Collation: [i–iv], 1–70, [71]. Leaf, 5¾ × 9¼. Binding, boards. Rubricated title. No imprint. Type, Caslon.

[270]

Friendship | By | Henry D. Thoreau | [*quotation*] | [*cut*] | New York | Thomas Y. Crowell & Co. | Publishers. [n. d.]

On reverse of title: D. B. Updike, The Merrymount Press, Boston. Collation: 1–55, [56]. Leaf, 5 × 7⅜. Binding, cloth. Rubricated throughout. With portrait. Type, Caslon.

[271]

Friendship's Offering | [*floret*] | Boston | The Merrymount Press | 1906.

Collation: [i–iv], 1–15, [16]. Leaf, 4½ × 7⅝. Binding, boards. Type, Caslon.

The Merrymount Press

Minor Printing

Reports: Lincoln House; Society of Arts & Crafts; Copley Society; Workingmen's Building Association; Annual Report of the President, Brown University, Providence.

Catalogues of Schools and Universities: Simmons College; St. Mark's School, Southborough, Mass.; Brown University, Providence; *also* Programme of Commencement Week; Departmental Circular; Announcement of Courses; *and* Announcement of Courses offered at the Women's College in Brown University, Providence; Boylston Medical Society of Harvard University.

Catalogues: Publications of Alfred Bartlett; Books and Manuscripts exhibited by Rudolph Haupt.

Church Missions House Publications, New York: Church Calendar for 1906; Mid-Day Intercessions for Missions.

The Society of Clinical Surgery, Statistics and Constitution; *also* Bibliography of Members Contributions to Literature.

American Medical Association, Committee on Arrangements, Preliminary Announcement; *also* Bulletin of Committee, Clinical Exhibits at Hospitals, Scientific Exhibit in New Buildings, Harvard Medical School; *and* Excursions.

Catalogue Fenway Court.

The Choral Art Society of Boston, Fifth Season, Second Programme; *also* Sixth Season, First Programme.

The Philadelphia Clericus, Philadelphia.

The Hawthorne Club, Boston, Massachusetts.

An International School of Peace, An Address.

Compositions of Ch. M. Loeffler.

Benvenuto Cellini, Artist and Writer, by Royal Cortissoz, New York.

Miss Winsor's School, 95 Beacon Street, Boston.

The Old South Meeting-House.

Bibliography

1907

[272]

The Will of | Charles Lounsbury | [*cut*] | Boston | Alfred Bartlett. [n. d.]

On reverse of title: The Merrymount Press, Boston. Collation: [i–iv], 1–7. Leaf, 3⅞ × 6¼. Binding, paper. Type, Mountjoye.

[273]

A Tenderfoot | Abroad | By | Justine Grayson | [*cut*] | Boston | W. A. Butterfield | 59 Bromfield St. | 1907.

On reverse of title: D. B. Updike, The Merrymount Press, Boston. Collation: i–viii, [i–ii], 1–98, [99–100]. Leaf, 5⅜ × 8¼. Binding, cloth. Type, Mountjoye.

[274]

Handbook | of | English Composition | a Compilation of Standard | Rules and Usage | by | Luella Clay Carson | Professor of Rhetoric and American Literature | University of Oregon | Revised Edition | [*publisher's mark*] | World Book Company | Yonkers-on-Hudson | New York | 1907.

On reverse of title: The Merrymount Press, Boston. Collation: i–x, [i–ii], 1–275. Leaf, 3⅝ × 5⅞. Binding, limp leather. Type, Scotch-face.

[275]

The Rhine-Gold | A Dramatic Poem by Richard | Wagner freely translated | in poetic narrative form by | Oliver Huckel | [*floret*] | Thomas Y. Crowell & Co. | Publishers New York. [n. d.]

On reverse of title: Composition and electrotype plates by D. B. Updike, The Merrymount Press, Boston. Collation: i–xxiv, 1–102, [103]. Leaf, 5 × 7⅜. Binding, cloth. Rubricated throughout. With 2 illustrations. Type, Clarendon.

[276]

[*within border*] Friendship | An Essay | by | Henry David Thoreau | from Thoreau's | Week on the Concord | and Merrimack | Rivers | [*floret*] | Boston | Alfred Bartlett | 1907.

The Merrymount Press

On reverse of title: The Merrymount Press, Boston. Collation: [i–iv], 1–42, [43]. Leaf, 4¼ × 7¼. Binding, boards. Type, Caslon.

[277]
Letters from The Raven | Being the Correspondence of | Lafcadio Hearn with | Henry Watkin | With Introduction and | Critical Comment by the Editor | Milton Bronner | [cut] | New York | Brentano's | 1907.

On reverse of title: D. B. Updike, The Merrymount Press, Boston. Collation: [i–ii], 1–201. Leaf, 5 × 7⅜. Binding, boards. Type, Caslon.

[278]
The First Book of | the Dofobs | [cut] | Printed for the | Society of the Dofobs | Chicago: MDCCCCVII.

Colophon: Fifty copies of this First Book of the Dofobs have been printed for the Members of The Society of the Dofobs on Italian hand-made paper by D. B. Updike, The Merrymount Press, Boston, in the month of April MDCCCCVII. Collation: [i–vi], 1–63, [64–65]. Leaf, 6⅜ × 9½. Binding, boards. With a signed reproduction of drawing by Howard Pyle and facsimile. Type, Mountjoye.

[279]
Debussy's | Pelléas et Mélisande | A Guide to the Opera | with Musical Examples | from the Score | By | Lawrence Gilman | Author of "Phases of Modern Music," "The Music of | To-morrow," "Stories of Symphonic Music," "Edward | Mac-Dowell" (in "Living Masters of Music" Series) | "Straus' 'Salome,'" etc. | [floret] | New York | G. Schirmer | 1907.

On reverse of title: D. B. Updike, The Merrymount Press, Boston. Collation: [i–viii], 1–84. Leaf, 4⅝ × 7¼. Binding, cloth. With portrait. Type, Scotch-face.

[280]
[within rules] The Greatest Fact | In Modern History | by Whitelaw Reid | [cut] | New York | Thomas Y. Crowell & Co. | Publishers. [n. d.]

On reverse of title: Composition and electrotype plates by D. B. Updike, The Merrymount Press, Boston. Collation: [i–vi], 1–39, [40]. Leaf, 5 × 7⅜. Binding, cloth. Rubricated throughout. With portrait. Type, Clarendon.

Bibliography

[281]

Madame de Treymes | By | Edith Wharton | [*floret*] | With Illustrations | New York | Charles Scribner's Sons | 1907.

On reverse of title: D. B. Updike, The Merrymount Press, Boston. Collation: [i–vi],[i–ii], 1–146, [147]. Leaf, 4⅞ × 7½. Binding, cloth. With 2 illustrations in colour. Type, Scotch-face.

[282]

[*within design*] Erasmus | Against War | With an Introduction by | J. W. Mackail | The Merrymount Press | Boston, MDCCCCVII.

Colophon: Of this volume which is edited by John W. Mackail with types & decorations by Herbert P. Horne ccciii copies were printed [*printer's mark*] by D. B. Updike at The Merrymount Press, Boston, Massachusetts, in the month of August MCMVII. Collation: i–xxxiv, 1–64,[65–66]. Leaf, 5⅝ × 9½. Binding, boards. Rubricated throughout. Type, Montallegro.

The Humanists' Library, Vol. II.

[283]

[*within rules*] A History of | The Episcopal Church | in Narragansett | Rhode Island | Including a History of Other Episcopal | Churches in the State | By Wilkins Updike | With a Transcript of the Narragansett Parish Register, from | 1718 to 1774; an Appendix containing a Reprint of a Work | entitled America Dissected by the Revd James MacSpar-|ran, D.D., and Copies of Other Old Papers; together with | Notes containing Genealogical and Biographical Accounts | of Distinguished Men, Families, &c. | Second Edition, newly edited, enlarged, and corrected by the | Reverend Daniel Goodwin, Ph.D., D.D. | sometime Rector of St. Paul's Church, Wickford, Narragansett | Illustrated by fifty Portraits after old Paintings; together | with six Views of Historic Localities, and several Facsimiles | [*volume numeral enclosed in printer's ornaments*] | Boston: Printed and Published by D. B. Updike | The Merrymount Press | 1907.

On reverse of title: The Merrymount Press, Boston. 3 vols. Collation: Vol. I, i–xlvi, 1–622; Vol. II, [i–ii], i–viii, [i–ii], 1–605; Vol. III, [i–ii], i–vi, 1–339. Leaf, 5½ × 8⅝. Binding, boards. Type, Caslon.

The Merrymount Press

[284]

The Idylls and the Ages | A Valuation of Tenny-|son's Idylls of the King | [*floret*] | Elucidated in Part by Comparisons between | Tennyson and Browning | By | John Franklin Genung | [*floret*] | Thomas Y. Crowell and Company | Publishers: New York: MDCCCCVII.

On reverse of title: Composition and electrotype plates by D. B. Updike, The Merrymount Press, Boston. Collation: i–viii, 1–80. Leaf, 5 × 7⅜. Binding, cloth. Rubricated throughout. Type, Clarendon.

[285]

Catalogue | of the | Boylston Medical Society | of Harvard University | December | 1906 | [*floret*] | Founded January 6, 1811 | Incorporated June 13, 1823 | Boston | The Merrymount Press | 1907.

On reverse of title: D. B. Updike, The Merrymount Press, Boston. Collation: [i–iv], 1–103, [104]. Leaf, 5¾ × 9⅛. Binding, boards. Type, Caslon. *Also issued in paper covers.*

[286]

[*within design*] Petrarch | and the Ancient World | by | Pierre | de Nolhac.

Colophon: Of this volume with types & decorations by Herbert P. Horne CCCIII copies were printed [*printer's mark*] by D. B. Updike at The Merrymount Press, Boston, Massachusetts, in the month of December MDCCCCVII. Collation: i–x, 1–120, [121–122]. Leaf, 5⅝ × 9½. Binding, boards. Rubricated throughout. Type, Montallegro.

The Humanists' Library, Vol. III.

[287]

[*within rules*] The Pure Gold of | Nineteenth Century | Literature | By William Lyon Phelps | Lampson Professor of English Literature at | Yale University | [*cut*] | New York | Thomas Y. Crowell & Co. | Publishers. [n. d.]

On reverse of title: D. B. Updike, The Merrymount Press, Boston. Collation: [i–x], 1–36, [37]. Leaf, 5 × 7⅜. Binding, cloth. Rubricated throughout. Type, Caslon.

[288]

The John Carter Brown Library | Three Proclamations |

Bibliography

concerning | The Lottery for | Virginia | 1613–1621 | [*arms*] |
Providence, Rhode Island | MDCCCCVII.

On reverse of title: One hundred copies printed at The Merrymount Press,
Boston, December, 1907. Collation: [i–vi], 1–4, [5–7]. Leaf, 12 × 16. Binding, boards. Rubricated title. With 3 facsimiles. Type, Merrymount.

[289]
[*within rules*] The Old Year | And the New | By | Charles
Edward Jefferson | Pastor of Broadway Tabernacle | New
York | [*cut*] | New York | Thomas Y. Crowell & Co. |
Publishers. [n. d.]

On reverse of title: Composition and electrotype plates by D. B. Updike,
The Merrymount Press, Boston. Collation: [i–ii], 1–60, [61]. Leaf, 5 × 7⅜.
Binding, cloth. Rubricated throughout. Type, Caslon.

[290]
The Proceedings of | the | Twenty-first Annual Meeting |
of | The Review Club | on the Evening of Saturday |
February ninth | MDCCCCVII | [*floret*] | Providence | Privately
printed | MDCCCCVII.

On reverse of title: D. B. Updike, The Merrymount Press, Boston. Collation: [i–vi], 1–97, [98]. Leaf, 5⅞ × 9. Binding, boards. Type, Mountjoye.

[291]
News from France | or | A Description of the Library | of
Cardinal Mazarin | Preceded by | The Surrender of | the
Library | (Now Newly Translated) | Two Tracts written |
by | Gabriel Naudé | [*floret*] | Chicago | A. C. McClurg
& Co. | MDCCCCVII.

Collation: 1–75, [76–77]. For full description, *see* No. 259.
Literature of Libraries, Vol. VI. Issued in May.

[292]
The Same.

For description, *see* No. 260.
Issued in May.

[135]

The Merrymount Press

[293]

A Brief Outline of | The History of | Libraries | By | Justus
Lipsius | Translated from the | Second Edition | (Antwerp,
The Plantin Press | John Moretus, 1607) | The Last from |
The Hand of the Author | By | John Cotton Dana | [*floret*] |
Chicago | A. C. McClurg & Co. | MDCCCCVII.

Collation: 1–121, [122–123]. For full description, *see* No. 259.
Literature of Libraries, Vol. VI. Issued in May.

[294]
The Same.

Large-paper edition. For description, *see* No. 260.
Issued in May.

[295]
A Christmas Anthology | Carols and Poems | Old and New |
[*cut*] | New York | Thomas Y. Crowell & Co. | Publishers.
[n. d.]

Leaf, 5 × 7⅜. Binding, cloth. Rubricated title. With 8 illustrations. Type,
Caslon.

*Imprint and collation are lacking in above description since no copies of this
book were obtainable. It is uniform, in general style, with No. 296.*

[296]
[*within border*] A Tennyson | Calendar | Selected and ar-
ranged by | Anna Harris Smith | [*printer's ornament*] | New
York | Thomas Y. Crowell & Co. | Publishers. [n. d.]

On reverse of title: Composition and electrotype plates by D. B. Updike,
The Merrymount Press, Boston. Collation: [i–iv], 1–133, [134]. Leaf,
5 × 7⅜. Binding, cloth. Rubricated title. With portrait. Type, Caslon.

[297]
Nelson Fairchild | [*floret*] | [*quotation*] | Privately printed.
[n. d.]

On reverse of title: The Merrymount Press, Boston. Collation: [i–vi],
1–191, [192–193]. Leaf, 6 × 9. Binding, boards. With 2 illustrations. Type,
Mountjoye.

Bibliography

[298]

In Memoriam | Ann Bent Winsor | March 23, 1830–
May 20, 1907 | Spoken by Theodore C. Williams | at the
Services held in Weston | May 22, 1907 | [*floret*] | Privately
printed | MDCCCCVII.

On reverse of title: The Merrymount Press. Collation: [i–ii], 1–8. Leaf,
5⅜ × 8¾. Binding, paper. Type, Mountjoye.

[299]

Mrs. Frederick Winsor | an Address made to the | Older
Classes in Miss Winsor's School | Monday, May 27, 1907 |
by | Mrs. Arthur Lyman | [*floret*] | Privately Printed |
MDCCCCVII.

On reverse of title: The Merrymount Press. Collation: [i–ii], 1–9. Leaf,
5⅜ × 8¾. Binding, paper. Type, Mountjoye.

[300]

How to preserve | the Local Self-Government | of the
States | A Brief Study of National Tendencies | A Speech de-
livered by Elihu Root at the | Dinner of the Pennsylvania
Society in | New York, Wednesday, December 12, 1906 |
Authorized and Correct | Edition | [*cut*] | New York: Bren-
tano's | 1907.

Collation: 1–14, [15]. Leaf, 5⅜ × 8⅜. Binding, paper. No imprint. Type,
Mountjoye.

Minor Printing

Reports: Copley Society of Boston; Workingmen's Building Association; Society of Arts & Crafts; Lincoln House; Annual Report of the President, Brown University, Providence.

Catalogues of Schools and Universities: Saint Mark's School,
Southborough, Massachusetts; Simmons College, Fifth Annual
Catalogue, 1906–1907 (*also* Sixth Annual Catalogue, 1907–1908);
Brown University, Providence; *also* Announcement of Courses;
Departmental Circular; *and* Announcement of Courses offered at
the Women's College in Brown University, 1907–1908.

The Domestic and Foreign Missionary Society Publications, New

The Merrymount Press

York: The Church Calendar for the Year of Our Lord Nineteen Hundred and Seven (*also for 1908*); Mid-Day Intercessions for Missions.

The Society of Clinical Surgery, Bibliography of Members Contributions to Literature, From September 1, 1906, to September 1, 1907.

Catalogue Fenway Court.

The Choral Art Society of Boston, Sixth Season, Second Programme.

Exercises in celebration of the Twentieth Anniversary of the Founding of Lincoln House.

Social Development, An Address given by Henry LeFavour.

A Woman's Opportunity in Business and the Industries, An Address by Henry Smith Pritchett.

Brookline Playgrounds by Desmond Fitzgerald, Brookline.

1908

[301]

Carla | Wenckebach | Pioneer | by | Margarethe Müller | [*floret*] | [*quotation*] | Ginn and Company | Boston and London | Publishers | 1908.

On reverse of title: D. B. Updike, The Merrymount Press, Boston. Collation: i–xiv, 1–289, [290]. Leaf, 5 × 7½. Binding, cloth. With 7 portraits. Type, Scotch-face.

[302]

[*within design*] The Defence of Poesie | A Letter to Q. Elizabeth | A Defence of Leicester | By Sir Philip Sidney | Edited by G. E. Woodberry | The Merrymount Press | Boston: MDCCCCVIII.

Colophon: Of this volume with initials and colophon by Herbert P. Horne and title-page by W. A. Dwiggins cccIII copies were printed [*printer's mark*] by D. B. Updike at The Merrymount Press, Boston, Massachusetts, in the month of May MDCCCCVIII. Collation: i–xx, 1–126, [127–128]. Leaf, 5¾ × 9½. Binding, boards. Rubricated throughout. Type, Montallegro.
The Humanists' Library, Vol. IV.

Bibliography

[303]

[*within border*] Christmas To-day | By | Hamilton Wright Mabie | [*floret*] | New York | Dodd, Mead & Company | 1908.

On reverse of title: Composition and electrotype plates by The Merrymount Press, Boston. Collation: [i–viii], 1–72, [73]. Leaf, 4⅜ × 7⅜. Binding, boards. Rubricated title. Type, Mountjoye.

[304]

The | Maid's Forgiveness | A Play | By | John Jay Chapman | [*floret*] | New York | Moffat, Yard & Co. | 1908.

On reverse of title: D. B. Updike, The Merrymount Press, Boston. Collation: [i–vi], 1–93, [94–95]. Leaf, 5 × 7. Binding, boards. Type, Scotch-face.

[305]

[*within border*] The Story of the | Old Boston Town House | 1658–1711 | By | Josiah Henry Benton, LL.D. | Author of "Samuel Slade Benton: his Ancestors and Descendants" | "A Notable Libel Case," "Early Census-Making | in Massachusetts, 1643–1765," &c. | With Portraits and Illustrations | [*floret*] | Boston | Privately printed | 1908.

On reverse of title: D. B. Updike, The Merrymount Press, Boston. Collation: i–xii, 1–60, [61]. Leaf, 6⅜ × 9⅝. Binding, boards. With 11 illustrations. Type, Scotch-face.

350 copies printed.

[306]

A Last Will | [*floret*] | Williston Fish | [*cut*] | Boston | Alfred Bartlett. [n. d.]

On reverse of title: The Merrymount Press, Boston. Collation: [i–iv], [i–ii], 1–17, [18]. Leaf, 3¾ × 6¼. Binding, boards. Rubricated throughout. Type, Mountjoye.

First published in 1907 as "The Will of Charles Lounsbury."

[307]

Twelve Lessons | in | The Fundamentals of | Voice Production | By | Arthur L. Manchester | Director of Music and

The Merrymount Press

Professor of Voice | Culture at Converse College | [*floret*] | [*cut*] | Boston | Oliver Ditson Company | New York: Chas. H. Ditson & Co. | Chicago: Lyon & Healy | Philadelphia: J. E. Ditson & Co. [n. d.]

Collation: [i–viii], 1–92. Leaf, 5¼ × 7¾. Binding, cloth. With 2 diagrams. No imprint. Type, Scotch-face.

Composition and electrotype plates only by the Press.

[308]
The Voyage of the | Oregon | from San Francisco | to Santiago in | 1898 | as told by | one of the Crew | [*cut*] | Privately printed | The Merrymount Press | Boston | 1908.

Collation: i–vi, 1–33, [34]. Leaf, 4⅜ × 7⅜. Binding, boards. Type, Caslon.

125 copies printed.

[309]
Leadership | The William Belden Noble Lectures | delivered at Sanders Theatre, Harvard University | December, 1907 | By the Rt. Rev. Charles H. Brent | Bishop of the Philippine Islands | [*floret*] | [*quotation*] | [*publisher's mark*] | Longmans, Green, and Co. | 91 and 93 Fifth Avenue, New York, | London and Bombay | 1908.

On reverse of title: Composition and electrotype plates by D. B. Updike, The Merrymount Press, Boston. Collation: i–xiv, 1–259, [260–264]. Leaf, 5 × 7⅜. Binding, cloth. Type, Scotch-face.

[310]
The Jesters | A Simple Story in Four Acts of Verse | adapted from the French of | Miguel Zamacoïs | By | John N. Raphael | [*floret*] | New York | Brentano's | 1908.

On reverse of title: D. B. Updike, The Merrymount Press, Boston. Collation: [i–iv], 1–175. Leaf, 5¼ × 8. Binding, cloth. Type, Scotch-face.

[311]
A Golden Vial full of | Odours | A Sermon | preached at the Old Narragansett Church | St. Paul's Parish, Wickford | Rhode Island | September ninth, MDCCCCVII | on the Two

Bibliography

Hundredth Anniversary | of its Erection | By | Rev. Daniel Goodwin, Ph.D., D.D. | sometime Rector of the Parish | [*cut*] | [*quotation*] | Printed by Members of the Parish | The Merrymount Press | Boston: MDCCCCVIII.

Collation: [i–ii], 1–22. Leaf, 5¼ × 8¼. Binding, paper. Type, Caslon.

[312]
Catechism | on the Seven Sacraments | and | the Religious Life | [*cut*] | Boston | 33 Bowdoin Street | [Price, 20 cents]. [n. d.]

On reverse of title: The Merrymount Press, Boston. Collation: 1–159. Leaf, 4⅜ × 6¼. Binding, paper. With 7 illustrations. Type, Caslon.

[313]
A Memorial of | My Mother | By | Cornelia Warren | [*floret*] | Boston | Privately printed | 1908.

On reverse of title: The Merrymount Press, Boston. Collation: [i–iv], 1–167, [168]. Leaf, 5⅞ × 9. Binding, boards. With 9 illustrations. Type, Mountjoye.

[314]
[*within rules*] Simmons College | The 1908 Class Book | [*seal*] | Boston | Published by the Class | 1908.

On reverse of title: D. B. Updike, The Merrymount Press, Boston. Collation: 1–78, [79–80]. Leaf, 7⅞ × 10¼. Binding, cloth. With portraits. Type, Scotch-face.

[315]
Lilies | of Eternal Peace | By | Lilian Whiting | Author of "The World Beautiful" | [*cut*] | New York | Thomas Y. Crowell & Co. | Publishers. [n. d.]

On reverse of title: D. B. Updike, The Merrymount Press, Boston. Collation: [i–vi], 1–40, [41]. Leaf, 5 × 7⅜. Binding, boards. Rubricated throughout. Type, Mountjoye.

[316]
The John Carter Brown Library | Providence, Rhode Island | A Facsimile | of the First Issue of the | Gazeta de Lima | the First South American Newspaper | with a Description

The Merrymount Press

of a File | for the Years | 1744–1763 | The Merrymount Press | Boston.

On reverse of title: Two hundred copies printed at The Merrymount Press, Boston, September, 1908. Collation: 1–31, [32]. Leaf, 5⅝ × 7⅞. Binding, paper. With facsimiles. Type, Caslon.

[317]

Carcassonne | Gustave Nadaud | Julia C. R. Dorr | [*floret*] | Privately printed | Christmas | 1908.

Colophon: Of this book seventy-five copies were printed for Thomas Nast Fairbanks at The Merrymount Press, in December, 1908. Collation: [1–21]. Leaf, 5 × 7⅝. Binding, boards. Type, Mountjoye.

[318]

Orchidaceae | Illustrations and Studies of | the Family Orchidaceae | Issued from the Ames Botanical Laboratory | North Easton, Massachusetts | By | Oakes Ames | A.M., F.L.S. | [*floret*] | Fascicle III | Boston | The Merrymount Press | 1908.

On reverse of title: D. B. Updike, The Merrymount Press, Boston. Collation: i–viii, 1–98, [99]. Leaf, 7 × 10. Binding, boards. Rubricated title. With 34 plates. Type, Scotch-face.

[319]

[*within design*] The | Poetical Works | of | John Milton | With a Life of the Author | and Illustrations | Boston | R. H. Hinkley Company. [n. d.]

Colophon: Of this hand-made paper edition of The Poetical Works of John Milton five hundred and fifty-five copies were printed by D. B. Updike at The Merrymount Press, Boston [*publisher's mark*]. Number —. 4 vols. Collation: Vol. I, [i–viii], 1–284, [285]; Vol. II, [i–viii], 1–251, [252–253]; Vol. III, [i–viii], 1–274, [275]; Vol. IV, i–xiv, 1–247, [248–249]. Leaf, 6¼ × 9½. Binding, full pigskin. Rubricated title, borders of illustrations, headpieces, tailpieces, and colophon. With 16 illustrations. Type, Mountjoye.

Title-page design and decorations by W. A. Dwiggins. The illustrations were adapted from Flaxman.

[320]

The Metropolitan Museum of Art | Catalogue | of a | Memorial

Bibliography

Exhibition | of the Works | of | Augustus Saint-Gaudens |
[*cut*] | New York: MDCCCCVIII.

On reverse of title: D. B. Updike, The Merrymount Press, Boston. Collation: [i–iv], 1–82. Leaf, 4¾ × 7⅞. Binding, paper. Type, Caslon.

[321]
The Same.

Leaf, 5¾ × 8⅞.
On hand-made paper.

[322]
A ✠ Ω | In Memoriam | Henry Yates Satterlee | D.D., LL.D. |
First Bishop of Washington | A Sermon by | Philip Mercer
Rhinelander | preached in St. John's Church, Washington,
D. C. | on the Second Sunday in Lent | March 15, 1908 |
[*floret*] | [Printed by request]. [n. d.]

On reverse of title: The Merrymount Press, Boston. Collation: [i–ii], 1–15.
Leaf, 5¼ × 8¼. Binding, paper. Type, Caslon.

[323]
Friendship's Offering | [*floret*] | Boston | W. B. Clarke Company | 1908.

On reverse of title: The Merrymount Press, Boston.
Reissue of No. 271.

[324]
The Plans and Elevations for | St. Thomas' Church | Made by
Cram, Goodhue and Ferguson | Approved by The Rector,
Wardens and | Vestrymen in May | MDCCCCVII | [*arms*] | New
York City | Published by the order of the Vestry | January:
MDCCCCVIII.

On reverse of title: D. B. Updike, The Merrymount Press, Boston. Collation: [i–iv], 1–13, [14–17]. Leaf, 8¾ × 11½. Binding, paper. With 4 illustrations and 7 plans. Type, Mountjoye.

[325]
Memorial Exercises | in honor of | Professor Albert Harkness | in Sayles Hall, Brown University | October the Thirty-

The Merrymount Press

first | MDCCCCVII | With Addresses by President W.H.P. Faunce |
Professor Thomas D. Seymour and | Professor Walter G.
Everett | [*floret*] | Providence | Published by the University.
[n. d.]

On reverse of title: D. B. Updike, The Merrymount Press, Boston. Collation: 1–55, [56]. Leaf, 5¾ × 9. Binding, paper. Type, Mountjoye.

Minor Printing

The Carnegie Foundation for the Advancement of Teaching,
Third Annual Report of the President and of the Treasurer, New
York.

Reports: Society of Arts & Crafts; Workingmen's Building Association; Lincoln House; Annual Report of the President, Brown
University, Providence.

Catalogues of Schools and Universities: Saint Mark's School,
Southborough, Massachusetts; Simmons College, Seventh Annual
Catalogue, 1908–1909; *also* The Summer Session, 1908; Brown Uni-
versity, 1908–1909, Providence; *also* Announcement of Courses;
Departmental Circular; *and* Announcement of Courses offered at
the Women's College in Brown University, 1908–1909.

The Domestic and Foreign Missionary Society Publications, New
York: The Church Calendar for the Year of Our Lord Nineteen
Hundred and Nine; Mid-Day Intercessions for Missions.

The Society of Clinical Surgery, Bibliography of Members Contributions to Literature, From September 1, 1907, to September 1,
1908.

The John Carter Brown Library, Providence, Rhode Island, Books
printed in Lima and Elsewhere in South America, after 1800.

By-Laws of The Winsor School.

Forty-third Annual Reunion of the Dartmouth Alumni Association of Boston and Vicinity.

Williams College, Order of Exercises for the Induction of Henry
Augustus Garfield, LL.D., into the Office of President, Williams-
town.

The Spirit of a Profession, An Address by James Hardy Ropes, D.D.

[144]

Bibliography

The Club of Odd Volumes, Providence Meeting; *also* Visit to The John Carter Brown Library, Providence.

An Appeal for Saint John's Church in Providence.

1909

[326]

The Witness of the Heart | and other Sermons | by the Rev. | Henry Morgan Stone | [*floret*] | Longmans, Green, and Co. | 91 and 93 Fifth Avenue, New York | London, Bombay, and Calcutta | 1909.

On reverse of title: D. B. Updike, The Merrymount Press, Boston. Collation: [i–xii], 1–203. Leaf, 5 × 7⅜. Binding, cloth. With 3 illustrations. Type, Scotch-face.

[327]

The | True Uses of Education | An Address | Delivered May 11, 1870 | at the Dedication of the | Main Building of Bradford Academy | Bradford, Massachusetts | by | Phillips Brooks | Bradford Academy | MDCCCCIX.

On reverse of title: The Merrymount Press, Boston. Collation: [i–iv], 1–12, [13]. Leaf, 4¾ × 7⅞. Binding, boards. Type, Mountjoye.
Also issued in paper covers.

[328]

The Easiest Way | An American Play concerning | a Particular Phase of | New York Life | In Four Acts and | Four Scenes | [*floret*] | By | Eugene Walter | Printed for the Author | MDCCCCIX.

Collation: i–xviii, 1–121, [122]. Leaf, 5¼ × 8¼. Binding, cloth. With 3 illustrations. No imprint. Type, Scotch-face.

[329]

The Same.

Collation: [i–viii], 1–121, [122]. Leaf, 6 × 9¼. Binding, three-quarter morocco.
On hand-made paper.

The Merrymount Press

[330]

A Sausage from | Bologna | A Comedy in Four Acts | By | John Jay Chapman | [*floret*] | [*quotation*] | New York | Moffat, Yard & Co. | 1909.

On reverse of title: D. B. Updike, The Merrymount Press, Boston. Collation: [i–viii], 1–113, [114–115]. Leaf, 5 × 6⅞. Binding, boards. Type, Scotch-face.

[331]

[*within design*] Christmas | Builders | by | Charles Edward | Jefferson | New York | Thomas Y. Crowell & Co. | Publishers. [n. d.]

On reverse of title: D. B. Updike, The Merrymount Press, Boston. Collation: [i–vi], 1–31, [32]. Leaf, 5 × 7⅜. Binding, boards. Rubricated. Type, Mountjoye.

Cover and title-page designs, 3 illustrations, and end-papers by W. A. Dwiggins.

[332]

The Valkyrie | (Die Walküre) | A Dramatic Poem by Richard | Wagner freely translated in | poetic narrative form by | Oliver Huckel | [*floret*] | Thomas Y. Crowell & Co. | Publishers New York. [n. d.]

On reverse of title: Composition and electrotype plates by D. B. Updike, The Merrymount Press, Boston. Collation: [i–ii], i–xxiv, 1–95, [96]. Leaf, 5 × 7⅜. Binding, cloth. Rubricated throughout. With 4 illustrations. Type, Clarendon.

[333]

The Golden Opportunity | an Address | delivered at the Fourth Annual Con-|vention of the American National | Retail Jewelers Association Omaha | Nebraska Wednesday August 4 1909 by | Ernest Miller Lunt | [*cut*] | Printed for the | Towle Manufacturing Company | Newburyport Massachusetts | at The Merrymount Press | Boston. [n. d.]

Collation: [i–iv], 1–25, [26]. Leaf, 5¾ × 8½. Binding, boards. With portrait. Type, Mountjoye.

[334]

[*within design*] Christus | a Story of Love | by | Grace

[146]

Bibliography

Hoffman White | [*floret*] | New York | Privately printed |
MDCCCCIX.

On reverse of title: D. B. Updike, The Merrymount Press, Boston. Collation: [i–iv], 1–64, [65]. Leaf, 5 × 7⅝. Binding, boards. Title in blue and black. Type, Caslon.

Title-page design by W. A. Dwiggins. 6 copies on hand-made paper were bound in full parchment.

[335]
Mr. Cleveland | A Personal Impression | by | Jesse Lynch Williams | [*floret*] | New York | Dodd, Mead & Company | 1909.

On reverse of title: Composition and electrotype plates by D. B. Updike, The Merrymount Press, Boston. Collation: [i–vi], 1–74, [75]. Leaf, 4½ × 7½. Binding, boards. With frontispiece. Type, Scotch-face.

[336]
E. W. Dennison | A Memorial | [*cut*] | Boston | 1909.

On reverse of title: D. B. Updike, The Merrymount Press, Boston. Collation: [i–iv], 1–102, [103]. Leaf, 5⅞ × 9⅛. Binding, cloth. With 10 illustrations and 2 facsimiles. Type, Mountjoye.

306 copies on hand-made paper were bound in full leather.

[337]
Inscriptions on the Grave-Stones | in the Old Church-yard of | St. Paul's Narragansett | North Kingstown Rhode Island | With a Record of the Inscriptions in the | Grave-yard of the Old Church at Wickford | compiled by | James N. Arnold | [*cut*] | Privately Printed | The Merry-mount Press | Boston. [n. d.]

Collation: i–viii, 1–36, [37]. Leaf, 5½ × 8½. Binding, paper. Type, Caslon.
Preface by D. B. Updike.

Minor Printing

The Carnegie Foundation for the Advancement of Teaching, Fourth Annual Report of the President and of the Treasurer, New York.

[147]

The Merrymount Press

Reports: Lincoln House; Society of Arts & Crafts; Working-men's Building Association; Annual Report of the President, Brown University, Providence.

Catalogues of Schools and Universities: Saint Mark's School, Southborough, Massachusetts; Simmons College, Eighth Annual Catalogue, 1909–1910; *also* Register of Graduates, 1908; *and* The Summer Library Class, 1909; Brown University, 1909–1910, Providence; *also* Announcement of Courses; *and* Announcement of Courses offered at the Women's College in Brown University, 1909–1910.

Catalogue Fenway Court.

The Society of Clinical Surgery, Bibliography of Members Contributions to Literature, From September 1, 1908, to September 1, 1909.

The Growth of Brown University in Recent Years, 1899–1909, Providence.

1910

[338]
A Catalogue | of the Engraved Plates | for | Picturesque Views | in England and Wales | with | Notes and Commentaries | Compiled by | Francis Bullard | [*cut*] | Boston | Privately printed | MDCCCCX.

Colophon: Two hundred and fifty copies printed at The Merrymount Press, Boston, October MDCCCCX. Collation: 1–102, [103]. Leaf, 5¾ × 9. Binding, boards. Rubricated title and initial in Introduction. Type, Caslon.
Also issued in paper covers.

[339]
Harvard Studies in Comparative Literature | Volume I | Three | Philosophical Poets | Lucretius, Dante, and Goethe | By | George Santayana | Professor of Philosophy in Harvard University | [*seal*] | Cambridge | Harvard University | 1910.

On reverse of title: D. B. Updike, The Merrymount Press, Boston. Collation: i–viii, 1–215. Leaf, 5⅝ × 8⅜. Binding, cloth. Type, Scotch-face.

[340]
[*within cut*] From | Passion to Peace | or | The Pathway of

the Pure | By | James Allen | Author of "As a Man Thinketh," "The Mastery | of Destiny," "From Poverty to Power," "Byways | of Blessedness," &c. | [*floret*] | New York | Thomas Y. Crowell & Co. [n. d.]

On reverse of title: Composition and electrotype plates by D. B. Updike, The Merrymount Press, Boston. Collation: i–x, 1–52, [53]. Leaf, 4⅝ × 7¼. Binding, boards. Rubricated title. Type, Caslon.

Border to title-page by W. A. Dwiggins.

[341]
Siegfried | A Dramatic Poem by Richard | Wagner freely translated in | poetic narrative form by | Oliver Huckel | [*floret*] | Thomas Y. Crowell & Co. | Publishers New York. [n. d.]

On reverse of title: Composition and electrotype plates by D. B. Updike, The Merrymount Press, Boston. Collation: i–xxiv, 1–105, [106]. Leaf, 5 × 7¼. Binding, cloth. Rubricated throughout. With 4 illustrations. Type, Clarendon.

[342]
A History of | the Eastern Diocese | By | Calvin R. Batchelder | [*floret*] | In Three Volumes | Volume | II | Printed for the Diocese of Massachusetts | and the Diocese of Rhode Island | at The Merrymount Press | Boston MDCCCX.

Collation: i–viii, 1–401. Leaf, 5⅝ × 8⅞. Binding, cloth. Type, Scotch-face.
This book was made uniform with Vol. I, which was printed elsewhere in 1876.

[343]
The High Court of | Parliament | and its Supremacy | an Historical Essay on the Boundaries | between Legislation and Adjudication | in England | By | Charles Howard McIlwain | Thomas Brackett Reed Professor of History and | Political Science in Bowdoin College | [*seal*] | New Haven: Yale University Press | London: Henry Frowde | Oxford University Press | MDCCCX.

Colophon: D. B. Updike, The Merrymount Press, Boston. Collation: i–xxii, 1–408, [409–410]. Leaf, 5¾ × 8⅝. Binding, cloth. Type, Scotch-face.

The Merrymount Press

[344]
Orchidaceae | Illustrations and Studies of | the Family Orchi-
daceae | Issued from the Ames Botanical Laboratory | North
Easton, Massachusetts | The Genus Habenaria in North
America | By | Oakes Ames | Director of the Botanic Garden
of Harvard University | With Twenty Etchings by | Blanche
Ames | [*floret*] | Fascicle IV | Boston | The Merrymount Press |
1910.

On reverse of title: D. B. Updike, The Merrymount Press, Boston. Collation: i–xiv, 1–287, [288]. Leaf, 7 × 10. Binding, boards. Type, Scotch-face.

[345]
[*within rules*] Early Days | on | Boston Common | By | Mary
Farwell Ayer | With many Illustrations after Old Prints |
[*printer's ornament*] | Boston | Privately Printed | 1910.

Colophon: Two hundred and fifty copies of this book were printed by
D. B. Updike, The Merrymount Press, Boston, in April, 1910. Collation:
i–viii, 1–78, [79–80]. Leaf, 7¼ × 10⅛. Binding, boards. With 24 illustrations. Type, Caslon.

[346]
The | Book of Common Prayer | Its Origin and Growth |
by | J. H. Benton, LL.D. | [*floret*] | [*quotation*] | Boston | Pri-
vately printed | 1910.

On reverse of title: D. B. Updike, The Merrymount Press, Boston. Collation: [i–ii], i–lxviii, [lxix]. Leaf, 6⅜ × 9⅝. Binding, boards. Type, Mountjoye.

[347]
The | Book of Common Prayer | and Books connected with |
its Origin and Growth | [*floret*] | Catalogue of the Collec-
tion of | Josiah Henry Benton, LL.D. | [*quotation*] | Boston |
Privately printed | 1910.

On reverse of title: D. B. Updike, The Merrymount Press, Boston. Collation: i–vi, 1–83, [84]. Leaf, 6⅜ × 9⅝. Binding, boards. Type, Oxford.

[348]
The Marolles Club | [*floret*] | Constitution | & | By-laws |
Boston: MDCCCCX.

Bibliography

On reverse of title: The Merrymount Press, Boston. Collation: 1–12, [13].
Leaf, 5¾ × 9. Binding, paper. With portrait. Type, Oxford.

[349]
The Carnegie Foundation | for the Advancement of Teach-
ing | Standard Forms for Financial Reports | of Colleges,
Universities, and | Technical Schools | Bulletin Number
Three | 576 Fifth Avenue | New York City. [n. d.]

On reverse of title: D. B. Updike, The Merrymount Press, Boston. Collation: [i–iv], 1–12, [13–37]. Leaf, 7⅜ × 10. Binding, paper. Type, Scotch-
face.

[350]
Medical Education | in the | United States and Canada | A
Report to | The Carnegie Foundation | for the Advancement
of Teaching | By | Abraham Flexner | With an Introduction
by | Henry S. Pritchett | President of the Foundation | Bul-
letin Number Four | 576 Fifth Avenue | New York City. [n. d.]

On reverse of title: D. B. Updike, The Merrymount Press, Boston. Collation: i–xviii, 1–346. Leaf, 7⅜ × 10. Binding, paper. Type, Scotch-face.

[351]
Academic and Industrial | Efficiency | A Report to | The
Carnegie Foundation | for the Advancement of Teaching |
By | Morris Llewellyn Cooke, M.E. | Member of the Amer-
ican Society of Mechanical Engineers | Bulletin Number Five |
576 Fifth Avenue | New York City. [n. d.]

On reverse of title: D. B. Updike, The Merrymount Press, Boston. Collation: i–viii, 1–134. Leaf, 7⅜ × 10. Binding, paper. Type, Scotch-face.

Minor Printing

The Carnegie Foundation for the Advancement of Teaching,
Fifth Annual Report of the President and of the Treasurer, New
York; *also* Rules for the Admission of Institutions and for the
Granting of Retiring Allowances.

Reports: Society of Arts & Crafts; Meeting of the Cancer Commission of Harvard University; Workingmen's Building Association; Lincoln House; Annual Report of the President, Brown
University, Providence.

The Merrymount Press

Catalogues of Schools and Universities: Saint Mark's School, Southborough, Massachusetts; Simmons College, Ninth Annual Catalogue, 1910–1911; *also* Register of Graduates, 1909; *and* The Summer Library Class, 1910; Brown University, 1910–1911, Providence; Rhode Island School of Design Year-Book, Providence.

Catalogues of Publications and Exhibitions: Publications of the Yale University Press, New Haven; *also* Supplement; Loan Exhibition of Pictures from the Collection of Henry C. Frick.

The Domestic and Foreign Missionary Society Publications, New York: The Church Calendar for the Year of Our Lord Nineteen Hundred and Ten; Mid-Day Intercessions for Missions.

Order of Service at the Presentation and Unveiling of the Memorial to Phillips Brooks, Trinity Church.

The Order for the Profession and Consecration of a Sister, Baltimore.

Office for the Reception of a Novice, Baltimore.

Minutes of the Meetings of the Executive Committee of the Joint Commission to bring about a World Conference on Faith and Order.

The Twenty-fifth Annual Dinner of K A [*Kappa Alpha*] in New England.

The Educated Woman, An Address by John D. Long, Bradford, Massachusetts.

1911

[352]
Records | of the | Brewster Congregational | Church | Brewster, Massachusetts | 1700–1792 | [*cut*] | Privately printed | A. D. 1911.

On reverse of title: Twenty-five copies printed at The Merrymount Press. Collation: [i–iv], 1–169. Leaf, 5½ × 8½. Binding, boards. Type, Caslon.

[353]
Reading | a | Poem | by | Wm. Makepeace Thackeray | [*cut*] | New York | The Grolier Club | 1911.

Colophon: [*device of club*] The Committee on Publications of The Grolier Club certifies that this copy of Reading a Poem is one of an edition of

Bibliography

two hundred and fifty copies. The head-piece and tail-piece in this volume are after sketches by Thackeray, re-drawn by W. A. Dwiggins, who also designed the title-page and colophon. Printed at The Merrymount Press, Boston, by D. B. Updike, in the month of February, 1911. Collation: i–x, 1–48, [49–51]. Leaf, 6 × 9⅛. Binding, boards. Type, Scotch-face.

[354]

[*within border*] The Silences of | the Moon | by | Henry Law Webb | [*cut*] | New York: John Lane Com-|pany. London: John Lane, | The Bodley Head, MDCCCXI.

On reverse of title: D. B. Updike, The Merrymount Press, Boston, U. S. A. Collation: [i–vi], 1–139, [140–141]. Leaf, 4¾ × 7⅜. Binding, cloth. Rubricated title. Type, Caslon.

[355]

Archives of the | General Convention | Edited by Order of | The Commission on Archives | by | Arthur Lowndes | Doctor in Divinity | Volume [*numeral*] | The Correspondence of | John Henry Hobart | [1757–1811] | New York | Privately printed | MDCCCXI [MDCCCXII].

Colophon: Two hundred and fifty copies printed at The Merrymount Press, Boston, by D. B. Updike. 6 vols. Collation: Vol. I, i–ccxiv, 1–396, [397–398]; Vol. II, i–xii, 1–551, [552–553]; Vol. III, i–xii, 1–603, [604–605]; Vol. IV, i–xii, 1–575, [576–577]; Vol. V, i–xiv, 1–601, [602–603] ; Vol. VI, i–xiv, 1–613, [614–615]. Leaf, 7¼ × 10½. Binding, cloth. Rubricated title. Type, Mountjoye and Oxford.

[356]

Letters | of | Bulwer-Lytton to Macready | With an Introduction by | Brander Matthews | [*within cut* 1836–1866] | Privately printed | The Carteret Book Club | Newark, New Jersey | 1911.

Colophon: One Hundred Copies printed in October, 1911, by D. B. Updike, at The Merrymount Press, Boston. Collation: i–xxii, 1–180, [181–182]. Leaf, 5¾ × 9⅛. Binding, boards. Type, Mountjoye.

[357]

In Memory of | Robert Treat Paine | [*cross*] | A Sermon preached at Trinity Church | in the City of Boston | by the

[153]

The Merrymount Press

Rev. Alexander Mann, D.D. | Advent Sunday, November 27 | A.D. MDCCCCX | Privately printed | MDCCCCXI.

On fourth page of cover: The Merrymount Press, Boston. Collation: [i–ii], 1–9. Leaf, 5⅜ × 8¾. Binding, paper. Type, Mountjoye.

[358]
[*within rules*] Joys of the Road | a Little Anthology | in Praise of | Walking | Compiled | by | W. R. B. | [*publisher's mark*] | Chicago | Browne's Bookstore | MDCCCCXI.

On reverse of title: The Merrymount Press, Boston. Collation: 1–103, [104]. Leaf, 4 × 6¼. Binding, cloth. Rubricated title. Type, Caslon and Oxford.

[359]
Forgotten Books | of | The American Nursery | A History of the Development of | the American Story-Book | by | Rosalie V. Halsey | [*cut*] | Boston | Charles E. Goodspeed & Co. | 1911.

On reverse of title: Of this book seven hundred copies were printed in November, 1911, by D. B. Updike, at The Merrymount Press, Boston. Collation: i–x, 1–244, [245]. Leaf, 6½ × 9⅞. Binding, boards. With 25 facsimiles. Type, Caslon.

[360]
Family Notes | [*floret*] | Desmond Fitzgerald | Privately printed | 1911.

On reverse of title: Seventy-five Copies printed at the Merrymount Press, Boston. Collation: i–vi, 1–143, [144]. Leaf, 6⅜ × 9¾. Binding, three-quarter morocco. With 9 illustrations and chart. Type, Caslon.

[361]
[*within border*] Depositio Cornuti | Typographici | That is | A Comical or Mirthful Play | Which can be performed without any | offence, at the Reception and Confirmation of | a Journeyman who has learned honestly the | Noble Art of Book-Printing, and by means | of which also in Future Times Young Men | can be Named, Confirmed, and Received as | Journeymen Printers, at the End of their | Apprenticeship.

Bibliography

Written in good Faith in | compliance with friendly Request and parti-|cular Desire, likewise to the imperishable | Honour of the High and Greatly Renowned | Art of Book-Printing | By | John Rist | [*floret*] | Originally Printed at Lüneburg: Reprinted as | acted at The Grolier Club, January 28, 1909 | New York: The Grolier Club | Anno Christi, MDCCCCXI.

Colophon: Of this Book, Two hundred and fifty copies were printed on Glaslan paper by D. B. Updike at The Merrymount Press, Boston, in the Month of February MDCCCCXI. Collation: i–viii, 1–34, [35–37]. Leaf, 6 × 9⅛. Binding, boards. Type, Caslon.

[362]
Alfred S. Woodworth | [*floret*] | In Memoriam | Privately printed | MDCCCCXI.

On reverse of title: D. B. Updike, The Merrymount Press, Boston. Collation: [i–iv], 1–9, [10]. Leaf, 5 × 7⅝. Binding, boards. With portrait. Type, Mountjoye.

[363]
Harriet W. Kennedy | November Twenty-Third | MDCCCCX | [*cut*] | Privately printed | MDCCCCXI.

On fourth page of cover: The Merrymount Press, Boston. Collation: [i–ii], [i–ii], 1–16, [17]. Leaf, 5¼ × 8⅛. Binding, paper. Type, Mountjoye.

[364]
The Vision of God | in the Open Heavens | A Sermon preached by | the Reverend Leighton Parks, D.D. | before the Graduating Class | of | the Episcopal Theological School | at Cambridge, Massachusetts | on Wednesday | June seventh, MDCCCCXI | [*cut*] | Privately printed | MDCCCCXI.

On reverse of title: The Merrymount Press, Boston. Collation: [i–ii], 1–14. Leaf, 5⅛ × 8¼. Binding, paper. Type, Caslon.

[365]
Addresses | which were delivered at a | Meeting held in Be-half of | the New Building | for the | Infants' Hospital, Bos-ton | on May 24, 1911 | by President A. Lawrence Lowell |

[155]

The Merrymount Press

Dr. J. Collins Warren | Rt. Rev. William Lawrence | and
Dr. Charles W. Eliot | [*floret*] | Boston: 1911.

On reverse of title: The Merrymount Press, Boston. Collation: [i–iv], 1–17,
[18–19]. Leaf, 6¼ × 8¾. Binding, paper. Type, Caslon.

[366]

Fundamental Articles | Charter, By-laws, and | Officers of
the | Episcopal Theological | School | Cambridge | Massa-
chusetts | [*seal*] | A.D. MDCCCXI.

On reverse of title: The Merrymount Press, Boston. Collation: [i–ii], 1–39.
Leaf, 4⅜ × 7⅜. Binding, cloth. Rubricated title. Type, Caslon.

[367]

The John Carter Brown Library | San Francisco Bay | and |
California | in 1776 | Three Maps, with Outline Sketches | re-
produced in Facsimile from the Original Manuscript | drawn
by Pedro Font, Chaplain and Cartographer | to the Expedi-
tion led by Juan Bautista De Ansa | which made the Over-
land Journey | from Northern Mexico to the California
Coast | during the Winter of 1775–1776 | [*floret*] | With an
Explanation by | Irving Berdine Richman | [*arms*] | Provi-
dence, Rhode Island | MDCCCXI.

On reverse of title: One hundred and twenty-five copies printed at The
Merrymount Press, Boston, June 1911. Collation: [i–iv], 1–7. Leaf, 12 × 16.
Binding, boards. With 9 facsimiles. Type, Merrymount.

[368]

The Dusk of the | Gods | (Götterdämmerung) | A Dramatic
Poem by Richard | Wagner freely translated in | poetic
narrative form by | Oliver Huckel | [*floret*] | Thomas Y.
Crowell & Company | Publishers New York. [n.d.]

On reverse of title: Composition and electrotype plates by D. B. Updike,
The Merrymount Press, Boston. Collation: i–xxiv, 1–100, [101]. Leaf,
5 × 7⅜. Binding, cloth. Rubricated throughout. With 4 illustrations. Type,
Clarendon.

[369]

The Order of Service for | the Consecration of | the Rev.

Bibliography

James DeWolf Perry, Jr. | as Bishop of Rhode Island | at Saint John's Church | in Providence | [*arms and motto*] | Feast of the Epiphany | A. D. MDCCCCXI.

On second page of cover: The Merrymount Press, Boston. Collation: [1–36]. Leaf, 5¼ × 8¼. Binding, paper. Rubricated cover. Type, Caslon.

Minor Printing

The Carnegie Foundation for the Advancement of Teaching, Sixth Annual Report of the President and of the Treasurer, New York; *also* Rules for the Admission of Institutions and for the Granting of Retiring Allowances.

Reports: John Carter Brown Library, Providence; Workingmen's Building Association; Annual Report of the President, Brown University, Providence.

Catalogues of Schools and Universities: Saint Mark's School, Southborough, Massachusetts; Middlebury College, Middlebury, Vermont; Trinity College, 1910–1911, Hartford; *also* Circular of Information supplement to the Catalogue; Simmons College, Tenth Annual Catalogue, 1911–1912; *also* Register of Graduates, 1910; Brown University, 1911–1912, Providence; *also* Announcement of Courses; *and* Announcement of Courses offered at the Women's College in Brown University, 1911–1912.

Catalogue of the Publications of the Yale University Press, New Haven; *also* Supplement.

The Domestic and Foreign Missionary Society Publications, New York: The Church Calendar for the Year of Our Lord Nineteen Hundred and Eleven; Mid-Day Intercessions for Missions.

Diocese of Pennsylvania: Order of Service for the Consecration of Philip Mercer Rhinelander as Bishop Coadjutor and Thomas James Garland as Suffragan Bishop, Philadelphia.

World Conference on Faith and Order Publications: Joint Commission appointed to arrange for a World Conference on Faith and Order (*also issued in Greek, Latin, Swedish, Italian, French, German, and Russian*); Report of the Committee on Plan and Scope.

An Office for the Anointing of the Sick, Hanover, New Hampshire.

The Year Book of the Winsor School, Boston.

The Merrymount Press

Catalogue Fenway Court.

Handbook of the John Hay Library in Brown University, Providence, Rhode Island.

Memorial Exhibition of the Works of Frederic Porter Vinton.

The Instructive District Nursing Association of Boston.

1912

[370]

A Day at Castrogiovanni | By | George Edward Woodberry | [*floret*] | Printed for the | Woodberry Society | 1912.

On reverse of title: The Merrymount Press, Boston. Colophon: Three hundred copies of this book have been printed for the Woodberry Society. Seventy-five are numbered and signed by the author. Collation: [i–viii], 1–29, [30]. Leaf, 5½ × 8½. Binding, boards. Type, Mountjoye.

[371]

Wendell Phillips | The Faith of an | American | By | George Edward Woodberry | [*cut*] | Printed for the | Woodberry Society | 1912.

Collation: [i–vi], 1–46. Leaf, 5½ × 8½. Binding, boards. No imprint. Type, Mountjoye.

[372]

[*within rules*] A History of | the | India Wharf Rats | 1886–1911 | Boston: Printed for the Club | The Merrymount Press | 1912.

Collation: 1–31, [32]. Leaf, 4¼ × 7¼. Binding, boards. Type, Caslon.

[373]

An | Address | delivered at Worcester | October 16, 1912 | before the | American Antiquarian Society | on the Occasion of the | One Hundredth Anniversary | of its | Foundation | By | Charles G. Washburn | Boston | Privately printed | 1912.

On reverse of title: D. B. Updike, The Merrymount Press, Boston. Collation: 1–45. Leaf, 5½ × 9. Binding, half morocco. Type, Oxford.
Also issued in paper covers.

Bibliography

[374]

Harvard Studies in Comparative Literature | Volume II | Chivalry | in English Literature | Chaucer, Malory, Spenser | and Shakespeare | By | William Henry Schofield | [*seal*] | Cambridge | Harvard University | 1912.

On reverse of title: D. B. Updike, The Merrymount Press, Boston, U.S.A. Collation: i–x, 1–294. Leaf, 5⅝ × 8½. Binding, cloth. Type, Scotch-face.

[375]

Submarine | Signals | [*cut*] | Submarine Signal Co. | 88 Broad Street | Boston. [n. d.]

On reverse of title: The Merrymount Press, Boston. Collation: 1–37, [38]. Leaf, 6 × 9. Binding, paper. With illustrations. Type, Caslon.

[376]

The Kingdom of All-Souls | And Two Other Poems | For Christmas | By | George Edward Woodberry | [*floret*] | Published for the | Woodberry Society | 1912.

On reverse of title: The Merrymount Press, Boston. Colophon: Three hundred copies of this book have been printed for the Woodberry Society. One hundred are numbered and signed by the author. Collation: [i–viii], 1–32, [33]. Leaf, 5½ × 8½. Binding, boards. Type, Oxford.

[377]

A Catalogue of an Exhibition of | Waltoniana | Consisting of Various Editions of "The | Compleat Angler," Walton's "Lives," Man-|uscripts, Portraits, Prints, Medals, &c. | From the Library of a Member of | The Club of Odd Volumes | [*floret*] | [*quotation*] | [*seal*] | Boston | The Club of Odd Volumes | 50 Mt. Vernon St. | [April 23 to May 2, 1912].

Colophon: One hundred and thirty copies of this catalogue were printed from type for the Club of Odd Volumes, at The Merrymount Press, Boston, in the month of April, 1912. Collation: i–x, 1–36, [37–38]. Leaf, 4½ × 7¼. Binding, paper. Type, Oxford.

[378]

Isaiah Thomas | Printer, Writer & Collector | A Paper read April 12, 1911, before | The Club of Odd Volumes | By | Charles Lemuel Nichols | With a Bibliography of the

The Merrymount Press

Books | printed by Isaiah Thomas | [*seal*] | Printed for | The Club of Odd Volumes | Boston: 1912.

Colophon: Of this Book One Hundred and Ten Copies were printed in the Month of March, 1912 [*seal*] The Merrymount Press, Boston. Collation: i–xii, 1–144, [145–146]. Leaf, 6¼ × 9⅜. Binding, boards. Type, Oxford.

[379]
[*within design*] The | Correspondence | of | Philip Sidney | and | Hubert Languet | [*floret*] | Edited by | William Aspen- wall | Bradley | [*floret*] | Boston | The Merrymount | Press | MDCCCCXII.

Colophon: [*floret*] This volume with title-page by W. A. Dwiggins was printed by D. B. Updike at The Merrymount Press, Boston, Massachusetts, in October MDCCCCXII [*floret*]. Collation: i–xxxii, 1–229, [230–231]. Leaf, 6⅛ × 9½. Binding, boards. Rubricated throughout. Type, Montallegro. *The Humanists' Library, Vol. V.*

[380]
The Master-singers | of Nuremberg | (Die Meistersinger von Nürnberg) | A Dramatic Poem by Richard | Wagner freely translated in | poetic narrative form by | Oliver Huckel | [*floret*] | Thomas Y. Crowell Company | Publishers New York. [n. d.]

On reverse of title: Composition and electrotype plates by D. B. Updike, The Merrymount Press, Boston. Collation: i–xxii, 1–127, [128]. Leaf, 5 × 7⅜. Binding, cloth. Rubricated throughout. With 5 illustrations. Type, Clarendon.

[381]
Whistler's Pastels | and other Modern Profiles | By | A. E. Gallatin | [*floret*] | New York | John Lane Company | Lon- don: John Lane, The Bodley Head | MDCCCCXII.

Colophon: Two hundred and fifty copies printed in December, 1911, by D. B. Updike at The Merrymount Press, Boston. Collation: [i–ii], i–x, 1–49, [50–54]. Leaf, 5½ × 8½. Binding, boards. With 21 illustrations. Type, Mountjoye.

[382]
Medical Education | in Europe | A Report to | The Carne- gie Foundation | for the Advancement of Teaching | By

Bibliography

Abraham Flexner | With an Introduction by | Henry S. Pritchett | President of the Foundation | Bulletin Number Six | 576 Fifth Avenue | New York City | 1912.

On reverse of title: D. B. Updike, The Merrymount Press, Boston. Collation, i–xx, 1–357. Leaf, 7⅜ × 10. Binding, paper. Type, Scotch-face.

[383]

In Memoriam | Whitcomb Field | An Address given by the Rev. Roderick | Stebbins in King's Chapel, Boston, Novem-| ber 30, 1912, at the Memorial Service to | Whitcomb Field, '05, who died in Port-|land, Oregon, November 20, 1912 | [*cut*] | Printed for the Class of 1905. [n. d.]

On reverse of title: The Merrymount Press, Boston. Collation: [1–6]. Leaf, 4¾ × 7½. Binding, paper. Type, Oxford.

Minor Printing

The Carnegie Foundation for the Advancement of Teaching, Seventh Annual Report of the President and of the Treasurer, New York.

Reports: John Carter Brown Library, Providence; Workingmen's Building Association; Annual Report of the President, Brown University, Providence.

Catalogues of Schools and Universities: Saint Mark's School, Southborough, Massachusetts; Simmons College, Eleventh Annual Catalogue, 1912–1913; Trinity College, 1911–1912, Hartford; Middlebury College, 1912–1913, Middlebury, Vermont; Bulletin of the State University of Iowa, Student Life, Iowa City; Brown University, 1912–1913, Providence; *also* Announcement of Courses; *and* Announcement of Courses offered at the Women's College in Brown University, 1912–1913.

World Conference on Faith and Order Publications: Joint Commission appointed to arrange for a World Conference on Faith and Order (*also issued in Dutch*); Report of the Committee on Plan and Scope; The World Conference and the Problem of Unity; An Official Statement by the Joint Commission of the Protestant Episcopal Church in the United States of America; Bibliography of Topics related to Church Unity; Ad Concilium Episcopale Ecclesiarum Catholicarum veterum Europaearum Epistola.

The Merrymount Press

The Rockefeller Institute for Medical Research, History, Organization and Equipment, New York.

Catalogue Fenway Court.

The By-Laws of the Board of Managers of the Cathedral House for Children, Laramie, Wyoming.

1913

[384]

The Portraits and | Caricatures of | James McNeill Whistler | An Iconography by | A. E. Gallatin | [*floret*] | With twenty examples | Ten hitherto unpublished | London: John Lane, The Bodley Head | New York: John Lane Company | Toronto: Bell & Cockburn | MDCCCXIII.

Colophon: Five hundred copies printed by D. B. Updike, The Merrymount Press, Boston, U. S. A., October, 1913. The first fifty copies printed on hand-made paper, numbered and signed by the author, of which this is No. —. Collation: i–xii, [i–ii], 1–51, [52–56]. Leaf, 5½ × 8½. Binding, half leather. Type, Oxford.

The machine-made paper copies were bound in full cloth.

[385]

American | and | English Studies | by | Whitelaw Reid | Vol. I | Government and Education [Vol. II | Biography, History and | Journalism] | New York | Charles Scribner's Sons | MDCCCXIII.

On reverse of title: D. B. Updike, The Merrymount Press, Boston. Collation: Vol. I, i–xii, 1–315, [316]; Vol. II, [i–vi], 1–343, [344]. Leaf, 5¾ × 8¾. Binding, cloth. Type, Mountjoye.

[386]

Sonnets & Quatrains | by | Antoinette De Coursey Patterson | [*cut*] | Philadelphia | H. W. Fisher & Company | MDCCCXIII.

On reverse of title: D. B. Updike, The Merrymount Press, Boston. Collation: i–xii, 1–45. Leaf, 5¼ × 7⅜. Binding, boards. Type, Caslon.

[387]

The Monroe Doctrine | an Obsolete Shibboleth | by | Hiram

Bibliography

Bingham | [*seal*] | New Haven: Yale University Press |
London: Humphrey Milford | Oxford University Press |
MDCCCCXIII.

On reverse of title: First printed August, 1913, One thousand five hundred copies. D. B. Updike, The Merrymount Press, Boston. Collation: i–x, 1–153, [154]. Leaf, 4½ × 7¼. Binding, cloth. Type, Oxford.

[388]
In Memory of | Eleanor Ladd Clark | October 29, 1878 |
December 7, 1912 | [*cut*] | Privately printed | 1913.

Colophon: The Merrymount Press, Boston. Collation: [1–11]. Leaf, 4¾ × 7½. Binding, boards. Type, Oxford.

[389]
Ordinary | and | Canon of the Mass | together with the Order
for | the Administration of | the Lord's Supper | or | Holy
Communion | and | the Holy Chant | [*floret*].

Colophon: The Text of this Book was prepared by Maurice W. Britton, Rector of S. Clement's Church, New York, and the Music by Charles Winfred Douglas, Canon of Fond du Lac. It was printed at The Merrymount Press, Boston, and is published by The H. W. Gray Company: New York, Agents for Novello & Co. Ltd., MDCCCXIII. Collation: [1–79]. Leaf, 9 × 12½. Issued in sheets. Rubricated throughout. Type, Merrymount.

[390]
The Story of | George Crowninshield's Yacht | Cleopatra's
Barge | on | a Voyage of Pleasure to the Western Islands |
and the Mediterranean | 1816–1817 | Compiled from Jour-
nals, Letters, and Log-Book by | Francis B. Crowninshield |
[*cut*] | Boston | Privately printed | 1913.

Colophon: [*within cut*] The Merrymount Press, Boston. Collation: i–xii, 1–259, [260]. Leaf, 8¼ × 11. Binding, cloth. Rubricated title. With 39 illustrations and facsimiles. Type, Scotch-face.

End-papers by W. A. Dwiggins.

[391]
Whistler's Pastels | and other Modern Profiles | By | A. E.
Gallatin | [*floret*] | New Edition | New York: John Lane Com-
pany | London: John Lane, The Bodley Head | MDCCCXIII.

The Merrymount Press

Colophon: [*floret*] Four hundred copies printed in February, 1913, by D. B. Updike at The Merrymount Press, Boston, U. S. A. Collation: [i–ii], i–x, 1–63, [64–68]. Leaf, 5½ × 8½. Binding, cloth. With 17 illustrations. Type, Mountjoye.

[392]
In Memory of | Royden Wolcott Allen | 1891–1913 | [*cut*] | Privately printed | 1913.

On reverse of title: The Merrymount Press, Boston. Collation: [i–vi], 1–15, [16–17]. Leaf, 4¾ × 7½. Binding, boards. With portrait. Type, Oxford.

[393]
Preliminary Report | of the Joint Commission on the | Support of the Clergy | [*floret*] | July: 1913.

On fourth page of cover: D. B. Updike, The Merrymount Press, Boston. Collation: [i–ii], i–viii, 1–118, [119]. Leaf, 5⅞ × 9⅛. Binding, paper. Type, Scotch-face.

[394]
[*within design*] Records of Journeys to Venice | and the Low Countries | By Albrecht Dürer | Edited by Roger Fry | The Merrymount Press | Boston: MDCCCXIII.

Colophon: This volume with title-page by W. A. Dwiggins was printed by D. B. Updike at The Merrymount Press, Boston, Massachusetts, in October MDCCCCXIII. Collation: i–xxvi, 1–117, [118–119]. Leaf, 6⅛ × 9½. Binding, boards. Rubricated throughout. Type, Montallegro.

The Humanists' Library, Vol. VI.

[395]
Beverly Public Library | [*floret*] | Proceedings | at the Opening of | the New Library Building | June 20, 1913 | [*seal*] | Beverly, Massachusetts | Printed for the Trustees | 1913.

On reverse of title: The Merrymount Press, Boston. Collation: [i–ii], 1–18. Leaf, 5¼ × 7⅞. Binding, paper. Type, Oxford.

[396]
Tristan and Isolda | (Tristan und Isolde) | A Dramatic Poem by Richard | Wagner freely translated in | poetic narrative

Bibliography

form by | Oliver Huckel | [*floret*] | Thomas Y. Crowell
Company | Publishers New York. [n. d.]

On reverse of title: Composition and electrotype plates by D. B. Updike,
The Merrymount Press, Boston. Collation: i–xvii, 1–72, [73]. Leaf, 5 × 7⅜.
Binding, cloth. Rubricated throughout. With 6 illustrations. Type, Clarendon.

[397]
[*cut*] | The Consecration of | The Chancel and Chapel | and
the Dedication of | The Parish House | of | Grace Church |
Providence | Tuesday, January Seventh | A.D. MDCCCXIII |
[*floret*].

On reverse of last page: D. B. Updike, The Merrymount Press, Boston.
Collation: 1–14, [15–16]. Leaf, 6 × 9¼. Binding, paper. Type, Caslon.

[398]
An Office of Prayer | for Missions | with Selected Psalms |
and Hymns | [*cut*] | New York | Published by the Domestic
& Foreign Missionary | Society of the Protestant Episcopal
Church in | The United States of America, at the Church |
Missions House, 281 Fourth Avenue. [n. d.]

Reissue of No. 79, in limp-cloth binding.

Minor Printing

The Carnegie Foundation for the Advancement of Teaching,
Eighth Annual Report of the President and of the Treasurer,
New York; *also* The Study of Legal Education, From the Report
of the President of the Carnegie Foundation for the Advancement
of Teaching for 1913.

Reports: John Carter Brown Library, Providence; Workingmen's
Building Association; Annual Report of the President, Brown
University, Providence.

Catalogues of Schools and Universities: Saint Mark's School,
Southborough, Massachusetts; The Browne & Nichols School,
Cambridge; Simmons College, Twelfth Annual Catalogue, 1913–
1914; Trinity College, 1911–1913, Hartford; Wheaton College,
1912–1913, Norton, Massachusetts; Brown University, 1913–1914,

The Merrymount Press

Providence; *also* Announcement of Courses; *and* Announcement of Courses offered at The Women's College in Brown University, 1913–1914; Middlebury College Bulletin, Middlebury, Vermont; *also* Courses of Study, 1913–1914.

Catalogue of the Publications of the Yale University Press, New Haven.

World Conference on Faith and Order Publications: Joint Commission appointed to arrange for a World Conference on Faith and Order (*also issued in Spanish*); Prayer and Unity, by a Layman; Bibliography of Topics related to Church Unity; Questions of Faith and Order for consideration by the Proposed Conference, by the Rt. Rev. A. C. A. Hall, D.D.; Unity or Union: Which? by the Rt. Rev. P. M. Rhinelander, D.D.; The Conference Spirit, by a Layman; List of Commissions already appointed; The Manifestation of Unity, by the Rt. Rev. C. P. Anderson, D.D.; Minutes of the Meetings of the Joint Commission appointed by the General Convention of 1910 to bring about a World Conference on Faith and Order.

The Order of Service for the Consecration of the Rev. Samuel Gavitt Babcock as Suffragan Bishop at Trinity Church in the City of Boston.

The University of Vermont and State Agricultural College, Burlington, Vermont, Concerning the History, Location, Scope, and Aims of the University, Burlington.

Some Facts about Bradford Academy, Bradford, Massachusetts.

Description of The Merrymount Press, Boston.

1914

[399]

[*within design*] A | Platonick Discourse | upon Love | by | Pico Della Mirandola | [*floret*] | Edited by | Edmund G. Gardner | Boston | The Merrymount Press.

Colophon: This volume with title-page by T. M. Cleland was printed by D. B. Updike at The Merrymount Press, Boston, U. S. A., MDCCCCXIV. Collation: i–xxviii, 1–83, [84–85]. Leaf, 6¼ × 9½. Binding, boards. Rubricated throughout. Type, Montallegro.

The Humanists' Library, Vol. VII.

Bibliography

[400]

Harvard Studies in Comparative Literature | Volume III |
The Comedies of | Holberg | by | Oscar James Campbell, Jr. |
Assistant Professor of English in the | University of Wis-
consin | [*arms*] | Cambridge | Harvard University Press | Lon-
don: Humphrey Milford | Oxford University Press | 1914.

On reverse of title: D. B. Updike, The Merrymount Press, Boston, U. S. A.
Collation: [i–ii], i–x, 1–363. Leaf, 5⅝ × 8½. Binding, cloth. Type, Oxford.

[401]

The | Book of Common Prayer | and Books connected with |
its Origin and Growth | [*floret*] | Catalogue of the Collec-
tion of | Josiah Henry Benton, LL.D. | [*quotation*] | Second
Edition prepared by | William Muss-Arnolt, B.D., Ph.D. |
Boston | Privately printed | 1914.

On reverse of title: D. B. Updike, The Merrymount Press, Boston. Collation: i–x, 1–142, [143]. Leaf, 6½ × 9¾. Binding, boards. Type, Oxford.

[402]

[*within design*] A | Lover's Moods | By Bertram Dobell |
Author of "Rosemary and Pansies" | "A Century of Son-
nets" | "Sidelights on Charles Lamb" | &c | Cleveland Ohio |
The Rowfant Club | MDCCCCXIV.

On page facing title: This edition consists of two hundred copies as follows: One hundred and twenty-five for The Rowfant Club and seventy-
five for the Author. This is Number —. On reverse of title: D. B. Updike,
The Merrymount Press, Boston. Collation: i–x, 1–61, [62]. Leaf, 5 × 6½.
Binding, boards. Rubricated title. Type, Caslon.

[403]

In Memoriam | Arthur Ryerson | An Address at the un-
veiling of a Tablet | in St. Luke's Hospital, Chicago | by
Cortland Parker | [*cut*] | Privately printed | 1914.

On reverse of title: The Merrymount Press, Boston. Collation: [i–vi], 1–13,
[14–15]. Leaf, 4¾ × 7½. Binding, cloth. With 2 illustrations. Type, Oxford.

[404]

An Account of | our Arresting Experience | by | Conway
Evans | [*floret*] | Privately printed | 1914.

The Merrymount Press

On reverse of title: 100 copies printed. D. B. Updike, The Merrymount Press, Boston. Collation: [i–iv], [i–ii], 1–30, [31]. Leaf, 4¾ × 7½. Binding, cloth. Type, Oxford.

[405]
John | Baskerville | Type-Founder | and Printer | 1706–1775 | [*printer's ornament*] | By | Josiah Henry Benton LL.D. | [*printer's ornament*] | Boston | Privately printed | 1914.

On reverse of title: D. B. Updike, The Merrymount Press, Boston. Collation: [i–vi], 1–78. Leaf, 6⅞ × 9½. Binding, boards. With portrait, facsimile, and illustration. Type, Caslon.

[406]
Two Phases of Criticism | Historical and Aesthetic | Lectures delivered on | the Larwill Foundation of Kenyon College | May seventh and eighth, 1913 | by | George Edward Woodberry | [*floret*] | Published for the | Woodberry Society | 1914.

On reverse of title: The Merrymount Press, Boston. Collation: [i–vi], 1–70. Leaf, 5½ × 8½. Binding, boards. Type, Oxford.

[407]
The | John Carter Brown | Library | A History | by | George Parker Winship | [*arms*] | Providence | 1914.

On reverse of title: D. B. Updike, The Merrymount Press, Boston. Collation: [i–iv], 1–96, [97]. Leaf, 6⅛ × 9½. Binding, boards. Type, Mountjoye.

[408]
[*within design*] A | Renaissance | Courtesy-Book | Galateo | of Manners & Behaviours | by | Giovanni Della Casa | [*floret*] | With an Introduction by | J. E. Spingarn | Boston | The Merrymount Press.

Colophon: This volume with title-page by T. M. Cleland was printed by D. B. Updike at The Merrymount Press, Boston, U.S.A., MDCCCCXIV. Collation: i–xxviii, 1–122, [123–124]. Leaf, 6⅛ × 9½. Binding, boards. Rubricated throughout. Type, Montallegro.

The Humanists' Library, Vol. VIII.

[409]
Comedies by Holberg | Jeppe of the Hill, The Political

Bibliography

Tinker | Erasmus Montanus | [*floret*] | Translated from the Danish by | Oscar James Campbell, Jr., Ph.D. | Assistant Professor of English in the University of Wisconsin | and | Frederic Schenck, B. Litt. Oxon. | Instructor in English in Harvard University | With an Introduction by | Oscar James Campbell, Jr. | New York | The American-Scandinavian Foundation | London: Humphrey Milford | Oxford University Press | 1914.

On reverse of title: D. B. Updike, The Merrymount Press, Boston, U.S.A. Collation: [i–ii], i–xvi, 1–178, [179–182]. Leaf, 5 × 7⅜. Binding, cloth. Type, Caslon.

Scandinavian Classics, Vol. I.

[410]
Poems by Tegnér | The Children of the Lord's Supper | Translated from the Swedish by | Henry Wadsworth Longfellow | and | Frithiof's Saga | Translated by Rev. W. Lewery Blackley | With an Introduction by | Paul Robert Lieder, A.M. | Harvard University | [*floret*] | New York | The American-Scandinavian | Foundation | 1914.

On reverse of title: D. B. Updike, The Merrymount Press, Boston, U.S.A. Collation: [i–ii], i–xxviii, 1–207, [208–209]. Leaf, 4⅞ × 7⅜. Binding, cloth. Type, Caslon.

Scandinavian Classics, Vol. II.

[411]
The | Voyages of the Norsemen | to America | by | William Hovgaard | Late Commander in the Royal Danish Navy | Professor of Naval Design and Construction in the | Massachusetts Institute of Technology | [*floret*] | With Eighty-three Illustrations | and Seven Maps | New York | The American-Scandinavian | Foundation | 1914.

On reverse of title: D. B. Updike, The Merrymount Press, Boston, U.S.A. Collation: [i–ii], i–xxii, 1–304, [305]. Leaf, 6¼ × 9¼. Binding, cloth. Type, Oxford.

Scandinavian Monographs, Vol. I.

The Merrymount Press

[412]
Eight Sermons | by | Daniel Merriman | [*floret*] | Boston | Privately printed | 1914.

On reverse of title: D. B. Updike, The Merrymount Press, Boston. Collation: [i–viii], 1–187. Leaf, 5¼ × 8¼. Binding, cloth. Type, Oxford.

[413]
The History of | Brown University | 1764–1914 | by | Walter C. Bronson, Litt.D. | Professor of English Literature | [*seal*] | Providence | Published by the University | 1914.

On reverse of title: D. B. Updike, The Merrymount Press, Boston. Collation: i–x, [i–ii], 1–547, [548]. Leaf, 6½ × 9¾. Binding, cloth. Type, Oxford.

[414]
Books in the Library of | Nelson W. Aldrich | Warwick, Rhode Island | [*floret*] | Part II | Literature, History | &c. | Privately Printed | 1914.

On reverse of title: D. B. Updike, The Merrymount Press, Boston. Collation: i–viii, 1–455, [456]. Leaf, 6¾ × 10. Binding, cloth. Rubricated title. Type, Oxford.

Part II was published before Part I.

[415]
Richard Wagner | The Man and his Work by | Oliver Huckel | [*floret*] | Thomas Y. Crowell Company | Publishers New York. [n. d.]

On reverse of title: Composition and electrotype plates by D. B. Updike, The Merrymount Press, Boston. Collation: [i–ii], i–xii, [i–ii], 1–121, [122]. Leaf, 5 × 7⅜. Binding, cloth. Rubricated throughout. With 5 illustrations. Type, Clarendon.

[416]
A Study of | Education in Vermont | Prepared by The Carnegie Foundation | for the Advancement of Teaching | at the Request of | the Vermont Educational Commission | Bulletin Number Seven | [*seal*] | New York City | 576 Fifth Avenue. [n. d.]

Bibliography

On reverse of title: D. B. Updike, The Merrymount Press, Boston. Collation: [i–iv], 1–241. Leaf, 7⅜ × 10. Binding, paper. Type, Scotch-face.

Part I issued separately in pamphlet form in 1913.

[417]
The Common Law and | the Case Method | in American University Law Schools | A Report to The Carnegie Foundation | for the Advancement of Teaching | By | Professor Dr. Josef Redlich | of the Faculty of Law and Political Science in | The University of Vienna | Bulletin Number Eight | [*seal*] | New York City | 576 Fifth Avenue. [n. d.]

On reverse of title: D. B. Updike, The Merrymount Press, Boston. Collation: i–xii, 1–84. Leaf, 7⅜ × 10. Binding, paper. Type, Scotch-face.

[418]
The Book of | The Official Acts of | The Bishop of Rhode Island | [*floret*] | Printed A.D. MDCCCCXIV.

Collation: [1–372]. Leaf, 8⅛ × 10¾. Binding, pigskin. Rubricated title. Type, Caslon.

1 copy printed. Single copies printed also for the Bishops of Maine, Western Massachusetts, Washington, and the Bishop Suffragan of Massachusetts. Information on imprint not obtainable.

Minor Printing

The Carnegie Foundation for the Advancement of Teaching, Ninth Annual Report of the President and of the Treasurer, New York; *also* Rules for the Admission of Institutions and for the Granting of Retiring Allowances.

Reports: John Carter Brown Library, Providence; Workingmen's Building Association; Annual Report of the President, Brown University, Providence; Wheaton College, President's Report, 1912–1913, Norton, Massachusetts.

Catalogues of Schools and Universities: Saint Mark's School, Southborough, Massachusetts; The Browne & Nichols School, Cambridge; Simmons College, Thirteenth Annual Catalogue, 1914–1915; Trinity College, 1913–1914, Hartford; Wheaton College, 1913–1914, Norton, Massachusetts; Brown University, 1914–1915, Providence; *also* Announcement of Courses; *and* Announce-

The Merrymount Press

ment of Courses offered at the Women's College in Brown University, 1914–1915; Middlebury College, 1914–1915; *also* Bulletin.

Catalogue of the Publications of the Yale University Press, New Haven; *also* Supplement.

World Conference on Faith and Order Publications: Report of the Committee on Church Unity of the National Council of Congregational Churches, 1913; A World Movement for Christian Unity, by the Rev. Lefferd M. A. Haughwout; Second Meeting of the Advisory Committee, Report of the Second Deputation to Great Britain, The Call for a Truce of God; Joint Commission appointed to arrange for a World Conference on Faith and Order (*in French*); Prayer and Unity, by a Layman; Unity or Union: Which? by the Rt. Rev. P. M. Rhinelander, D.D.; The Conference Spirit, by a Layman; Minutes of the Meetings of the Joint Commission appointed by the General Convention of 1910 to bring about a World Conference on Faith and Order, May 20, 1913, to May 14, 1914; List of Commissions already appointed, March 20, 1914; An Official Statement by the Joint Commission of the Protestant Episcopal Church in the United States of America; Report of the Joint Commission to the General Convention of the Protestant Episcopal Church, 1913.

The By-Laws of the Board of Managers of the Cathedral Home for Children, Laramie, Wyoming.

The Society of Printers, Reports of President and Treasurer with Constitution, By-Laws, and List of Members.

University Dinner to Delegates and other Guests on the occasion of the One Hundred and Fiftieth Anniversary of the Founding of Brown University, Providence.

1915

[419]
The Jonny-Cake Papers of | "Shepherd Tom " | Together with | Reminiscences of Narragansett | Schools of Former Days | by | Thomas Robinson Hazard | With a Biographical Sketch and Notes by | Rowland Gibson Hazard | Illustrated by Rudolph Ruzicka | [*crest*] | Boston | Printed for the Subscribers | 1915.

Bibliography

Colophon: Of this edition six hundred copies have been printed on French hand-made paper for the subscribers, and six hundred additional copies on antique wove paper for general distribution, by D. B. Updike, The Merrymount Press, Boston, September, 1915. Collation: [i–ii], i–xx, [i–ii], 1–429, [430–431]. Leaf of antique-wove-paper edition, 5⅞ × 8¾; leaf of hand-made-paper edition, 5⅞ × 9. Binding, boards. Illustrated with 23 woodcuts. Type, Oxford.

[420]

The Sesquicentennial | of | Brown University | 1764–1914 | A Commemoration | [seal] | Published by the University | 1915.

On reverse of title: D. B. Updike, The Merrymount Press, Boston. Collation: i–x, 1–306, [307]. Leaf, 6⅜ × 9¾. Binding, boards. Type, Mountjoye.

[421]

Napoleon | an Essay by | William Makepeace Thackeray | Together with Reproductions of | Five Original Sketches | by the Author | [cut] | Privately printed | 1915.

Colophon: Seventy-five copies of this book were printed by D. B. Updike, The Merrymount Press, Boston, in the month of March, 1915. Collation: [i–ii], 1–23, [24–39]. Leaf, 7⅜ × 8⅞. Binding, boards. Type, Mountjoye.

[422]

In Memory of | Robert Parkman Blake | 1870–1914 | [floret] | [quotation] | Boston | Privately printed | 1915.

On reverse of title: D. B. Updike, The Merrymount Press, Boston. Collation: [i–iv], 1–30, [31–33]. Leaf, 5⅛ × 8¼. Binding, boards. Type, Mountjoye.

[423]

Comedies by Holberg | Jeppe of the Hill, The Political Tinker | Erasmus Montanus | [floret] | Translated from the Danish by | Oscar James Campbell, Jr., Ph.D. | Assistant Professor of English in the University of Wisconsin | and | Frederic Schenck, B.Litt.Oxon. | Instructor in English in Harvard University | With an Introduction by | Oscar James Campbell, Jr. | Third Impression | New York | The American-

[173]

The Merrymount Press

Scandinavian Foundation | London: Humphrey Milford |
Oxford University Press | 1914.
Reissue of No. 409.

[424]
In Memoriam | Francis Bishop Harrington | 1854–1914 |
[*floret*] | Boston | Privately printed | 1915.

On reverse of title: D. B. Updike, The Merrymount Press, Boston. Collation: [i–vi], 1–41. Leaf, 5¼ × 8¼. Binding, cloth. With 2 illustrations and
2 facsimiles. Type, Mountjoye.

[425]
Wellesley College | Restoration and Endowment Fund |
[*floret*] | Record of a Meeting in | Celebration of its Com-
pletion | Held January 15 | 1915 | Published by the Col-
lege | Wellesley, Massachusetts | 1915.

On reverse of title: D. B. Updike, The Merrymount Press, Boston. Collation: 1–32, [33–35]. Leaf, 5½ × 8¼. Binding, boards. Type, Oxford.
Also issued in paper covers, with leaf measuring 5½ × 8.

[426]
A Memorial of | the Seventy-fifth Anniversary | of the
Founding of | The University of Michigan | Held in Com-
mencement Week | June 23 to June 27 | 1912 | [*seal*] | Ann
Arbor | Published by the University | 1915.

On reverse of title: D. B. Updike, The Merrymount Press, Boston. Collation: i–vii, 1–216, [217]. Leaf, 6⅜ × 9¾. Binding, cloth. Type, Mountjoye.

[427]
[*within border*] Bill Pratt | The Saw-Buck | Philosopher |
[*floret*] | An Appreciation of the | Life, Public Services, and |
Speeches of One who for | over half a Century | ministered
to the En-|tertainment and Edifi-|cation of the Students | of
Williams College. By | John Sheridan Zelie of | the Class of
'Eighty-|seven, and Carroll Perry | of the Class of 'Ninety. |
[*florets*] | Williamstown, MDCCCXCV.

Bibliography

Colophon: The Merrymount Press, Boston. Collation: [i–iv], i–x, 1–156, [157–159]. Leaf, 5⅝ × 7½.
Reissue of No. 13, with new matter.

[428]
Brookline | Thursday Club | Founded December, 1871 | [*floret*] | Constitution and List of | Officers and Members | Printed for the Club | 1915.

On reverse of title: D. B. Updike, The Merrymount Press, Boston. Collation: 1–23. Leaf, 5¼ × 8¼. Binding, cloth. Type, Oxford.

[429]
Orchidaceae | Illustrations and Studies of | the Family Orchidaceae | Issued from the Ames Botanical Laboratory | North Easton, Massachusetts | The Genera and Species of | Philippine Orchids | By | Oakes Ames | Director of the Botanic Garden of Harvard University | [*floret*] | Fascicle V | Boston | The Merrymount Press | 1915.

On reverse of title: D. B. Updike, The Merrymount Press, Boston. Collation: i–xiv, 1–270, [271]. Leaf, 7 × 10. Binding, boards. Rubricated title. With map. Type, Scotch-face.

[430]
Poems and Songs | by | Björnstjerne Björnson | [*floret*] | Translated from the Norwegian | in the Original Meters | by | Arthur Hubbell Palmer | Professor of the German Language and Literature | in Yale University | New York | The American-Scandinavian | Foundation | 1915.

On reverse of title: D. B. Updike, The Merrymount Press, Boston, U. S. A. Collation: [i–ii], i–xxii, 1–264, [265–267]. Leaf, 5 × 7⅜. Binding, cloth. Type, Caslon.
Scandinavian Classics, Vol. III.

[431]
Master Olof | A Drama in Five Acts | By August Strindberg | [*floret*] | Translated from the Swedish | with an Introduction by | Edwin Björkman | From the Prose Version of 1872 |

The Merrymount Press

[*floret*] | New York | The American-Scandinavian Foundation | London: Humphrey Milford | Oxford University Press |
1915.

On reverse of title: D. B. Updike, The Merrymount Press, Boston, U. S. A.
Collation: [i–ii], i–xxiv, 1–125, [126–128]. Leaf, 5 × 7⅜. Binding, cloth.
Type, Caslon.

Scandinavian Classics, Vol. IV.

[432]
The Early Years of Brown University | 1764–1770 | [*floret*] |
William Williams Keen, M.D., LL.D. [n. d.]

On fourth page of cover: D. B. Updike, The Merrymount Press, Boston.
Collation: 1–36, [37]. Leaf, 6¼ × 9¾. Binding, paper. No title. Type,
Mountjoye.

[433]
William and Mary Ann Appleton | 1815 | and their Descendants | 1915 | Boston | Privately Printed | 1915.

On reverse of title: D. B. Updike, The Merrymount Press, Boston. Collation: [1–7]. Leaf, 6 × 8¾. Binding, cloth. With arms, genealogical chart, and 3 illustrations. Type, Caslon.

Minor Printing

The Carnegie Foundation for the Advancement of Teaching, Tenth Annual Report of the President and of the Treasurer, New York; *also* Study of Legal Education, From the Report of the President.

Reports: John Carter Brown Library, Providence; Annual Report of the President, Brown University, Providence; Wheaton College, President's Report, 1913–1914, Norton, Massachusetts.

Catalogues of Schools and Universities: Saint Mark's School, Fiftieth Year, 1865–1915, Southborough, Massachusetts; The Browne & Nichols School, Cambridge; Simmons College, Fourteenth Annual Catalogue, 1915–1916; Trinity College, 1914–1915, Hartford; Wheaton College, 1914–1915, Norton, Massachusetts; Brown University, 1915–1916, Providence; *also* Announcement of Courses; *and* Announcement of Courses offered at the Women's College in Brown University, 1915–1916; Middlebury College, Middlebury, Vermont.

Bibliography

World Conference on Faith and Order Publications: A First Preliminary Conference; The Object and Method of Conference; A Manual of Prayer for Unity; Second Meeting of the Advisory Committee, Report of the Second Deputation to Great Britain; List of Commissions already appointed, October 22, 1915.

The Church Pension Fund, To accompany the Report of the Special Diocesan Committee, New York.

The Cathedral, a Letter from William Lawrence, Bishop of Massachusetts.

The Rockefeller Institute for Medical Research, History, Organization, and Equipment, New York.

Vassar College, Fiftieth Anniversary, Publications, Poughkeepsie: General Programme; Receptions; Pageant of Athena; After-Dinner Addresses, "The College and the Community"; Historical Exhibition of Physical Training at Vassar College; Calendar, A. D. 1916.

The Sesquicentennial of Brown University, 1764–1914, Historical Address by Charles Evans Hughes, LL.D., Providence.

The Place in Letters of Henry Norman Hudson, Middlebury, Vermont.

Ground Rent and Taxes, by Jonas M. Miles.

1916

[434]

The Fiftieth Anniversary | of | The Opening of Vassar College | October 10 to 13, 1915 | [*floret*] | A Record | Vassar College | Poughkeepsie New York | 1916.

On reverse of title: D. B. Updike, The Merrymount Press, Boston. Collation: i–xviii, 1–337. Leaf, 5⅝ × 8¼. Binding, boards. With 4 illustrations. Type, Oxford.

[435]

Ballad Criticism | in Scandinavia and Great Britain | during the Eighteenth Century | by | Sigurd Bernhard Hustvedt, Ph.D. | Instructor in English in the University of Illinois |

The Merrymount Press

[*floret*] | New York | The American-Scandinavian Founda-
tion | London: Humphrey Milford | Oxford University
Press | 1916.

On reverse of title: D. B. Updike, The Merrymount Press, Boston, U.S.A.
Collation: [i–ii], i–x, 1–335, [336–338]. Leaf, 6¼ × 9¼. Binding, cloth.
Type, Oxford.

[436]
Verses | by | Sarah Orne Jewett | [*floret*] | Boston | Printed
for her Friends | 1916.

On reverse of title: D. B. Updike, The Merrymount Press, Boston. Collation: [i–ii], i–vi, [i–ii], 1–33. Leaf, 5⅛ × 7⅜. Binding, boards. Type,
Caslon.

[437]
A Catalogue of | The Collection of Prints from the | Liber
Studiorum | of | Joseph Mallord William Turner | formed
by the late Francis Bullard | of Boston Massachusetts | and
bequeathed by him to the | Museum of Fine Arts | in
Boston | [*floret*] | Boston | Privately printed | 1916.

On reverse of title: D. B. Updike, The Merrymount Press, Boston. Collation: [i–x], 1–203, [204]. Leaf, 9 × 12½. Binding, boards. Rubricated
title. With 91 illustrations. Type, Oxford.

300 copies printed.

[438]
The Observations of | Professor Maturin | By | Clyde Furst |
[*publisher's mark*] | New York | Columbia University Press |
1916 | All rights reserved.

On reverse of title: D. B. Updike, The Merrymount Press, Boston. Collation: i–xii, 1–224, [225]. Leaf, 4⅝ × 7. Binding, boards. Type, Caslon.

[439]
[*border*] | The Steel Flea | Translated from the Russian of |
Nikolai Semyonovitch Lyeskoff | by | Isabel F. Hapgood |
[*floret*] | Privately printed for the | Company of Gentlemen
Adventurers | at The Merrymount Press, Boston | 1916 |
[*border*].

Bibliography

Colophon: Three hundred copies were printed by D. B. Updike, at The Merrymount Press, Boston, in October, 1916, of which this is Number —. Collation: i–viii, 1–94, [95–96]. Leaf, 4⅞ × 7¾. Binding, boards. Type, Caslon.

[440]
Report | of the Joint Commission on | The Book of Common Prayer | Appointed by | The General Convention of 1913 | [*floret*] | Boston | D. B. Updike, The Merrymount Press | 1916 | [Price, $1.00].

On reverse of title: D. B. Updike, The Merrymount Press, Boston. Collation: i–xii, 1–177, [178]. Leaf, 5 × 7. Binding, paper. Type, Oxford.

[441]
Walter Henry McDaniels | [*floret*] | Two Notices and an | Appreciation | Privately printed | 1916.

On reverse of title: D. B. Updike, The Merrymount Press, Boston. Collation: [1–17]. Leaf, 4¾ × 7½. Binding, cloth. Type, Oxford.
Also issued in paper covers.

[442]
Letters | of | Henry Weston Farnsworth | of the Foreign Legion | [*floret*] | Boston | Privately printed | 1916.

On reverse of title: D. B. Updike, The Merrymount Press, Boston. Collation: i–xviii, 1–219. Leaf, 4¼ × 6¾. Binding, cloth. With 2 illustrations. Type, Oxford.

[443]
Responsive Readings | Selected and arranged by | The Boys of St. Paul's School | for Use in the Chapel of | St. Paul's School | [*floret*] | Concord | New Hampshire | 1916.

On reverse of title: D. B. Updike, The Merrymount Press, Boston. Collation: [i–ii], i–xii, 1–202. Leaf, 4¼ × 6½. Binding, cloth. Type, Oxford.

[444]
[*within border*] New | Nursery Rhymes | On Old Lines | By an American [*Sara Norton*] | [*cut and quotation*] | Privately printed, Boston, 1916.

The Merrymount Press

On reverse of title: Printed at the Merrymount Press, Boston, U.S.A.
Collation: [1–56]. Leaf, 5×7. Binding, paper. Type, Caslon.

[445]
Books in the Library of | Nelson W. Aldrich | Warwick,
Rhode Island | [*floret*] | Part I | Economics | Privately
printed | 1916.

On reverse of title: D. B. Updike, The Merrymount Press, Boston. Collation: i–x, 1–372, [373]. Leaf, 6¾×10. Binding, cloth. Rubricated title.
With portrait. Type, Oxford.

Part II (No. 414) was printed before Part I, in 1914.

[446]
Letters | from Rowland Hazard | to his Wife | Written in
the Year | 1876 | [*arms*] | Privately printed | 1916.

Colophon: Fifty copies printed at The Merrymount Press, Boston, of which
this is Number —. Collation: [i–viii], 1–131, [132–133]. Leaf, 5¼×8¼.
Binding, cloth. Type, Oxford.

[447]
James Robert Dunbar | A Memorial | [*floret*] | Boston |
Privately printed | 1916.

On reverse of title: D. B. Updike, The Merrymount Press, Boston. Collation: [i–iv], 1–44, [45]. Leaf, 4¾×7¾. Binding, cloth. With portrait.
Type, Mountjoye.

[448]
Certain Contemporaries | A Set of Notes in Art Criticism |
by | A. E. Gallatin | [*floret*] | New York: John Lane Com-
pany | London: John Lane, The Bodley Head | MDCCCCXVI.

Colophon: Two hundred and fifty copies printed during April, 1916, by
D. B. Updike, The Merrymount Press, Boston, U.S.A. Collation: [i–ii],
i–viii, 1–63, [64–68]. Leaf, 6¼×8½. Binding, boards. With 24 illustrations. Type, Mountjoye.

[449]
Shakespeare | an Address | By | George Edward Wood-
berry | [*floret*] | Printed for the | Woodberry Society |
1916.

Bibliography

On reverse of title: The Merrymount Press, Boston. Colophon: Three hundred copies of this book have been printed for the Woodberry Society. Seventy-five are numbered and signed by the Author. Collation: [i–vi], 1–36, [37]. Leaf, 5⅜ × 8½. Binding, boards. Type, Mountjoye.

[450]

In Memoriam | Cornelia Stewart Butler | [*cut and inscription*] | Privately printed | MDCCCCXVI.

On reverse of title: The Merrymount Press, Boston. Collation: [i–iv], 1–9, [10]. Leaf, 4¾ × 7¾. Binding, boards. Type, Mountjoye.

[451]

The | Book of the Homeless | (Le Livre des Sans-Foyer) | Edited by Edith Wharton | Original Articles in Verse and Prose | Illustrations reproduced from Original Paintings & Drawings | [*floret*] | The Book is sold | for the Benefit of the American Hostels for Refugees | (with the Foyer Franco-Belge) | and of the Children of Flanders Rescue Committee | New York | Charles Scribner's Sons | MDCCCCXVI.

On reverse of title: D. B. Updike, The Merrymount Press, Boston, U. S. A. Colophon: Of this book, in addition to the regular edition, there have been printed and numbered one hundred and seventy-five copies de luxe, of larger format. Numbers 1–50 on French hand-made paper, containing four facsimiles of manuscripts and a second set of illustrations in portfolio. Numbers 51–175 on Van Gelder paper. Collation: i–xxvi, 1–154, [155–157]. Leaf, 8⅛ × 10¾. Binding, boards. With 22 illustrations. Type, Mountjoye.

With extra title-page engraved on wood by Rudolph Ruzicka.

[452]
The Same.

Colophon: Same as in small-paper editions, but numbered. Leaf, 9⅝ × 12¾.
Printed on hand-made paper.

[453]
The | Story of India Wharf | From an Address by | Herbert F. Otis | Delivered on the Centennial of the | Erection of India Wharf Building | With Illustrations | [*cut*] | Printed for | The India Wharf Rats | 1916.

[181]

The Merrymount Press

Colophon: One hundred copies printed at The Merrymount Press, Boston, December, 1916. Collation: 1–19, [20–47]. Leaf, 9⅜ × 12¼. Binding, boards. With 16 illustrations and plans. Type, Scotch-face.

[454]
The Prose Edda | By | Snorri Sturluson | [*floret*] | Translated from the Icelandic | with an Introduction | by | Arthur Gilchrist Brodeur, Ph.D. | Instructor in English Philology in the University of California | New York | The American-Scandinavian Foundation | London: Humphrey Milford | Oxford University Press | 1916.

On reverse of title: D. B. Updike, The Merrymount Press, Boston, U. S. A. Collation: [i–ii], i–xxii, 1–266, [267–269]. Leaf, 5 × 7⅜. Binding, cloth. Type, Caslon.

Scandinavian Classics, Vol. V.

[455]
Modern Icelandic Plays | Eyvind of the Hills | The Hraun Farm | By | Jóhann Sigurjónsson | [*floret*] | Translated by | Henninge Krohn Schanche | New York | The American-Scandinavian Foundation | London: Humphrey Milford | Oxford University Press | 1916.

On reverse of title: D. B. Updike, The Merrymount Press, Boston, U. S. A. Collation: [i–ii], i–xii, 1–131, [132–137]. Leaf, 5 × 7⅜. Binding, cloth. Type, Caslon.

Scandinavian Classics, Vol. VI.

[456]
[*within border*] A Bundle of Letters from | Belgian Friends | [*floret*] | With Prefatory Note by H. S. N. [*Helen S. North*] | and Illustrations. [n. d.]

On reverse of title: D. B. Updike, The Merrymount Press, Boston. Collation: 1–39, [40]. Leaf, 5⅜ × 7⅜. Issued in loose sheets. With 8 illustrations. Type, Oxford.

[457]
The Carnegie Foundation | for the Advancement of Teaching | [*printer's ornament*] | A Comprehensive Plan of In-

Bibliography

surance | and Annuities for College Teachers | By | Henry S. Pritchett | President of The Carnegie Foundation | Bulletin Number Nine | [*seal*] | 576 Fifth Avenue | New York City | 1916.

On reverse of title: D. B. Updike, The Merrymount Press, Boston. Collation: i–xx, 1–67. Leaf, 7⅜ × 10. Binding, paper. Type, Scotch-face.

[458]
A Brief History of | St. Mary's Church, South Portsmouth | & | Holy Cross Chapel, Middletown | Rhode Island | 1843–1916 | [*cut*] | Privately Printed | A. D. 1916.

On reverse of title: D. B. Updike, The Merrymount Press, Boston. Collation: [i–vi], 1–23. Leaf, 5¼ × 8¼. Binding, paper. Type, Caslon.

[459]
Intercessory | Prayers | for | a Day of Devotion | [*cut*] | Guild of All Saints' Church | Peterborough, New Hampshire. [n.d.]

Collation: 1–23, [24–26]. Leaf, 3 × 4½. Binding, paper. No imprint. Type, Scotch-face.

Minor Printing

Carnegie Foundation for the Advancement of Teaching, Eleventh Annual Report of the President and of the Treasurer, New York; *also* The Study of Legal Education, From the Report of the President.

Reports: John Carter Brown Library, Providence; Annual Report of the President, Brown University, Providence; Wheaton College, President's Report, 1914–1915, Norton, Massachusetts.

Catalogues of Schools and Universities: Saint Mark's School, Southborough, Massachusetts; The Browne & Nichols School, Cambridge; Simmons College, Fifteenth Annual Catalogue, 1916–1917; Trinity College, 1915–1916, Hartford; Wheaton College, 1915–1916, Norton, Massachusetts; Brown University, 1916–1917, Providence; *also* Announcement of Courses; *and* Announcement of Courses offered at the Women's College in Brown University, 1916–1917.

Catalogue of the Writings of Aurelius Palmieri, O.S.A., D.D., Part I.

World Conference on Faith and Order Publications: North Amer-

The Merrymount Press

ican Preparatory Conference, Garden City, Long Island, New York, Report of Progress by the Secretary, *etc.*; Minutes of the Meeting of the North American Preparatory Conference, Garden City, Long Island, New York, 1916; The Object and the Method of Conference; Report of the Joint Commission to the General Convention of the Protestant Episcopal Church, 1916; Plans for further Procedure with regard to the World Conference on Faith and Order.

Catalogue Fenway Court.

Wheaton College, Founder's Day, Norton, Massachusetts.

Concerning the Founding of a Church School for Boys in North Carolina, Southborough, Massachusetts.

The Philanthropic Boards established by John D. Rockefeller, New York.

The Rockefeller Foundation, International Health Board, New York.

Citizens Calendar for the Year A.D. 1917.

1917

[460]

Newark | A Series of Engravings on Wood by | Rudolph Ruzicka | With an Appreciation of | the Pictorial Aspects of the Town | by Walter Pritchard Eaton | [*arms*] | The Carteret Book Club | Newark, New Jersey | 1917.

Colophon: Two hundred copies of this book were printed for The Carteret Book Club of Newark, New Jersey, in November, 1917; the 5 full-page illustrations in color being printed by Rudolph Ruzicka, New York, and the text and other illustrations by D. B. Updike, The Merrymount Press, Boston. Collation: i–xvi, 1–52, [53–54]. Leaf, 9⅛ × 12. Binding, boards. Title in green and black. With 17 woodcuts. Type, Caslon.

Also issued in paper covers.

[461]

Dedication | of the | Memorial Pulpit | to | Robert Treat Paine | Former Vestryman and Junior Warden | of Trinity Church, Boston | on Sunday, December 10, 1916 | Boston | Privately printed | 1917.

Bibliography

On reverse of title: D. B. Updike, The Merrymount Press, Boston. Collation: [i–vi], 1–16, [17]. Leaf, 5¼ × 7⅞. Binding, boards. With 3 illustrations. Type, Oxford.

Also issued in paper covers.

[462]

Paul Manship | A Critical Essay on his Sculpture | and an Iconography | by | A. E. Gallatin | With Eight Illustrations | [*floret*] | New York | John Lane Company | MDCCCCXVII.

Colophon: One hundred and fifty copies printed by D. B. Updike, The Merrymount Press, Boston, U. S. A., February, 1917. Collation: [i–vi], 1–15, [16–33]. Leaf, 6¼ × 8½. Binding, boards. Type, Oxford and Mountjoye.

[463]

The Boston Book | Market | 1679–1700 | by Worthington Chauncey Ford | [*seal*] | Boston | The Club of Odd Volumes | 1917.

On reverse of title: D. B. Updike, The Merrymount Press, Boston. Collation: i–xii, 1–197, [198]. Leaf, 6¼ × 9⅜. Binding, boards. Rubricated title. Type, Mountjoye and Oxford.

151 copies printed.

[464]

The Portraits of | Albert Gallatin | by | A. E. Gallatin | Privately printed | 1917.

Colophon: Fifty copies printed during February, 1917, by D. B. Updike, The Merrymount Press, Boston, U. S. A. Collation: i–xiv, 1–28, [29]. Leaf, 6⅛ × 8½. Binding, boards. With three portraits. Type, Oxford.

[465]

William Howe McElwain | 1867–1908 | by | Henry Greenleaf Pearson | [*floret*] | [*quotation*] | Boston | Privately printed | 1917.

On reverse of title: The Merrymount Press, Boston. Collation: [i–viii], 1–188, [189]. Leaf, 5 × 7½. Binding, cloth. With 5 illustrations and facsimiles. Type, Oxford.

[466]

The Story of the | Sargent Industrial School | at Beacon, New York | 1891–1916 | Told by | Sarah Louise Arnold |

[185]

The Merrymount Press

Dean of Simmons College, Boston | [*cut*] | Printed for the Scholars | 1917.

On reverse of title: D. B. Updike, The Merrymount Press, Boston. Collation: i–xiv, 1–77. Leaf, 5⅝ × 8¼. Binding, cloth. With 10 illustrations. Type, Oxford.

[467]

[*within cut*] The | Metropolitan | Museum of Art | A | Catalogue | of | Italian | Renaissance | Woodcuts | by | William M. Ivins, Jr. | New York: MDCCCCXVII.

Colophon: Of this Catalogue one thousand copies have been printed by D. B. Updike, The Merrymount Press, Boston, in November, 1917. Collation: [i–x], 1–65, [66–67]. Leaf, 6¼ × 9½. Binding, boards. With 15 illustrations. Type, Caslon.

Also issued in paper covers.

[468]

[*within rules*] The Parochial | Library | of the | Eighteenth | Century | in | Christ Church | Boston | by | A Proprietor of Christ Church [*Percival Merritt*] | [*cut*] | Boston | Privately printed at The Merrymount Press in the | Year of our Lord MDCCCCXVII.

Collation: [i–vi], 1–81. Leaf, 5⅝ × 8¼. Binding, boards. Type, Caslon.

200 copies printed.

[469]

Massachusetts General Hospital | The Moseley Memorial | Building | Dedicated October Sixteenth | 1916 | [*seal*] | Boston | Privately printed | 1917.

On reverse of title: D. B. Updike, The Merrymount Press, Boston. Collation: i–x, 1–19, [20–67]. Leaf, 6¼ × 8½. Binding, cloth. With 27 illustrations and plans. Type, Mountjoye.

Also issued in paper covers.

[470]

Responsive Readings | [*cut*] | Groton School | 1917.

On reverse of title: D. B. Updike, The Merrymount Press, Boston. Collation: [i–ii], i–xii, 1–202. Leaf, 4¼ × 6½. Binding, cloth. Type, Oxford.

Identical with "Responsive Readings," St. Paul's School; see No. 443.

Bibliography

[471]

Ideal Passion | Sonnets | By | George Edward Woodberry | [*floret*] | [*quotation*] | Printed for the | Woodberry Society | 1917.

On reverse of title: The Merrymount Press, Boston. Colophon: Four hundred copies of this book have been printed for the Woodberry Society. One hundred are numbered and signed by the author. Collation: 1–49, [50–51]. Leaf, 5¾ × 8½. Binding, boards. Type, Oxford.

[472]

John Chipman Gray | [*floret*] | Boston | Privately printed | MDCCCCXVII.

On reverse of title: D. B. Updike, The Merrymount Press, Boston. Collation: i–vi, 1–142, [143]. Leaf, 6¼ × 9½. Binding, cloth. With portrait and book-plate. Type, Mountjoye.

[473]

Pierrot's Verses | by Maria de Acosta Sargent | [*cut*] | Privately printed | MDCCCCXVII.

On reverse of title: The Merrymount Press. Collation: [i–ii], 1–27, [28–29]. Leaf, 4¼ × 6. Binding, boards. Type, Oxford.

[474]

The Wood-Engravings of | Rudolph Ruzicka | By W. M. Ivins, Jr. | [*floret*] | The Newark Museum Association | Newark, New Jersey | 1917.

On reverse of title: D. B. Updike, The Merrymount Press, Boston. Collation: [i–iv], 1–8, [9]. Leaf, 4⅜ × 6⅞. Binding, paper. With woodcut in two colours. Type, Oxford.

[475]

Memoirs of the Private Life | of | Marie Antoinette | to which are added Personal Recollections | Illustrative of the Reigns of Louis XIV, XV, XVI | by | Jeanne Louise Henriette Campan | First Lady-in-Waiting to the Queen | [*floret*] | With a Memoir of Madame Campan by | F. Barrière. New Edition revised by | F. M. Graves, with an Introduction | and Notes by J. Holland Rose, Litt.D. | With Illustrations | Volume I [II] | New York: Brentano's | 1917.

The Merrymount Press

On reverse of title: D. B. Updike, The Merrymount Press, Boston. Colla-tion: Vol. I, [i–ii], i–cxxviii, 1–309, [310]; Vol. II, [i–ii], i–x, 1–460, [461]. Leaf, 5⅞ × 9¼. Binding, cloth. With 32 illustrations in photogravure. Type, Mountjoye.

With extra title-page adapted from an engraving by C. P. Marillier. The design of the binding was copied from a book bound by Derôme.

[476]
[*within border*] James Browne | His Writings | In Prose and Verse | Concerning the First Settling of the Town | of Providence and a Memorandum of his | Efforts to prevent a Separation in the Bap-|tist Congregation there in Octo-ber, 1731: | Together with Some Metrical Observations | [*quotation*] | [*printer's ornament*] | Printed by D. B. Updike at The Merry-|mount Press in Boston, Massachusetts, 1917.

Collation: [i–iv], 1–24. Leaf, 4⅜ × 7¼. Binding, boards. Type, Caslon.

[477]
Poems and Songs | by | Björnstjerne Björnson | [*floret*] | Translated from the Norwegian | in the Original Meters | by | Arthur Hubbell Palmer | Professor of the German Lan-guage and Literature | in Yale University | New York | The American-Scandinavian | Foundation | 1915.

Reissue of No. 430.

[478]
Marie Grubbe | A Lady of the Seventeenth Century | by | J. P. Jacobsen | [*floret*] | Translated from the Danish | by | Hanna Astrup Larsen | New York | The American-Scandi-navian Foundation | London: Humphrey Milford | Oxford University Press | 1917.

On reverse of title: D. B. Updike, The Merrymount Press, Boston, U. S. A. Collation: [i–ii], i–xvi, 1–261, [262–265]. Leaf, 5 × 7⅜. Binding, cloth. Type, Caslon.

Scandinavian Classics, Vol. VII.

[479]
Arnljot Gelline | by | Björnstjerne Björnson | [*floret*] | Trans-

Bibliography

lated from the Norwegian | with Introduction and Notes | by | William Morton Payne, LL.D. | New York | The American-Scandinavian Foundation | London: Humphrey Milford | Oxford University Press | 1917.

On reverse of title: D. B. Updike, The Merrymount Press, Boston, U. S. A. Collation: [i–ii], i–xiv, 1–155, [156–159]. Leaf, 5 × 7⅜. Binding, cloth. Type, Caslon.
Scandinavian Classics, Vol. VIII.

[480]
Anthology of Swedish | Lyrics | from 1750 to 1915 | [*floret*] | Translated in the Original Meters by | Charles Wharton Stork | Author of "Sea and Bay"; Translator of "Selected Poems | of Gustaf Fröding" | New York | The American-Scandinavian Foundation | London: Humphrey Milford | Oxford University Press | 1917.

On reverse of title: D. B. Updike, The Merrymount Press, Boston, U. S. A. Collation: [i–ii], i–xl, 1–280, [281–285]. Leaf, 5 × 7⅜. Binding, cloth. Type, Caslon.
Scandinavian Classics, Vol. IX.

[481]
[*within rules*] The Heart of Europe | An Address delivered by Charles | Pergler in Washington, December | 11, 1916, at a Conference of Oppressed | or Dependent Nationalities. With | a Foreword by Professor Alois F. | Kovarik, Ph.D., D.Sc., Yale University | [*cut*] | Published by the Bohemian (Czech) | National Alliance, at Number 3639 | West 26th Street, Chicago, Illinois.

Colophon: This volume, with drawings by Fred. T. Chapman and J. C. Vondrous, was designed by Vojtech Preissig, and printed at the Merrymount Press, Boston, 1917. Collation: 1–39, [40]. Leaf, 6 × 9. Binding, boards. With 4 illustrations and map. Type, Caslon.

[482]
Mary Anna Ingell | January 21, 1845: November 28, 1916 | [*floret*] | Privately printed | Boston: 1917.

On reverse of title: The Merrymount Press, Boston. Collation: [i–iv], 1–26, [27]. Leaf, 5¼ × 8⅛. Binding, paper. Type, Mountjoye.

The Merrymount Press

[483]

Federal Aid for | Vocational Education | A Report to The Carnegie Foundation | for the Advancement of Teaching | By I. L. Kandel | M.A. Manchester; Ph.D., Columbia | Bulletin Number Ten | [*seal*] | New York City | 576 Fifth Avenue. [n. d.]

On reverse of title: D. B. Updike, The Merrymount Press, Boston. Collation: i–vi, 1–127. Leaf, 7⅜ × 10. Binding, paper. Type, Scotch-face.

[484]

Curricula | designed for the Professional Preparation of Teachers | for American Public Schools | [*floret*] | Provisional Suggestions formulated and issued by The Carnegie Foundation for the Advancement of | Teaching for coöperative discussion on the part of Training Institutions and Students of Education | 576 Fifth Avenue | New York City | [February, 1917].

On reverse of title: D. B. Updike, The Merrymount Press, Boston. Collation: [1–54]. Leaf, 12⅜ × 9¼ oblong. Binding, paper. Type, Scotch-face.

[485]

Medical Education | in the | United States and Canada | A Report to | The Carnegie Foundation | for the Advancement of Teaching | By | Abraham Flexner | With an Introduction by | Henry S. Pritchett | President of the Foundation | Bulletin Number Four | 576 Fifth Avenue | New York City. [n. d.]

Reissue of No. 350.

Minor Printing

The Carnegie Foundation for the Advancement of Teaching, Twelfth Annual Report of the President and of the Treasurer, New York; *also* Index of the First Ten Annual Reports of the Carnegie Foundation; Publications of the Foundation; Report to the Trustees of the Carnegie Foundation by the Commission chosen to consider a Plan of Insurance and Annuities; *and* The Study of Legal Education, From the Report of the President, 1917.

Bibliography

Reports: John Carter Brown Library, Providence; Annual Report of the President, Brown University, Providence; Wheaton College, President's Report, 1915–1916, Norton, Massachusetts.

Catalogues of Schools and Universities: Saint Mark's School, Southborough, Massachusetts; The Browne & Nichols School, Cambridge; Simmons College, Sixteenth Annual Catalogue, 1917–1918; Trinity College, 1916–1917, Hartford; Wheaton College, 1916–1917, Norton, Massachusetts; Brown University, 1917–1918, Providence; *also* Announcement of Courses.

World Conference on Faith and Order Publications: Epistolae Nomine Ssmi Domini Benedicti XV Humaniter Missae ab Eminentissimo Viro Petro Gasparri, c.s.r.e., Coetui Virorum Delectorum ad Congressum Orbis Christiani Parandum ut Favente Deo Controversiae de Fide et Constitutione Ecclesiae Christi rite Delucidentur atque Explorentur; Joint Commission appointed to arrange for a World Conference on Faith and Order (*in Russian*); Prayer and Unity, by a Layman; Unity or Union: Which? by the Rt. Rev. P. M. Rhinelander, D.D.; List of Commissions already Appointed, September, 1917; The Object and Method of Conference; A Manual of Prayer for Unity; De Unione Ecclesiarum ac totius Christianae Societatis Congressu (Vulgo "The World Conference") pro Quaestionibus ad Fidem Ordinemque Ecclesiae spectantibus rite Explorandis et Perpendendis.

Women's College in Brown University, Twenty-fifth Anniversary, 1892–1917, Providence; *also* The Women's College in Brown University.

Familiar Prayers, St. Paul's School, Concord, New Hampshire.

A Service of Praise and Thanksgiving to Almighty God upon the Completion of the Church Pension Fund.

The Rockefeller Institute for Medical Research, Organization and Equipment, New York.

Address Delivered at the Presentation by the American Institute of Electrical Engineers of the Edison Medal to Mr. Nikola Tesla, New York City, by B. A. Behrend, New York.

Description of The Merrymount Press, Boston (*illustrated*).

The Merrymount Press
1918

[486]
An Easter Ode | 1918 | By George Edward Woodberry |
[*floret*] | Printed for the Woodberry Society | 1918.

Colophon: Two hundred and fifty copies of this Poem have been printed
for the Woodberry Society by D. B. Updike, The Merrymount Press, Boston. One hundred are numbered and signed by the Author. Collation: 1–11,
[12]. Leaf, 8 × 10⅝. Binding, paper. Type, Janson.

[487]
Abroad with Jane | By | Edward Sandford Martin | [*floret*] |
Privately printed | 1918.

On reverse of title: D. B. Updike, The Merrymount Press, Boston. Collation: [i–iv], 1–119. Leaf, 4¼ × 6¾. Binding, boards. With portrait. Type,
Oxford.

[488]
Loan Exhibition | of Paintings, Watercolors, Drawings |
Etchings & Sculpture | by | Arthur B. Davis | [*floret*] | Mac-
beth Galleries | 450 Fifth Avenue, New York | 1918.

On reverse of title: Typography and presswork by The Merrymount Press,
Boston. Photogravures by A. W. Elson & Company, Belmont, Masstts. Collation: 1–16, [17–87]. Leaf, 6⅛ × 9½. Binding, boards. With 35 illustrations. Type, Mountjoye and Oxford.

[489]
Anna Cabot Mills Lodge | [*floret*] | [*quotation*] | Privately
printed | MDCCCCXVIII.

On reverse of title: D. B. Updike, The Merrymount Press, Boston. Collation: [i–vi], 1–59, [60]. Leaf, 9½ × 12⅝. Binding, boards. Rubricated title.
With portrait. Type, Mountjoye and Oxford.

[490]
In Memoriam | H. W. W. [*Herbert Wheelwright Windeler*] |
1897–1917 | [*floret*] | Printed for his Friends | 1918.

On reverse of title: D. B. Updike, The Merrymount Press, Boston. Collation: 1–27, [28]. Leaf, 5 × 7½. Binding, paper. With portrait. Type, Oxford.

Bibliography

[491]

Collection A. E. Gallatin | Modern Paintings, Drawings | &c. | With a Preface by Guy Pène du Bois | Exhibited for the Benefit of the American War Relief | January 2 to February 2, 1918 | [cut] | Bourgeois Galleries| 668 Fifth Avenue, New York. [n.d.]

On reverse of title: D. B. Updike, The Merrymount Press, Boston. Collation: 1–22, [23–47]. Leaf, 6¼ × 8½. Binding, paper. With 12 illustrations. Type, Mountjoye and Oxford.

Illustrated edition limited to 110 copies. Also issued without illustrations; collation: 1–22.

[492]

Portraits of Whistler | A Critical Study and an Iconography | By A. E. Gallatin | With Forty Illustrations | [*floret*] | [*quotation*] | New York: John Lane Company | London: John Lane, The Bodley Head | 1918.

Colophon: Two hundred and fifty copies printed during November, 1918, by D. B. Updike, The Merrymount Press, Boston, U. S. A. Collation: [i–ii], i–xii, 1–81, [82–83]. Leaf, 7⅞ × 10¾. Binding, boards. Rubricated title. Type, Mountjoye and Oxford.

[493]

In Memoriam | A.C.M.L. [*Anna Cabot Mills Lodge*] | [*floret*] | By C.S.-R. [*Cecil Spring-Rice*] | Privately Printed | MDCCCCXVIII.

On reverse of title: D. B. Updike, The Merrymount Press, Boston. Collation: [i–iv], 1–46. Leaf, 5¾ × 8½. Binding, boards. Type, Oxford.

[494]

Gösta Berling's Saga | by | Selma Lagerlöf | [*floret*] | Translated from the Swedish | by Lillie Tudeer | Part I [II] | New York | The American-Scandinavian Foundation | London: Humphrey Milford | Oxford University Press | 1918.

On reverse of title: D. B. Updike, The Merrymount Press, Boston, U. S. A. Collation: Part I, [i–ii], i–xii, 1–294; Part II, [i–ii], i–vi, 1–315, [316]. Leaf, 4⅞ × 7⅜. Binding, cloth. Type, Caslon.

Scandinavian Classics, Vols. X and XI.

[495]

The Carnegie Foundation | for the Advancement of Teaching | Pensions for | Public School Teachers | A Report for the

The Merrymount Press

Committee on Salaries, Pensions | and Tenure, of the National Education Association | By | Clyde Furst and I. L. Kandel | Bulletin Number Twelve | [*seal*] | New York City | 576 Fifth Avenue. [n. d.]

On reverse of title: D. B. Updike, The Merrymount Press, Boston. Collation: i–xii, 1–85. Leaf, 7⅜ × 10. Binding, paper. Type, Scotch-face.

[496]
A Study of Engineering | Education | Prepared for the Joint Committee on Engineering | Education of the National Engineering Societies | By | Charles Riborg Mann | Bulletin Number Eleven | [*seal*] | New York City | 576 Fifth Avenue. [n. d.]

On reverse of title: D. B. Updike, The Merrymount Press, Boston. Collation: i–xii, 1–139. Leaf, 7⅜ × 10. Binding, paper. Type, Scotch-face.

[497]
The Legion | By Gustave Babin | [*cut*] | From "L'Illustration" of January 19, 1918 | Translated by E. F. L. [n. d.]

On second page of cover: D. B. Updike, The Merrymount Press, Boston. Collation: 1–22. Leaf, 5¼ × 8¼. Binding, paper. Type, Oxford.

Minor Printing

The Carnegie Foundation for the Advancement of Teaching, Thirteenth Annual Report of the President and of the Treasurer, New York; *also* A Statement to the Teachers in the Associated Colleges and Universities; Rules for the Admission of Institutions and for the Granting of Retiring Allowances; Publications of the Foundation; *and* Legal Education during the War, by Alfred Z. Reed, From the Thirteenth Annual Report of the President.

John Carter Brown Library, Providence, Rhode Island, Report to the Corporation of Brown University, Providence.

Catalogues of Schools and Universities: Saint Mark's School, Southborough, Massachusetts; The Browne & Nichols School, Cambridge; Simmons College, Seventeenth Annual Catalogue, 1918–1919; *also* Announcement of Courses; Trinity College, 1917–1918, Hartford; Wheaton College, 1917–1918, Norton, Massachusetts;

Bibliography

Brown University, 1918–1919, Providence; *also* Announcement of Courses, 1918–1919.

World Conference on Faith and Order Publications: An Official Statement by the Joint Commission of the Protestant Episcopal Church in the United States of America; The Conference Spirit, by a Layman; Suggestions for the Octave of Prayer for Christian Unity; Suggestions for a Paper or Discourse on the Significance of the Incarnation for Present World Needs; Report of the Joint Commission to the General Convention of the Protestant Episcopal Church, 1916.

Catalogue Fenway Court.

Harvard College, Class of 1881, Thirty-fifth Anniversary, Cambridge.

National Shawmut Bank, Roll of Honor.

The Trustees of The Metropolitan Museum of Art, New York, Minute upon the Service rendered the Museum by the late John Pierpont Morgan, New York.

1919

[498]
Poems by Tegnér | The Children of the Lord's Supper | Translated from the Swedish by | Henry Wadsworth Longfellow | and | Frithiof's Saga | Translated by Rev. W. Lewery Blackley | With an Introduction by | Paul Robert Lieder, A.M. | Harvard University | [*floret*] | Second Impression | New York | The American-Scandinavian | Foundation | 1914.

Reissue of No. 410.

[499]
Sara Videbeck | and | The Chapel | by C. J. L. Almquist | Translated from the Swedish | by Adolph Burnett Benson | Author of "Swedish Romanticism" | [*floret*] | New York | The American-Scandinavian Foundation | London: Humphrey Milford | Oxford University Press | 1919.

The Merrymount Press

On reverse of title: D. B. Updike, The Merrymount Press, Boston, U. S. A. Collation: [i–ii], i–xxiv, 1–229, [230–233]. Leaf, 4⅞ × 7⅜. Binding, cloth. Type, Caslon.

Scandinavian Classics, Vol. XII.

[500]
Modern Icelandic Plays | Eyvind of the Hills | The Hraun Farm | by | Jóhann Sigurjónsson | [*floret*] | Translated by | Henninge Krohn Schanche | New York | The American-Scandinavian Foundation | London: Humphrey Milford | Oxford University Press | 1916.

Reissue of No. 454.

[501]
Journal | of a Canteen Worker | A Record of Service with the | American Red Cross in Flanders | by | Herbert Mason Sears | [*arms*] | Boston | Privately printed | 1919.

On reverse of title: The Merrymount Press, Boston. Collation: i–xii, 1–213. Leaf, 4¼ × 6¾. Binding, cloth. With 12 illustrations and map. Type, Oxford.

[502]
List of Books | Privately Printed by William K. Bixby | And those Privately Printed by Book Clubs | from Manuscripts in his Collection | Including short Sketches written by | Mr. Bixby for Book Clubs | [*floret*] | St. Louis | Printed for Libraries & Collectors | 1919.

Colophon: Sixty Copies of this List were printed by D. B. Updike, The Merrymount Press, Boston, in June, 1919. Collation: [i–vi], 1–18. Leaf, 8 × 11. Binding, boards. Type, Caslon.

[503]
Marcus Perrin Knowlton | Late Chief Justice | of the Supreme Judicial Court of the | Commonwealth of Massachusetts | A Memorial | [*floret*] | Privately printed | 1919.

On reverse of title: D. B. Updike, The Merrymount Press, Boston. Collation: [i–ii], i–vi, 1–55, [56]. Leaf, 6¼ × 9½. Binding, cloth. With portrait. Type, Mountjoye.

Bibliography

[504]
Two Letters | from | General William Tecumseh Sherman | to General Ulysses S. Grant | & | William T. McPherson | In the Collection of W. K. Bixby of Saint Louis | [*printer's ornament*] | Privately Printed | 1919.

Colophon: Fifty copies of this book were printed for W. K. Bixby, Saint Louis, by D. B. Updike, The Merrymount Press, Boston. Collation: 1–18, [19]. Leaf, 6½ × 8¾. Binding, boards. Type, Caslon.

[505]
The | Czechoslovak | State | by | Charles Pergler | Commissioner of the Czechoslovak Republic | in the United States | [*arms*] | New York | Czechoslovak Arts Club | 1919.

Colophon: D. B. Updike, The Merrymount Press, Boston. Collation: [i–ii], 1–32, [33–34]. Leaf, 5¾ × 8½. Binding, boards. With portrait and map. Type, Mountjoye.

Also issued in paper covers, with leaf measuring 5½ × 8⅛.

[506]
Exhibition of Paintings by | Abbott H. Thayer | [*floret*] | Pittsburgh | Carnegie Institute | 1919.

On reverse of title: D. B. Updike, The Merrymount Press, Boston. Collation: 1–40, [41]. Leaf, 5⅞ × 8⅞. Binding, boards. With 6 illustrations. Type, Mountjoye and Oxford.

[507]
Exhibition of Paintings by | Abbott H. Thayer | Held at Carnegie Institute | Pittsburgh | April 24–June 30 | [*floret*] | Pittsburgh | Carnegie Institute | 1919.

On reverse of title: D. B. Updike, The Merrymount Press, Boston. Collation: 1–34, [35]. Leaf, 5¾ × 8⅞. Binding, paper. Type, Mountjoye and Oxford.

[508]
Bibliotheca Americana | Catalogue of the | John Carter Brown | Library | in Brown University | Providence, Rhode Island | Volume I [*Parts I, II*] | [*arms*] | Providence | Published by the Library | 1919.

[197]

The Merrymount Press

On reverse of title: D. B. Updike, The Merrymount Press, Boston. Collation: Part I, [i–ii], i–viii, 1–240; Part II, [i–ii], 241–510, [511]. Leaf, 7 × 10½. Binding, cloth. Rubricated title to each volume. Portrait in Part I; illustration in Part II. Type, Oxford.

In 3 volumes. Vols. I and II of 2 parts each, each part bound separately.

[509]
The Same.

Binding, boards. With two copies of the portrait with and without inscription in Part I, and of the illustration with and without inscription in Part II.

Printed on hand-made paper.

[510]
Niels Lyhne | by | J. P. Jacobsen | Translated from the Danish | by Hanna Astrup Larsen | [*floret*] | New York | The American-Scandinavian Foundation | London: Humphrey Milford | Oxford University Press | 1919.

On reverse of title: D. B. Updike, The Merrymount Press, Boston, U. S. A. Collation: [i–ii], i–xii, 1–284, [285–287]. Leaf, 4⅞ × 7⅜. Binding, cloth. Type, Caslon.

Scandinavian Classics, Vol. XIII.

[511]
Justice and the Poor | A Study of the Present Denial of Justice to the Poor | and of the Agencies making more Equal | their Position before the Law | with Particular Reference to Legal Aid Work | in the United States | By | Reginald Heber Smith | of the Boston Bar | Bulletin Number Thirteen | [*seal*] | New York City | 576 Fifth Avenue. [n. d.]

On reverse of title: D. B. Updike, The Merrymount Press. Collation: i–xiv, 1–271. Leaf, 7⅜ × 10. Binding, paper. With 3 charts. Type, Scotchface.

Issued in cloth in the same year by Charles Scribner's Sons.

[512]
A Study of Engineering | Education | Prepared for the Joint Committee on Engineering | Education of the National Engineering Societies | By | Charles Riborg Mann | Bulletin

Bibliography

Number Eleven | [*seal*] | New York City | 576 Fifth Avenue. [n. d.]

Reissue of No. 496.

[513]
Helen Homans in France | 1915–1918 | [*floret*] | [*quotation*] | Boston | 1919.

On reverse of title: The Merrymount Press, Boston. Collation: 1–38, [39]. Leaf, 4⅞ × 7⅛. Binding, paper. Type, Oxford.

[514]
The | Music of Bohemia | by | Ladislav Urban | [*floret*] | Czechoslovak Arts Club | of New York City | 1919.

On reverse of title: D. B. Updike, The Merrymount Press, Boston. Collation: 1–50. Leaf, 5 × 7. Binding, paper. With 4 illustrations and music. Type, Oxford.

[515]
Museum of French Art | French Institute in the United States | National in Scope | Catalogue | of the | Second Annual Official Loan Exhibition of | French Art | Periods of Louis XV | & | Louis XVI | Held at the Gallery of the Museum | in the City of New York | January 14 to January 29, 1919 | [*floret*] | Privately Printed. [n. d.]

Colophon: [*printer's mark*] D. B. Updike, The Merrymount Press. Collation: 1–59, [60–63]. Leaf, 11½ × 16⅜. Binding, cloth. Rubricated title. With 11 illustrations. Type, Caslon.

Minor Printing

The Carnegie Foundation for the Advancement of Teaching, Fourteenth Annual Report of the President and of the Treasurer, New York; *also* Publications of the Foundation; The Study of Legal Education, From the Report of the President; *and* Memorandum concerning Participation in the Teachers Insurance and Annuity Association of America by Institutions associated with the Carnegie Foundation.

Reports: John Carter Brown Library, Providence; The Manhat-

The Merrymount Press

tanville Nursery Association, New York; Annual Report of the President, Brown University, Providence.

Catalogues of Schools and Universities: Saint Mark's School, Southborough, Massachusetts; The Browne & Nichols School, Cambridge; Simmons College, Eighteenth Annual Catalogue, 1919–1920; Trinity College, 1918–1919, Hartford; Wheaton College, 1918–1919, Norton, Massachusetts; Brown University, 1919–1920, Providence; *also* Announcement of Courses.

World Conference on Faith and Order Publications: The World Conference of all the Christian Confessions (*also issued in Italian*); Unity or Union: Which? by the Rt. Rev. P. M. Rhinelander, D.D.; Second Meeting of the Advisory Committee, Report of the Second Deputation to Great Britain, The Call for a Truce of God; Report of the Deputation to Europe and the East (*also issued in Italian and French*); Report of the Joint Commission to the General Convention of the Protestant Episcopal Church; North American Preparatory Conference, Garden City, Long Island, New York, Report of Progress by the Secretary, *etc.*; The Conference Spirit, by a Layman; List of Commissions already Appointed, October 4, 1919; Statement of the Position of the Protestant Episcopal Church on Questions of Faith and Order prepared by the Commission of that Church on the World Conference; Notes for the Octave of Prayer for Christian Unity.

An Appeal for the Phillips Brooks Memorial Endowment Fund for Trinity Church in the City of Boston.

The Metabolic Clinic established at Santa Barbara, California, by Dr. Nathaniel Bowditch Potter, Santa Barbara.

The Durant Guest House of Wellesley College.

Jennie Barrell Woodman, In Memoriam.

The Merrymount Press, Boston, Its Aims, Work, and Equipment.

Town of Westwood, Certificate of Honor, Westwood, Massachusetts.

The Club of Odd Volumes, List of Officers, Anno Domini MDCCCXIX.

Bibliography

1920

[516]

On the Field of Honor | A Collection of War Letters and Reminiscences | of Three Harvard Undergraduates | who gave their Lives in | the Great Cause | [*floret*] | Edited by Paul B. Elliott | Boston | Printed for their Friends | 1920.

On reverse of title: D. B. Updike, The Merrymount Press, Boston. Collation: i–xii, 1–121, [122–123]. Leaf, 6⅞ × 9½. Binding, cloth. With 5 portraits. Type, Mountjoye.

[517]

Russell Sturgis Hubbard | 1863–1918 | Written for his Sons by their Mother | Elizabeth Russell Perry Hubbard | [*floret*] | Boston | Privately printed | 1920.

On reverse of title: D. B. Updike, The Merrymount Press, Boston. Collation: i–xviii, 1–124, [125–126]. Leaf, 6 × 9¼. Binding, cloth. With 4 illustrations. Type, Mountjoye.

[518]

Alice Cogswell Bemis | A Sketch by a Friend | [*floret*] | Boston | Privately printed | 1920.

On reverse of title: The Merrymount Press, Boston. Collation: [i–iv], 1–57. Leaf, 4¼ × 6¾. Binding, boards. With 6 illustrations. Type, Oxford.

[519]

A Catalogue of | The First Coles Exhibition | [*floret*] | Abraham Coles: J. Ackerman Coles | Emilie S. Coles | Newark, New Jersey | The Newark Museum Association | 1920.

On reverse of title: The Merrymount Press, Boston. Collation: 1–40. Leaf, 6 × 9. Binding, boards. With 14 illustrations. Type, Oxford.

Also issued in paper covers.

[520]

In Memory of | Betsey Shipman Gates Mills | [*floret*] | Privately printed | 1920.

The Merrymount Press

On reverse of title: The Merrymount Press, Boston. Collation: [i–vi], 1–14. Leaf, 5¼ × 8¼. Binding, cloth. With 5 illustrations. Type, Oxford. *Also bound in full leather.*

[521]

The | Inferno of Dante | with Text and Translation | by | Eleanor Vinton Murray | [*floret*] | Boston | Privately printed | 1920.

On reverse of title: D. B. Updike, The Merrymount Press, Boston. Collation: [i–ii], i–viii, 1–393. Leaf, 6 × 8½. Binding, boards. Type, Oxford.

[522]

[*within rules*] The Cultivation of | Vineyards | in Southwestern France | By | Alicia du Pont de Nemours | [*cut*] | New York: Brentano's | 1920.

On reverse of title: D. B. Updike, The Merrymount Press, Boston. Collation: i–xii, 1–273. Leaf, 4⅞ × 7⅜. Binding, boards. With 8 illustrations. Type, Caslon.

[523]

The Isles of Pines | 1668 | An Essay in Bibliography | by | Worthington Chauncey Ford | [*seal*] | Boston | The Club of Odd Volumes | 1920.

On page facing title: Edition limited to 151 copies. On reverse of title: D. B. Updike, The Merrymount Press, Boston. Collation: i–xii, 1–116, [117]. Leaf, 6¾ × 8½. Binding, boards. Rubricated title. With 15 illustrations. Type, Caslon and Janson.

[524]

Saint George's School | in the War | [*cut*] | [*quotation*] | Printed for the Alumni Association of | Saint George's School | 1920.

On reverse of title: D. B. Updike, The Merrymount Press, Boston. Collation: i–xiv, 1–168, [169]. Leaf, 5⅞ × 9⅛. Binding, cloth. With 20 illustrations. Type, Oxford.

[525]

The Family at Gilje | A Domestic Story of the Forties | By | Jonas Lie | [*floret*] | Translated from the Norwegian | by

Bibliography

Samuel Coffin Eastman | With an Introduction by Julius Emil Olson | New York | The American-Scandinavian Foundation | London: Humphrey Milford | Oxford University Press | 1920.

On reverse of title: D. B. Updike, The Merrymount Press, Boston, U. S. A. Collation: [i–ii], i–xxxii, 1–245, [246–250]. Leaf, 5 × 7⅜. Binding, cloth. Type, Caslon.

Scandinavian Classics, Vol. XIV.

[526]
One Hundredth Anniversary of | The Diocese of Maine | 1820–1920 | Christ Church, Gardiner, Maine | May thirtieth to June third | [*floret*] | Gardiner, Maine | 1920.

On reverse of title: D. B. Updike, The Merrymount Press, Boston. Collation: i–xii, 1–159, [160–161]. Leaf, 7½ × 10¾. Binding, cloth. With numerous illustrations. Type, Scotch-face.

[527]
Orchidaceae | Illustrations and Studies of | the Family Orchidaceae | Issued from the Ames Botanical Laboratory | North Easton, Massachusetts | The Orchids of Mount Kinabalu | British North Borneo | by Oakes Ames and Charles Schweinfurth | Notes on Philippine Orchids VII by Oakes Ames | Director of the Botanic Gardens of Harvard University | With Twenty-two Etchings by Blanche Ames | [*floret*] | Fascicle VI | Boston | The Merrymount Press | 1920.

On reverse of title: D. B. Updike, The Merrymount Press, Boston. Collation: i–xiv, 1–334, [335]. Leaf, 7 × 9⅞. Binding, boards. Rubricated title. Type, Scotch-face.

[528]
The Charles Men | by | Verner von | Heidenstam | [*floret*] | Translated from the Swedish | by Charles Wharton Stork | With an Introduction by Fredrik Böök | Part I [II] | New York | The American-Scandinavian Foundation | London: Humphrey Milford | Oxford University Press | 1920.

On reverse of title: D. B. Updike, The Merrymount Press, Boston, U. S. A.

[203]

The Merrymount Press

Collation: Part I, [i–ii], i–xxvi, 1–269; Part II, [i–viii], 1–286, [287–290].
Leaf, 4⅞ × 7⅜. Binding, cloth. Type, Caslon.
Scandinavian Classics, Vol. XV.

[529]
Verses to My Wife. [n. d.]

On reverse of title: D. B. Updike, The Merrymount Press, Boston. Collation: i–xvii. Leaf, 6⅜ × 4⅛ oblong. Binding, boards. Rubricated throughout. Type, Batarde.

[530]
The Round Clock | by | Beatrice Nickerson | Drawings by Catherine Richardson | [*floret*] | Privately printed | 1920.

On reverse of title: D. B. Updike, The Merrymount Press. Collation:[i–iv],
1–36. Leaf, 5 × 6⅝. Binding, paper. Type, Oxford.

[531]
The Professional Preparation | of Teachers for | American Public Schools | A Study based upon an Examination of Tax-supported | Normal Schools in the State of Missouri | By | William S. Learned, William C. Bagley | And Charles A. McMurry, George D. Strayer | Walter F. Dearborn, Isaac L. Kandel, Homer W. Josselyn | [*seal*] | New York | The Carnegie Foundation | for the Advancement of Teaching | 576 Fifth Avenue. [n. d.]

On reverse of title: D. B. Updike, The Merrymount Press, Boston. Collation: i–xx, 1–475. Leaf, 7⅜ × 10. Binding, paper. Type, Scotch-face.

[532]
An Explorer in the | Air Service | By | Hiram Bingham | formerly Lieutenant-Colonel, Air Service, U. S. A. | [*seal*] | New Haven | Yale University Press | London: Humphrey Milford, Oxford University Press | MDCCCCXX.

On reverse of title: D. B. Updike, The Merrymount Press, Boston. Collation: i–xiv, 1–260. Leaf, 5¾ × 8⅞. Binding, boards. With 46 illustrations.
Type, Oxford.

[533]
Comedies by Holberg | Jeppe of the Hill, The Political

Bibliography

Tinker | Erasmus Montanus | [*floret*] | Translated from the Danish by | Oscar James Campbell, Jr., Ph.D. | Assistant Professor of English in the University of Wisconsin | and | Frederic Schenck, B.Litt.Oxon. | Instructor in English in Harvard University | With an Introduction by | Oscar James Campbell, Jr. | Second Impression | New York | The American-Scandinavian Foundation | London: Humphrey Milford | Oxford University Press | 1914.

Reissue of No. 409.

Minor Printing

The Carnegie Foundation for the Advancement of Teaching, Fifteenth Annual Report of the President and of the Treasurer, New York; *also* Publications of the Foundation; *and* Act of Incorporation, By-Laws, Rules for the Admission of Institutions and for the Granting of Retiring Allowances.

Reports: John Carter Brown Library, Providence; Annual Report of the President, Brown University, Providence; Wheaton College President's Report, 1918–1919, Norton, Massachusetts; The Commonwealth Fund, New York; Twenty-ninth Meeting of the Society of Clinical Surgery; *also* Thirtieth Meeting.

Catalogues of Schools and Universities: The Browne & Nichols School, Cambridge; Simmons College, Nineteenth Annual Catalogue, 1920–1921; Trinity College, 1919–1920, Hartford; Wheaton College, 1919–1920, Norton, Massachusetts; Brown University, 1920–1921, Providence; *also* Announcement of Courses; Middlebury College Bulletin, Middlebury, Vermont.

Catalogue of the First and Preliminary Exhibition of Gifts from Dr. J. Ackerman Coles to the City of Newark.

World Conference on Faith and Order Publications: Rapport de la mission envoyée en Europe dans l'Orient; Ein neuer Versuch die Wiedervereinigung der Christenheit Herbeizufuehren; Une nouvelle tentative pour préparer la réunion des Églises; Joint Commission appointed to arrange for a World Conference on Faith and Order (*in Greek*); An Official Statement by the Joint Commission of the Protestant Episcopal Church in the United States of America; List of Commissions already Appointed, February 24 and June 1, 1920; Prayer and Unity, by a Layman; Unity or Union: Which? by the Rt. Rev. P. M. Rhinelander, D.D.; The

The Merrymount Press

Conference Spirit, by a Layman; A World Movement for Christian Unity by the Rev. Lefferd M. A. Haughwout; Report of the Deputation to Europe and the East (*in French*); De Unione Ecclesiarum ac totius Christianae Societatis Congressu (Vulgo "The World Conference") pro Quaestionibus ad Fidem Ordinemque Ecclesiae spectantibus rite Explorandis et Perpendendis.

The Society of Clinical Surgery, Statistics and Constitution.

Catalogue Fenway Court.

Mary's Little Lamb, with the Holiday Greetings of Mr. and Mrs. W. K. Bixby, St. Louis.

A Letter from Sir John Bowring, with his Hymn, "Watchman! Tell us of the Night," Reproduced from Originals in the Collection of Mr. W. K. Bixby, St. Louis.

Art Directors Club, New York.

1921

[534]
Lucasta | The Poems of | Richard Lovelace | Esquire | With an Introductory Note by | William Lyon Phelps | Volume I [II] | [*seal*] | Chicago | The Caxton Club | 1921.

On reverse of title: The Merrymount Press, Boston. 2 vols. Collation: Vol. I, i–xvi, 1–174; Vol. II, i–xii, 1–184, [185]. Leaf, 4⅝ × 7⅛. Binding, boards. Rubricated title. Type, Oxford.

[535]
Catalogue of an Exhibition of | Wood-Engravings | Etchings and Drawings | by Rudolph Ruzicka | November 28 to December 10, 1921 | [*cut*] | The Anderson Galleries | Park Avenue & 59th Street, New York. [n. d.]

Colophon: A special edition of this Catalogue, numbering 125 copies, has been issued. It contains a wood-engraving in black and two colors, printed and signed by Mr. Ruzicka. Collation: 1–14, [15]. Leaf, 6⅛ × 8½. Binding, paper. Title in blue and black. Type, Caslon.

[536]
The Same.

Colophon: One hundred and twenty-five copies of this Catalogue were

Bibliography

printed by D. B. Updike, The Merrymount Press, Boston. The wood-engraving in black and two colors, "An East River Night; In Memoriam F. R. S." was printed by Rudolph Ruzicka. Leaf, 6¼ × 8¾.

[537]
Note-Book | of | a Journey to Japan, Korea | and China | 1919 | [cut] | Privately printed | for the Family and Friends of W. K. Bixby | 1921.

Colophon: Sixty copies of this "Note-Book of a Journey to Japan, Korea, and China" were printed by D. B. Updike, The Merrymount Press, Boston, in December, 1921. Collation: [i–vi], 1–281, [282–283]. Leaf, 6⅞ × 9½. Binding, boards. Title in brown and black. Type, Caslon.

[538]
Justice and the Poor | A Study of the Present Denial of Justice to the Poor | and of the Agencies making more Equal | their Position before the Law | with Particular Reference to Legal Aid Work | in the United States | By | Reginald Heber Smith | of the Boston Bar | Bulletin Number Thirteen | [Second Edition] | [seal] | New York City | 576 Fifth Avenue. [n. d.]

Reissue of No. 511.

[539]
Julian Alden Weir | An Appreciation | of his Life and Works | With Illustrations | [floret] | New York | The Century Club | 1921.

On reverse of title: D. B. Updike, The Merrymount Press, Boston. Collation: i–x, 1–140, [141]. Leaf, 8½ × 11⅛. Binding, boards. Rubricated title. With 25 illustrations. Type, Caslon.

[540]
History | of | Lee, Higginson & Company | 1848–1918 | by | Professor Barrett Wendell | Boston | Privately printed | 1921.

On reverse of title: D. B. Updike, The Merrymount Press, Boston. Collation: 1–46, [47]. Leaf, 6 × 8¼. Binding, paper. Type, Oxford.

[207]

The Merrymount Press

[541]
Many Children | by | Mrs. Schuyler Van Rensselaer | With Drawings by | Florence Wyman Ivins | [cut] | [quotation] | Boston | The Atlantic Monthly Press | 1921.

On reverse of title: D. B. Updike, The Merrymount Press, Boston. Collation: i–xii, 1–83, [84]. Leaf, 4¾ × 6⅞. Binding, cloth. Type, Caslon.

[542]
Notes and Journal | of | Travel in Europe | 1804–1805 | by | Washington Irving | With an Introduction by William P. Trent and | Title-page and Illustrations in Aquatint | Designed and Engraved by | Rudolph Ruzicka | In Three Volumes | Volume I [II] [III] | New York | The Grolier Club | 1921.

Colophon: Of Irving's Notes and Journal two hundred and fifty-seven sets on rag paper (seven of which are for presentation and copyright) and three sets on Japanese vellum were printed for The Grolier Club by D. B. Updike, The Merrymount Press, Boston, in the month of September, 1921. Collation: Vol. I, i–xliv, 1–167; Vol. II, [i–vi], [i–ii], 1–188; Vol. III, [i–vi], [i–ii], 1–199, [200]. Leaf, 4¼ × 6⅞. Binding, cloth. With extra title-page in aquatint in each volume and 3 illustrations. Type, Oxford.

[543]
Enclaves of Single Tax | being a Compendium | of the Legal Documents involved | together with a Historical Description | by | Charles White Huntington | [floret] | Published by Fiske Warren | Harvard Massachusetts | 1921.

On reverse of title: Printed at The Merrymount Press, Boston. Collation: i–x, 1–149, [150]. Leaf, 5⅞ × 8⅛. Binding, cloth. Type, Scotch-face.

[544]
In Loving Memory of | Annie Louise Clarke | who departed this life | July fifteenth | 1920 | [floret] | Privately printed | 1921.

On reverse of title: The Merrymount Press, Boston. Collation: [i–iv], 1–11, [12]. Leaf, 5⅞ × 9. Binding, paper. With portrait. Type, Mountjoye.

[545]
Training | for the Public Profession | of the Law | Historical Development and | Principal Contemporary Prob-

Bibliography

lems | of Legal Education in the United States | with Some
Account of | Conditions in England and Canada | By |
Alfred Zantzinger Reed | Bulletin Number Fifteen | [*seal*] |
New York City | 522 Fifth Avenue | 1921.

On reverse of title: D. B. Updike, The Merrymount Press, Boston. Collation: i–xviii, 1–498. Leaf, 6⅛ × 9¼. Binding, paper. Type, Scotch-face.

[546]
The Carnegie Foundation | for the Advancement of Teaching | Standard Forms for Financial Reports | of Colleges,
Universities, and | Technical Schools | Bulletin Number
Three | [Second Edition] | 522 Fifth Avenue | New York
City. [n. d.]

Reissue of No. 349.

Minor Printing

The Carnegie Foundation for the Advancement of Teaching,
Sixteenth Annual Report of the President and of the Treasurer,
New York; *also* Progress of the Contractual Plan of Old Age Annuities; Publications of the Foundation; *and* The Study of Legal Education, Recommendations of the American Bar Association, List of Law Schools, From the Report of the President.

Reports: John Carter Brown Library, Providence; The Commonwealth Fund, New York; Thirty-second Meeting of the Society of Clinical Surgery.

Catalogues of Schools and Universities: The Browne & Nichols
School, Cambridge; Simmons College, Twentieth Annual Catalogue, 1921–1922; Trinity College, 1920–1921, Hartford; Wheaton
College, 1920–1921, Norton, Massachusetts; Brown University,
1921–1922, Providence.

Catalogues of Exhibitions: Frederick R. Shaler Memorial Exhibition, New York; The Albert Felix Schmitt Exhibition.

Order of Service for the Supreme Council, Ancient Accepted
Scottish Rite, Northern Masonic Jurisdiction, U. S. A.

American Orthopedic Association, Programme of the Twenty-fifth Annual Session, Boston.

Description of The Merrymount Press, Boston (*illustrated*).

The Merrymount Press

1922

[547]

M. L. Gordon's | Experiences in the Civil War | from his
Narrative, Letters | and Diary | Edited by Donald Gordon |
[*cut*] | With Illustrations | Boston | Privately printed | 1922.

On reverse of title: D. B. Updike, The Merrymount Press, Boston. Collation: [i–xii], 1–72. Leaf, 8 × 10¾. Binding, boards. Rubricated title. With
16 portraits and facsimiles. Type, Mountjoye.

[548]

Printing Types | Their History, Forms, and Use | A Study in
Survivals | by | Daniel Berkeley Updike | With Illustra-
tions | [*quotation*] | Volume I [II] | [*seal*] | Cambridge | Har-
vard University Press | London: Humphrey Milford | Ox-
ford University Press | 1922.

On reverse of title: D. B. Updike, The Merrymount Press, Boston, U. S. A.
Collation: Vol. I, i–xxxii, 1–276; Vol. II, i–xx, 1–308. Leaf, 6¼ × 9¼. Binding, cloth. With 367 illustrations. Type, Oxford.

[549]

Oliver Ames, Jr. | 1895–1918 | by M. A. DeWolfe Howe |
[*floret*] | [*quotation*] | [*cut*] | Boston | Privately printed | 1922.

On reverse of title: The Merrymount Press, Boston. Collation: 1–84, [85].
Leaf, 5 × 7⅝. Binding, cloth. With 6 illustrations. Type, Oxford.

[550]

[*printer's ornament*] | The Felicities of | Sixty | By Isaac H.
Lionberger | [*printer's ornament*] | Boston | The Club of Odd
Volumes | 1922 | [*printer's ornament*].

Colophon: [*seal*] One hundred and one copies of The Felicities of Sixty
have been printed for the Club of Odd Volumes by D. B. Updike, The
Merrymount Press, Boston, in December, 1922. Collation: [i–vi], 1–35,
[36–37]. Leaf, 5 × 7⅝. Binding, cloth. Type, Janson.

[551]

Letters of | Rowland Gibson Hazard | With a Biographical
Sketch by | Caroline Hazard | and Two Appreciations | [*arms*] |
Privately printed | 1922.

Bibliography

On reverse of title: D. B. Updike, The Merrymount Press, Boston. Collation: i–xvi, 1–349, [350–351]. Leaf, 6 × 8⅜. Binding, boards. With 9 illustrations. Type, Caslon.

[552]
Selections from the Diaries of | William Appleton | 1786–1862 | [*floret*] | Boston | Privately printed | 1922.

On reverse of title: D. B. Updike, The Merrymount Press, Boston. Collation: [i–x], 1–250, [251]. Leaf, 6¼ × 8¾. Binding, boards. With 6 illustrations. Type, Caslon.

[553]
Dibdin's Ghost | & | Boccaccio | [*floret*] | MDCCCCXXII | [*floret*].

Colophon: Five hundred copies of "Dibdin's Ghost" and "Boccaccio," by Eugene Field, were printed for W. K. Bixby, by D. B. Updike, The Merrymount Press, Boston, in May, 1922. Collation: [1–27]. Leaf, 4⅞ × 6⅝. Binding, boards. Rubricated throughout. Type, Oxford.

[554]
[*within rules*] Two Poems | by Eugene Field | Reproduced from the Original MSS. | [*printer's ornament*] | Seein' Things at Night | [*printer's ornament*] | To M. L. Gray | [*monogram*] | Privately Printed for W. K. Bixby.

Colophon: Two hundred and fifty copies of "Two Poems by Eugene Field" were printed for W. K. Bixby by D. B. Updike, The Merrymount Press, Boston, in April, 1922. Collation: [1–16]. Leaf, 7¾ × 10. Binding, boards. Printed in blue and black. Type, Old Style.

[555]
Two Letters | I | Anthony Wayne and Lake George | Letter from General Anthony Wayne to General Schuyler | Ticonderoga, March 23, 1777 | II | Washington's Announcement of | Arnold's Treason | Letter from George Washington to the | Judge Advocate General | September 26, 1780 | [*seal*] | Privately Printed by W. K. Bixby | For Historical Societies and Personal Friends | 1922.

Colophon: Two hundred and fifty copies of this book were printed for W. K. Bixby by D. B. Updike, The Merrymount Press, Boston, in the month

The Merrymount Press

of May, 1922. Collation: [1–7]. Leaf, 8¼ × 13½. Binding, boards. Rubricated title. With facsimile reproductions of the letters. Type, Caslon.
Cover-paper design adapted by W. A. Dwiggins from an old toile de Jouy.

[556]
Note-Book of a Trip | to Gibraltar, Madeira, Monaco, Nice,
Algiers | Naples, Pompeii, Rome, Cairo | Luxor & Athens |
1921 | [*initials within cut*] | Privately Printed | For the Family
and Friends of | W. K. Bixby | 1922.

Colophon: Sixty copies of this Note-Book of a Trip to Gibraltar, Madeira,
Monaco, Nice, etc., were printed by D. B.Updike, The Merrymount Press,
Boston, in January, 1922. Collation: 1–75, [76–77]. Leaf, 4¼ × 6⅞. Binding, boards. Type, Oxford.

[557]
James Whitcomb Riley's | Letter from Boston | Written
when he first felt that he was gaining | Recognition | [*cut*] |
Privately Printed | For a few Friends by W. K. Bixby | Saint
Louis | 1922.

Colophon: Five hundred copies of A Letter of James Whitcomb Riley,
with view of the Doorway of the Longfellow House, Cambridge, engraved
on wood by Rudolph Ruzicka, were printed by D. B. Updike, The Merrymount Press, Boston, in September, 1922. Collation: [1–9]. Leaf, 5½ × 8½.
Binding, paper. Title in black and yellow. With facsimile of letter. Type,
Oxford.

[558]
Dedication Exercises | of the | Oscar C. Tugo Circle | Pasteur & Longwood Avenues, Boston | October 18, 1921 | In
Memory of the First Enlisted Man in | the American Expeditionary Force | to be killed by the Enemy | [*cut*] | Boston |
Privately printed | 1922.

On reverse of title: The Merrymount Press, Boston. Collation: [i–ii], 1–33,
[34]. Leaf, 5⅞ × 9⅜. Binding, boards. With 3 illustrations. Type, Mountjoye.
Also issued in paper covers.

[559]
A Catalogue of | the Napoleon Collection | formed by |
William Henry Hoffman | 1867–1916 | Given to Brown

Bibliography

University in 1921 | by Mira H. Hoffman | [*seal*] | Published
by the University | Providence Rhode Island | 1922.

On reverse of title: One hundred copies printed on Kelmscott hand-made
paper and three hundred copies on machine-made paper. D. B. Updike,
The Merrymount Press, Boston. Collation: [i–vi], 1–77. Leaf, 8 × 10¾.
Binding, paper. Type, Mountjoye and Oxford.

[560]
A Choice of Manuscripts | and Bookbindings | from | the
Library of | Isabella Stewart Gardner | Fenway Court | [*cut*] |
MDCCCCXXII.

On reverse of title: D. B. Updike, The Merrymount Press, Boston. Collation: [i–iv], 1–103. Leaf, 5¾ × 9⅛. Binding, boards. Rubricated title. Type,
Caslon.

[561]
Charles Lamb | A Letter regarding Roast Pig to William
Hazlitt | and | A Letter on Friendship to Robert Lloyd | to-
gether with | A Dissertation on Roast Pig | [*cut*] | Privately
Printed for his Friends by | W. K. Bixby | 1922.

Colophon: Two hundred and fifty copies of Two Letters of Charles Lamb
were printed in October, 1922 [*name of Press within cut*]. Collation: [1–35].
Leaf, 6½ × 8½. Binding, boards. Type, Scotch-face.

[562]
Enclaves of Single Tax | or Economic Rent | Being a Com-
pendium | of the Legal Documents Involved | together with
a Historical Description | by | Charles White Huntington |
[*floret*] | Second Annual Volume | Published by Fiske War-
ren | Harvard Massachusetts | 1922.

On reverse of title: Printed at The Merrymount Press, Boston. Collation:
i–xii, 1–223, [224–225]. Leaf, 5⅞ × 8⅛. Binding, cloth. With numerous
maps. Type, Scotch-face.

[563]
Benjamin Franklin | on Balloons | A Letter written from
Passy, France, January Sixteenth | MDCCLXXXIV | [*quotation*] |
[*cut, with caption*] | Privately printed for his Friends by W. K.
Bixby | Saint Louis: MDCCCCXXII.

The Merrymount Press

Colophon: Two hundred and fifty copies of Benjamin Franklin's Letter on Balloons were printed on Vidalon paper for W. K. Bixby by D. B. Updike, The Merrymount Press, Boston, October, 1922. Collation: [1–10]. Leaf, 8 × 9⅝. Binding, boards. With facsimile of letter. Type, Caslon.
Cover-paper design adapted by W. A. Dwiggins from an eighteenth-century toile de Jouy.

[564]
The Portraits of | Sir Francis Bernard | by | Albert Matthews | [*seal*] | Boston | The Club of Odd Volumes | 1922.

On fourth page of cover: The Merrymount Press, Boston. Collation: 1–15, [16]. Leaf, 6 × 9⅛. Binding, paper. With portrait. Type, Caslon.
100 copies printed.

[565]
Orchidaceae | Illustrations and Studies of | the Family Orchidaceae | Issued from the Ames Botanical Laboratory | North Easton, Massachusetts | Pogonia and its Allies | in the Northeastern United States | and Other Papers | By Oakes Ames | With thirteen plates by Blanche Ames | [*floret*] | Fascicle VII | Boston | The Merrymount Press | 1922.

On reverse of title: D. B. Updike, The Merrymount Press, Boston. Collation: [i–x], 1–174. Leaf, 7 × 9⅞. Binding, boards. Type, Scotch-face.

[566]
Diocese of Massachusetts | The Order of Service for the | Consecration | of | Charles Lewis Slattery | as | Bishop Coadjutor | at Trinity Church | in the City of Boston | [*seal*] | The Eve of All Saints | A. D. MDCCCXXII.

On second page of cover: D. B. Updike, The Merrymount Press, Boston. Collation: 1–39, [40]. Leaf, 5½ × 8¾. Binding, paper. Rubricated throughout. Type, Caslon.

[567]
The | Wedding Journey | of | Charles and Martha Babcock Amory | Letters of Mrs. Amory to her Mother | Mrs. Gardiner Greene | 1833–1834 | Volume the First | France

Bibliography

and Italy | [Volume the Second | Switzerland, Holland and Germany] | [*cut*] | Boston | Privately printed | 1922.

Colophon: [*cut*] One hundred copies of The Wedding Journey of Charles and Martha Babcock Amory were printed by Daniel Berkeley Updike, The Merrymount Press, Boston, in February, 1922. Collation: Vol. I, i–xii, 1–234; Vol. II, i–x, 1–260, [261]. Leaf, 7¼ × 9⅛. Binding, cloth. With 2 portraits. Type, Mountjoye.

Printed for Mrs. Amory's daughter, the late Mrs. F. Gordon Dexter. Preface by D. B. Updike. The binding copies the tooling of the blank-book in which the letters were written.

[568]

Martha Washington's Letter | Written from Philadelphia, June 15, 1794 | To Mrs. Frances Washington | [*cut*] | Privately printed for W. K. Bixby | Saint Louis | 1922.

Colophon: [*name of Press within cut*] Two Hundred and Fifty copies of Martha Washington's Letter to Mrs. Frances Washington were printed for W. K. Bixby by D. B. Updike, The Merrymount Press, in the month of October, 1922. Collation: 1–9. Leaf, 7⅜ × 9. Binding, boards. Rubricated title. With facsimile of letter. Type, Oxford.

Cover-paper design the same as on the Wayne and Washington Letters (No. 555).

[569]

Education | in the Maritime Provinces of | Canada | By | William S. Learned | and | Kenneth C. M. Sills | [*seal*] | New York | The Carnegie Foundation | for the Advancement of Teaching | 522 Fifth Avenue | 1922.

On reverse of title: D. B. Updike, The Merrymount Press, Boston. Collation: [i–vi], 1–50. Leaf, 7⅜ × 10. Binding, paper. With map. Type, Scotch-face.

Bulletin Number Sixteen.

[570]

Bibliotheca Americana | Catalogue of the | John Carter Brown | Library | in Brown University | Providence, Rhode Island | Volume II [*Part I*] | [*arms*] | Providence | Published by the Library | 1922.

On reverse of title: The Merrymount Press, Boston. Collation: [i–vi], 1–250. Leaf, 7 × 10½. Binding, cloth. Rubricated title. With portrait. Type, Oxford.

In 3 volumes. Vols. I and II of 2 parts each, each part bound separately.

The Merrymount Press

The Same.

Binding, boards. With two copies of the portrait, with and without inscription.

Printed on hand-made paper.

Minor Printing

The Carnegie Foundation for the Advancement of Teaching, Seventeenth Annual Report of the President and of the Treasurer, New York; *also* Publications of the Foundation; The Progress of Legal Education, The Washington Conference and the Association of American Law Schools, *etc.*, Advance Extract from the Seventeenth Annual Report of the President; *and* Act of Incorporation, By-Laws, Rules for the Admission of Institutions and for the Granting of Retiring Allowances.

Reports: John Carter Brown Library, Providence; Annual Report of the President, Brown University, Providence; Metropolitan Museum of Art, Report to the Committee on Educational Work, New York; Carnegie Corporation of New York, Report of the Acting President, New York.

Catalogues of Schools and Universities: Saint Mark's School, Southborough, Massachusetts; Simmons College, Twenty-first Annual Catalogue, 1922–1923; Trinity College, 1921–1922, Hartford; Wheaton College, 1921–1922, Norton, Massachusetts; Brown University, 1922–1923, Providence.

Catalogue of an Exhibition illustrating the Varied Interests of Book Buyers, 1450–1600, The Club of Odd Volumes.

Order of Service for the Feast of the Paschal Lamb, Mount Olivet Chapter of Rose Croix, A.A.S.R.

Office for the Reception of a Novice, Baltimore.

Draft of a Plan for a National Association of Legal Aid Organizations, A Report submitted by the Committee on By-Laws appointed by the President of the National Alliance of Legal Aid Societies.

The Study of Literature, reprinted from the Educational Review, New York.

Bulletin of Class of 1879 [*Harvard College*], May 31, 1922.

Bibliography

1923

[572]

[*within border*] The Journal of | Mrs. John Amory | (Katharine Greene) | 1775–1777 | With Letters from her Father | Rufus Greene | 1759–1777 | [*floret*] | Edited and Arranged from Manuscripts and | Illustrated from Portraits in the Possession of Mrs. Amory's Great-Great-Granddaughter | Martha C. Codman | Boston | Privately printed | 1923.

Colophon: One hundred copies of The Journal of Mrs. John Amory were printed by D. B. Updike, The Merrymount Press, Boston, in the Month of July, 1923. Collation: i–x, 1–101, [102–103]. Leaf, 7¾ × 10¼. Binding, cloth. With 13 illustrations and facsimiles. Type, Mountjoye.

Printed for Miss Martha C. Codman of Washington.

[573]

Lithography | by | Bolton Brown | New York | Fitzroy Carrington | 1923.

On reverse of title: D. B. Updike, The Merrymount Press, Boston. Collation: 1–27, [28–29]. Leaf, 5½ × 8½. Binding, boards. Type, Caslon.

[574]

[*border*] | Lida Shaw King | An Appreciation | By | Mary E. Woolley | President of Mount Holyoke College | South Hadley, Massachusetts | With Reproduction of a Portrait by | Frank W. Benson | [*printer's ornament*] | Privately printed | MDCCCCXXIII | [*border*].

Colophon: Six hundred and fifty copies of this Appreciation were printed by D. B. Updike, The Merrymount Press, Boston, in November, 1923. Collation: [i–vi], 1–12, [13]. Leaf, 5⅝ × 8¼. Binding, boards. Type, Caslon.

[575]

[*within border*] Stephen Crane | By | Thomas L. Raymond | Newark New Jersey | The Carteret Book Club | 1923.

Colophon: Two hundred and fifty copies of this book were printed for The Carteret Book Club of Newark, New Jersey, in May, 1923, by D. B. Updike, The Merrymount Press, Boston, Massachusetts. Collation: i–x, 1–42, [43–45]. Leaf, 5⅛ × 7⅞. Binding, boards. With portrait. Type, Oxford.

[217]

The Merrymount Press

[576]

The Diary of | Ellen Birdseye Wheaton | With Notes by | Donald Gordon | [*floret*] | Boston | Privately printed | 1923.

On reverse of title: D. B. Updike, The Merrymount Press, Boston. Collation: i–xviii, 1–419, [420]. Leaf, 6 × 8⅜. Binding, boards. Rubricated title. With 10 illustrations. Type, Caslon.

[577]

Address | upon the Unveiling of a Tablet to mark | No. 38 Winthrop Street, Cambridge, where | Theodore Roosevelt | lived while a Student at Harvard University | Delivered on Saturday, October 27, 1923 | By Charles G. Washburn | Boston | Privately printed | 1923.

On reverse of title: D. B. Updike, The Merrymount Press, Boston. Collation: 1–15. Leaf, 5⅝ × 8¼. Binding, boards. With 3 illustrations. Type, Caslon.

200 copies printed.

[578]

A Journey to India | 1921–1922 | Casual Comment by | Albert Farwell Bemis | [*cut*] | Boston | Privately printed | 1923.

On reverse of title: D. B. Updike, The Merrymount Press, Boston. Collation: i–xiv, 1–97, [98]. Leaf, 5½ × 7⅝. Binding, boards. With 51 illustrations. Type, Oxford.

[579]

The City's Voice | A Book of Verse | By | Morris Gray | [*publisher's mark*] | Boston | Marshall Jones Company. [n.d.]

On reverse of title: D. B. Updike, The Merrymount Press, Boston. Collation: i–xii, 1–135, [136]. Leaf, 4⅝ × 7¾. Binding, cloth. Type, Caslon.

[580]

The Carnegie Foundation | for the Advancement of Teaching | Pensions for | Public School Teachers | A Report for the Committee on Salaries, Pensions | and Tenure, of the National Education Association | By | Clyde Furst and I. L. Kandel | Bulletin Number Twelve | [*seal*] | New York City | 576 Fifth Avenue. [n.d.]

Reissue of No. 495.

[218]

Bibliography

[581]

In Memoriam | Bellamy Storer | With Personal Remembrances of | President McKinley, President Roosevelt | and John Ireland, Archbishop of St. Paul | By | Maria Longworth Storer | [*cut*] | Privately printed | 1923.

On reverse of title: The Merrymount Press, Boston. Collation: [i–viii], 1–119, [120]. Leaf, 7 × 9⅝. Binding, cloth. With 2 illustrations. Type, Mountjoye.

[582]

A Book of Verse | By | Theodora Taylor | [*printer's ornament*] | Newport | Privately printed | MDCCCCXXIII.

On reverse of title: D. B. Updike, The Merrymount Press, Boston. Collation: i–viii, 1–39, [40]. Leaf, 4⅝ × 7¾. Binding, cloth. Type, Caslon.

[583]

Pro Vita Monastica | An Essay in Defence of | the Contemplative Vir-|tues by Henry Dwight Sedgwick | Author of "Life of Marcus Aurelius," "Dante," | "An Apology for Old Maids," "Italy in the Thir-|teenth Century," "A Short History of Italy," &c. | Boston | The Atlantic Monthly Press | MDCCCCXXIII.

On reverse of title: D. B. Updike, The Merrymount Press, Boston. Collation: i–xviii, 1–164. Leaf, 5½ × 8⅛. Binding, cloth. Rubricated title. Type, Caslon.

[584]

[*border*] | Minor Parts | Six Poems | by | Mary Byers Smith | [*printer's ornament*] | Boston | Privately printed | 1923 | [*border*].

On reverse of title: D. B. Updike, The Merrymount Press, Boston. Collation: 1–11, [12]. Leaf, 5 × 7⅞. Binding, paper. Type, Caslon.
100 copies printed.

[585]

Glimpses of | An Old Social Capital | (Portsmouth, New Hampshire) | As illustrated by the Life of the | Reverend Arthur Browne | and his Circle | By | Mary Cochrane Rogers | [*floret*] | Boston | Printed for the Subscribers | MDCCCCXXIII.

The Merrymount Press

On reverse of title: D. B. Updike, The Merrymount Press, Boston. Collation: i–xiv, 1–92, [93]. Leaf, 7⅝ × 10¼. Binding, boards. With 22 illustrations. Type, Caslon.

[586]
Doctor | Johnson | A Play | By | A. Edward Newton, Esq. | Author of | The Amenities of | Book-Collecting | and Kindred | Affections | A Magnificent | Farce & Other | Diversions of | a Book-Collector | [cut] | Boston | The Atlantic Monthly Press | MDCCCCXXIII.

On reverse of title: D. B. Updike, The Merrymount Press, Boston. Collation: i–xviii, 1–120. Leaf, 6¾ × 8⅝. Binding, boards. Rubricated title. With frontispiece in colour and 8 half-tone reproductions. Type, Caslon.

[587]
The Same.

On page following half-title: Of the five hundred and eighty-five copies of this Hand-made Paper Edition, this is copy number —. On reverse of title: D. B. Updike, The Merrymount Press, Boston. Collation: [i–ii], i–xviii, 1–20. Leaf, 6¾ × 8¾. Binding, boards. With 16 illustrations and facsimile.

[588]
The Reminiscences of | Frederick Ayer | [floret] | Boston | Privately printed | 1923.

On reverse of title: D. B. Updike, The Merrymount Press, Boston. Collation: [i–x], 1–84, [85]. Leaf, 5⅞ × 9⅜. Binding, full morocco. Rubricated title. With 23 illustrations and map. Type, Caslon.

[589]
Chinese Painting | As Reflected in the Thought and Art of | Li Lung-Mien | 1070–1106 | By Agnes E. Meyer | New York | Duffield & Company | 1923.

On reverse of title: D. B. Updike, The Merrymount Press, Boston. Collation: i–xiv, 1–251, [252]. Leaf, 8¾ × 11¼. Binding, boards. With 12 illustrations. Type, Mountjoye and Oxford.

[590]
The Same.

Colophon: Of this edition of Chinese Painting as Reflected in the Thought and Art of Li Lung-Mien, three hundred copies have been printed by D. B.

Bibliography

Updike, The Merrymount Press, Boston, of which this is No.—. This volume is accompanied by a portfolio containing twenty photographic reproductions by W. A. Livingstone, of Detroit, from the paintings of Li Lung-Mien. Collation: i–xiv, 1–423, [424–425].

[591]

The Prize Day Address [*Groton School, June 15, 1923*] | by | Professor Julian Lowell Coolidge | of Harvard University | [*floret*] | Privately Printed. [n. d.]

On reverse of last page of text: D. B. Updike, The Merrymount Press, Boston. Collation: 1–31, [32], Leaf, 5½ × 8½. Binding, paper. Type, Caslon.

[592]

Training | for Library Service | A Report prepared for | The Carnegie Corporation of New York | By | Charles C. Williamson | New York | 1923.

On reverse of title: D. B. Updike, The Merrymount Press, Boston. Collation: [i–viii], 1–165. Leaf, 6⅛ × 9¼. Binding, paper. With map. Type, Scotch-face.

[593]

Catalogue of the | John Carter Brown Library | Volume II | Part II. [n. d.]

Collation: [i–ii], 251–521, [522]. Leaf, 7 × 10½. Binding, cloth. With illustration. No imprint. Type, Oxford.

In 3 volumes. Vols. I and II of 2 parts each, each part bound separately.

[594]

The Same.

Binding, boards. With two copies of the illustration, with and without inscription.

Printed on hand-made paper.

[595]

Frederick David Ely | Justice of the Municipal Court | In the City of Boston | [*floret*] | Memorial of Norfolk County Bar Association | as presented | to the Supreme Judicial Court | at Dedham, Massachusetts April 2, 1923 | Boston | Privately printed | 1923.

The Merrymount Press

Colophon: Two hundred copies of this Memorial have been printed by D. B. Updike, The Merrymount Press, Boston, in December, 1923. This is Number —. Collation: [i-vi], 1-23, [24-25]. Leaf, 5½ × 8½. Binding, boards. Type, Caslon.

[596]
The Order of Service for the | Institution | of | Henry Knox Sherrill | as | Rector | of Trinity Church | in the City of Boston | [cut] | Trinity Sunday | A.D. MDCCCCXXIII.

On reverse of title: D. B. Updike, The Merrymount Press, Boston. Collation: 1-15, [16]. Leaf, 5½ × 8¾. Binding, paper. Rubricated throughout. Type, Caslon.

[597]
A Description of | The Reredos and Mural Paintings | in | Emmanuel Church | Newport, Rhode Island | By | Alice May Elliot | [floret] | Newport | Privately Printed. [n. d.]

On reverse of title: D. B. Updike, The Merrymount Press, Boston. Collation: [i-x], 1-17. Leaf, 5¼ × 8¼. Binding, paper. Type, Caslon.

Minor Printing

The Carnegie Foundation for the Advancement of Teaching, Eighteenth Annual Report of the President and of the Treasurer, New York; *also* Publications of the Foundation; *and* The World and Yesterday, by Clyde Furst, Secretary of the Carnegie Foundation.

Reports: John Carter Brown Library, Providence; Annual Report of the President, Brown University, Providence; Wheaton College, President's Report, Norton, Massachusetts; Carnegie Corporation of New York, Report of the Acting President for the Year ended September 30, 1923, New York.

Catalogues of Schools and Universities: Saint Mark's School, Southborough, Massachusetts; The Browne & Nichols School, Cambridge; Simmons College, Twenty-second Annual Catalogue, 1923-1924; Trinity College, 1922-1923, Hartford; Wheaton College, 1922-1923, Norton, Massachusetts; Brown University, Providence.

All Saints' Church, Peterborough, New Hampshire.

Bibliography

The Society of Clinical Surgery, Statistics.

Catalogue Fenway Court.

Methods and Results of Psychological Tests given at Brown University by Professor Stephen S. Colvin, Providence.

The School in Cambridge, by William Lawrence, Bishop of Massachusetts, Cambridge.

Bulletin of Class of 1879 [*Harvard College*], May 31, 1923.

Grand & Upright Pianofortes, Mason & Hamlin Co. (*also miniature catalogue*).

1924

[598]
Mark Gordon | 1794–1886 | By | Donald Gordon | [*floret*] | Privately printed | 1924.
On reverse of title: D. B. Updike, The Merrymount Press, Boston. Collation: [i–vi], 1–32. Leaf, 5½ × 8⅝. Binding, cloth. With 13 illustrations. Type, Caslon.

[599]
John Shaw Billings | Creator of the National Medical Library | and its Catalogue | First Director of the New York | Public Library | By | Harry Miller Lydenberg | Chief Reference Librarian of the | New York Public Library | [*florets*] | Chicago | American Library Association | 1924.
Colophon: One thousand copies of this book were printed by D. B. Updike, The Merrymount Press, Boston, in June, 1924, of which five hundred are numbered. Collation: [i–viii], 1–94, [95–96]. Leaf, 5⅝ × 8¾. Binding, boards. With portrait. Type, Caslon.
American Library Pioneers, Vol. I.

[600]
An Enumeration of the | Orchids | of the United States | and Canada | Prepared for the | American Orchid Society | By Oakes Ames | [*floret*] | Boston | The American Orchid Society | 1924.
On reverse of title: D. B. Updike, The Merrymount Press, Boston. Collation: i–viii, 1–120. Leaf, 5¼ × 8¼. Binding, boards. Rubricated title. Type, Oxford.

[223]

The Merrymount Press

[601]

South County Studies | Of Some Eighteenth Century Persons | Places & Conditions | In that Portion of Rhode Island called | Narragansett | By Esther Bernon Carpenter | With an Introduction by Caroline Hazard | compiled largely from Letters now first published | by Oliver Wendell Holmes | [*floret*] | Boston | Printed for the Subscribers | 1924.

On reverse of title: D. B. Updike, The Merrymount Press, Boston. Collation: i–xvi, 1–296, [297]. Leaf, 5⅞ × 9. Binding, boards. With frontispiece. Type, Oxford.

750 copies printed.

[602]

William Lowell Putnam | A little of the fragrance of his life gathered together here | by his wife | [*arms*] | Boston | Privately printed | 1924.

On reverse of title: D B. Updike, The Merrymount Press, Boston. Collation: [i–vi], 1–37, [38]. Leaf, 5⅛ × 7½. Binding, boards. With portrait. Type, Caslon.

[603]

The | American Public Library | and the | Diffusion of Knowledge | By | William S. Learned | of the Staff of the Carnegie Foundation | for the Advancement of Teaching | New York | Harcourt, Brace and Company. [n. d.]

On reverse of title: D. B. Updike, The Merrymount Press, Boston. Collation: [i–ii], i–viii, 1–89. Leaf, 6¼ × 9½. Binding, boards. With table and map. Type, Scotch-face.

[604]

[*border*] | In the Day's Work | By | Daniel Berkeley Updike | Author of "Printing Types: Their | History, Forms, and Use" | [*arms within printer's ornament*] | Cambridge | Harvard University Press | 1924 | [*border*].

On reverse of title: Printed by D. B. Updike, The Merrymount Press, Boston, U. S. A. Collation: [i–viii], 1–69, [70]. Leaf, 5½ × 8⅜. Binding, boards. Type, Caslon.

Bibliography

[605]

[*within border*] In the Day's Work | By | Daniel Berkeley Updike | Limited Edition | [*arms*] | Cambridge | Harvard University Press | 1924.

Colophon: Two hundred and sixty copies of this edition of "In the Day's Work," of which two hundred and fifty are for sale, were printed at The Merrymount Press, Boston, September, 1924 [*acrostic*]. This copy is Number —. Collation: [i–x], 1–69, [70–71]. Leaf, 5½ × 8½. Binding, cloth. Rubricated title and colophon. With 11 examples of typography, some in colour. Type, Caslon.

[606]

Justice and the Poor | A Study of the Present Denial of Justice to the Poor | and of the Agencies making more Equal | their Position before the Law | with Particular Reference to Legal Aid Work | in the United States | By | Reginald Heber Smith | of the Boston Bar | Bulletin Number Thirteen | [Third Edition] | [*seal*] | New York City | 522 Fifth Avenue | 1924.

Reissue of No. 511.

[607]

[*within border*] A Dissertation | upon | English Typographical Founders | And Founderies | By | Edward Rowe Mores | A.M., A.S.S. | With Appendix by John Nichols | &c. &c. | Edited by D. B. Updike | [*seal of printer's ornaments*] | New York | The Grolier Club | 1924.

Colophon: [*seal of printer's ornaments*] The Committee on Publications of The Grolier Club certifies that this copy of Edward Rowe Mores' "Dissertation upon English Typographical Founders and Founderies " is one of an edition of two hundred and fifty copies printed on Vidalon paper by D. B. Updike, The Merrymount Press, Boston. The press-work was completed in June, 1924. Collation: i–xl, 1–103, [104–105]. Leaf, 5⅞ × 9½. Binding, cloth. With portrait, genealogical table, and facsimiles. Type, Caslon.

[608]

Gaston Lachaise | Sixteen Reproductions in Collotype | of the Sculptor's Work | Edited with an Introduction | by

The Merrymount Press

A. E. Gallatin | [*printer's ornament*] | New York | E. P. Dutton & Company | 1924.

Colophon: [*printer's ornament*] Of this Book 400 copies were printed by D. B. Updike, The Merrymount Press, Boston, June, 1924. Collation: [i–viii], 1–52, [53–55]. Leaf, 7⅞ × 10⅞. Binding, boards. Type, Caslon.

[609]
Citations by | President | William Herbert Perry Faunce | for | Honorary Degrees | granted by Brown University | MDCCCC–MDCCCCXXIV. [n. d.]

On reverse of title: D. B. Updike, The Merrymount Press, Boston. Collation: [i–vi], 1–48, [49]. Leaf, 6⅛ × 9¼. Binding, paper. Type, Montallegro.

[610]
The Same.

Leaf, 6¼ × 9½. Binding, boards.
On hand-made paper.

[611]
[*within border*] Home! Sweet Home! | By John Howard Payne | A Reproduction of the Author's Manuscript of the Poem | [*cut*] | With the Season's Greetings from | Mr. & Mrs. W. K. Bixby.

Colophon: [*border*] [*cut*] Five hundred Copies printed by D. B. Updike, The Merrymount Press, Boston, in the Month of December 1924 [*border*]. Collation: [1–7]. Leaf, 8½ × 7¼ oblong. Binding, paper. Type, Scotch-face.

[612]
Chapel Services | Saint Paul's School | [*cut*] | Concord | New Hampshire | 1924.

On reverse of title: D. B. Updike, The Merrymount Press, Boston. Collation: 1–49. Leaf, 4⅜ × 6½. Binding, boards. Type, Oxford.

[613]
Order of Service | for the Laying of the | Foundation Stone | of | Saint George's Chapel | June fourteenth | A. D. MDCCCCXXIIII | [*floret*] | [*inscription*] | Saint George's School | Middletown, Rhode Island. [n. d.]

[226]

Bibliography

On fourth page of cover: D. B. Updike, The Merrymount Press, Boston. Collation: 1–9, [10–12]. Leaf, 5½ × 8¾. Binding, paper. Rubricated throughout. Type, Caslon.

[614]
Inveni Portam | Joseph Conrad | By | R. B. Cunninghame Graham | [*printer's ornament*] | The Rowfant Club | Cleveland | 1924.

Colophon: One hundred & fifty-seven copies of this book were printed for The Rowfant Club of Cleveland, Ohio, by D. B. Updike at The Merrymount Press, Boston, in the month of December, 1924. This is Number —. Collation: [i–vi], 1–14, [15–17]. Leaf, 5 × 7⅞. Binding, paper. Type, Poliphilus.

Minor Printing

The Carnegie Foundation for the Advancement of Teaching, Nineteenth Annual Report of the President and of the Treasurer, New York; *also* Condensed Edition of Nineteenth Annual Report; Publications of the Foundation; *and* Standards and Standardizers in Legal Education, Bar Admission Requirements, *etc.*, Advance Extract from the Nineteenth Annual Report of the President.

Reports: John Carter Brown Library, Providence; Annual Report of the President, Brown University, Providence; Carnegie Corporation of New York, Report of the President and of the Treasurer, New York.

Catalogues of Schools and Universities: Saint Mark's School, Southborough, Massachusetts; Trinity College, 1923–1924, Hartford; Wheaton College, 1923–1924, Norton, Massachusetts; Brown University, 1924–1925, Providence.

Twenty-four Views of Wheaton College, Norton, Massachusetts, with Foreword and Descriptive Notes, Norton.

Notes on an Exhibition of Early American Lithographs, 1819–1859, The Club of Odd Volumes.

Grand & Upright Pianofortes, Mason & Hamlin Co.

Press Notices of the Work of Albert Felix Schmitt, Cambridge.

All Saints' Church, Peterborough, New Hampshire.

The Merrymount Press

1925

[615]

A Note | on the Discovery of a New Page of Poetry | in | William Blake's Milton | By | S. Foster Damon | Illustrated by Facsimile Reproductions | from the Original | in the Possession of a Member of | The Club of Odd Volumes | Boston | Printed for The Club of Odd Volumes | The Merrymount Press | 1925.

On page facing title: Edition limited to one hundred and fifty copies. On reverse of title: D. B. Updike, The Merrymount Press, Boston. Collation: [i–vi], 1–14. Leaf, 8½ × 11. Binding, cloth. With 3 illustrations in colour. Type, Scotch-face.

[616]

The Richard C. Jenkinson | Collection of Books | chosen to show the Work of | the Best Printers | [*floret*] | The Public Library | By Order of its Board of Trustees | Newark New Jersey | 1925.

Colophon: Five hundred copies of this Catalogue were printed by D. B. Updike, The Merrymount Press, Boston, in June, 1925. Collation: i–x, 1–69, [70–71]. Leaf, 5⅜ × 7⅞. Binding, boards. Type, Caslon.

Also issued in paper covers.

[617]

Letters | written on the Occasion of | a Dinner given to | George Edward Woodberry | New York, May Twelfth | 1925 | Printed for | The Woodberry Society | 1925.

Colophon: One hundred and twenty-five copies of this book were printed by D. B. Updike, The Merrymount Press, Boston, in July, 1925. This is Number —. Collation: [i–viii], 1–19, [20–21]. Leaf, 5 × 7⅝. Binding, paper. Type, Oxford.

[618]

Breezes from Cape Cod | By Helen Freeman Stevens | Illustrated by | Arthur W. Wheelwright | [*cut*] | Chatham-on-Cape-Cod | MCMXXV.

On reverse of title: D. B. Updike, The Merrymount Press, Boston. Collation: [i–viii], [i–ii], 1–17, [18]. Leaf, 5⅛ × 7¼. Binding, paper. Type, Oxford.

Bibliography

[619]
The Professional Preparation | of Teachers for | American
Public Schools | A Study based upon an Examination of Tax-
supported | Normal Schools in the State of Missouri | By |
William S. Learned, William C. Bagley | And Charles A.
McMurry, George D. Strayer | Walter F. Dearborn, Isaac L.
Kandel, Homer W. Josselyn | [*seal*] | New York | The Car-
negie Foundation | for the Advancement of Teaching | 576
Fifth Avenue. [n. d.]

Reissue of No. 531.

[620]
An Account of the Dedication of | The West Window | of
St. John's Church, Beverly Farms | Whitsunday, May thirty-
first | MDCCCCXXV | [*printer's ornament*] | Privately printed |
MDCCCCXXV.

Colophon: Of this volume one hundred and thirty copies were printed by
D. B. Updike, The Merrymount Press, Boston, October, 1925. Collation:
[i–vi], 1–21, [22–23]. Leaf, 8⅜ × 11½. Binding, morocco. Rubricated
throughout. With plate and diagram. Type, Poliphilus.

[621]
[*cross*] | Order of Service | for the Dedication of | Grace
Chapel | Trinity Methodist Episcopal Church | Springfield,
Massachusetts | on Sunday afternoon, June Seventh | Anno
Domini MDCCCCXXV | at four o'clock | [*floret*] | [*quotation*].
[n. d.]

On last page: D. B. Updike, The Merrymount Press, Boston. Collation:
[i–ii], 1–20, [21–22]. Leaf, 6¼ × 8⅝. Binding, paper. Rubricated throughout. With 7 illustrations. Type, Caslon.

[622]
The Book of | The Jacob Wendell | Scholars | [*floret*] | Bos-
ton | Privately printed | 1925.

Colophon: Of this book one hundred and fifty copies were printed by D. B.
Updike, The Merrymount Press, Boston, in the month of July 1925. Col-
lation: [i–x], 1–90, [91]. Leaf, 6 × 9. Binding, cloth. With 2 portraits. Type,
Caslon.

[229]

The Merrymount Press

[623]

[*within rules*] In Memoriam | Ruth Sibley Hilton | September 14, 1908 | March 15, 1925 | [*floret*]. [n. d.]

Colophon: The Merrymount Press, Boston. Collation: [1–13]. Leaf, 5¾ × 8⅛. Binding, paper. Rubricated throughout. With portrait. Type, Blado.

[624]

The | First Baptist Church | of | Pittsburgh | [*cut*] | Pittsburgh, Pennsylvania | A. D. MDCCCCXXV.

On reverse of title: D. B. Updike, The Merrymount Press, Boston. Collation: i–x, 1–91, [92]. Leaf, 7½ × 10. Binding, paper. With 53 illustrations. Type, Caslon.

[625]

[*within border*] The Public Latin School | of Boston | in the World War | 1914–1918 | [*printer's ornament*] | A Roll of Honor | Boston | 1925.

Colophon: Twenty-six copies of this Book were printed for the Boston Latin School Association by D. B. Updike, The Merrymount Press, Boston, in December 1925. Collation: 1–278. Leaf, 10⅜ × 13⅞. Binding, boards. Rubricated title. Type, Poliphilus and Blado.

[626]

The Record | of Those who Gave to an Endowment Fund collected by | The National Society of | The Colonial Dames of America | for the Maintenance of | Sulgrave Manor | The Home of the Ancestors of George Washington | in Sulgrave, Northamptonshire, England | [*arms*] | Printed for the National Society | MDCCCCXXV.

Colophon: [*arms*] Forty-eight Copies of this Book were printed for The National Society of The Colonial Dames of America by D. B. Updike, The Merrymount Press, Boston, in the Month of June MDCCCCXXV [*floret*]. This is number —. Collation: i–x, 1–108, [109–113]. Leaf, 12½ × 18⅞. Binding, boards. Rubricated title and colophon. Type, Monotype and hand-set Caslon.

[627]

The Metropolitan Museum of Art | Addresses | on the Occasion of the | Opening of | The American Wing | [*printer's ornament*] | New York | 1925.

[230]

Bibliography

Colophon: Of this volume Five Hundred copies were printed in March, 1925 [*printer's ornament*] By D. B. Updike, The Merrymount Press, Boston [*printer's ornament*]. The ornaments used were among the earliest productions of American typefounders, being made by Binney and Ronaldson, of Philadelphia, in 1812. Collation: [i–viii], 1–33, [34–35]. Leaf, 6¼ × 9⅜. Binding, cloth. Type, Caslon.

[628]
1885–1920 | Class of 1885 | Williams College | [*printer's ornament*] | Thirty-Fifth Reunion | [*printer's ornament*] | Secretary's Report | & | Dinner Verses. [n. d.]

On reverse of title: D. B. Updike, The Merrymount Press, Boston. Collation: 1–15. Leaf, 5½ × 8½. Binding, paper. With 2 illustrations. Type, Caslon.

[629]
The History | of | Little Billy | & | His Grand-Pa | A Tale | For Young and Old | Adorn'd with Cuts | Barnstable | Printed for, and to be had from, the | Author. MDCCCXXV.

Colophon: Two Copies Printed By D. B. Updike, The Merrymount Press, Boston. Collation: i–viii, 1–10, [11]. Leaf, 3 × 4. Binding, paper. Type, Caslon.

A second impression of 11 copies was printed in the same month of the same year.

[630]
Eight Songs | for | The Daughters of Hope | [*cut*] | Privately Printed | Providence | 1925.

On reverse of title: D. B. Updike, The Merrymount Press, Boston. Collation: [i–vi], 1–12. Leaf, 5⅛ × 7⅜. Binding, paper. Type, Caslon.

[631]
W. G. M. | Swampscott | August Twelfth | 1891 [*Home Dedication Hymn*]. [n. d.]

On reverse of last page of text: The Merrymount Press, Boston. Collation: [1–8]. Leaf, 3½ × 4⅝. Binding, leather. Type, Caslon.

[632]
[*within rules with arms*] The Book of Remembrance | Being a Record of Gifts to | The Glebe-House | or Parsonage | at

The Merrymount Press

Woodbury, Connecticut | The Birthplace of | American Episcopacy. [n. d.]

On reverse of title: The Merrymount Press, Boston. Collation: [1–48]. Leaf, 9½ × 12. Rubricated throughout. Type, Caslon and Black-letter.

1 copy printed. Printed sheets only supplied by the Press.

Minor Printing

The Carnegie Foundation for the Advancement of Teaching, Twentieth Annual Report of the President and of the Treasurer, New York; *also* Publications of the Foundation.

Reports: John Carter Brown Library, Providence; Annual Report of the President, Brown University, Providence; Carnegie Corporation of New York, Report of the President & of the Treasurer, New York; *also* Report of the Treasurer.

Catalogues of Schools and Universities: Saint Mark's School, Southborough, Massachusetts; The Browne & Nichols School, Cambridge; The Beaver Country Day School, Incorporated, Chestnut Hill, Massachusetts; Pomfret School, 1924–25, Pomfret, Connecticut; Trinity College, 1924–1925, Hartford; Wheaton College, 1924–1925, Norton, Massachusetts; Brown University, 1925–1926, Providence.

Catalogues of Exhibitions: An Exhibition of Sporting Books and Sporting Prints, The Club of Odd Volumes; Exhibition of Etchings by Rembrandt, 1606–1669, New York; Exhibition of Etchings and Dry Points by Whistler, New York.

Catalogue Fenway Court; *also* Catalogue Isabella Stewart Gardner Museum, Fenway Court.

Boston College, The New Library Building, University Heights, Chestnut Hill, Massachusetts.

Bulletin of Class of 1879 [*Harvard College*], June 1, 1925.

The Rescue and Education of Russian Children & Youth in Exile, 1915–1925.

Club of Odd Volumes, Officers for 1925.

Bibliography

1926

[633]

[*within border*] The Ghost in | the Attic | and Other Verses by | George S. Bryan | New York | Alfred A. Knopf | 1926.

On reverse of title: Printed by D. B. Updike, The Merrymount Press, Boston, U. S. A. Collation: i–x, 1–145, [146]. Leaf, 5⅛×7¼. Binding, boards. Type, Oxford.

[634]

Occasional Verses | 1873–1923 | By | Robert Grant | [*cut*] | Boston | Privately Printed | 1926.

Colophon: Three hundred copies of this book were printed by D. B. Updike, The Merrymount Press, Boston, in December, 1926. Collation: i–xiv, 1–165, [166–167]. Leaf, 5×7¼. Binding, cloth. Type, Oxford.

[635]

James Colles | 1788–1883 | Life & Letters | By | Emily Johnston De Forest | [*crest*] | New York | Privately printed | 1926.

Colophon: Of this volume four hundred copies were printed by D. B. Updike, The Merrymount Press, Boston, in March, 1926. Collation: i–xvi, 1–299, [300–301]. Leaf, 6¼×9½. Binding, boards. With 30 illustrations. Type, Caslon Monotype.

[636]

Essays & Verses | About Books | By | Beverly Chew | [*cut*] | New York | 1926.

Colophon: Of this Book Two hundred and seventy-five copies have been printed by D. B. Updike, The Merrymount Press, Boston, in November, 1926. Collation: i–xii, [i–ii], 1–107, [108–109]. Leaf, 6¼×9⅝. Binding, boards. Rubricated title. With woodcut by Rudolph Ruzicka and 18 facsimile reproductions of title-pages. Type, Caslon.

[637]

The Beginnings of a Parish | A Paper read before the Men's Guild of the | Church of the Advent | December 31, 1925 | By | George O. G. Coale | [*cut*] | Boston | Printed for the Guild | A.D. 1926.

The Merrymount Press

On reverse of title: D. B. Updike, The Merrymount Press, Boston. Collation: [i–ii], 1–32. Leaf, 5¼ × 8⅛. Binding, paper. Type, Caslon.

[638]
Events | which led to the Development | of the Literature of | the Middle Ages | By | Thomas L. Raymond | [*florets*] | Public Library | Newark, New Jersey | 1926.

On reverse of title: The Merrymount Press, Boston. Collation: i–viii, [i–ii], 1–32, [33]. Leaf, 4⅝ × 6⅞. Binding, boards. Type, Caslon.
Also issued in paper covers.

[639]
From Sheep Pasture to | Flower Garden | A Paper | read at a Meeting of the | Castine Garden Club | by | a Member | [*printer's ornament*] | Boston | Privately printed | 1926.

On reverse of title: D. B. Updike, The Merrymount Press, Boston. Collation: [i–ii], 1–10. Leaf, 4½ × 6⅞. Binding, paper. Type, Caslon.

[640]
The Metropolitan Museum of Art | Memorial | Exhibition | of the Work | of | John Singer | Sargent | [*floret*] | New York | January 4 through February 14 | 1926.

Colophon: Of this Catalogue two thousand copies have been printed by D. B. Updike, The Merrymount Press, Boston, in January, 1926. One hundred additional copies have also been printed on larger paper. Collation: i–xxiv, 1–14, [15–93]. Leaf, 6½ × 9⅝. Binding, paper. With 72 illustrations. Type, Oxford.

[641]
The Same.

Colophon: Of this Catalogue two thousand copies have been printed by D. B. Updike, The Merrymount Press, Boston, in January, 1926. This is one of a hundred additional copies printed on larger paper. Leaf, 6⅞ × 10⅜. Binding, boards.

[642]
Gleanings from Forefathers' | A Memorial Souvenir | by | Charles B. Wright | [*printer's ornament*] | Middlebury Historical Society | Middlebury, Vermont | 1926.

Bibliography

Colophon: Three hundred copies of this book were printed by D. B. Updike, The Merrymount Press, Boston, in December, 1926. Collation: i–xvi, 1–96, [97–99]. Leaf, 4½ × 7⅛. Binding, boards. With frontispiece. Type, Caslon.

[643]
A Completed Century | 1826–1926 | The Story of | Heywood-Wakefield Company | [*florets*] | Boston | Printed for the Company | 1926.

On reverse of title: D. B. Updike, The Merrymount Press, Boston. Collation: i–viii, 1–111, [112]. Leaf, 7⅝ × 10⅛. Binding, cloth. Rubricated title. With numerous illustrations. Type, Caslon.

[644]
The | Benjamin Crehore | Piano | An Account in the Form of Notes | Compiled by | Charles L. Crehore | [*cut*] | Boston | Privately Printed | 1926.

Colophon: Of this book fifty copies were printed by D. B Updike, The Merrymount Press, Boston, in the month of July, 1926. Collation: [i–viii], 1–28, [29–31]. Leaf, 6×9. Binding, boards. With 6 illustrations. Type, Caslon.

[645]
A Book of Sonnets | Chosen by | Elizabeth Walker Pontefract | [*floret*] | Privately Printed | 1926.

On reverse of title: D. B. Updike, The Merrymount Press, Boston. Collation: i–xiv, 1–214, [215]. Leaf, 4¼ × 5¼. Binding, leather. Type, Caslon. *75 copies printed.*

[646]
Samuel Swett Green | By | Robert Kendall Shaw | Librarian, Worcester Public Library | [*floret*] | Chicago | American Library Association | 1926.

Colophon: One thousand copies of this book were printed by D. B. Updike, The Merrymount Press, Boston, in April, 1926, of which five hundred are numbered. Collation: [i–viii], 1–92, [93–94]. Leaf, 5½ × 8⅜. Binding, boards. With portraits. Type, Caslon.
American Library Pioneers, Vol. II.

[647]
Yesterday & To-morrow | A Sermon | preached at St. John's

The Merrymount Press

Church | Wilkinsonville, Massachusetts | on the One Hundredth Anniversary | of the Parish, June 24, 1925 | by | Rev. Samuel S. Drury | [*cut*] | Privately printed | 1926.

On reverse of title: D. B. Updike, The Merrymount Press, Boston. Collation: [i–vi], [i–ii], 1–13, [14]. Leaf, 4¾ × 7⅝. Binding, cloth. Rubricated title. Type, Oxford.

[648]
Edith Carpenter Macy | February | 1925 | [*monogram*] | New York | 1926.

Colophon: One hundred copies printed by D. B. Updike, The Merrymount Press, Boston. Collation: [i–vi], 1–132, [133–135]. Leaf, 7½ × 9⅞. Binding, boards. With portrait. Type, Mountjoye.

8 copies were bound in full leather.

[649]
The Carnegie Foundation | for the Advancement of Teaching | Bulletin Number Seventeen | Retiring Allowances for Officers | and Teachers in Virginia Public Schools | A Study made at the request of | the Virginia State Teachers Association and | the State Board of Education | By Clyde Furst, Raymond L. Mattocks, and | Howard J. Savage | of The Carnegie Foundation | With a Preface | By Henry S. Pritchett | President of The Foundation | [*seal*] | New York | 1926.

On reverse of title: D. B. Updike, The Merrymount Press, Boston. Collation: i–vi, 1–70. Leaf, 6⅛ × 9¼. Binding, paper. With chart. Type, Scotch-face.

[650]
Dental Education | in the United States and Canada | A Report to The Carnegie Foundation | for the Advancement of Teaching | By | William J. Gies | With a Preface by Henry S. Pritchett | President of The Foundation | Bulletin Number Nineteen | [*seal*] | New York | The Carnegie Foundation | for the Advancement of Teaching | 522 Fifth Avenue | 1926.

On reverse of title: D. B. Updike, The Merrymount Press, Boston. Collation: i–xxii, 1–692. Leaf, 7⅜ × 10. Binding, paper. Type, Scotch-face.

Bibliography

Minor Printing

The Carnegie Foundation for the Advancement of Teaching, Twenty-first Annual Report of the President and of the Treasurer, New York.

Reports: John Carter Brown Library, Providence; Annual Report of the President, Brown University, Providence.

Catalogues of Schools and Universities: Saint Mark's School, Southborough, Massachusetts (*1925–1926 and 1926–1927 issued in 1926*); The Browne & Nichols School, Cambridge; Wheaton College, 1925–1926, Norton, Massachusetts; Brown University, 1926–1927, Providence.

Catalogue Isabella Stewart Gardner Museum, Fenway Court.

The Metropolitan Museum of Art, Membership MCMXXVI, New York.

Tileston & Hollingsworth Company, Calendar for February.

New Fifth Avenue Office of the Farmers' Loan & Trust Company, New York.

The Club of Odd Volumes, Officers for the Year 1926.

The Merrymount Press, Boston, Its Aims, Work, and Equipment.

1927

[651]

[*within border*] The American Institute of Graphic Arts | A Plan of | Printing Instruction | for | Public Schools | [*printer's ornament*] | By Henry H. Taylor | New York: The John Day Company, MDCCCCXXVII.

On reverse of title: D. B. Updike, The Merrymount Press, Boston. Collation: i–xxii, 1–35, [36]. Leaf, 5⅜ × 8. Binding, cloth. With facsimile reproduction. Type, Caslon.

[652]

Thoughts | on | Religion and Morality | By | James Eddy | [*floret*] | [*quotation*] | Privately printed | The Merrymount Press | Boston | 1927.

The Merrymount Press

Collation: i–xii, 1–50, [51]. Leaf, 4½ × 7⅛. Binding, cloth. With portrait. Type, Caslon.

[653]

The | Higher Citizenship | Two Addresses | By Alfred L. Baker | [*floret*] | Chicago | Privately printed | 1927.

Colophon: Seven hundred and fifty copies of this book, of which two hundred and fifty are on handmade paper, were printed by D. B. Updike, The Merrymount Press, Boston, in November, 1927. Collation: 1–41, [42–43]. Leaf, 5⅛ × 7⅞. Binding, boards. Rubricated. Type, Lutetia.

[654]

The Same.

Leaf, 5⅛ × 8. Binding, half morocco.

[655]

Games and Sports | in | British Schools and Universities | By | Howard J. Savage | Staff Member | The Carnegie Foundation for the Advancement of Teaching | [*seal*] | New York | The Carnegie Foundation | for the Advancement of Teaching | 522 Fifth Avenue. [n. d.]

On reverse of title: D. B. Updike, The Merrymount Press, Boston. Collation: i–viii, 1–252. Leaf, 7⅜ × 10. Binding, paper. Type, Scotch-face.
Bulletin Number Eighteen.

[656]

Arnold Green | A Sketch by | Frances M. G. Wayland | 1840–1926 | [*floret*] | Privately printed | 1927.

Colophon: One hundred and seventy-five copies printed by D. B. Updike, The Merrymount Press, Boston, in December, 1927. Collation: i–x, 1–77, [78–79]. Leaf, 4¼ × 6⅞. Binding, cloth. With 6 photogravures. Type, Oxford.

[657]

The Quality of | the Educational Process | in the United States and | in Europe | By | William S. Learned | [*floret*] | First printed in the Annual Reports of | The Carnegie Foundation | [*seal*] | New York | The Carnegie Foundation | for the Advancement of Teaching | 522 Fifth Avenue. [n. d.]

Bibliography

On reverse of title: D. B. Updike, The Merrymount Press, Boston. Collation: i–x, 1–133. Leaf, 7⅜ × 10. Binding, paper. With table. Type, Scotchface.

Bulletin Number Twenty.

[658]
At Burn Side | Verses by Two Friends | [*cut*] | Privately printed | 1927.

Colophon: One hundred and fifty copies of this book were printed by D. B. Updike, The Merrymount Press, Boston, in January, 1927. This is Number —. Collation: [i–vi], 1–18, [19–21]. Leaf, 4⅞ × 7¼. Binding, boards. Type, Oxford.

[659]
Memoirs | of | Mary Baker Eddy | By | Adam H. Dickey, C.S.D. | [*floret*] | Published by | Lillian S. Dickey, C.S.B. | Brookline, Massachusetts | 1927.

On reverse of title: The Merrymount Press, Boston. Collation: i–xviii, 1–141. Leaf, 5½ × 8. Binding, cloth. With portrait and facsimiles. Type, Mountjoye.

This book was suppressed at the instance of the Christian Science authorities and as many copies were recalled as possible.

[660]
Lord Byron | to | Tom Moore | A Facsimile | of the Original Manuscript of | "My boat is on the shore" | St. Louis | Privately printed | 1927.

Colophon: Four hundred copies printed by D. B. Updike, The Merrymount Press, Boston, December, 1927. Collation: [1–9]. Leaf, 4⅜ × 6⅜. Binding, paper. Type, Scotch-face.

[661]
[*within cut*] An | Accomplished | Female | Friend | Christmas | MCMXXVII.

Colophon: Printed in an Edition of 100 copies for Mr. and Mrs. John Munro Woolsey at The Merrymount Press, Christmas, 1927. Collation: [1–7]. Leaf, 3¾ × 5⅞. Binding, paper. Type, Scotch-face.

[662]
Occasional Verses | 1873–1923 | By | Robert Grant | [*cut*] | New York | Charles Scribner's Sons | 1927.

The Merrymount Press

On reverse of title: D. B. Updike, The Merrymount Press, Boston. Collation: [i–ii], i–xiv, 1–165.

Reissue of No. 634.

Minor Printing

The Carnegie Foundation for the Advancement of Teaching, Twenty-second Annual Report of the President and of the Treasurer, New York; *also* The Study of English, by Clyde Furst, Secretary to the Carnegie Foundation; College Athletics and Scholarship; *and* Publications of the Foundation.

Reports: John Carter Brown Library, Providence; Annual Report of the President, Brown University, Providence; Ninety-first Annual Report, Providence Athenaeum, Providence.

Catalogues of Schools and Universities: Avon Old Farms, Avon, Connecticut; Brown University, 1927–1928, Providence; *also* The Graduate School.

The Metropolitan Museum of Art, Substance of a Statement made to the Board of Trustees by the President, Robert W. DeForest, New York, 1926; *also* The Metropolitan Museum of Art, What It Is & What It Does, A Dictionary of Museum Facts and Activities; *and* The Metropolitan Museum of Art, Reproductions on Sale of Objects in the Collections.

Tricennial Exhibition of the Society of Arts & Crafts.

The Club of Odd Volumes of Boston, List of Officers and Members; *also* Officers for the Year 1927.

All Saints' Church, Peterborough, New Hampshire.

Helen Choate Bell, by Paulina Cony Drown, Cambridge.

1928

[663]

Musical | Discourse | From The New York Times | By | Richard Aldrich | [*cut*] | Oxford University Press | London: Humphrey Milford | New York Toronto Melbourne | Cape Town Bombay | 1928.

On reverse of title: D. B. Updike, The Merrymount Press, Boston. Collation: [i–viii], 1–304, [305]. Leaf, 5 × 7¼. Binding, boards. Type, Scotch-face.

Bibliography

[664]

The | House on the Down | and Other Poems | By | Dorothy
Davis Coburn | [*floret*] | Illustrated by Harold Field Kellogg |
Boston | Privately Printed | 1928.

On reverse of title: D. B. Updike, The Merrymount Press, Boston. Collation: i–x, 1–98. Leaf, 5 × 7¼. Binding, boards. Type, Oxford.

[665]

Notes | By | Lady Louisa Stuart | on | George Selwyn and
His Contemporaries | By John Heneage Jesse | Edited from
the Original Manuscript by | W. S. Lewis | New York | Ox-
ford University Press | London: Humphrey Milford | 1928.

On page facing title: Of this volume five hundred copies have been printed
in November, 1928, by D. B. Updike, The Merrymount Press, U. S. A.,
Boston. Of this number four hundred and seventy are for sale. This copy
is number —. Collation: i–xiv, 1–65. Leaf, 7½ × 9¾. Binding, boards. With
portrait and facsimile. Type, Caslon.

[666]

The | Complete Angler | or | The Contemplative Man's |
Recreation | By Isaac Walton | With an Introduction by |
Bliss Perry | and Decorations by | W. A. Dwiggins | [*flo-
ret*] | Boston | C. E. Goodspeed & Co. | 1928.

Colophon: [*floret*] Of this Edition of The Complete Angler six hundred
copies have been printed by D. B. Updike, The Merrymount Press, Boston,
in the Month of April, 1928. Collation: i–xxxii, 1–323, [324–325]. Leaf,
4⅝ × 7. Binding, boards. Rubricated title. With 5 illustrations in colours.
Type, Oxford.
Binding designed by W. A. Dwiggins.

[667]

A Memorial Tablet | Placed in Remembrance of | Nettie
Fowler McCormick | In the Pope Memorial Church | North
Cohasset, Massachusetts | Dedicated Anno Domini 1927 |
[*cut*] | Privately printed | 1928.

Colophon: One hundred copies of this book were printed, by D. B. Updike,
The Merrymount Press, Boston, in the Month of June, 1928 [*floret*]. Collation: 1–20, [21–23]. Leaf, 7⅜ × 9⅞. Binding, morocco. Title in blue and
black. With illustration in colour. Type, Lutetia.

[241]

The Merrymount Press

[668]

Thoughts | on | Religion and Morality | By | James Eddy | [*floret*] | [*quotation*] | Privately printed | The Merrymount Press | Boston | 1927.

Reissue of No. 652.

[669]

A Chronological List of the Books | Printed at The Kelmscott Press [*floret*] | With Illustrative Material from | a Collection made by William Mor-|ris and Henry C. Marillier [*floret*] Now | in the Library of Marsden J. Perry | of Providence Rhode Island.

Colophon: [*floret*] Eight hundred copies printed at The Merrymount Press, Boston, in the Month of May, MDCCCCXXVIII. Collation: i–viii, [i–ii], 1–42, [43–44]. Leaf, 5⅝ × 8⅛. Binding, paper. Type, Poliphilus.
Printed for presentation to members of the Grolier Club, New York.

[670]

Egyptian Literature | A Lecture by | Arthur Cruttenden Mace | Late Associate Curator | Department of Egyptian Art | [*cut*] | New York | The Metropolitan Museum of Art | 1928.

On reverse of title: D. B. Updike, The Merrymount Press, Boston. Collation: [i–vi], 1–32. Leaf, 6 × 9½. Binding, boards. Type, Lutetia.
250 copies printed.

[671]

The Silversmiths of | Little Rest | By | William Davis Miller | [*cut*] | Kingston | Rhode Island | 1928.

On reverse of title: D. B. Updike, The Merrymount Press, Boston. Collation: i–xii, 1–50. Leaf, 7½ × 9⅞. Binding, boards. With 19 illustrations. Type, Caslon.

[672]

Present-Day Law Schools | in the United States | and Canada | By | Alfred Zantzinger Reed | Bulletin Number Twenty-one | [*seal*] | New York City | 522 Fifth Avenue | 1928.

On reverse of title: D. B. Updike, The Merrymount Press, Boston. Collation: i–xvi, 1–598. Leaf, 6⅛ × 9¼. Binding, paper. With 3 tables. Type, Scotch-face.

Bibliography

[673]

West-running | Brook | By | Robert Frost | [*publisher's mark*] |
New York | Henry Holt and Company. [n. d.]

On page preceding half-title: One thousand copies of West-running Brook
have been specially printed and bound, and have been signed by the
Author. Of these, nine hundred and eighty copies are for sale. This copy
is Number —. On reverse of title: D. B. Updike, The Merrymount Press,
Boston. Collation: [i–ii], i–viii, 1–58. Leaf, 6 × 9. Binding, boards. With
4 illustrations. Type, Poliphilus.

Illustrations by J. J. Lankes.

[674]

Hunt Clubs | and | Country Clubs | in America | [*cut*] | Bos-
ton | Privately printed | 1928.

On reverse of title: D. B. Updike, The Merrymount Press, Boston. Collation: i–xxiv, 1–95. Leaf, 6⅛ × 8½. Binding, cloth. With 24 illustrations.
Type, Oxford.

[675]

Games and Sports | in | British Schools and Universities |
By | Howard J. Savage | Staff Member | The Carnegie Foun-
dation for the Advancement of Teaching | [Second Edition] |
[*seal*] | New York | The Carnegie Foundation | for the Ad-
vancement of Teaching | 522 Fifth Avenue. [n. d.]

Reissue of No. 655.

[676]

The Quality of | the Educational Process | in the United
States and | in Europe | By William S. Learned | [*floret*] |
First printed in the Annual Reports of | The Carnegie Foun-
dation | [*seal*] | New York | The Carnegie Foundation | for
the Advancement of Teaching | 522 Fifth Avenue. [n. d.]

Reissue of No. 657.

[677]

Harvard Boathouse | Memorial | [*floret*] | Description | [*print-
er's ornament*] | Boathouse History | Privately printed | July
1928.

[243]

The Merrymount Press

On reverse of title: D. B. Updike, The Merrymount Press, Boston. Collation: [i–iv], 1–22, [23–25]. Leaf, 7¾ × 10¾. Binding, boards. With 5 illustrations. Type, Scotch-face.

[678]
An Account of | the Dedicatory Ceremonies | in connection with the | Base Hospital No. 5 | Memorial | [*floret*] | Privately printed | 1928.

On reverse of title: D. B. Updike, The Merrymount Press, Boston. Collation: 1–19, [20]. Leaf, 5½ × 8⅛. Binding, paper. With 5 illustrations. Type, Caslon.

[679]
[*floret*] The Form of | Consecration of | St. George's Chapel | April xxiii, Anno Domini | MDCCCCXXVIII [*florets*] | St. George's School | Middletown, Rhode Island.

Colophon: Six hundred copies printed at The Merrymount Press, Boston, April, 1928. Collation: [i–iv], 1–57, [58–60]. Leaf, 4¼ × 6⅜. Binding, cloth. Rubricated throughout. Type, Janson.

[680]
The Carnegie Foundation | for the Advancement of Teaching | Bulletin Number Twenty-two | A Retirement Plan for | Colorado Public Schools | A Study made at the Request of | The Colorado Education Association and the | State Department of Public Instruction | By | Howard J. Savage, Carnegie Foundation, and Edmund S. Cogswell, Consulting Actuary | With an Introduction by | Clyde Furst | Secretary of the Foundation | [*seal*] | New York | 1928.

On reverse of title: D. B. Updike, The Merrymount Press, Boston. Collation: i–x, 1–72. Leaf, 6⅛ × 9¼. Binding, paper. Type, Scotch-face.

Minor Printing

The Carnegie Foundation for the Advancement of Teaching, Twenty-third Annual Report of the President and of the Treasurer, New York; *also* Publications of the Foundation; Program for a Study of the Relations of Secondary and Higher Education in Pennsylvania, Abstract of a Report, *etc.*; Study of the Relations of

Bibliography

Higher Education in Pennsylvania, Memorandum of Procedure in Section II, in 1928; *and* Review of Legal Education in the United States and Canada for the Years 1926 and 1927, by Alfred Z. Reed.

Reports: John Carter Brown Library, Providence; Annual Report of the President, Brown University, Providence; Ninety-second Annual Report, Providence Athenaeum, Providence.

Catalogues of Schools and Universities: Saint Mark's School, Southborough, Massachusetts; Avon Old Farms, Avon, Connecticut; Brown University, 1928–1929, Providence; *also* The Women's College in Brown University, 1927–1928.

Catalogue Isabella Stewart Gardner Museum, Fenway Court.

Cowley, A Quarterly Magazine, Vol. I [*Nos. 1, 2, 3, 4*], Cambridge.

Club of Odd Volumes of Boston, List of Officers and Members, March first, 1928.

Specimen Pamphlet, Encyclopaedia of the Social Sciences, Editor-in-Chief Edwin R. A. Seligman, LL.D., HON.D., New York.

Lancaster in the Great War, 1914–1918, Roll of Honor, Lancaster, Massachusetts.

Description of The Merrymount Press, Boston (*illustrated*).

1929

[681]

American First Editions | Bibliographic Check Lists of the Works | of One Hundred and Five | American Authors | [*floret*] | Edited by Merle Johnson | Compiler of A Bibliography of Mark Twain, A Bibliographic Check List | of James Branch Cabell, High Spots of American Literature, | &c., &c. | New York | R. R. Bowker Co. | 1929.

On reverse of title: Printed in a limited edition of 1,000 copies by D. B. Updike, The Merrymount Press, Boston. Collation: i–viii, 1–242. Leaf, 6¼ × 9¼. Binding, cloth. Type, Caslon.

[682]

[*within rules*] Quarto Club | Papers | MCMXXVII–MCMXXVIII | [*cut*] | New York | Printed for the Members | MCMXXIX.

The Merrymount Press

Colophon: [*seal*] Of this, the Second Collection of Quarto Club Papers, ninety-nine numbered copies have been printed by D. B. Updike, The Merrymount Press, Boston, in the month of March, 1929. This is number —. Collation: [i–x], 1–152, [153–155]. Leaf, 6⅛ × 8⅜. Binding, cloth. Title, chapter-initials, and colophon in black and burnt ochre. Type, Oxford.

[683]

Old Mrs. Chundle | A Short Story | By | Thomas Hardy | [*cut*] | New York | Crosby Gaige | 1929.

Colophon: Of this story—written about 1880–1890 and probably intended to be included in the volume entitled "Life's Little Ironies," or "Wessex Tales,"—742 copies have been printed on Zanders hand-made paper, and 13 on gray French Ingres paper, by D. B. Updike, The Merrymount Press, Boston, January, 1929. Of these, 700 copies, numbered from 1 to 700, inclusive, are for sale, and will be distributed by Random House. This is copy number —. Collation: [i–iv], [i–ii], 1–26, [27–29]. Leaf, 5⅞ × 8⅜. Binding, boards. Type, Janson.

[684]

[*border*] | Charles Lemuel Nichols | A Tribute | [*floret*] | William Vail Kellen | Boston | Privately printed | 1929 | [*border*].

Colophon: [*printer's ornament*] One hundred and forty-nine copies printed by D. B. Updike, The Merrymount Press, Boston, in the Month of June, 1929 [*printer's ornament*]. Collation: [i–vi], 1–37, [38–39]. Leaf, 5 × 7⅞. Binding, cloth. Type, Janson.

[685]

[*within border*] The | First American Bible | A Leaf | from a Copy of the Bible translated into | the Indian Language by John Eliot and | printed at Cambridge in New England in | the Year 1663 | With an Account of the Translator and his Labors, | and of the two Printers who produced the Book, by | George Parker Winship | Boston | Printed by D. B. Updike at The Merrymount Press for | Charles E. Goodspeed and Company, Anno Dni 1929.

Collation: [i–iv], 1–20. Leaf, 5⅞ × 7⅝. Binding, cloth. Type, Janson. *Edition limited to 157 copies.*

[686]

Letters | from an Old Sportsman | to a Young One | By

Bibliography

A. Henry Higginson | With a Foreword by Redmond C. Stewart | and | Illustrated by Lionel Edwards | [*cut*] | Doubleday, Doran & Company, Inc. | Garden City, New York | 1929.

Colophon: This book is set in Scotch-face and printed on Wove Antique paper by D. B. Updike, The Merrymount Press, Boston [*floret*]. First Regular Edition, of 1500 copies, published October 25, 1929. Collation: i–xvi, 1–248, [249–251]. Leaf, 6 × 9⅛. Binding, cloth. With 15 illustrations. Type, Scotch-face.

[687]
The Same.

Colophon: This book is set in Scotch-face and printed on Aurelian paper by D. B. Updike, The Merrymount Press, Boston [*floret*]. First published on October 11, 1929, in an edition of 201 copies, of which this is Number —. Collation: i–xviii, 1–248, [249–251]. Leaf, 6¼ × 9¼. Rubricated title.

[688]
Punch and Judy, | With Twenty-eight Illustrations | by | George Cruikshank | Accompanied by the Dialogue of the Puppet-show | an Account of its Origin, and of Puppet-plays | in England by John Payne Collier | Together with a Foreword | By Tony Sarg | And a Bibliographical Note by | Anne Lyon Haight | [*cut*] | New York | Rimimgton & Hooper | 1929.

Colophon: The Savoy Editions, Issue Number Two [*publisher's mark*]. This is Number — of an Edition of 376 copies, designed and printed by D. B. Updike, The Merrymount Press, Boston. Set in Scotch-face Type and printed on Wove Antique paper. Distributed by Doubleday, Doran and Company, Inc., Garden City, New York. Published October 25, 1929. Collation: i–xviii, 1–148, [149]. Leaf, 5 × 8. Binding, boards. Type, Scotch-face.

[689]
Icones Farlowianae | Illustrations of the Larger Fungi | of Eastern North America | By | William Gilson Farlow | With Descriptive Text by | Edward Angus Burt | [*floret*] | The Farlow Library and Herbarium of | Harvard University | Cambridge, Massachusetts | 1929.

The Merrymount Press

On reverse of title: D. B. Updike, The Merrymount Press, Boston. Collation: i–x, 1–120. Leaf, 11⅛ × 14. Binding, cloth. With illustrations in colour. Type, Caslon.

Text only printed by the Press.

[690]
[*within border*] A Soldier's | Manuscript | [*printer's ornament*] | Cornelius Winant | Privately printed | 1929.

Colophon: [*printer's ornament*] Of this book, 250 copies were printed on hand-made paper and 750 on machine-made paper by D. B. Updike, The Merrymount Press, Boston, in November, 1929 [*printer's ornament*]. Collation: i–viii, 1–140, [141–143]. Leaf, 5¼ × 8. Binding, boards. With portrait. Type, Janson.

The hand-made paper edition was bound in half leather.

[691]
Thoughts | on | Religion and Morality | By | James Eddy | [*floret*] | [*quotation*] | Privately printed | The Merrymount Press | Boston | 1927.

Reissue of No. 652.

[692]
[*within border*] Franklin | Evans | or The Inebriate | A Tale of the Times | By | Walter Whitman | With Introduction by | Emory Halloway | [*cut*] | New York: Random House | MDCCCCXXIX.

Colophon: [*cut*] Seven hundred copies of Franklin Evans were printed by D. B. Updike, The Merrymount Press, Boston [*cut*]. Collation: i–xxiv, 1–248, [249–251]. Leaf, 4⅞ × 7⅞. Binding, cloth. Type, Scotch-face.

[693]
Life in Carolina and | New England | During the Nineteenth Century | As Illustrated by Reminiscences and Letters of | The Middleton Family of Charleston | South Carolina | And of the De Wolf Family of Bristol | Rhode Island | [*floret*] | Bristol, Rhode Island | Privately printed | 1929.

Colophon: Five hundred copies of this book were printed by D. B. Updike, The Merrymount Press, Boston, in the Month of August, 1929. Collation: i–xiv, 1–233, [234]. Leaf, 7½ × 9⅝. Binding, cloth. With 50 illustrations. Type, Oxford.

Bibliography

[694]

An Early American | Queen Anne Escritoire | 1715–1730 |
[*floret*] | Privately Printed.

Colophon: Two hundred copies printed by D. B. Updike, The Merrymount
Press, Boston, in the Month of October, 1929. Collation: 1–10, [11]. Leaf,
7½ × 9⅞. Binding, boards. With 5 illustrations. Type, Caslon.

[695]

The Richard C. Jenkinson | Collection of Books | Chosen
to show the Work of | the Best Printers | [*floret*] | Book II |
The Public Library | By Order of its Board of Trustees |
Newark New Jersey | 1929.

Colophon: Five hundred copies of this Catalogue were printed by D. B.
Updike, The Merrymount Press, Boston, in June, 1929. Collation: i–x,
1–189, [190–191]. Leaf, 5⅜ × 7⅞. Binding, boards. Type, Caslon.

Also issued in paper covers.

[696]

A Precious Heritage | An Account of the Life of Rowland
Hazard | and his Wife Margaret Anna Rood | who estab-
lished their Home | Oakwoods, in Peace Dale | Rhode
Island | 1854 | By their Daughter | Caroline Hazard | Peace
Dale, Rhode Island | Privately printed | 1929.

On reverse of title: D. B. Updike, The Merrymount Press, Boston. Collation: i–xiv, 1–367, [368]. Leaf, 5⅞ × 8⅞. Binding, boards. With 8 illustrations. Type, Caslon.

[697]

Recollections of | Joshua Francis Fisher | Written in 1864 |
[*floret*] | Arranged by Sophia Cadwalader | Privately Printed |
1929.

On reverse of title: D. B. Updike, The Merrymount Press, Boston. Collation: i–xii, 1–282, [283]. Leaf, 6 × 9. Binding, cloth. With portrait. Type,
Caslon.

[698]

American College | Athletics | By | Howard J. Savage |
Staff Member, Carnegie Foundation for the Advancement
of Teaching | and | Harold W. Bentley, John T. McGovern,

The Merrymount Press

Dean F. Smiley, M.D. | With a Preface by | Henry S. Pritchett | President of the Foundation | Bulletin Number Twenty-three | [*seal*] | New York | The Carnegie Foundation | for the Advancement of Teaching | 522 Fifth Avenue | 1929.

On reverse of title: D. B. Updike, The Merrymount Press, Boston. Collation: i–xxii, 1–383. Leaf, 7⅜ × 10. Binding, paper. Type, Scotch-face. *1000 copies were bound in cloth.*

[699]
Our Guests | Mary Ann and Her Predecessors | By Lucy Maynard Salmon | [*cut*] | Privately printed | 1929.

Colophon: [*cut*] One hundred copies of Our Guests were printed at The Merrymount Press in April, 1929. Collation: i–vi, 1–33, [34–35]. Leaf, 5 × 7¼. Binding, cloth. Type, Scotch-face.

[700]
A Catalogue | of Medical Incunabula contained in | The William Norton Bullard | Loan Collection | deposited in | The Boston Medical Library | [*floret*] | Compiled by James F. Ballard | Boston | Privately printed | 1929.

Colophon: Two hundred and fifty copies of this catalogue were printed by D. B. Updike, The Merrymount Press, Boston, in the month of July, 1929. Collation: i–viii, 1–75, [76–77]. Leaf, 7½ × 9⅞. Binding, cloth. With facsimile illustration. Type, Caslon.

[701]
William Bradford Homer Dowse | A Memoir | By William Vail Kellen | [*floret*] | Boston | Privately Printed | 1929.

On reverse of title: One hundred and fifty copies printed by D. B. Updike, The Merrymount Press, Boston, September, 1929. Collation: [i–iv], 1–43, [44]. Leaf, 5 × 7½. Binding, cloth. With portrait. Type, Janson.

[702]
An Appreciation | Eliza Greene Chace | March 2, 1851–December 9, 1924 | [*floret*] | Providence | Privately printed | 1929.

Colophon: One hundred copies printed by D. B. Updike, The Merrymount Press, Boston, in the month of May, 1929 [*floret*]. Collation: [i–vi], [i–ii], 1–32, [33–35]. Leaf, 5⅛ × 8. Binding, cloth. With portrait. Type, Mountjoye.

Bibliography

[703]

The Diversions of a Will Collector | A Dialogue | Mark G. Holstein.

Colophon: Of this Paper, which was read by the author to the Quarto Club in New York City, two hundred and fifty-one copies have been privately printed by D. B. Updike, The Merrymount Press, Boston, U. S. A., in 1929. Collation: 1–39, [40]. Leaf, 6⅛ × 8⅜. Binding, paper. Rubricated initial. Type, Oxford.

[704]

The Literature of | American School and College | Athletics | By | W. Carson Ryan, Jr. | With a Foreword by | Henry S. Pritchett | President of The Carnegie Foundation | [*floret*] | Bulletin Number Twenty-four | [*seal*] | New York | The Carnegie Foundation | for the Advancement of Teaching | 522 Fifth Avenue | 1929.

On reverse of title: D. B. Updike, The Merrymount Press, Boston. Collation: i–xlvi, 1–305. Leaf, 7⅜ × 10. Binding, paper. Type, Scotch-face.

Minor Printing

The Carnegie Foundation for the Advancement of Teaching, Twenty-fourth Annual Report of the President and of the Treasurer, New York; *also* Publications of the Foundation; Letter of Gift, Act of Incorporation, By-Laws, Rules for the Admission of Institutions and for the Granting of Retiring Allowances; Study of the Relations of Secondary and Higher Education in Pennsylvania, A Review of the First Year's Progress, 1928–1929; Athletics, An Element in the Evolution of the American University, by Henry S. Pritchett; *and* Review of Legal Education in the United States and Canada for the Year 1928, by Alfred Z. Reed.

Reports: John Carter Brown Library, Providence; Annual Report of the President, Brown University, Providence; Ninety-third Annual Report, Providence Athenaeum, Providence.

Catalogues of Schools and Universities: Saint Mark's School, Southborough, Massachusetts; Brown University, 1928–1929, Providence; *also* Pembroke College in Brown University, 1928–1929; *and* The Graduate School, 1929–1930.

Catalogue Isabella Stewart Gardner Museum, Fenway Court.

The Merrymount Press

Washington Cathedral, A Form for the Dedication of the Chapel of St. Augustine in the College of Preachers, Washington, D. C.; *also* A Form for the Dedication of the Building of the College of Preachers, Washington, D. C.

The Women's Republican Club of Massachusetts, Programme of Statecraft Institute.

The Limited Editions Club, Incorporated, The Classics of the World's Literature, New York.

Cowley, A Quarterly Magazine, Vol. II [*Nos. 1, 2, 3*], Cambridge.

1930

[705]
The Three Wayfarers | A Play in One Act | By | Thomas Hardy | Dramatized from his story "The Three Strangers" | Illustrated by William H. Cotton | [*floret*] | New York: The Fountain Press | London: The Cayme Press | 1930.

Colophon: Of this book five hundred and forty-two copies, of which five hundred are for sale, were printed by D. B. Updike, The Merrymount Press, Boston, U. S. A., in February, 1930. Distributed in America by Random House, and in Great Britain by Humphrey Toulmin at The Cayme Press, Ltd. This is Number —. Collation: [i–viii], 1–34, [35–37]. Leaf, 7½ × 9⅞. Binding, half leather. With 4 illustrations in colour. Type, Janson.

[706]
Pineapples | of Finest Flavour | or | A Selection of Sundry Unpublished Letters | of the English Roscius, David Garrick | [*floret*] | Edited with an Introduction and Notes by | David Mason Little | Cambridge | Harvard University Press | 1930.

Colophon: Printed by D. B. Updike, The Merrymount Press, Boston, in the month of February, 1930, in an edition limited to four hundred copies, of which this is Number —. Collation: i–xx, 1–100, [101–103]. Leaf, 7¾ × 10½. Binding, cloth. With 3 facsimile letters. Type, Janson.

[707]
The Boston Society of | Natural History | 1830–1930 | [*quotation*] | [*seal*] | Boston | Printed for the Society | 1930.

Bibliography

Colophon: D. B. Updike, The Merrymount Press, Boston. Collation: i–xii, 1–117, [118–119]. Leaf, 7½ × 9⅞. Binding, boards. With 39 illustrations. Type, Scotch-face.

The title on the cover is "Milestones."

[708]

[*border*] | All About | Mother Goose | By | Vincent Starrett | [*printer's ornament*] | The Apellicon Press | 1930. | [*border*].

Colophon: Of this book, 275 copies have been printed (of which 250 are for sale), by D. B. Updike, The Merrymount Press, Boston, in April, 1930. Collation: [i–iv], [i–ii], 1–40, [41]. Leaf, 5¾ × 8¼. Binding, boards. Type, Janson.

[709]

The Glory of the Nightingales | By | Edward Arlington Robinson | [*floret*] | New York | The Macmillan Company | 1930.

Colophon: Of this edition, 500 copies have been printed by D. B. Updike, The Merrymount Press, Boston. This is copy No. —. Collation: [i–viii], 1–82, [83–85]. Leaf, 5¾ × 8½. Binding, cloth. Rubricated title. Type, Janson.

[710]

As Hounds Ran | Four Centuries of Foxhunting | Edited by A. Henry Higginson | With Forewords by John Masefield | and Edgar Astley Milne | Illustrated with Contemporary Prints and with New Drawings by | Cecil Aldin & Lionel Edwards | [*floret*] | New York: Huntington Press: MDCCCXXX.

Colophon: Printed by D. B. Updike, The Merrymount Press, Boston, the text hand set in Janson type, printed on Leipsig paper. Of an edition of 990 copies for America & England this is Number —. Collation: i–xxviii, 1–240, [241]. Leaf, 7½ × 9⅞. Binding, cloth. With 30 illustrations. Type, Janson.

[711]

The Fables of | Jean de la Fontaine | Newly translated into English Verse | by Joseph Auslander and | Jacques Le Clercq | With Title-page and Decorations engraved on Copper | by Rudolph Ruzicka | [*floret*] | Volume I | Books I–VI translated by | Joseph Auslander | [Volume II | Books VII–XII

The Merrymount Press

translated by | Jacques Le Clercq] | New York | The Limited Editions Club | 1930.

Colophon: This is Copy Number — of fifteen hundred copies of this Limited Edition of The Fables of La Fontaine translated by Joseph Auslander and Jacques Le Clercq, illustrated with engravings on copper by Rudolph Ruzicka, printed for the members of The Limited Editions Club by D. B. Updike, The Merrymount Press, Boston, U. S. A., and signed· by the illustrator. Collation: Vol. I, i–xxii, 1–265, [266]; Vol. II, i–xiv, 1–398, [399–404]. Leaf, 5½ × 8⅝. Binding, cloth. With titles and 12 half-title decorations engraved. Type, Janson.

[712]
[*within border*] Bill Pratt | The Saw-Buck | Philosopher | [*floret*] | An Appreciation of the | Life, Public Services, and | Speeches of One who for | over half a Century | ministered to the En-|tertainment and Edifi-|cation of the Students | of Williams College. By | John Sheridan Zelie of | the Class of 'Eighty-|seven, and Carroll Perry | of the Class of 'Ninety. | [*florets*] | Williamstown, MDCCCXCV.

Reissue of No. 13.

[713]
The Book of | Common Prayer | and Administration of the Sacraments | and Other Rites and Ceremonies | of the Church | According to the Use of the | Protestant Episcopal Church | in the United States of America | [*floret*] | Together with The Psalter | or Psalms of David | Printed for the Commission |
A. D. MDCCCCXXVIII.

Colophon: Of this standard edition of The Book of Common Prayer five hundred copies were printed by D. B. Updike, The Merrymount Press, Boston, Massachusetts, A. D. MDCCCCXXX. Collation: i–xlii, 1–611, [612–613]. Leaf, 9½ × 13⅜. Binding, leather. Rubricated throughout. Type, Janson.
The date on the title-page refers to the year of the Prayer Book revision, that in the colophon to the year of issue.

[714]
[*within rules*] War Books | By | H. M. Tomlinson | A Lecture | Given at Manchester University | February 15, 1929 | The Rowfant Club | Cleveland, Ohio | 1930.

[254]

Bibliography

Colophon: [*printer's ornament*] Of this book, 215 copies were printed by D. B. Updike, The Merrymount Press, Boston, U.S.A., in the month of February, 1930. No. — [*printer's ornament*]. Collation: [i–iv], 1–36, [37]. Leaf, 5¼ × 8. Binding, boards. Rubricated title and colophon. Type, Janson.

[715]
The Master of the Voids | By | Walter Maxwell | Author of "Wayside Verses" | &c., &c. | [*floret*] | Washington | 1930.

On reverse of title: D. B. Updike, The Merrymount Press, Boston, U.S.A. Collation: [i–iv], [i–ii], 1–11. Leaf, 5¼ × 7⅜. Binding, cloth. Type, Caslon. *150 copies printed.*

[716]
The Philippine | Club | [*floret*] | Privately Printed | 1930.

Colophon: Of this book, 500 copies have been printed by D. B. Updike, The Merrymount Press, Boston, in the month of June, 1930. Collation: [i–vi], 1–40, [41]. Leaf, 5 × 7⅝. Binding, cloth. With 12 illustrations. Type, Janson.

[717]
Sunshine & Stardust | By | Constance Witherby | [*floret*] | Born September 5, 1913 | Died August 30, 1929 | Privately Printed | 1930.

Colophon: Of this book, seven hundred and fifty copies were printed by D. B. Updike, The Merrymount Press, Boston, in the month of April, 1930. Collation: i–xii, 1–121, [122–123]. Leaf, 5¾ × 8½. Binding, boards. With portrait. Type, Oxford.

[718]
Nailer Tom's Diary | Otherwise | The Journal of Thomas B. Hazard | of Kingstown Rhode Island | 1778 to 1840 | Which includes Observations on the Weather | Records of Births Marriages and Deaths | Transactions by Barter and Money of Varying Value | Preaching Friends and Neighborhood Gossip | Printed as Written and Introduced by | Caroline Hazard | Author of "College Tom" "The Narragansett Friends Meeting" | "Anchors of Tradition" | [*floret*] | Boston | The Merrymount Press | 1930.

The Merrymount Press

On reverse of title: D. B. Updike, The Merrymount Press, Boston. Collation: i–xxiv, 1–808. Leaf, 8¼ × 10¾. Binding, cloth. Type, Caslon monotype. *400 copies printed.*

[719]
John Cotton Dana | 1856–1929 | [*floret*] | Newark, New Jersey | 1930.

Colophon: [*floret*] Five hundred copies of this book have been printed by D. B. Updike, The Merrymount Press, Boston, in July, 1930. Collation: i–viii, 1–125, [126–127]. Leaf, 5⅞ × 8⅜. Binding, boards. With portrait. Type, Caslon.

[720]
A New Bedford Merchant | By Horatio Hathaway | Being Notes taken from Records in the Office | of the late Thomas Schuyler Hathaway | a Successful Shipowner of the | Nineteenth Century | [*floret*] | Privately printed. [n. d.]

On reverse of title: D. B. Updike, The Merrymount Press, Boston. Collation: i–xiv, 1–74, [75]. Leaf, 6½ × 8⅞. Binding, boards. With 15 illustrations and facsimiles. Type, Caslon.
50 copies printed.

[721]
Charles Adelbert | Canfield | By | Caspar Whitney | [*printer's ornament*] | [*printer's ornament*] | New York | Privately Printed | 1930.

Colophon: Of this book, twenty-five copies bound in leather and one hundred and seventy-five bound in boards were printed by D. B. Updike, The Merrymount Press, Boston, in December, 1930. Collation: i–viii, 1–217, [218–219]. Leaf, 9⅛ × 12. Binding, boards. With 14 illustrations. Type, Bodoni.

[722]
Merlin | By Clyde Furst | [*floret*] | New York | 1930.

Colophon: Three hundred copies printed by D. B. Updike, The Merrymount Press, Boston. Collation: [i–vi], 1–22, [23–25]. Leaf, 6¾ × 10. Binding, paper. Type, Janson.

[723]
Anthology of Swedish | Lyrics | from 1750 to 1925 | [*floret*] | Translated in the Original Meters by | Charles Wharton

Bibliography

Stork | Author of "Sea and Bay"; Translator of "Selected Poems | of Gustav Fröding" | New York | The American-Scandinavian Foundation | London: Humphrey Milford | Oxford University Press | 1930.

Collation: [i–ii], i–xl, 1–294, [295–301]. Leaf, 4⅞ × 7⅜.
Reissue of Volume IX of Scandinavian Classics, with additions; see No. 480.

[724]
In Memoriam | William Amory Gardner | A Sermon | preached in Groton School Chapel | by Mr. Peabody | Sunday, February 16 | 1930 | [*cut*] | Groton School | 1930.

On reverse of title: D. B. Updike, The Merrymount Press, Boston. Collation: [i–iv], 1–16. Leaf, 4⅝ × 7⅝. Binding, paper. Type, Oxford.

[725]
John Taylor Bottomley. [n. d.]

On reverse of page iv: The Merrymount Press, Boston. Collation: [i–iv], 1–19, [20]. Leaf, 5 × 7⅝. Binding, cloth. Type, Caslon.

[726]
An Altar Guild | Manual | by | Edith Weir Perry | [*floret*] | Published by | The Diocesan Altar Guild | of Rhode Island. [n. d.]

On reverse of title: D. B. Updike, The Merrymount Press, Boston. Collation: i–xii, 1–59, [60]. Leaf, 4½ × 6⅞. Binding, paper. Type, Caslon.

[727]
Diocese of Massachusetts | The Order of Service for the | Consecration | of | Henry Knox Sherrill | as | Bishop of Massachusetts | at Trinity Church | in the City of Boston | [*seal*] | October the Fourteenth | A. D. MDCCCCXXX.

On reverse of title: D. B. Updike, The Merrymount Press, Boston. Collation: 1–35, [36]. Leaf, 5½ × 8¾. Binding, paper. Rubricated throughout. Type, Caslon.

[728]
The Social Philosophy of | Pensions | With a Review of Existing Pension | Systems for Professional Groups | By |

The Merrymount Press

Henry S. Pritchett | President of the Carnegie Foundation |
Bulletin Number Twenty-five | [*seal*] | New York | The Car-
negie Foundation | for the Advancement of Teaching | 522
Fifth Avenue | 1930.

On reverse of title: D. B. Updike, The Merrymount Press, Boston. Collation: i–iv, 1–85. Leaf, 6⅛ × 9¼. Binding, paper. Type, Scotch-face.

Minor Printing

The Carnegie Foundation for the Advancement of Teaching,
Twenty-fifth Annual Report of the President and of the Treasurer, New York; *also* Study of the Relations of Secondary and
Higher Education in Pennsylvania, the College Sophomore Examination; *and* Review of Legal Education in the United States
and Canada for the Year 1929, by Alfred Z. Reed.

Reports: John Carter Brown Library, Providence; Annual Report
of the President, Brown University, Providence; Ninety-fourth
Annual Report, Providence Athenaeum, Providence.

Catalogues of Schools and Universities: Saint Mark's School,
Southborough, Massachusetts; Brown University, 1929–1930, Providence; *also* Pembroke College in Brown University, 1929–1930;
and The Graduate School, 1930–1931.

Catalogue Isabella Stewart Gardner Museum, Fenway Court.

General Theological Seminary of the Protestant Episcopal
Church.

Introduction by Caroline Hazard to "Nailer Tom's Diary" Otherwise the Journal of Thomas B. Hazard of Kingstown, Rhode
Island, 1778–1840.

The Metropolitan Museum of Art, Reproductions on Sale of
Objects in the Collections, A Cyclopedia of Information, New
York.

Susanna Shanklin Browne, Wyoming, New York.

Cowley, A Quarterly Magazine, Vol. II [*No. 4*], Vol. III [*Nos. 9, 10,
11, 12*], Cambridge.

Rules for Judicial Conduct, Things necessary to be continually
had in Remembrance, by Sir Matthew Hale, Kt., New York.

Bibliography

1931

[729]

The Colonial Printer | By | Lawrence C. Wroth | [*seal*] | New York | The Grolier Club | 1931.

Colophon: The Committee on Publications of The Grolier Club certifies that this copy of "The Colonial Printer" is one of an edition of 300 copies printed by D. B. Updike at The Merrymount Press, Boston, Massachusetts. The presswork was completed in the month of February, 1931. Collation: i–xviii, 1–271, [272–273]. Leaf, 6¾ × 10⅛. Binding, cloth. Rubricated title. With 15 illustrations. Type, Mountjoye.

[730]

Sidney Lawton Smith | Designer, Etcher, Engraver | With Extracts from his Diary | and a Check-list of his | Book-plates | [*publisher's mark*] | Boston | Charles E. Goodspeed & Co. | 1931.

Colophon: Of this book, two hundred copies—fifty for private distribution and one hundred and fifty for sale—were printed by D. B. Updike, The Merrymount Press, Boston, in March, 1931. Collation: i–xii, 1–135, [136–137]. Leaf, 6¾ × 9½. Binding, boards. With 31 illustrations. Type, Scotch-face.

[731]

Manual | of the Fellowship of | St. John | [*floret*] | in Association with the | Society of St. John the Evangelist. [n. d.]

On reverse of title: The Merrymount Press, Boston. Collation: [i–ii], i–iv, 1–62, [63]. Leaf, 3⅞ × 5⅞. Binding, cloth. Type, Caslon.

[732]

A Litany | of the Fellowship of | St. John | [*floret*]. [n. d.]

Collation: 1–11, [12]. Leaf, 3⅞ × 5⅞. Binding, paper. No title. No imprint. Type, Caslon.

[733]

Pius XI | on | Christian Marriage | In the Original Latin with | English Translation | [*arms*] | New York | The Barry Vail Corporation | A. D. MDCCCCXXXI.

Colophon: One thousand copies of this edition, of which five hundred and eighty are for sale, were printed in the month of June, Pius XI happily

The Merrymount Press

reigning, A. D. MDCCCCXXXI, by D. B. Updike, The Merrymount Press, Boston, Massachusetts, U. S. A. Collation: [i–iv], 1–133, [134–135]. Leaf, 9½ × 12¼. Binding, half morocco. Rubricated title. With portrait. Type, Bodoni.

[734]
Pius XI | on | Christian Marriage | The English Translation | [*arms*] | New York | The Barry Vail Corporation |
A. D. MDCCCCXXXI.

Colophon: Twenty-five thousand copies were printed in the month of June, Pius XI happily reigning, Anno Domini MDCCCCXXXI, by D. B. Updike, The Merrymount Press, Boston, Massachusetts, U. S. A. Collation: [i–iv], 1–73, [74–75]. Leaf, 5⅞ × 8½. Binding, cloth. With portrait. Type, Lutetia.

[735]
The Isabella Stewart Gardner Museum | Catalogue | of the | Exhibited Paintings and Drawings | By Philip Hendy | [*floret*] | Boston: Printed for the Trustees: 1931.

On reverse of title: Printed by D. B. Updike, The Merrymount Press, Boston, U. S. A. Collation: i–x, 1–447. Leaf, 6 × 9⅛. Binding, cloth. With numerous illustrations. Type, Janson.

[736]
Matthias at the Door | By | Edwin Arlington Robinson | [*floret*] | New York | The Macmillan Company | 1931.

Colophon: Of this Edition, 500 copies have been printed by D. B. Updike, The Merrymount Press, Boston. This is copy No.—. Collation: [i–viii], 1–99, [100–101]. Leaf, 6 × 9⅛. Binding, cloth. Rubricated title. Type, Janson.

[737]
Ellen Terry | and | Bernard Shaw | A Correspondence | [*floret*] | Edited by | Christopher St. John | New York: The Fountain Press | London: Constable & Co. Ltd | 1931.

Colophon: Of this, the first edition of Ellen Terry and Bernard Shaw: A Correspondence, there have been printed by D. B. Updike, The Merrymount Press, Boston, Massachusetts, 3,000 copies for sale, numbered from 1 to 3,000, and 50 copies for presentation numbered from I to L. Distribution in the United States of America by G. P. Putnam's Sons. This is Number —. Collation: i–xl, 1–370, [371]. Leaf, 6¼ × 9⅞. Binding, cloth. Rubricated title. Type, Janson.

Bibliography

[738]
Bibliotheca Americana | Catalogue of the | John Carter Brown | Library | in Brown University | Providence, Rhode Island | Volume III | [*arms*] | Providence | Published by the Library | 1931.

On reverse of title: The Merrymount Press, Boston. Collation: [i–vi], 1–310. Leaf, 7 × 10½. Binding, cloth. Rubricated title. With portrait. Type, Oxford.

[739]
The Same.

Binding, boards. With two copies of the portrait, with and without inscription.

Printed on hand-made paper.

[740]
Charles Ammi Cutter | by | William Parker Cutter | [*florets*] | Chicago | American Library Association | 1931.

Colophon: One thousand copies of this book were printed by D. B. Updike, The Merrymount Press, Boston, in September, 1931, of which five hundred are numbered. Collation: [i–viii], 1–66, [67–68]. Leaf, 5½ × 8¼. Binding, boards. With 5 illustrations. Type, Caslon monotype.

American Library Pioneers, Vol. III.

[741]
Opus V | [*cut*] | Boston | Privately printed | 1931.

Colophon: Of this book twenty-five copies were printed by D. B. Updike, The Merrymount Press, Boston, in October, 1931. Collation: i–vi, [i–ii], 1–82, [83]. Leaf, 6⅞ × 9⅝. Binding, half leather. Rubricated title. Type, Janson.

12 of these copies were bound in full leather.

[742]
A Catalogue of | the Altschul Collection of | George Meredith | in the Yale University Library | Compiled by Bertha Coolidge | [*floret*] | With an Introduction by | Chauncey Brewster Tinker | Privately printed | 1931.

Colophon: Of this Catalogue, Five hundred copies have been printed by D. B. Updike, The Merrymount Press, Boston, in the Month of April, 1931. Collation: i–xviii, 1–195, [196–197]. Leaf, 7 × 10½. Binding, boards. Rubricated title. Type, Oxford.

The Merrymount Press

[743]
In Memoriam | Mary Whiton Calkins | 1863–1930.

Colophon: Five hundred copies were printed by D. B. Updike, The Merrymount Press, Boston, in June, 1931. Collation: [i–iv], 1–50, [51–55]. Leaf, 6 × 8½. Binding, paper. With portrait. Type, Caslon.

[744]
An Altar Guild | Manual | by | Edith Weir Perry | [*floret*] | Published by | The Diocesan Altar Guild | of Rhode Island. [n. d.]

Reissue of No. 726.

[745]
A | Journal | kept at | Nootka Sound | by | John R. Jewitt | One of the Survivors of the Crew of | the Ship Boston | during a Captivity among the Indians | from March, 1803, to July, 1805 | Reprinted from the Original Edition, Boston, 1807 | [*printer's ornament*] | With an Introduction and a Check List of | Later Accounts of Jewitt's Captivity by | Norman L. Dodge | [*printer's ornament*] | Boston | Charles E. Goodspeed & Co. | 1931.

On reverse of title: One hundred copies Printed by D. B. Updike, The Merrymount Press. Collation: i–xxiv, 1–91. Leaf, 4¼ × 6¾. Binding, cloth. With frontispiece. Type, Oxford.

[746]
[*within border*] The Walpole Society | In Praise of Antiquaries | By | Norman M. Isham | [*floret*] | Printed by the Society | 1931.

Colophon: [*printer's ornament*] Of this Volume one hundred and ten copies were printed for the members of The Walpole Society by D. B. Updike, The Merrymount Press, Boston, October, 1931, of which thirty-five copies are offered for sale [*printer's ornament*]. Collation: [i–vi], 1–22, [23]. Leaf, 5 × 7¾. Binding, cloth. With portrait. Type, Scotch-face.

Binding arranged from a design used by Roger Payne.

[747]
Current Developments in | American College Sport | By Howard J. Savage, John T. McGovern, Harold W. Bentley | With a Preface by | Henry Suzzallo | President of the Foun-

Bibliography

dation | Bulletin Number Twenty-six | [*seal*] | New York | The Carnegie Foundation | for the Advancement of Teaching | 522 Fifth Avenue | 1931.

On reverse of title: D. B. Updike, The Merrymount Press, Boston. Collation: [i–vi], 1–58. Leaf, 7⅜ × 10. Binding, paper. Type, Scotch-face.

Minor Printing

The Carnegie Foundation for the Advancement of Teaching, Twenty-sixth Annual Report of the President and of the Treasurer, New York; *also* Publications of the Foundation; A List of those having Expectations of Benefits from the Carnegie Foundation, Effective as of May 1, 1929; The Missing Element in Legal Education, Practical Training and Ethical Standards; Officers of Administration, Trustees, Associated Institutions; Study of the Relations of Secondary and Higher Education in Pennsylvania, Testing College Students; *and* Review of Legal Education in the United States and Canada for the Year 1930, by Alfred Z. Reed.

Reports: John Carter Brown Library, Providence; Annual Report of the President, Brown University, Providence; *also* Report of the Librarian; Ninety-fifth Annual Report, Providence Athenaeum, Providence; *also* Ninety-sixth Annual Report.

Catalogue of Brown University, 1931–1932; *also* Pembroke College in Brown University, 1930–1931; *and* The Graduate School, 1930–1931 (*also 1931–1932*).

The Book of Common Prayer and Administration of the Sacraments and Other Rites and Ceremonies of the Church, According to the Use of the Protestant Episcopal Church in the United States of America, Together with The Psalter or Psalms of David (*circular*).

James Whitcomb Riley's Reply to a Request for his Autograph, Melrose, Massachusetts.

Cowley, A Quarterly Magazine, Vol. IV [*Nos. 13, 14, 15, 16*], Cambridge.

The Society of Printers for the Study & Advancement of the Art of Printing, List of Members, 1930–1931.

Exhibition for the Zamorano Club of examples from the Collection of Merrymount Press Books made by Max Farrand, San Marino, California.

The Merrymount Press

1932

[748]
The Jaunts and Jollities | of that Renowned Sporting Citizen | Mr. John Jorrocks | of St. Botolph Lane and Great Coram Street | By R. S. Surtees | [*floret*] | With Illustrations in Water-color by Gordon Ross | and an Introduction by A. Edward Newton | New York | The Limited Editions Club | 1932.

Colophon: [*club emblem*] Of this edition of The Jaunts and Jollities of that Renowned Sporting Citizen Mr. John Jorrocks, illustrated by Gordon Ross, fifteen hundred copies have been printed by D. B. Updike, The Merrymount Press, Boston, for the members of The Limited Editions Club, this being number —. Signed by [*Gordon Ross*]. Collation: i–xviii, 1–218, [219–221]. Leaf, 7⅜ × 10⅛. Binding, cloth. With 10 illustrations. Rubricated title. Type, Janson.

[749]
Pembroke College in Brown University | Exercises Commemorative | of | Lida Shaw King | Dean of Pembroke College | 1905–1922 | [*floret*] | Held in Alumnae Hall | March 3, 1932 | Pembroke College | Providence, Rhode Island | MDCCCCXXXII.

Colophon: Five hundred copies of this book bound in paper designed and executed by Rosamond B. Loring were printed at the expense of a Friend of Pembroke College by D. B. Updike, The Merrymount Press, Boston, May, 1932. Collation: [i–iv], 1–22, [23–25]. Leaf, 5¼ × 8¼. Binding, boards. Type, Lutetia.

[750]
A Century of Scholars | Rhode Island Alpha of | Phi Beta Kappa | 1830–1930 | [*floret*] | Edited by William T. Hastings, '03 | Chapter Secretary | Providence | Rhode Island | 1932.

On reverse of title: D. B. Updike, The Merrymount Press, Boston. Collation: [i–viii], 1–227. Leaf, 6⅛ × 9¼. Binding, cloth. Type, Janson.

[751]
Thoughts | on | Religion and Morality | By | James Eddy | [*floret*] | [*quotation*] | Privately printed | The Merrymount Press | Boston | 1927.

Reissue of No. 652.

Bibliography

[752]

The Rockefeller McCormick Tapestries | Three Early Sixteenth Century | Tapestries | With a Discussion of the History of the | Tree of Life | [*floret*] | Phyllis Ackerman | New York | Oxford University Press | London, Toronto, Melbourne & Bombay. [n. d.]

On reverse of title: D. B. Updike, The Merrymount Press, Boston. Collation: [i–ii], [i–vi], 1–48. Leaf, 15⅜ × 20⅝. Binding, portfolio, boards. Rubricated title. With 43 plates at the back in loose sheets, of which 6 are in colour. Type, Janson and Caslon.

[753]

Old Houses | in the South County of Rhode Island | Compiled by the | National Society of the Colonial Dames | in the State of Rhode Island and | Providence Plantations | [*floret*] | Part First | Providence | Printed for the Society | 1932.

On reverse of title: Printed by D. B. Updike, The Merrymount Press, Boston. Collation: i–xii, 1–68. Leaf, 7⅞ × 10¾. Binding, cloth. With 95 illustrations and decorative end-papers. Type, Janson.

Also issued in paper covers.

[754]

Local Provision for Higher Education | in Saskatchewan | An Advisory Memorandum on University Policy proposed | at the Request of the University of Saskatchewan | By W. S. Learned | Staff Member, Carnegie Foundation for the Advancement of Teaching | and | E. W. Wallace | Chancellor, Victoria University, Toronto | With a Foreword by Henry Suzzallo | President of the Foundation | Bulletin Number Twenty-seven | [*seal*] | New York | The Carnegie Foundation | for the Advancement of Teaching | 522 Fifth Avenue | 1932.

On reverse of title: D. B. Updike, The Merrymount Press, Boston. Collation: [i–vi], 1–30. Leaf, 7⅜ × 9⅞. Binding, paper. Type, Scotch-face.

[755]

The Scythian Wonder | Or, The Vegetable Lamb of Tartary | by | Lucy Eugenia Osborne. [n. d.]

The Merrymount Press

Collation: [1–15]. Leaf, 8½ × 10½. Binding, boards. With illustration. Type, Janson.

Printed as an insert for Part Ten of " The Colophon." 1 copy bound.

Minor Printing

The Carnegie Foundation for the Advancement of Teaching, Twenty-seventh Annual Report of the President and of the Treasurer, New York; *also* Review of Legal Education in the United States and Canada for the Year 1931, by Alfred Z. Reed.

John Carter Brown Library, Providence, Rhode Island, Report to the Corporation of Brown University, Providence.

Catalogue of Pembroke College, Brown University, 1931–1932, Providence.

Boston Surgical Society, Incorporated.

The Merrymount Press, Boston, Its Aims, Work, and Equipment.

1933

[756]
The Brothers Karamazov | A Novel | in Four Parts and an Epilogue | by | Fyodor Dostoevsky | The Translation by Constance Garnett | Revised, with an Introduction | by Avrahm Yarmolinsky | With Eighteen Portrait Illustrations | by Alexander King | Volume I [II, III] | [*cut*] | New York | The Limited Editions Club | 1933.

Colophon: This edition of The Brothers Karamazov consists of fifteen hundred copies printed for members of The Limited Editions Club by D. B. Updike, The Merrymount Press, Boston, with illustrations by Alexander King [*cut*]. This is Copy Number — and it is signed by [*Alexander King*]. Collation: Vol. I, i–xxx, 1–408; Vol. II, i–viii, 1–352; Vol. III, i–viii, 1–396, [397]. Leaf, 5½ × 8⅛. Binding, boards. With 18 illustrations in colour. Type, Granjon.

[757]
Reality | [*floret*] | [*quotation*] | Privately Printed | 1933.

On reverse of title: D. B. Updike, The Merrymount Press, Boston. Collation: [i–iv], 1–267. Leaf, 5 × 7¼. Binding, cloth. Type, Scotch-face.

Bibliography

[758]

[*within rules*] [*quotation and arms*] The Book of Remembrance | Being a Record of Gifts | made to | Christ Church | at Cambridge, Massachusetts | Founded Anno Domini | 1759. [n. d.]

On reverse of title: D. B. Updike, The Merrymount Press, Boston. Collation: [1–100]. Leaf, 9½ × 12. Binding, leather. Rubricated throughout. Type, Caslon and Black-letter.

1 copy printed.

[759]

[*within rules*] Picturesque Word Origins | With forty-five Illustrative Drawings | [*seal*] | G. & C. Merriam Company, Springfield, Massachusetts, U. S. A. [n. d.]

On reverse of title: D. B. Updike, The Merrymount Press, Boston, U. S. A. Collation: i–vi, 1–134. Leaf, 9⅞ × 6¾ oblong. Binding, cloth. Type, Janson and Garamond.

The drawings and design for binding were supplied by the publishers.

[760]

In Memoriam | Sherrard Billings | A Sermon | Preached in Groton School Chapel | by Endicott Peabody | Sunday, May 14 | 1933 | [*cross*] | Groton School | 1933.

On reverse of title: D. B. Updike, The Merrymount Press, Boston. Collation: [i–iv], 1–18. Leaf, 4⅝ × 7⅝. Binding, paper. Type, Oxford.

[761]

Trinity Church | in the City of Boston | Massachusetts | 1733–1933 | Boston | Printed for the Wardens & Vestry | of Trinity Church | 1933.

On reverse of title: D. B. Updike, The Merrymount Press, Boston. Collation: [i–x], 1–220. Leaf, 6⅛ × 9¼. Binding, cloth. With 17 illustrations. Type, Janson.

[762]

The Book of | The Official Acts of | The Bishop of Albany | [*floret*] | Printed A. D. MDCCCXXXIII.

On reverse of title: D. B. Updike, The Merrymount Press, Boston. Collation: [1–422]. Leaf, 8⅛ × 10¾. Binding, cloth. Rubricated title. Type, Caslon.

[267]

The Merrymount Press

1 copy printed. Single copies printed also for the Bishops of Maine, Vermont, Southern Ohio, and Chicago, and the Missionary Bishops of Wyoming, San Joaquin, Liberia, and Tohoku.

Minor Printing

The Carnegie Foundation for the Advancement of Teaching, Publications of the Foundation, New York; *also* Review of Legal Education in the United States and Canada for the Year 1932, by Alfred Z. Reed; *and* Education and the Economic Situation, Reprinted from the Twenty-seventh Annual Report.

Wheaton College, Norton, Massachusetts.

The Living God.

Tileston & Hollingsworth Company, Calendar for March.

Supplementary Bibliography
1934-1949

Supplementary Bibliography

1934

[763]

[*within rules*] The Life of | Our Lord | Written during the years 1846–1849 | By Charles Dickens | for His Children | And now first published | [*cut*] | New York | Simon and Schuster | 1934.

Colophon: This edition is specially designed by D. B. Updike, The Merrymount Press, Boston, and is limited to 2387 numbered copies, which are published simultaneously with the regular first trade edition. [*publisher's mark*] This copy is number —. Collation: i–xii, 1–128, [129]. Leaf, 5⅛ × 7¾. Binding, boards. Rubricated title. With illustration. Type, Caslon Monotype and Lettre Batarde.

[764]

Gallatin Iconography | By | Albert Eugene Gallatin | [*floret*] | Privately Printed | 1934.

Colophon: One hundred copies printed by D. B. Updike, The Merrymount Press, Boston in March, 1934. Collation: i–viii, 1–53, [54]. Leaf, 7½ × 10. Binding, cloth. With 57 illustrations. Type, Caslon Monotype.

[765]

Codex Quartus Sancti Iacobi | De Expedimento et Conversione Yspanic et | Gallecie Editus a Beato Turpino Archiepi- | scopo (Turpin's Chronicle).

Colophon: Three hundred copies are printed at The Merrymount Press, Boston for Ward Thoron May, 1934. Collation: [i–viii], [1–53]. Leaf, 7 × 10. Binding, boards. With 3 illustrations. Type, Caslon Monotype.

[766]

Some Unrecorded Letters of | Caroline Norton | in the Altschul Collection of the | Yale University Library | By | Bertha Coolidge | [*floret*] | Privately Printed | 1934.

Colophon: [*printer's device*] Seventy-five copies printed for private distribution by D. B. Updike, The Merrymount Press, Boston February, 1934. Collation: [i–iv], 1–25, [26–27]. Leaf, 7 × 10½. Binding, boards. Rubricated title. Type, Oxford.

Paste paper on cover designed and executed by Rosamond B. Loring.

The Merrymount Press

[767]

Robert Grosseteste | and the Jews | By | Lee M. Friedman |
[*seal*] | Cambridge | Harvard University Press | 1934.

On reverse of title: D. B. Updike, The Merrymount Press, Boston. Collation: [i–vi], 1–34. Leaf, 7½ × 9⅞. Binding, cloth. With 3 illustrations.
Type, Caslon Monotype.

[768]

The Catalogue | of the Collection of | Joseph T. Tower, Jr. |
Class of 1921 | in the Institute of Geographical Exploration |
Harvard University | [*cut*] | Privately Printed | 1933.

On reverse of title: [One hundred and ten copies printed] D. B. Updike,
The Merrymount Press, Boston. Collation: i–viii, 1–184. Leaf, 6½ × 9¾.
Binding, cloth. Rubricated title. Type, Oxford.
10 copies were bound in full Red French Levant.

[769]

John Adams's Book | Being Notes on | A Record of Births, Mar-
riages & Deaths | of Three Generations of the | Adams Family |
1734–1807 | [*type ornament*] | Compiled by Henry Adams |
Printed for the Boston Athenæum | 1934.

Colophon: One hundred and fifty copies printed by D. B. Updike, The
Merrymount Press, Boston in the Month of May, 1934. Collation: 1–7,
[8–9]. Leaf, 8⅜ × 13⅝. Binding, boards. With facsimile illustration.
Type, Caslon Monotype.

[770]

[*within rules*] The | Preface | to | Johnson's | Dictionary | of the |
English Language | 1755 | [*cut*] | Cleveland | The Rowfant Club |
1934.

Colophon: [*rules*] [*cut*] Reprinted from the First Edition of the Dictionary in
the Charles Orr Memorial Collection of the Rowfant Club Library, by
D. B. Updike, The Merrymount Press, Boston. One hundred ten copies
have been printed, of which this is number — [*rules*]. Collation: [i–iv], 1–32,
[33]. Leaf, 7½ × 10⅛. Binding, boards. Rubricated title. Type, Caslon
Monotype.

[771]

A Christmas Carol | in Prose | Being a Ghost Story of Christ-
mas | By | Charles Dickens | [*floret*] | With Illustrations by Gor-

Bibliography

don Ross | and an Introduction by Stephen Leacock | Boston |
Printed for the Members of The Limited Editions Club at | The
Merrymount Press, Christmas, 1934.

Colophon: [*club emblem*] This edition is designed and printed by D. B.
Updike, The Merrymount Press, Boston, fifteen hundred copies being prepared for issue to the members of The Limited Editions Club Christmas
1934. The illustrations are by Gordon Ross, who signs here: [*Gordon Ross*]
This copy number —. Collation: i–xii, 1–100, [101]. Leaf, 7 × 10. Binding,
boards. With 6 illustrations in colour. Type, Caslon Monotype.
Paste paper on cover designed and executed by Rosamond B. Loring.

[772]
Notes | on The Merrymount Press & its Work | By Daniel
Berkeley Updike | With a Bibliographical List of Books |
printed at the Press | 1893–1933 | By Julian Pearce Smith | With
Views of the Press at Various Periods | Specimen of Types al-
luded to | &c. &c. &c. | [*seal*] | Cambridge | Harvard University
Press | 1934.

On reverse of title: D. B. Updike, The Merrymount Press, Boston, U.S.A.
Colophon: This edition, limited to five hundred copies printed on machine-
made paper at the Merrymount Press, Boston, was completed and type
distributed in March, 1934. Collation: i–x, 1–279, [280–281]. Leaf, 5⅞ ×
8⅞. Binding, cloth. With 13 illustrations. Type, Janson.

[773]
The Same

Colophon: Twenty-five copies of this book were printed on Glaslan hand-
made paper at The Merrymount Press, in March, 1934. [*floret*] This is
Number —. Binding, boards.
Paste paper on cover designed and executed by Rosamond B. Loring.

[774]
In Memorian | Mary Frazer Smith | Eleanor Acheson McCulloch
Gamble | [*floret*] | Wellesley College | 1934.

On reverse of title: D. B. Updike, The Merrymount Press, Boston. Collation: i–iv, 1–41, [42]. Leaf, 6 × 8½. Binding, paper. Type, Caslon Monotype.

The Merrymount Press

[775]

Chapel Services | Saint Paul's School | [*cut*] | Concord | New Hampshire | 1934.

On reverse of title: D. B. Updike, The Merrymount Press, Boston. Collation: 1–54. Leaf, 4¼ × 6½. Binding, cloth. Rubricated title. Type, Oxford.

[776]

The Writings of | A. Kingsley Porter | 1883–1933 | A Bibliography | Compiled under the Direction of | Lucy Kingsley Porter | ter | The Fogg Art Museum | Cambridge | 1934.

On reverse of title: D. B. Updike, The Merrymount Press, Boston. Collation: i–iv, 1–15, [16]. Leaf, 5⅝ × 8⅛. Binding, paper. Type, Caslon Monotype.

[777]

Henry Suzzallo | 1875–1933 | [*floret*] | A Memorial Gathering held in the Milbank | Memorial Chapel, Teachers College | Columbia University | on December the eighteenth | 1933 | New York | 1934.

Colophon: D. B. Updike, The Merrymount Press, Boston, Collation: [i–iv], 1–22, [23]. Leaf, 6¼ × 9¼. Binding, paper. With collotype portrait. Type, Caslon Monotype.

Minor Printing

The Carnegie Foundation for the Advancement of Teaching, Twenty-ninth Annual Report of the President and of the Treasurer, New York; *also* Review of Legal Education in the United States and Canada for the Year 1933, by Alfred Z. Reed.

Catalogues of Schools: Roxbury Latin School, 1933–1934; Manter Hall School, Cambridge.

On Choosing a School (The Beaver Country Day School, Chestnut Hill).

Message to the Gold Star Mothers of France.

Athenæum Items.

John Carter Brown Library, Providence, Rhode Island, Report to the Corporation of Brown University, Providence.

Bibliography

1935

[778]

The | Public Schools of Colonial Boston | 1635–1775 | By | Robert Francis Seybolt | Professor of the History of Education | University of Illinois | [*seal*] | Cambridge | Harvard University Press | 1935.

On reverse of title: Printed in the United States of America by D. B. Updike, The Merrymount Press, Boston, Massachusetts. Collation: i–x, 1–101. Leaf, 5⅝ × 8½. Binding, cloth. Type, Caslon Monotype.

[779]

Whistler | in Belgium and Holland | By | Howard Mansfield | M. Knoedler & Company, Inc. | 14 East Fifty-seventh Street | New York. [n.d.].

Colophon: Of this book there have been printed, by D. B. Updike, The Merrymount Press, Boston, Massachusetts, five hundred and twenty-five numbered copies. Of these Numbers 1–25 are for the Author, Numbers 26–50 are for presentation, and Numbers 51–525 are for sale. This is Number —. Collation: 1–25, [26–27]. Leaf, 6⅛ × 9¼. Binding, boards. Type, Caslon Monotype.

Issued as a companion volume to No. 780.

[780]

Whistler | as a Critic of His Own Prints | By | Howard Mansfield | M. Knoedler & Company, Inc. | 14 East Fifty-seventh Street | New York. [n.d.]

Colophon: Of this book there have been printed, by D. B. Updike, The Merrymount Press, Boston, Massachusetts, five hundred and twenty-five numbered copies. Of these Numbers 1–25 are for the Author, Numbers 26–50 are for presentation, and Numbers 51–525 are for sale. This is number —. Collation: 1–33, [34–35]. Leaf, 6⅛ × 9¼. Binding, boards. Type, Caslon Monotype.

Issued as a companion volume to No. 779.

[781]

Dedication | Being | Later Letters from the Writer of | "Reality" | [*floret*] | Privately Printed | 1935.

The Merrymount Press

On reverse of title: D. B. Updike, The Merrymount Press, Boston. Collation: [i–iv], 1–414. Leaf, 5 × 7¼. Binding, cloth. Type, Scotch-face Monotype.

[782]
Publications | of | The Colonial Society of Massachusetts | Volume XXI | [*printer's ornaments*] | Collections | [*seal*] | Boston | Published by the Society | 1935.

On reverse of title: D. B. Updike, The Merrymount Press, Boston, U.S.A. Collation: [i–xiv], 1–534. Leaf, 6½ × 9⅜. Binding, cloth. With 2 illustrations. Type, Caslon Monotype.

[783]
Her Recollections | [*rule*] | [*cut*] | [*rule*] | Privately Printed | 1935.

On reverse of title: D. B. Updike, The Merrymount Press, Boston. Collation: i–xii, 1–102, [103]. Leaf, 5⅞ × 8⅞. Binding, cloth. With 24 illustrations. Type, Caslon Monotype.

[784]
The Twenty-Fifth | Anniversary Meeting of | The Walpole Society | [*cut*] | Printed by the Society | 1935.

Colophon: Of this Volume there were printed by D. B. Updike, The Merrymount Press, Boston, in October, 1935, for the Members of the Walpole Society fifty copies on Worthy Permanent Book, bound in paper designed and executed by Rosamond B. Loring, and fifty copies on Aurelian paper, bound in marbled paper. Collation: i–iv, 1–55, [56]. Leaf, 6⅛ × 9⅛. Binding, boards. Rubricated title. Type, Caslon Monotype.

[785]
Securities and Dividends | of a | Banker's Daughter | By Marjorie Wiggin Prescott | [*printer's ornaments*] | Privately Printed.

Colophon: Of this book there have been printed, by D. B. Updike, The Merrymount Press, Boston, Massachusetts, U.S.A., one hundred and fifty copies for the author's distribution, December 2, 1935. Collation: [i–vi], 1–103, [104–105]. Leaf, 6⅛ × 9⅛. Binding, boards. With 2 illustrations. Type, Caslon Monotype.

[786]
Timothy Cole | Wood-Engraver | By | Alphaeus P. Cole | and |

Bibliography

Margaret Ward Cole | Limited Edition | Illustrated with nineteen of Timothy Cole's finest Wood-engravings | [*floret*] | New York | The Pioneer Associates | 11 West Forty-second Street | 1935.

On reverse of title: D. B. Updike, The Merrymount Press, Boston, U.S.A. Colophon: [*at front*] This edition of Timothy Cole: Wood-Engraver was designed and printed by D. B. Updike, The Merrymount Press, Boston, Massachusetts, U.S.A., in December, 1935, and consists of 750 numbered and autographed copies. This copy is No. —. (*Alphaeus P. Cole, Margaret W. Cole*). Collation: [i–ii], i–xx, 1–172. Leaf, 7 × 10. Binding, cloth. Type, Caslon Monotype.

[787]

The Life and Works | of | Joseph Rodman Drake | (1795–1820) | A Memoir | and complete text of His Poems & Prose | including much never before printed | Prepared by | Frank Lester Pleadwell, M.D. | Captain, Medical Corps, U.S.N. Retired | Editor (with Thomas O. Mabbott) of | "The Life and Works of Edward Coote Pinkney" | [*printer's ornament*] | Boston | Printed for the Author by | The Merrymount Press | 1935.

Colophon: Of this Edition of the Life and Works of Joseph Rodman Drake seven hundred and fifty copies have been printed by D. B. Updike, The Merrymount Press, Boston, U.S.A., in the month of December, 1935. Collation: i–xx, 1–424, [425]. Leaf, 5½ × 8. Binding, cloth. With 16 illustrations. Type, Scotch-face Monotype.

[788]

In Memoriam | [*cut*] | Gladys Emily Streibert | 1885–1930 | New York | 1935.

On reverse of title: D. B. Updike, The Merrymount Press, Boston. Collation: [i–iv], 1–12, [13]. Leaf, 6 × 8⅜. Binding, paper. With photogravure portrait. Type, Caslon Monotype.

[789]

The Carnegie Foundation | for the Advancement of Teaching | Early Papers of the Foundation | [*seal*] | 522 Fifth Avenue | New York City | 1935.

On reverse of title: D. B. Updike, The Merrymount Press, Boston. Collation: i–viii, 1–57. Leaf, 7¼ × 10. Binding, paper. Type, Caslon Monotype.

The Merrymount Press

[790]

[*border*] | Catalogue 250 | Books, Prints, Autographs, | Book-plates | With a Foreword by Charles E. Goodspeed | Goodspeed's Book Shop, Incorporated | 7 Ashburton Place | Boston, Massachusetts, U.S.A. | [*border*]. [n.d.]

On outside back cover: D. B. Updike, The Merrymount Press, Boston. Collation: [i–ii], i–xviii, 1–107, [108]. Leaf, 6 × 9. Binding, paper. Type, Scotch-face Monotype.

[791]

Poems | By | Sophia Metcalf Baker | [*floret*] | Privately Printed [n.d.]

On reverse of title: D. B. Updike, The Merrymount Press, Boston. Collation: i–xii, 1–183, [184]. Leaf, 5 × 7⅜. Binding, cloth. With photogravure portrait. Type, Caslon Monotype.

[792]

The Right Side of the Ship | [*printer's ornaments*] | [*quotation*] | [*floret*] | The Church Society for College Work | 3805 Locust Street, Philadelphia | Pennsylvania | 1935.

On reverse of title: The Merrymount Press, Boston. Collation: [i–vi], 1–23, [24–25]. Leaf, 5 × 7¾. Binding, paper. Type, Caslon Monotype.

[793]

Friendship | [*floret*] | Boston | Privately Printed | 1935.

On reverse of title: The Merrymount Press, Boston. Collation: [i–iv], 1–12. Leaf, 4½ × 6⅞. Binding, paper. Type, Caslon Monotype.

[794]

Report on the Award | of | The Middlesex Competitive | Prize Scholarships | 1935 | Middlesex School | Concord, Massachusetts | 1935.

On reverse of title: The Merrymount Press, Boston. Collation: [i–iv], 1–17, [18]. Leaf, 6 × 8⅜. Binding, paper. Type, Caslon Monotype.

Bibliography

Minor Printing

The Carnegie Foundation for the Advancement of Teaching, Thirtieth Annual Report of the President and of the Treasurer; *also* Publications of the Foundation *and* Review of Legal Education in the United States and Canada for the Year 1934, by Alfred Z. Reed.

Athenæum Items.

Thomas Fishing Rods.

Washington's Farewell Address, A Reprint on Strathmore Permanent

Catalogue of the Roxbury Latin School, 1934–1935.

The Messenger, National Society of Colonial Dames of America, June 1935.

Boston Symphony Orchestra Announcement, Fifty-fifth Season 1935–1936.

Reports: John Carter Brown Library, Providence, Rhode Island, Report to the Corporation of Brown University, Providence; Ninety-ninth and One hundredth Annual Reports, Providence Athenæum, Providence.

In Memoriam M. T. B. H. (Maria Theresa Burnham Hopkins).

Catalogue Isabella Stewart Gardner Museum, Fenway Court.

Eightieth Anniversary M. F. P. (Mrs. Henry Parkman).

1936

[795]

Shakespeare's Sonnets | Edited with Introduction and Notes | by | Tucker Brooke | [*printer's ornament*] | Oxford University Press | London, New York | 1936.

On reverse of title: D. B. Updike, The Merrymount Press, Boston. Collation: i–viii, 1–346. Leaf, 5½ × 8. Binding, cloth. Type, Caslon Monotype.

[796]

George Arthur Plimpton | 1855–1936.

On reverse of title: D. B. Updike, The Merrymount Press, Boston. Collation: [i–ii], 1–12. Leaf, 5¾ × 8½. Binding, paper. With photogravure portrait. Type, Janson.

The Merrymount Press

[797]

A Memoir | of the | Reverend John Bartlett | Harvard, A.B.
1805, A.M. 1808 | By | Willard Reed | [*printer's ornament*] |
Boston | Privately Printed for Mrs. J. B. Noyes | The Merry-
mount Press | 1936.

Collation: i–vi, 1–49, [50]. Leaf, 5½ × 8. Binding, boards. Type, Baskerville Monotype.

[798]

[*border*] | Southboro Recipes | Old and New | [*floret*] | This little
Book is compiled of Recipes | given by Members and Friends of
the | Southboro Village Society | and is sold for the benefit of |
The Community House | [*border*]. [n.d.]

On reverse of title: The Merrymount Press, Boston. Collation: [i–ii], 1–85.
Leaf, 5⅛ × 7½. Binding, paper. Type, Caslon Monotype.

[799]

Tales | of a Sportsman's Wife | By | Marjorie Wiggin Pres-
cott | [*printer's ornament*] | Privately Printed. [n.d.]

Colophon: Printed by D. B. Updike, The Merrymount Press, Boston,
Massachusetts, U.S.A. Collation: [i–vi], 1–17, [18–21]. Leaf, 5¾ × 8¼.
Binding, boards. With 2 illustrations. Type, Janson.

[800]

The Carnegie Foundation for the Advancement of Teaching |
The Colleges and | the Courts | Judicial Decisions regarding In-
stitutions | of Higher Education in the | United States | By |
Edward C. Elliott | President, Purdue University | and | M. M.
Chambers | Member Staff, American Youth Commission | of
the American Council on Education | [*florets*] | New York City |
522 Fifth Avenue | 1936.

On last page: D. B. Updike, The Merrymount Press, Boston. Collation:
i–x, 1–563. Leaf, 6 × 9. Binding, cloth. Type, Caslon Monotype.
Also issued in paper covers.

[801]

Snow on Cholera | Being | A Reprint of Two Papers | By | John
Snow, M.D. | together with | A Biographical Memoir | By |

Bibliography

B. W. Richardson, M.D. | and | An Introduction | By | Wade Hampton Frost, M.D. | Professor of Epidemiology, The Johns Hopkins School | of Hygiene and Public Health | New York | The Commonwealth Fund | London: Humphrey Milford: Oxford University Press | 1936.

On reverse of title: D. B. Updike, The Merrymount Press, Boston. Collation: i–xlviii, [i–ii], i–viii, 1–191. Leaf, 5⁷⁄₁₆ × 8⅞. Binding, cloth. With frontispiece and 2 folding maps. Type, Scotch-face Monotype.

[802]
Boswell's Journal | of | A Tour to the Hebrides | with | Samuel Johnson, LL.D. | Now First Published from the Original Manuscript | [*printer's ornaments*] | Prepared for the Press, with Preface and Notes | by Frederick A. Pottle and Charles H. Bennett | [*printer's ornaments*] | New York: The Viking Press | London: William Heinemann, Ltd. | 1936.

Colophon: Set by The Haddon Craftsmen in Monotype Baskerville. Printed by D. B. Updike, at The Merrymount Press on Worthy Hand and Arrows All-Rag Paper. Aquatone Illustrations by Edward Stern & Co. Bound by George McKibbin & Son. Title-page designed by Richard Ellis. Planned and supervised by M. B. Glick. Collation: i–xviii, 1–435, [436–438]. Leaf, 7 × 10. Binding, boards. Rubricated title.

[803]
Opus VI | [*cut*] | Boston | Privately Printed | 1936.

Colophon: Of this book fifteen copies were printed by D. B. Updike, The Merrymount Press, Boston in September, 1936. Collation: [i–vi], 1–77, [78–79]. Leaf, 6⅞ × 9¾, Binding, boards. Rubricated title. Type Janson. *5 copies were bound in half red French Levant.*

[804]
Trinity Church | in Newport, Rhode Island | A History of the Fabric | By | Norman Morrison Isham | A.M., F.A.I.A. | [*floret*] | Boston | Printed for the Subscribers | MDCCCCXXXVI.

On reverse of title: D. B. Updike, The Merrymount Press, Boston. Collation: i–xii, 1–111. Leaf, 7⅝ × 10⅛. Binding, boards. With 33 illustrations. Type, Caslon Monotype.

[281]

The Merrymount Press

[805]

Harvard College | Class of 1926 | [*printer's ornaments*] | The Decennial Report | [*seal*] | Cambridge | Printed for the Class | 1936.

On reverse of title: D. B. Updike, The Merrymount Press, Boston. Collation: i–xii, [i–ii], 1–235, [236–237]. Leaf, 6 × 9. Binding, cloth. Type, Caslon Monotype.

[806]

Walden | or Life in the Woods | By Henry David Thoreau | [*dash*] | Illustrated with Photographs | Taken at Various Seasons at Walden Pond by | Edward Steichen | And with an Introduction by | Henry Seidel Canby | [*printer's ornament*] | Boston | [*dash*] | Printed at The Merrymount Press | for the Members of | The Limited Editions Club | MDCCCCXXXVI.

Colophon: Of this book fifteen hundred copies have been made for the Members of The Limited Editions Club by D. B. Updike, The Merrymount Press, Boston, the illustrations being reproduced from photographs made at Walden Pond by Edward Steichen who here signs (*Steichen*). This copy Number —. Collation: i–xiv, 1–290, [291]. Leaf, 7 × 9¾. Binding, boards. Rubricated title. With 16 illustrations. Type, Scotch-face Monotype.
Paste paper on cover designed and executed by Rosamond B. Loring.

[807]

Forain | Draughtsman, Lithographer | Etcher | By | Campbell Dodgson | M. Knoedler & Company, Inc. | 14 East Fifty-seventh Street | New York. [n.d.]

Colophon: Of this book there have been printed, by D. B. Updike, The Merrymount Press, Boston, Massachusetts, four hundred and twenty-five numbered copies. Of these Numbers 1–25 are for the Author, Numbers 26–50 are for presentation, and Numbers 51–425 are for sale. This is Number —. Collation: 1–66, [67–69]. Leaf, 6 × 9¼. Binding, boards. Type, Caslon Monotype.

[808]

Boston | Paper Trade Association | A Review of Fifty Years | 1886–1936 | [*printer's ornament*] | With By-Laws | Chronological List of Officers | Portraits of Presidents | and | Membership Roll | Boston, Massachusetts | 1936.

Bibliography

On reverse of title: The Merrymount Press, Boston. Collation: [i–ii], 1–46. Leaf, 5 × 7¼. Binding, boards. Type, Caslon Monotype.

[809]

Thoughts | on | Thomas Jefferson | or | What Jefferson was Not | By | Harold Jefferson Coolidge | [*seal*] | Boston | The Club of Odd Volumes | M.DCCCC.XXXVI.

On reverse of title: D. B. Updike, The Merrymount Press, Boston. Collation: [i–x], 1–45. Leaf, 6¼ × 9⁵⁄₁₆. Binding, boards. With frontispiece portrait in colour and 3 facsimile letters. Type, Caslon Monotype.

[810]

[*within border*] The | Events | of the Year | MDCCCXXXV | Being an Address lately delivered before | The Members of | The Colonial Society of | Massachusetts | at a Collation following its Annual Assembly | November 21, 1935 | [*rule*] | By Doctor Samuel Eliot Morison | (of the College of New Town, vulgarly called Cambridge,) | President of the Society | [*rule*] | Micah VI. 5. | O my People, remember now what Balak King of Moab consulted, | and what Balaam the Son of Beor answered him from Shittim unto | Gilgal; that ye may know the Righteousness of the Lord. | [*rule*] | Boston | Printed at The Merrymount Press at the Request of | a Member of the Society aforesaid, Anno Domini 1936.

Collation: [i–ii], 1–5. Leaf, 5⅜ × 7¼. Binding, paper. Type, Janson.

[811]

The By-Laws of | The Colonial Society of Massachusetts | With the | Certificate of Incorporation | [*seal*] | Boston | Printed for the Society | 1936.

On reverse of title: D. B. Updike, The Merrymount Press, Boston, U.S.A. Collation: 1–13. Leaf, 6½ × 9⅜. Binding, paper. Type, Caslon Monotype.

[812]

Boston Symphony Orchestra | Charcoal Drawings of its Members | With Biographical Sketches | By | Gerome Brush | [*floret*] | Boston | Printed for the Orchestra | 1936.

[283]

The Merrymount Press

On reverse of title: The Merrymount Press, Boston. Colophon: [*at front*] A specially bound limited edition of 300 copies of this book has been printed and signed by the artist, in September, 1936. This is Copy No. —. Collation: i–viii, 1–218, [219]. Leaf, 7¾ × 10. Binding, boards. Type, Caslon Monotype.

Also issued in paper covers.

[813]
Report | on the | Second Annual Competition | for the | Middlesex Prize Scholarships | April, 1936 | [*printer's ornament*] | Middlesex School | Concord | Massachusetts | 1936.

On reverse of title: The Merrymount Press, Boston. Collation: [i–ii], 1–12, [13]. Leaf, 6 × 8⅜. Binding, paper. Type, Caslon Monotype.

[814]
Examinations | and Their Substitutes | in the United States | By I. L. Kandel, M.A., Ph.D. | Professor of Education and | Associate in the International Institute | Teachers College, Columbia University | With a Preface by Walter A. Jessup | President of the Foundation | Bulletin Number Twenty-eight | [*seal*] | New York | The Carnegie Foundation | for the Advancement of Teaching | 552 Fifth Avenue | 1936.

On reverse of title: D. B. Updike, The Merrymount Press, Boston. Collation: i–xii, 1–183. Leaf, 7⅜ × 10. Binding, paper. Type, Scotch-face Monotype.

Minor Printing

The Carnegie Foundation for the Advancement of Teaching, Thirty-first Annual Report of the President and of the Treasurer, New York.

Testimonial Dinner to Chief Henry A. Fox, Boston Fire Department.

Goodspeed's Book Shop, Catalogue 274, First Editions of New England Authors.

Athenæum Items.

On Choosing a School (The Beaver Country Day School, Chestnut Hill).

Catalogue Isabella Stewart Gardner Museum, Fenway Court.

[284]

Bibliography

Dedication of a Tablet Placed in the State House at Concord by the Society of Mayflower Descendants in the State of New Hampshire November twenty-first A.D. 1936.

John Carter Brown Library, Providence, Rhode Island, Report to the Corporation of Brown University, Providence.

1937

[815]

[*within border*] [Number 25] | Two Centuries of | Bruce Rogers | with a Prologue | "B R's Secret Passion" | By | Christopher Morley [*printer's ornaments*] | Philip C. Duschnes | 507 Fifth Avenue, New York.

On reverse of title: Five hundred and fifty copies of this catalogue were printed, February, 1937, by D. B. Updike, The Merrymount Press, Boston, U.S.A. Collation: [i–ii], iii–iv, [v], 1–43, [44–45]. Leaf, 4⅝ × 7¼. Binding, paper. With collotype illustration. Type, Caslon Monotype.

[816]

An Introduction to | The Mellon Collection | By | Royal Cortissoz | Author of "The Painter's Craft" | "Personalities in Art" | "American Artists," etc. | [*floret*] | Privately Printed | The Merrymount Press | 1937.

On reverse of title: D. B. Updike, The Merrymount Press, Boston. Collation: [i–x], [1–3], 4–46. Leaf, 4⅝ × 7¼. Binding, cloth. With 16 illustrations in half-tone. Type, Caslon Monotype.

[817]

[*within border*] The Old Farm | By | Gertrude Weld Arnold | [*rule*] | [*cut*] | [*rule*] | Boston | Privately Printed | 1937.

On reverse of title: D. B. Updike, The Merrymount Press, Boston. Collation: [i–vi], vii–xiv, 1–78, [79–80]. Leaf, 6 × 8⅜. Binding, cloth. With 16 illustrations in collotype. Type, Caslon Monotype.

[818]

The Mother Church | A History of the Building of the | Original Edifice of | The First Church of Christ, Scientist | in Boston, Massachusetts | [*floret*] | By Joseph Armstrong | Boston | The

The Merrymount Press

Christian Science Publishing Society | One, Norway Street. [n.d.]

On reverse of title: D. B. Updike, The Merrymount Press, Boston. Collation: [i–iv], v–xii, 1–96, [97]. Leaf, 5¾ × 8. Binding, cloth. With 18 illustrations. Type, Caslon Monotype.

[819]

Printing Types | Their History, Forms, and Use | A Study in Survivals | by | Daniel Berkeley Updike | With Illustrations | [*quotation*] | Volume I [II] | [*seal*] | Second Edition | Cambridge | Harvard University Press | London: Humphrey Milford | Oxford University Press | 1937.

On reverse of title: D. B. Updike, The Merrymount Press, Boston, U.S.A. Collation: Vol. I, i–xl, 1–292; Vol. II, i–xx, 1–326. Leaf, 6¼ × 9¼. Binding, cloth. Type, Oxford.

Second Edition of No. 548. Contains 16 pages of Supplementary Notes in Volume I and 20 pages in Volume II. In addition, minor textual changes appear throughout.

[820]

Tales | of a Sportsman's Wife | By | Marjorie Wiggin Prescott | [*printer's ornament*] | Fishing | Privately Printed. [n.d.]

Colophon: Printed by D. B. Updike, The Merrymount Press, Boston, Massachusetts, U.S.A. Collation: [i–iv], 1–56, [57–60]. Leaf, 5¾ × 8¼. Binding, boards. Type, Janson.

[821]

Slow Boat | Reflections from the Sea | by | J. Lionberger Davis | [*printer's ornament*] | Privately Printed | 1937.

On reverse of title: D. B. Updike, The Merrymount Press, Boston. Collation: [i–viii], 1–27, [28]. Leaf, 4⅝ × 7½. Binding, paper. Type, Caslon Monotype.

[822]

A Modern | Prometheus | by | J. Lionberger Davis | Privately Printed | 1937.

On reverse of title: D. B. Updike, The Merrymount Press, Boston. Collation: [i–vi], 1–8, [9]. Leaf, 4⅝ × 7½. Binding, paper. Type, Caslon Monotype.

Bibliography

[823]

[*within border*] Jessie Thomas | Vincent | (Mrs. Leon Vincent) |
[*printer's ornaments*] | Boston | 1937.

On reverse of title: D. B. Updike, The Merrymount Press, Boston. Collation: [i–vi], 1–57, [58]. Leaf, 5⅜ × 8⅝. Binding, cloth. With 2 photogravure portraits. Type, Scotch-face Monotype.

[824]

Richard Smith | First English Settler of the | Narragansett Coun-
try, Rhode Island | With a Series of Letters written by his Son |
Richard Smith, Jr., to members of the Winthrop Family | and
Notes on Cocumscussuc, Smith's Estate | in Narragansett | By
Daniel Berkeley Updike | With Illustrations from Drawings
by | Edmund Hort New | [*arms*] | Boston | The Merrymount
Press | 1937.

On reverse of title: The Merrymount Press, Boston. Collation: i–xx, 1–
118. Leaf, 6¼ × 9⅜. Binding, cloth. With 4 illustrations. Type, Caslon
Monotype.

[825]

[*border*] | Lantern Slides | by | Mary Cadwalader Jones | [*floret*] |
Privately Printed | 1937 | [*border*].

On reverse of title: D. B. Updike, The Merrymount Press, Boston. Colla-
tion: i–viii, 1–128, [129]. Leaf, 5¼ × 8⅛. Binding, boards. Type, Caslon
Monotype.
Paste paper on cover designed and executed by Rosamond B. Loring.

[826]

William Crowninshield | Endicott | By | William Lawrence |
[*floret*] | Privately Printed. [n.d.]

Colophon: The Merrymount Press, Boston. Collation: [i–iv], 1–17, [18–19].
Leaf, 5 × 7⅝. Binding, cloth. With photogravure portrait. Type, Oxford.

[827]

Publications | of | The Colonial Society of Massachusetts | Vol-
ume XXXII | [*printer's ornaments*] | Transactions | 1933–1937 |
[*seal*] | Boston | Published by the Society | 1937.

On reverse of title: D. B. Updike, The Merrymount Press, Boston, U.S.A.
Collation: i–xviii, 1–569. Leaf, 6½ × 9⅜. Binding, cloth. With 11 collotype
illustrations. Type, Caslon Monotype.

[287]

The Merrymount Press

[828]

Phi Beta Kappa | Keys at Brown | By | William T. Hastings |
[*cut*] | Providence | Rhode Island | 1937.

On reverse of title: D. B. Updike, The Merrymount Press, Boston. Collation: [i–iv], 1–20. Leaf, 6⅛ × 9¼. Binding, paper. Rubricated title. Type,
Caslon Monotype.

[829]

Catalogue | of Antique Furniture and | Objects of Art | in the
Pingree House | Salem | The Gift of Francis Shaw, Jr. | and
Miriam Shaw | in Memory of Their Father | Francis Shaw,
Esq. | 1935 | Salem | The Essex Institute | 1937.

On reverse of title: The Merrymount Press, Boston. Collation: 1–13, [14].
Leaf, 4½ × 7. Binding, paper. Type, Caslon Monotype.

[830]

[*cross*] | Services at the Funeral of | William Crowninshield
Endicott | held at | Grace Church and Harmony Grove | Salem,
Massachusetts | December First | A.D. 1936.

Collation: [i–ii], 1–14. Leaf, 5⅛ × 7⅜. Binding, paper. Type, Caslon
Monotype.

50 copies printed.

[831]

The Pilgrim Fathers, Their Significance in History | [*rule*] |
An | Address | at the Unveiling of | A Tablet | to the | May-
flower Pilgrims | in the State House at Concord, New Hamp-
shire | November 21, 1936 | Being the | Three Hundred and
Sixteenth | Anniversary | of the Signing of | The Mayflower
Compact | [*rule*] | By | Samuel Eliot Morison | Professor of His-
tory at Harvard University and President of the | Colonial So-
ciety of Massachusetts | [*rule*] | [*printer's ornaments*] | [*rule*] |
Concord | Printed for the Society of Mayflower Descendants |
in the State of New Hampshire | 1937.

On reverse of title: D. B. Updike, The Merrymount Press, Boston. Collation: [i–iv], 1–27. Leaf, 6 × 9. Binding, paper. Type, Caslon Monotype.

Bibliography

[832]

Report | on the | Third Annual Competition | for the | Middle-sex Prize Scholarships | Held | April 3, 1937 | [*printer's orna-ment*] | Middlesex School | Concord, Massachusetts | 1937.

On outside back cover: D. B. Updike, The Merrymount Press, Boston. Collation: [i–ii], 1–5, [6]. Leaf, 6 × 8⅜. Binding, paper. Type, Caslon Mono-type.

[833]

"So You think It's New" | by | Wilfred J. Funk | Drawings by Russell Sherman | [*cut*] | Funk & Wagnalls Company | New York and London. [n.d.]

Collation: [i–ix], x, 1–198. Leaf, 6 × 8. Binding, cloth. With 47 illustra-tions. Type, Scotch-face Monotype.
Composition and presswork only by the Press.

Minor Printing

The Carnegie Foundation for the Advancement of Teaching, Thirty-second Annual Report of the President and of the Treasurer, New York; *also* Announcements of a General Record Examination *and* Tested Achievements of Prospective Teachers in Pennsylvania, Reprinted from the Thirty-first Annual Report.

Goodspeed's Book Shop, Catalogue Number 278, Rare Books.

Athenæum Items.

Hints on Popularity, Angelo Patri.

Matilda Campbell Markoe.

Reports: John Carter Brown Library, Providence, Rhode Island, Report to the Corporation of Brown University, Providence; One Hundred & First and Second Annual Reports, Providence Athenæum, Providence.

Reprints from Colonial Society of Massachusetts Transactions: A Voyage to the Mediterranean during the Napoleonic Wars by Robert E. Peabody (Volume XXXII); Two Winthrops and A Mouse, 1640, by Stewart Mitchell (Volume XXXII); The Discovery of a Lost Cambridge Imprint, John Eliot's Genesis, 1655, by Wilberforce Eames (Volume XXXIV).

[289]

The Merrymount Press
1938

[834]

Meditations in Season | On the Elements of Christian | Philoso-
phy | by | Herber Wallace Schneider | Professor of Religion,
Columbia University | [cut] | Oxford University Press | New
York, London, Toronto | 1938.

Collation: [i–viii], 1–82, [83]. Leaf, 5⅛ × 7⅝. Binding, cloth. Type, Caslon
Monotype.

[835]

The Wall-Paintings of India | Central Asia & Ceylon | A Com-
parative Study | By Benjamin Rowland, Jr. | With an | Intro-
ductory Essay on The Nature of Buddist Art | By Ananda K.
Coomaraswamy | [floret] | With a Foreword by A. Townshend
Johnson and | Colour Plates by F. Bailey Vanderhoef, Jr. | Bos-
ton | Printed at The Merrymount Press | 1938.

On reverse of title: D. B. Updike, The Merrymount Press, Boston. Collation: [i–ii], i–xiv, 1–94. Leaf, 11 × 13⅞. Binding, Portfolio, cloth. Rubricated title. With 30 plates in colour at the back in loose sheets. Type,
Janson.

[836]

Poems to Vera | by | George Sterling | [rule] | [printer's orna-
ment] | [rule] | New York | Oxford University Press | 1938.

On reverse of title: D. B. Updike, The Merrymount Press, Boston. Collation: i–vi, 1–38, [39]. Leaf, 4⅝ × 7¼. Binding, cloth. Rubricated title.
With collotype frontispiece. Type, Baskerville Monotype.

[837]

Study of the Relations of Secondary and Higher Education in |
Pennsylvania | The Student | and His Knowledge | A Report to
The Carnegie Foundation on the Results | of High School and
College Examinations of | 1928, 1930, and 1932 | By William S.
Learned | Staff Member, Carnegie Foundation for the Advance-
ment of Teaching | And Ben D. Wood | Director of Collegiate
Educational Research, Columbia College | With a Foreword by
Walter A. Jessup | President of the Foundation | Bulletin Num-

[290]

Bibliography

ber Twenty-nine | [*seal*] | New York | The Carnegie Founda-
tion | for the Advancement of Teaching | 1938.

On reverse of title: D. B. Updike, The Merrymount Press, Boston. Collation: i–xx, 1–406. Leaf, 7⅜ × 10. Binding, paper. Type, Scotch-face
Monotype.

[838]
A College Friendship | A Series of Letters | from | John Hay to
Hannah Angell | [*printer's ornament*] | [*cut*] | [*printer's ornament*] |
Boston | Privately Printed | 1938.

Colophon: Three hundred and fifty copies of this book were printed by D.
B. Updike, The Merrymount Press, Boston, in the month of April, 1938.
Collation: i–x, 1–65, [66–67]. Leaf, 6⅛ × 8⅜. Binding, cloth. With photo-
gravure portrait. Type, Oxford.

[839]
[*printer's ornament*] | The Commonwealth Fund | Fellows |
1925–1937 | [*printer's ornament*] | New York | The Common-
wealth Fund | 1938 | [*printer's ornament*].

On reverse of title: D. B. Updike, The Merrymount Press, Boston. Collation: [i–vi], 1–204, [205]. Leaf, 5 × 7½. Binding, cloth. Type, Caslon
Monotype.

[840]
A Catalogue of the Books of | John Quincy Adams | Deposited
in the Boston Athenæum | With Notes on | Books, Adams Seals
and Bookplates | By Henry Adams | With an Introduction by |
Worthington Chauncey Ford | [*seal*] | Boston | Printed for the
Athenæum | 1938.

Colophon: [*seal*] Of this book 300 copies were printed by D. B. Updike, The
Merrymount Press, Boston, Massachusetts June, 1938. Collation: [i–viii],
1–152, [153]. Leaf, 6¼ × 9⅜. Binding, cloth. With 13 photogravure illustrations. Type, Caslon Monotype and Janson.

[841]
The Hispanic Society of America | Handbook | Museum and
Library Collections | [*seal*] | Printed by Order of | The Trus-
tees | New York | 1938.

[291]

The Merrymount Press

Collation: [i–x], 1–442, [443]. Leaf, 6¼ × 8⅞. Binding, cloth. Type, Cheltenham Monotype.

[842]

[*within cut*] The | Pickwick Papers | Some Bibliographical Remarks | An Address | Delivered before The Caxton Club | January sixteenth, 1937 | By | J. Christian Bay | Librarian, The John Crerar Library, Chicago | Chicago | The Caxton Club | 1938.

Colophon: [*seal*] Two hundred and fifty copies of this book were printed by D. B. Updike at The Merrymount Press, Boston, 1938. Collation: [i–vi], 1–28, [29]. Leaf, 6 × 8⅞. Binding, cloth. With 4 photogravure illustrations. Type, Scotch-face Monotype.

[843]

Vision | Being the Continuation of | "Reality" and "Dedication" | (from 1931 to 1937) | [*floret*] | Privately Printed | 1938.

On reverse of title: D. B. Updike, The Merrymount Press, Boston. Collation: [i–vi], 1–353. Leaf, 5 × 7¼. Binding, cloth. Type, Scotch-face Monotype.

[844]

[*printer's ornament*] | The | Classics | By | Campbell Dodgson | [*floret*] | Privately Printed | M. Knoedler & Company, Inc. | New York | [*printer's ornament*].

On reverse of title: D. B. Updike, The Merrymount Press, Boston, Massachusetts, U.S.A. Colophon: [*printer's ornament*] Of this book there have been printed three hundred and seventy-five numbered copies, for presentation to the Friends of M. Knoedler & Company, Inc. and twenty-five lettered copies for the Author Christmas, 1938. [*rule*] This is Number —. [*printer's ornament*]. Collation: [i–iv], 1–22, [23]. Leaf, 4⅛ × 6⅜. Binding, boards. Type, Baskerville Monotype.

[845]

Recollections of | Henry Sargent Hunnewell | [*printer's ornaments*] | Boston | Privately Printed | 1938.

On reverse of title: D. B. Updike, The Merrymount Press, Boston. Collation: [i–iv], 1–31, [32–33]. Leaf, 4¾ × 7½. Binding, cloth. Type, Caslon Monotype.

Bibliography

[846]

[*within cut*] A Catalogue | of the | Thirteenth | Annual Exhibition | of | Engravings, Woodcuts | Etchings | of | the XV and XVI | Centuries | April 4th to April 30th, | 1938 | M. Knoedler & Company, Inc. | 14 East Fifty-seventh Street | New York.

Colophon: [*cut*] Of this catalogue there have been printed by D. B. Updike, The Merrymount Press, Boston, Massachusetts one thousand five hundred copies for M. Knoedler & Company, Inc. and their friends April, 1938. Collation: i–iv, 1–79, [80–81]. Leaf, 5¾ × 8⅝. Binding, paper. With 36 illustrations. Type, Caslon Monotype.

[847]

[*cut*] | Carita Fiorentina | Privately Printed. [n.d.]

Colophon: Two hundred copies printed by D. B. Updike, The Merrymount Press, Boston, U.S.A. Collation: [i–vi], 1–16, [17–18]. Leaf, 4¾ × 7½. Binding, paper. Type, Caslon Monotype.

[848]

[*rule*] | The Provenance | of | A Country Law Library | and | Court House | at | Petersham | Massachusetts.

Colophon: One hundred copies printed by The Merrymount Press, Boston, for John Munro Woolsey in honor of The Centennial of the building of The Country Law Library and Court House, and The Visit of The Walpole Society thereto on Saturday, September 24, 1938. Collation: 1–11, [12–13]. Leaf, 4¾ × 7. Binding, paper. Type, Scotch-face Monotype.

[849]

Address by Daniel Berkeley Updike | at the Official Opening | of the New Installation of the | Updike Collection of Books on Printing | at the Providence Public Library | December sixteenth | 1937.

Colophon: One hundred and seventy-five copies printed. The Merrymount Press, Boston. Collation: [i–ii], 1–9, [10]. Leaf, 4⅝ × 7. Binding, paper. Type, Oxford.

[850]

[*quotation*] | [*printer's ornament*] | Colby's Roman | Julian Daniel Taylor | By | Bertha Louise Soule | [*seal*] | Colby College, Waterville, Maine. [n.d.]

The Merrymount Press

On reverse of title: The Athenæum Press. Collation: i–xiv, 1–141, [142]. Leaf, 5½ × 8⅛. Binding, cloth. With 20 illustrations. Type, Granjon Linotype.

Presswork only by the Press.

Minor Printing

The Carnegie Foundation for the Advancement of Teaching, Thirty-third Annual Report of the President and of the Treasurer, New York; *also* Announcement of the Graduate Record Examination; Act of Incorporation, By-Laws, Rules for the Granting of Retiring Allowances; The Student and His Knowledge, Reprinted from Bulletin Number Twenty-nine; *and* Appreciations.

Goodspeed's Book Shop, Catalogue 294, Manuscripts & Early Printed Books.

Footnotes, The Bulletin of the Friends of the Library, Massachusetts Institute of Technology.

Athenæum Items.

The Larz Anderson House in Washington, Society of the Cincinnati.

The Month at Goodspeed's.

Reports: John Carter Brown Library, Providence, Rhode Island, Report to the Corporation of Brown University, Providence; One Hundred and Third Annual Report, Providence Athenæum, Providence.

1939

[851]

Friendship | By | Ralph Waldo | Emerson | [*floret*] | Worcester | Achille J. St. Onge | 1939.

Colophon: [*floret*] Of this book 950 copies were printed from Times New Roman type, upon Worthy Hand and Arrows paper by D. B. Updike, The Merrymount Press, Boston, U.S.A. [*floret*]. Collation: [i–iv], 1–82, [83] Leaf, 1½ × 2¼. Binding, leather. With half-tone portrait. Type, Times Roman.

Some copies of this book were bound at the direction of the publisher in Niger Morocco by Sangorski of London.

[852]

Strangers & Pilgrims | Studies | in Classics of Christian Devo-

Bibliography

tion | By Willard L. Sperry | Dean of the Harvard Divinity School | [*cut*] | Boston | Little, Brown & Company | 1939.

On reverse of title: Printed in the United States of America by D. B. Updike, The Merrymount Press, Boston, Massachusetts. Collation: i–xvi, 1–165, [166–167]. Leaf, 5½ × 8½. Binding, cloth. Type, Baskerville Monotype.

[853]
[*within border*] Holmes | of the | Breakfast Table | By | M. A. DeWolfe Howe | [*cut*] | Oxford University Press | London · New York | 1939.

On reverse of title: D. B. Updike, The Merrymount Press, Boston. Collation: i–x, 1–172. Leaf, 5½ × 8⅛. Binding, cloth. With 8 illustrations in collotype. Type, Baskerville Monotype.

[854]
[*within cut*] A Catalogue | of the | Fourteenth | Annual Exhibition | of | Engravings, Etchings | Woodcuts | of the XV and XVI | Centuries | March 7th to March 25th | 1939 | M. Knoedler & Company, Inc. | 14 East Fifty-seventh Street | New York

Colophon: [*cut*] Of this catalogue there have been printed by D. B. Updike, The Merrymount Press, Boston, Massachusetts one thousand five hundred copies for M. Knoedler & Company, Inc. and their friends March, 1939. Collation: i–vi, 1–117, [118–119]. Leaf, 5¾ × 8⅝. Binding, paper. With 48 illustrations. Type, Times Roman Monotype.

[855]
Bread and Honey | By | Frances H. Savage | [*printer's ornament*] | [*cut*] | [*printer's ornament*] | New York | Privately Printed | 1939.

On reverse of title: D. B. Updike, The Merrymount Press, Boston. Collation: i–viii, 1–59. Leaf, 4⅝ × 7¼. Binding, paper. Type, Baskerville Monotype.

100 copies printed.

[856]
The | Grolier Club | Founded 1884 | Officers, Committees | Constitution and By-Laws | Members | Reports of Officers and Committees | for the Year | 1938 | [*floret*] | New York | 47 East Sixtieth Street | MCMXXXIX.

[295]

The Merrymount Press

Colophon: Printed by D. B. Updike, The Merrymount Press, Boston. Collation: 1–117, [118–119]. Leaf, 4¼ × 6⅝. Binding, paper. Type, Caslon Monotype.

[857]
Addison Gallery | of American Art | [*printer's ornaments*] | Handbook | of Paintings, Sculpture, Prints | and Drawings | in the Permanent Collection | [*floret*] | Phillips Academy | Andover, Massachusetts | 1939.

On reverse of title: D. B. Updike, The Merrymount Press, Boston. Collation: i–x, 1–133. Leaf, 5½ × 8½. Binding, cloth. Type, Times Roman Monotype.

[858]
[*within border*] Pietas in Patria | [*rule*] | Dr. Morison's | Farewell | to | The Colonial Society of | Massachusetts | Being a Review of the Events of | A.D. MDCCCXXXVIII | [*rule*] | Delivered at the Annual Dinner of the Society aforesaid | held on Monday, the Twenty-first Day of November, 1938 | [*rule*] | [*cut*] | [*rule*] | Boston in New England: Printed at the expense of | the Society at The Merrymount Press, A.D. 1939.

Collation: [i–ii], 1–9. Leaf, 5⅜ × 7⅜. Binding, paper. Type, Janson.

[859]
The | Century Association | Year-Book | 1939 | [*border*] | [*floret*] | [*border*] | New York | 1939.

On reverse of title: D. B. Updike, The Merrymount Press, Boston. Collation: [i–vi], 1–132. Leaf, 5⅜ × 6¾. Binding, cloth. Type, Times Roman Monotype.

[860]
Century | Memorials | 1938 | [*border*] | [*floret*] | [*border*] | New York | 1939.

On reverse of title: D. B. Updike, The Merrymount Press, Boston. Collation: [i–iv], 1–92. Leaf, 5½ × 8⅜. Binding, cloth. Type, Baskerville Monotype.

[861]
A Garland of | Friendship | Gathered from Many Gardens | for Irene Johnson | [*cut*] | Privately Printed | MCMXXXIX.

[296]

Bibliography

Collation: [i–ii], 1–40, [41]. Leaf, 6¼ × 8⅛. Binding, boards. Title printed in 2 colours. Type, Poliphilus and Bembo.

Only the title-page and shelf-back lettering were set by the Press.

[862]

Nansen | By Anna Gertrude Hall | Illustrated by Boris Artzy-basheff | [*cut*] | New York | Published by The Viking Press | 1940.

On reverse of title: Set by The Merrymount Press in the Times and Perpetua Types of the Monotype Corporation Limited. Collation: 1–165. Leaf, 6⅛ × 9¼. Binding, cloth. With 21 illustrations in gravure. Type, Times Roman and Perpetua.

Text printed by The Country Life Press.

[863]

Counterfeiting | in Colonial Pennsylvania | by | Harrold E. Gillingham | [*seal*] | The American Numismatic Society | Broadway at 156th Street | New York | 1939.

On reverse of title: The Merrymount Press, Boston, U.S.A. Collation: [i–vi], 1–52. Leaf, 4½ × 6⅝. Binding, paper. With illustration in collotype. Type, Caslon Monotype.

Numismatic Notes and Monographs No. 86.

[864]

[*within rules and border*] Westminster Abbey | By | An American Visitor | [*floret*].

Colophon: [*border and rule*] Printed at The Merrymount Press, Boston, Massachusetts, 1939. By permission of *The Guardian*, London [*rule and border*]. Collation: [1–7]. Leaf, 7½ × 10. Binding, paper. Rubricated throughout. Type, Lutetia.

[865]

Andrew McCance | Born at Killyleagh, County Down, Ireland | September 21, 1863 | Died at Arlington, Massachusetts | August 30, 1939 | [*floret*] | Boston | Privately Printed | 1939.

On reverse of title: [*printer's ornament*] D. B. Updike, The Merrymount Press, Boston [*printer's ornament*]. Collation: [i–iv], 1–19. Leaf, 6 × 9. Binding, paper. With photogravure portrait. Type, Baskerville Monotype and Janson.

[297]

The Merrymount Press

[866]

Tales | of a Sportsman's Wife | By | Marjorie Wiggin Prescott | [*printer's ornament*] | Shooting | Privately Printed. [n.d.]

Colophon: Printed by D. B. Updike, The Merrymount Press, Boston, Massachusetts, U.S.A. Collation: [i–vi], 1–79, [80–81]. Leaf, 5¾ × 8¼. Binding, boards. With 2 illustrations. Type, Janson.

[867]

Family Jottings | Roger Wolcott | [*floret*] | Privately Printed | 1939.

On reverse of title: [*printer's ornament*] D. B. Updike, The Merrymount Press, Boston [*printer's ornament*]. Collation: i–x, 1–120. Leaf, 5⅞ × 8⅞. Binding, cloth. Type, Caslon Monotype.

[868]

A Preliminary Check List of | Cambridge, Massachusetts | Imprints | 1638–1692 | Prepared, and with a Foreword | By George Parker Winship | [*seal*] | Boston | The Colonial Society of Massachusetts | 1939.

Collation: i–xii, 1–40. Leaf, 6⅜ × 9¼. Binding, paper. Type, Caslon Monotype, Janson and Black Letter.
No imprint.

[869]

To | Herbert Putnam | Librarian of Congress | 1899–1939 | [*floret*] | An Address | in Appreciation of His Services | to Scholarship | and | to the Advancement of Knowledge | Presented on behalf of | the Scholars of the United States | By the American Council of | Learned Societies | [*floret*]. [n.d.]

On reverse of title: D. B. Updike, The Merrymount Press, Boston. Collation: [1–14]. Leaf, 6¾ × 10. Binding, paper. Rubricated title. Type, Caslon Monotype.
Also issued in large folio. See No. 872.

[870]

[*cut*] | Proceedings | Had on November 3, 1939 | in the | United States District Court | for the Southern District of New York | on the | One Hundred and Fiftieth Anniversary | of its Organization | [*rule*].

Bibliography

On reverse of title: Printed in an edition of three hundred copies for Southern District Court Reporters by The Merrymount Press, Boston, Massachusetts. Collation: 1–26. Leaf, 6⅛ × 9¼. Binding, paper. Type, Bulmer Monotype.

[871]
Songs | To Our Lady | By | Francesco Petrarca | Translated by | Eleanor Vinton Murray | [cut] | Privately Printed | 1939.

Colophon: The Merrymount Press, Boston. Collation: [i–iv], 1–23, [24]. Leaf, 4¾ × 6½. Binding, paper. Type, Baskerville Monotype.

[872]
To | Herbert Putnam | Librarian of Congress | 1899–1939 | [floret] | An Address | in Appreciation of His Services | To Scholarship | and | To the Advancement of Knowledge | Presented on Behalf of | The Scholars of the United States | By The American Council of | Learned Societies | [floret]. [n.d.]

On reverse of title: D. B. Updike, The Merrymount Press, Boston. Collation: [i–ii], [1–3]. Leaf, 11½ × 16¾. Binding, paper. Rubricated title. Type, Janson.
6 copies printed.

[873]
A Memorial to | Frank Edward Winsor | 1870–1939 | Chief Engineer from 1926 to 1939 | of the | Metropolitan District Water Supply Commission | of the Commonwealth of Massachusetts | [floret] | Prepared by the Commission | Eugene C. Hultman | Chairman | Thomas D. Lavelle Edward J. Kelley | Associate Commissioners | [floret]. [n.d.]

On reverse of title: D. B. Updike, The Merrymount Press, Boston. Collation: [i–ii], [1–3]. Leaf, 11½ × 16¾. Binding, paper. Rubricated title. Type, Janson.
40 copies printed.

[874]
Studies in | Early Graduate Education | The Johns Hopkins, Clark University, | The University of Chicago | By W. Carson Ryan | Staff Associate | Carnegie Foundation for the Advancement of Teaching | With a Preface by Walter A. Jessup | Presi-

[299]

The Merrymount Press

dent of the Foundation | Bulletin Number Thirty | [*seal*] | New York | The Carnegie Foundation | for the Advancement of Teaching | 552 Fifth Avenue | 1939.

On reverse of title: D. B. Updike, The Merrymount Press, Boston. Collation: i–viii, 1–167. Leaf, 7⅜ × 10. Binding, paper. Type, Scotch-face Monotype.

Minor Printing

The Carnegie Foundation for the Advance of Teaching, Thirty-fourth Annual Report of the President and of the Treasurer, New York; *also* Announcement of the Graduate Record Examination *and* Life Insurance for College Teachers, Reprinted from the Thirty-third Annual Report.

The Month at Goodspeed's.

Athenæum Items.

Massachusetts Historical Society, List of Members.

"— called St. Michael's (St. Michael's Episcopal Church, Marblehead, Massachusetts).

Reports: John Carter Brown Library, Providence, Rhode Island, Report to the Corporation of Brown University, Providence; Boston Athenæum, Reports of the Library Committee and the Librarian for the Year 1938.

George T. Goodspeed, The "First American" Queen Mab (insert for "The Colophon").

The Management of Boston Metal Investors, Incorporated.

Gold and Metal Shares as Investments.

1940

[875]

The Cheney Award | A Record of its First Ten Years | 1928–1938 | With an Introduction by | Mrs. William H. Schofield | (Mary Lyon Cheney Schofield) | [*printer's ornaments*] | Privately Printed | Peterborough, New Hampshire | 1940.

On reverse of title: D. B. Updike, The Merrymount Press, Boston. Collation: [i–iv], 1–18, [19–45]. Leaf, 8½ × 11⅛. Binding, cloth. With 28 illustrations. Type, Times Roman Monotype.

Bibliography

[876]

An Account of | Calligraphy | & | Printing | in the Sixteenth
Century | from Dialogues attributed to | Christopher Plantin |
Printed and Published by him at Antwerp, in | 1567. French and
Flemist Text in facsimile, Eng- | lish Translation and Notes by
Ray Nash and | Foreword by Stanley Morison | [cut] | Cam-
bridge | Massachusetts | Department of Printing and Graphic
Arts | Harvard College Library | 1940.

Colophon: [at front] Two hundred and fifty copies have been printed by
D. B. Updike, The Merrymount Press, Boston, in January, 1940, as the
first publication of the Department of Printing and Graphic Arts, in the
Harvard College Library, Cambridge, Massachusetts. Collation: i–viii,
1–30, [31]. Leaf, 4⅝ × 7. Binding, boards. With 40 collotype illustrations.
Type, Caslon Monotype.
Paste paper on cover designed and executed by Rosamond B. Loring.

[877]

Pride and Prejudice | By | Jane Austen | with Preface by Frank
Swinnerton | and Illustrations by | Helen Sewell | [cut] | Boston:
Printed for the Members of | The Limited Editions Club | at
The Merrymount Press | 1940.

Colophon: [cut] Of this Edition of "Pride and Prejuduce" fifteen hundred
copies have been made for the Members of the Limited Editions Club by
D. B. Updike, The Merrymount Press, Boston, the Illustrations being
drawn by Helen Sewell who signs here — this Copy, which is Number —.
Collation: i–xvi, 1–411, [412–413]. Leaf, 6 × 9⅛. Binding, leather. With 46
illustrations. Type, Baskerville Monotype.

[878]

Documents | Relating to | The Frick Collection | [floret] | New
York | 1940.

On reverse of title: [printer's ornament] The Merrymount Press, Boston
[printer's ornament]. Collation: [i–vi], 1–37. Leaf, 6 × 9. Binding, cloth.
Type, Bulmer Monotype.

[879]

It's No Fun to | Grow Up | A Handbook of Information | for
Precocious Adults | By Horton W. Reed | [printer's ornament] |
Illustrated by Monnie Dunlop | [floret] | Boston, 1940.

The Merrymount Press

On reverse of title: The Merrymount Press, Boston. Collation: i–viii, 1–42. Leaf, 6⅛ × 9⅛. Binding, boards. With 12 illustrations. Type, Times Roman Monotype and Astree.

[880]

Rabbi Haim Isaac Carigal | His Newport Sermon and | His Yale Portrait | By | Lee M. Friedman | [*floret*] | Boston | Privately Printed | 1940.

On reverse of title: [*printer's ornament*] D. B. Updike, The Merrymount Press, Boston [*printer's ornament*]. Collation: [i–vi], 1–43, [44–45]. Leaf, 5¾ × 8½. Binding, boards. With photogravure portrait. Type, Caslon Monotype and Janson.

[881]

The | Grolier Club | Founded 1884 | Officers, Committees | Constitution and By-Laws | Members | Reports of Officers | and Committees | for the Year | 1939 | [*floret*] | New York | 47 East Sixtieth Street | MCMXL.

Colophon: Printed by D. B. Updike, The Merrymount Press, Boston, Massachusetts, U.S.A. Collation: 1–111, [112–113]. Leaf, 4¼ × 6⅝. Binding, paper. Type, Caslon Monotype.

[882]

The | Century Association | Year-Book | 1940 | [*border*] | [*floret*] | [*border*] | New York | 1940.

On reverse of title: [*printer's ornament*] D. B. Updike, The Merrymount Press, Boston [*printer's ornament*]. Collation: [i–vi], 1–134. Leaf, 5⅜ × 6¾. Binding, cloth. Type, Times Roman Monotype.

[883]

[*cut*] | A Keepsake | printed in the year of the | Five Hundredth Anniversary of the | Invention of Printing | and Commemorating the Thirty-fifth year | since the Inauguration of | The Society of Printers | Being the Address of | William Dana Orcutt, Esqr. | at the First Meeting of the Society | February 24, 1905 | [*rule*].

Colophon: This Edition, limited to 300 copies, is arranged and printed by D. B. Updike, The Merrymount Press, Boston in the Month of May 19 [*printer's ornament*] 40. This is Number —. Collation: i–viii, 1–7, [8]. Leaf, 4¼ × 6¾. Binding, cloth. Rubricated title. Type, Bulmer Monotype.

Bibliography

[884]

The Elements of | Lettering | By | John Howard Benson | and | Arthur Graham Carey | [cut] | John Stevens | Newport, Rhode Island | 1940.

Colophon: Printed for John Stevens, Newport, Rhode Island, by D B. Updike, The Merrymount Press, Boston, in the Month of May, 1940. Collation: i–x, 1–125, [126]. Leaf, 7½ × 10. Binding, cloth. Type, Times Roman Monotype.

100 copies were also printed on rag paper and numbered.

[885]

John Graham Brooks | Helen Lawrence Brooks | 1846–1938 | [*floret*] | A Memorial | Boston | Privately Printed | 1940.

On reverse of title: D. B. Updike, The Merrymount Press, Boston. Collation: [i–vi], 1–63. Leaf, 5½ × 8½. Binding, cloth. With 9 photogravure illustrations. Type, Baskerville Monotype.

[886]

Study of the Relations of Secondary and Higher Education in | Pennsylvania | An Experiment | in Responsible Learning | A Report to the Carnegie Foundation on Projects | in Evaluation of Secondary School Progress | 1929–1938 | By William S. Learned | Staff Member, Carnegie Foundation for the Advancement of Teaching | And Anna L. Rose Hawkes | Staff Assistant for the Pennsylvania Inquiry | With a Foreword by Walter A. Jessup | President of the Foundation | Bulletin Number Thirty-one | [*seal*] | New York | The Carnegie Foundation | for the Advancement of Teaching | 1940.

On reverse of title: [*printer's ornament*] D. B. Updike, The Merrymount Press, Boston [*printer's ornament*]. Collation: [i–vi], 1–61. Leaf, 7⅜ × 10. Binding, paper. With 16 illustrations. Type, Scotch-face Monotype.

[887]

Century | Memorials | 1939 | [*border*] | [*floret*] | [*border*] | New York | 1940.

On reverse of title: [*printer's ornament*] D. B. Updike, The Merrymount Press, Boston [*printer's ornament*]. Collation: [i–iv], 1–76. Leaf, 5⅜ × 8⅜. Binding, cloth. Type, Baskerville Monotype and Janson.

[303]

The Merrymount Press

[888]

Publications | of | The Colonial Society of Massachusetts | Volume XXXIII | [*printer's ornaments*] | Collections | [*seal*] | Boston | Published by the Society | 1940.

On reverse of title: D. B. Updike, The Merrymount Press, Boston, U.S.A. Collation: [i–ii], i–xl, 1–237. Leaf, 6½ × 9⅜. Binding, cloth. Type, Caslon Monotype.

[889]

[*printer's ornament*] | John Cotton Dana | A Life | By Frank Kingdon | President of the University of Newark | Newark | The Public Library and Museum | 1940 | [*printer's ornament*].

On reverse of title: [*printer's ornament*] D. B. Updike, The Merrymount Press, Boston, U.S.A. [*printer's ornament*]. Collation: [i–x], 1–175. Leaf, 5⅝ × 8½. Binding, cloth. With photogravure frontispiece. Type, Baskerville Monotype.

[890]

Temples of Rome | as Coin Types | By | Donald F. Brown | [*seal*] | The American Numismatic Society | Broadway at 156th Street | New York | 1940.

On reverse of title: The Merrymount Press, Boston, U.S.A. Collation: [i–iv], 1–51, [52]. Leaf, 4½ × 6⅝. Binding, paper. With 9 collotype plates. Type, Caslon Monotype.
Numismatic Notes and Monographs No. 90.

[891]

Butler Hospital | Incorporated 1844 | For the Treatment of Nervous and | Mental Illness | [*cut*] | Arthur H. Ruggles, M.D. | Superintendent | 305 Blackstone Boulevard, Providence, Rhode Island. [n.d.]

On reverse of title: The Merrymount Press, Boston. Collation: 1–19, [20]. Leaf, 5¾ × 8. Binding, paper. With 15 illustrations. Type, Baskerville Monotype.

[892]

The Carnegie Foundation for the Advancement of Teaching | A Third of a Century of | Teachers Retirement | Records of

[304]

Bibliography

Measures Adopted to carry out | the Purposes of the Founder | [*seal*] | 522 Fifth Avenue | New York City | 1940.

On reverse of title: [*printer's ornament*] D. B. Updike, The Merrymount Press, Boston [*printer's ornament*]. Collation: i–viii, 1–102. Leaf, 7⅜ × 10. Binding, cloth. With illustration. Type, Scotch-face Monotype.
Also issued in paper covers.

[893]
The Syrian Tetradrachms | Of | Caracalla and Macrinus | By | Alfred R. Bellinger | Lampson Professor of Latin in Yale College | Fellow of Saybrook College | Numismatic Studies | No. 3 | [*seal*] | The American Numismatic Society | New York | 1940.

On reverse of title: D. B. Updike, The Merrymount Press, Boston, U.S.A. Collation: 1–116, [117]. Leaf, 7¾ × 10¾. Binding, paper. With 26 plates in collotype. Type, Caslon Monotype.

[894]
The Athenæum Gallery | 1827–1873 | The Boston Athenæum as an | Early Patron of Art | By | Mabel Munson Swan | With an Introduction by | Charles Knowles Bolton | [*seal*] | Printed from the Income of the | Robert Charles Billings Fund | The Boston Athenæum | 1940.

On reverse of title: [*printer's ornament*] D. B. Updike, The Merrymount Press, Boston [*printer's ornament*]. Collation: [i–ii], i–xiv, 1–312. Leaf, 6¼ × 8¾. Binding, cloth. With 10 photogravure illustrations. Type, Caslon Monotype.

[895]
The Earlier Staters | of Heraclea Lucaniae | By | Eunice Work | [*seal*] | The American Numismatic Society | Broadway at 156th Street | New York | 1940.

On reverse of title: The Merrymount Press, Boston, U.S.A. Collation: [i–iv], 1–40. Leaf, 4½ × 6⅝. Binding, paper. With 8 collotype plates. Type, Caslon Monotype.
Numismatic Notes and Monographs No. 91.

[896]
Chester Noyes Greenough | An Account of His Life as |

[305]

The Merrymount Press

Teacher, Dean, Master & Scholar | By Ruth Hornblower Greenough | [*cut*] | [*quotation*] | Printed at The Merrymount Press | Harvard Cooperative Society | Distributors, Cambridge | 1940.

On reverse of title: [*printer's ornament*] D. B. Updike, The Merrymount Press, Boston, U.S.A. [*printer's ornament*]. Collation: i–xvi, 1–335. Leaf, 6¼ × 9⅜. Binding, cloth. With 20 photogravure illustrations. Type, Caslon Monotype and Janson.
Frontispiece wood-engraving in colour by Rudolph Ruzicka.

[897]
Collected Studies by | Chester Noyes Greenough | With an Introduction by | Wilbur Cortez Abbott | [*cut*] | Printed at The Merrymount Press | Harvard Cooperative Society | Distributors, Cambridge | 1940.

On reverse of title: [*printer's ornament*] D. B. Updike, The Merrymount Press, Boston, U.S.A. [*printer's ornament*]. Collation: i–xii, 1–303. Leaf, 6¼ × 9⅜. Binding, cloth. Type, Caslon Monotype and Janson.
Companion Volume to No. 896.

[898]
Six Hundred Years | of | Sport | A Catalogue of an Exhibition held at | The Grolier Club | December 12, 1940 through February 4, 1941 | [*seal*] | New York | The Grolier Club | 1940.

On reverse of title: The Committee on Publications of The Grolier Club certifies that this copy of *Six Hundred Years of Sport* is one of an edition of five hundred copies, printed by D. B. Updike, The Merrymount Press in the month of December, 1940. Collation: i–x, 1–37. Leaf, 5½ × 8⅜. Binding, paper. With illustration. Type, Baskerville Monotype and Bulmer.

[899]
[*within border*] Five | American | Immortals | By | Joseph | Auslander | [*floret*] | Worcester | Achille J. St. Onge | 1940.

Colophon: [*printer's ornament*] Of this book 475 copies have been printed from Caslon type, on Glenbourne Deckle Edge Book by D. B. Updike, The Merrymount Press, Boston, Massachusetts, U.S.A. [*printer's ornament*]. Collation: [i–iv], 1–50, [51]. Leaf, 2 × 3. Binding, cloth. Five postage stamps used as illustrations for the five essays. Type, Caslon Monotype.

Bibliography

Minor Printing

The Carnegie Foundation for the Advancement of Teaching, Thirty-fifth Annual Report of the President and of the Treasurer, New York; *also* Announcement of the Graduate Record Examination; Act of Incorporation, By-Laws, Rules for the Granting of Retiring Allowances; The Carnegie Foundation for the Advancement of Teaching, Reprinted from the Thirty-second Annual Report; Accrediting Agencies, Reprinted from the Thirty-fourth Annual Report; Publications of the Foundation; *and* Graduate Record Examination, Books I and II.

The Month at Goodspeed's.

Athenæum Items.

Reports: John Carter Brown Library, Providence, Rhode Island, Report to the Corporation of Brown University, Providence; Butler Hospital for the Treatment of Nervous and Mental Illness, Reports Presented to the Corporation at its Annual Meeting January 24, 1940 (Ninety-sixth Annual Report); One Hundred & Fourth and Fifth Annual Reports, Providence Athenæum, Providence; Boston Athenæum, Reports of the Library Committee and the Librarian for the Year 1939.

Goodspeed's Book Shop, Catalogue 326, Association Books.

Four Thousand and One Buttons, An Exhibition at the Cooper Union.

To Clarence E. Sherman, Providence Public Library (Testimonial).

Will of Joseph B. Thomas, Dated April 19, 1887.

Friends of the Harvard Forest.

The Harvard Forest at Petersham, Massachusetts.

Matt Bushnell Jones May 15, 1871–July 1, 1941 (Broadside).

Catalogue Isabella Stewart Gardner Museum, Fenway Court.

Service of Dedication of the All Saints Memorial Window, Church of Our Saviour, Longwood.

1941

[900]

[*on pictorial background*] The Flowering of | New England | By Van Wyck Brooks | With an Introduction by M. A. DeWolfe Howe and | Illustrations by R. J. Holden | Boston | Printed for

The Merrymount Press

the Members of | The Limited Editions Club | at The Merrymount Press | 1941.

Colophon: [*within illustration*] The Flowering of New England was awarded The Limited Editions Club's Gold Medal in November, 1938. This edition was prepared for the Members of the Club by D. B. Updike, The Merrymount Press, Boston. The edition consists of fifteen hundred numbered copies. The illustrations were made by Ray J. Holden, who here signs —. Collation: i–xxii, 1–468, [469]. Leaf, 7 × 10. Binding, cloth. With 40 illustrations in sanguine collotype. Type, Bulmer Monotype.

The binding is an all-over pattern of oak leaves and acorns.

[901]

[*within border*] Some Poems | and | A Devotion | of | John Donne | The Poet of the Month | New Directions | Norfolk, Connecticut | 1941.

Colophon: [*border*] Some Poems and A Devotion of John Donne was printed from Caslon type on Glenbourne Deckle Edge Book for New Directions, Norfolk, Conn., by D. B. Updike, The Merrymount Press, Boston, U.S.A. [*border*]. Collation: [i–iv], [1–28]. Leaf, 5 ⅞ × 9. Binding, boards. Type, Caslon Monotype and Janson.

Also issued in paper covers. Reprinted in 1941, 1942, and 1945 without textual changes.

[902]

Plant Illustration | before 1850 | A Catalogue of an Exhibition | of Books, Drawings and Prints | Held by The Garden Club of America | and The Grolier Club | From February 20 to March 31, 1941 | [*seal*] | New York | The Grolier Club | 1941.

Colophon: [*at front*] The Committee on Publications of The Grolier Club certifies that this copy of *Plant Illustration before 1850* is one of an edition o six hundred copies, printed by D. B. Updike, The Merrymount Press, in the month of February, 1941. Collation: i–xiv, 1–33. Leaf, 5 ⅝ × 8 ⅜. Binding, paper. With illustration. Type, Caslon Monotype.

[903]

Early Houses | of the King's Province | in | The Narragansett Country | By William Davis Miller | With Drawings by | Norman Morrison Isham | [*printer's ornament*] | Wakefield | Rhode Island | 1941.

[308]

Bibliography

Colophon: [*between printer's ornaments*] Of this book 150 copies, of which 50 are for sale, were printed by D. B. Updike, at The Merrymount Press, Boston, U.S.A. in May, 1941. Collation: [i–vi], 1–33, [34–35]. Leaf, 4⅝ × 7¼. Binding, boards. Rubricated title and colophon. With 12 collotype illustrations. Type, Caslon Monotype.

[904]
The | Century Association | Year-Book | 1941 | [*border*] |
[*floret*] | [*border*] | New York | 1941.

On reverse of title: [*printer's ornament*] D. B. Updike, The Merrymount. Press, Boston [*printer's ornament*]. Collation: [i–vi], 1–138. Leaf, 5⅜ × 6¾ Binding, cloth. Type, Times Roman Monotype.

[905]
Fiftieth Anniversary of | Phi Beta Epsilon | Fraternity of | The Massachusetts Institute | of Technology | 1890–1940 | [*cut*] | Cambridge | Massachusetts | 1941.

On reverse of title: [*printer's ornament*] D. B. Updike, The Merrymount Press, Boston, U.S.A. [*printer's ornament*]. Collation: [i–vi], 1–71. Leaf, 8⅝ × 11⅝. Binding, cloth. With 39 collotype illustrations. Type, Times Roman Monotype.

[906]
Harvard College | Class of 1926 | [*printer's ornament*] | The Quindecennial Report | [*seal between rules*] | Cambridge | Printed for the Class | 1941.

On reverse of title: D. B. Updike, The Merrymount Press, Boston, U.S.A. Collation: i–xx, 1–275, [276]. Leaf, 6 × 9. Binding, cloth. Type, Caslon Monotype and Janson.

[907]
[*within cut*] The | Making | of a Modern | Museum | By | Eleanor | Garnier | Hewitt. [n.d.]

On reverse of title: The Merrymount Press, Boston, Collation: [i–iv], 1–20. Leaf, 6⅛ × 9⅛. Binding, paper. Title printed in 2 colours. Type, Baskerville Monotype.

[908]
Some Aspects of | Printing | Old and New | By | Daniel Berkeley Updike | [*cut*] | New Haven | William Edwin Rudge | 1941.

The Merrymount Press

Colophon: Printed by D. B. Updike at The Merrymount Press, Boston, Massachusetts, U.S.A. Collation: [i–vi], 1–72, [73–74]. Leaf, 7⅜ × 10⅛. Binding, cloth. With collotype illustration. Type, Time Roman Monotype and Perpetua Titling.

75 copies were specially bound in boards for The Society of Printers of Boston and autographed.

[909]
Georgine Holmes Thomas | 1848–1940 | [*printer's ornament*] | Stewart Mitchell | Boston | 1941.

Colophon: One hundred and twenty-five copies were printed for private distribution by D. B. Updike, The Merrymount Press, Boston, in June, 1941. Collation: [i–iv], 1–25, [26–29]. Leaf, 5 × 7¾. Binding, cloth. With 2 photogravure illustrations. Type, Lutetia.

[910]
Century | Memorials | 1940 | [*border*] | [*floret*] | [*border*] | New York | 1941.

On reverse of title: [*printer's ornament*] D. B. Updike, The Merrymount Press, Boston [*printer's ornament*]. Collation: [i–iv], 1–62. Leaf, 5½ × 8½. Binding, cloth. Type, Baskerville Monotype.

[911]
Required | Mathematics | for the New York City Public Schools | [*cut*] | Grade 8A | by | Henrietta D. Antoville | Catherine M. Trube | General Editor | William Jansen, Ed.D. | [*rule*] | Noble & Noble, Publishers, Inc. | 100 Fifth Avenue, New York City. [n.d.]

Collation: i–x, 1–288. Leaf, 5½ × 7½. Binding, cloth. Type, Times Roman Monotype and Perpetua Titling.
Composition and electrotype plates only supplied by the Press.

[912]
Required | Mathematics | for the New York City Public Schools | [*cut*] | Grade 8B | by | Henrietta D. Antoville | Catherine M. Trube | General Editor | William Jansen, Ed.D. | [*rule*] | Noble & Noble, Publishers, Inc. | 100 Fifth Avenue, New York City. [n.d.]

Bibliography

Collation: i–x, 1–274. Leaf, 5 ½ × 7 ½. Binding, cloth. Type, Times Roman Monotype and Perpetua Titling.
Composition and electrotype plates only supplied by the Press.

[913]
The Carnegie Foundation for the Advancement of Teaching | The Colleges and | The Courts | 1936–40 | Recent Judicial Decisions Regarding | Higher Education in the United States | By M. M. Chambers | Chief, Student Project Planning Section | Division of Student Work, National Youth Administration | With a Foreword | By Edward C. Elliott | President, Purdue University | [*florets*] | New York City | 522 Fifth Avenue | 1941.

On reverse of title: D. B. Updike, The Merrymount Press, Boston. Collation: i–xiv, 1–126. Leaf, 6 × 9. Binding, cloth. Type, Caslon Monotype.
Also issued in paper covers.

[914]
Foreign Imitations | of the English Noble | By | Herbert E. Ives | [*seal*] | The American Numismatic Society | Broadway at 156th Street | New York | 1941.

On reverse of title: The Merrymount Press, Boston, U.S.A. Collation: [i–iv], 1–36, [37]. Leaf, 4½ × 6⅝. Binding, paper. With 5 collotype plates. Type, Caslon Monotype.
Numismatic Notes and Mongraphs No. 93.

[915]
Harvard College | Class of 1880 | [*printer's ornaments*] | Secretary's Report XI | 1941 | [*border*] | [*seal*] | [*border*] | Boston | Printed for the Class | The Merrymount Press | 1941.

Collation: i–x, 1–69, [70]. Leaf, 6 × 9. Binding, cloth. Type, Caslon Monotype.

[916]
William Coddington | of Rhode Island | A Sketch | By | Emily Coddington Williams | [*border*] | [*floret*] | [*border*] | Newport, Rhode Island | Privately Printed | 1941.

On reverse of title: The Merrymount Press, Boston. Collation: i–viii, 1–80. Leaf, 6¼ × 9⅜. Binding, cloth. Type, Caslon Monotype.

The Merrymount Press

[917]

Voyages of the "Columbia" | to the Northwest Coast | 1787–
1790 and 1790–1793 | Edited by | Frederic W. Howay | [*seal*] |
The Massachusetts Historical Society | 1941.

On reverse of title: D. B. Updike, The Merrymount Press, Boston, U.S.A.
Collation: i–xxxii, 1–518. Leaf, 7 × 9½. Binding, boards. With 12 collotype
illustrations. Type, Caslon Monotype.

[918]

The Graduate Record | Examination | A Memorandum on the
General Character | and Purpose of the Examination | Including
a Summary of Initial Studies | of its Validity | [*printer's orna-
ment*] | New York | The Carnegie Foundation | for the Advance-
ment of Teaching | 1941.

On reverse of title: D. B. Updike, The Merrymount Press, Boston. Colla-
tion: [i–ii], 1–38. Leaf, 5¾ × 8⅝. Binding, paper. Type, Scotch-face
Monotype.
With folding chart at back.

[919]

The | Grolier Club | Founded 1884 | Officers, Committees |
Constitution and By-Laws | Members | Reports of Officers |
and Committees | for the Year | 1940 | [*floret*] | New York | 47
East Sixtieth Street | MCMXLI.

Colophon: Printed by D. B. Updike, The Merrymount Press, Boston, Massachusetts, U.S.A. Collation: 1–121, [122–123]. Leaf, 4¼ × 6⅝. Binding,
paper. Type, Caslon Monotype.

[920]

Rare Americana | from the Collection of | Matt B. Jones | [*cut*] |
Catalogue 345 | Goodspeed's Book Shop, Inc. | 18 Beacon St.,
Boston, Massachusetts, U.S.A. [n.d.]

On reverse of title: [*printer's ornament*] D. B. Updike, The Merrymount
Press, Boston [*printer's ornament*]. Collation: i–vi, 1–57. Leaf, 5½ × 8¼.
Binding, paper. Type, Times Roman Monotype.

[921]

A Catalogue of | Books | Published by the Syndics of the | Cam-

Bibliography

bridge University Press | (England) | 1941 | [*arms*] | Agents in America | The Macmillan Company.

On last page: The Merrymount Press, Boston. Collation: i–xii, 1–119, [120]. Leaf, 6⅛ × 9¼. Binding, paper. Type, Times Roman Monotype.

[922]
[*within cut*] A Pinch of | Salt | By | Frances H. Savage | [*printer's ornament*] | New York | Privately Printed | 1941.

On reverse of title: D. B. Updike, The Merrymount Press, Boston. Collation: i–viii, 1–69. Leaf, 4⅝ × 7¼. Binding, boards. Type, Baskerville Monotype.

100 copies printed.

Minor Printing

The Carnegie Foundation for the Advancement of Teaching, Thirty-sixth Annual Report of the President and of the Treasurer, New York; *also* Education and Turmoil by Walter A. Jessup, President. Reprinted from the Thirty-fifth Annual Report; Symposium on Student Appraisal, by William S. Learned. Reprinted from the Thirty-sixth Annual Report; *and* Graduate Record Examination, Books I and II.

The Month at Goodspeed's.

Athenæum Items.

Reports: John Carter Brown Library, Providence, Rhode Island, Report to the Corporation of Brown University, Providence; Massachusetts Historical Society, Annual Reports of the Council, Treasurer, Director, and Cabinet Keeper; Boston Athenæum, Reports of the Library Committee and the Librarian for the Year 1940; Butler Hospital for the Treatment of Mental and Nervous Illness, Reports Presented to the Corporation at its Annual Meeting January 22, 1941 (Ninety-seventh Annual Report); Sixty-Third Annual Report of the Providence Public Library; American Merchant Marine Library, Nineteenth Annual Report of the Trustees.

With Hammer and Tongs. Malleable Metals in Diverse Designs, An Exhibition at the Cooper Union.

To William Davis Miller of the Providence Public Library (Testimonial).

To Mary Lavinia Lamprey, Ames Free Library, Easton, Massachusetts (Testimonial).

The Merrymount Press

The Frick Collection, Lecture Schedule, October 1, 1941–January 31, 1942.

A Parting Word (William Arms Fisher).

1942

[923]
Practical | Mathematics | Book I | [*cut*] | by | Henrietta D. Antoville | Catherine M. Trube | General Editor | William Jansen, Ed.D. | [*rule*] | Noble & Noble, Publishers, Inc. | 100 Fifth Avenue, New York City. [n.d.]

Collation: i–x, 1–337. Leaf, 5 ½ × 7 ½. Binding, cloth. Type, Times Roman Monotype and Perpetua Titling.
Composition and electrotype plates only supplied by the Press.

[924]
Practical | Mathematics | Book II | [*cut*] | by | Henrietta D. Antoville | Catherine M. Trube | General Editor | William Jansen, Ed.D. | [*rule*] | Noble & Noble, Publishers, Inc. | 100 Fifth Avenue, New York City. [n.d.]

Collation: i–x, 1–342. Leaf, 5 ½ × 7 ½. Binding, cloth. Type, Times Roman Monotype and Perpetua Titling.
Composition and electrotype plates only supplied by the Press.

[925]
Harriet Hildreth Heard | (Mrs. Lanier Dunn) | 1856–1936 | By Her Daughter Hildreth | [*floret*] | Boston | Privately Printed | 1942.

On reverse of title: The Merrymount Press, Boston, U.S.A. Collation: [i–vi], 1–112. Leaf, 5 ⅞ × 8 ⅞. Binding, cloth. With 13 photogravure illustrations. Type, Caslon Monotype and Janson.

[926]
The Education of | Henry Adams | An Autobiography | [*printer's ornaments*] | Illustrated with Twelve Etchings by | Samuel Chamberlain | and with an Introduction by | Henry Seidel Canby | [*floret*] | Boston: Printed for the Members of | The Limited Editions Club | at The Merrymount Press | 1942.

[314]

Bibliography

Colophon: Of this edition of "The Education of Henry Adams" fifteen hundred copies have been made for the members of the Limited Editions Club by D. B. Updike, The Merrymount Press, Boston. The etchings have been printed from the artist's plates by Charles Furth in New York [*floret*]. This copy is number — and it is signed by the illustrator. Collation: i–xviii, 1–485, [486]. Leaf, 7 × 10. Binding, cloth. Rubricated title. Type, Times Roman Monotype and Perpetua Titling.

[927]

Las Artes del | Libro | en los Estados Unidos | 1931–1941 | Nueva York | Instituto Norteamericano | de Artes Gráficas | 1942.

On reverse of title: D. B. Updike, The Merrymount Press, Boston, Mass., U.S.A. Collation: i–xii, [1–75]. Leaf, 6⅞ × 9⅛. Binding. paper, Type, Times Roman Monotype and Perpetua Titling.
An edition with a cover and title in Portuguese was also printed.

[928]

[*within border*] The Sword on the Table | Thomas Dorr's Rebellion | By Winfield Townley Scott | [*printer's ornament*] | [*quotation*] | [*printer's ornament*] | The Poet of the Month | New Directions | Norfolk, Conn. [n.d.]

Colophon: [*border*] The Sword on the Table was designed by and printed at The Merrymount Press, Boston. The types used are Scotch Roman [*border*]. Collation: [i–iv], [1–28]. Leaf, 5⅞ × 8⅛. Binding, boards. Type, Scotchface Monotype.
Also issued in paper covers.

[929]

Poem of the Cid | Reprinted from the Unique Manuscript | at Madrid | With Translation and Notes | By Archer M. Huntington, M.A. | [*seal*] | The Hispanic Society of America | 1942.

Collation: [i–iv], [1–507]. Leaf, 5¼ × 8½. Binding, cloth. Type, Tudor Black.
Only the title and half-titles set by the Press. Text reproduced from a previous edition and entire volume printed by offset lithography.

[930]

The | Seamen's Handbook | for Shore Leave | By | Mrs. Henry Howard | [*cut*] | Seventh Edition | New York | American Merchant Marine | Library Association | 45 Broadway. [n.d.]

[315]

The Merrymount Press

On reverse of title: Printed in the United States of America by The Merrymount Press, Boston, Mass. Collation: i–xl, 1–348. Leaf, 3½ × 5¾. Binding: cloth. Type, Times Roman Monotype.

With folding map inside back cover. Also appeared with following imprint on title: Published by | The Mitre Press | Mitre Chambers, Mitre Street | London.

[931]
Century | Memorials | 1941 | [*border*] | [*floret*] | [*border*] | New York | 1942.

On reverse of title: [*printer's ornament*] D. B. Updike, The Merrymount Press, Boston [*printer's ornament*]. Collation: [i–iv], 1–66. Leaf, 5½ × 8¾. Binding, cloth. Type, Baskerville Monotype and Janson.

[932]
Proceedings | of the | Massachusetts Historical Society | Volume LXVI | October, 1936–May, 1941 | [*seal*] | Boston | Published by the Society | 1942.

On reverse of title: The Merrymount Press, Boston, Mass., U.S.A. Collation: i–xiv, 1–613. Leaf, 6¼ × 9½. Binding, cloth. With 2 photogravure and 6 collotype illustrations. Type, Caslon Monotype.

[933]
Educational | Opportunities | at The Massachusetts | Institute of Technology | [*dash*] | [*cut*] | [*dash*] | Cambridge | Massachusetts Institute of Technology | February, 1942.

On reverse of title: The Merrymount Press, Boston. Collation: [i–viii], 1–44. Leaf, 6 × 9. Binding, paper. With 2 illustrations. Type, Times Roman Monotype.

[934]
A History of | Scroll and Key | 1842–1942 | By Maynard Mack | [*cut*] | Printed for the Society | 1942.

On reverse of title: This edition limited to five copies of which this is number —. Printed by D. B. Updike, The Merrymount Press, Boston under the Direction of the Yale University Press. Collation: i–xiv, 1–306. Leaf, 9¼ × 12¼. Binding, cloth. Type, Caslon Monotype and Janson.

[935]
Emma Pendleton Bradley Home | Barrington Parkway, East Providence, R. I. | Report | for the First Ten Years | April 8,

Bibliography

1931–April 8, 1941 | A Memorial Hospital for Children | up to Twelve Years of Age, of Normal Intelligence, who suffer from | Nervous and Behavior Disorders. [n.d.]

On reverse of title: The Merrymount Press, Boston. Collation: 1–42. Leaf, 5 × 7½. Binding, paper. With 9 half-tone illustrations. Type, Times Roman Monotype.

[936]
The | Century Association | Year-Book | 1942 | [*border*] | [*floret*] | [*border*] | New York | 1942.

On reverse of title: [*printer's ornament*] D. B. Updike, The Merrymount Press, Boston [*printer's ornament*]. Collation: [i–vi], 1–140. Leaf, 5⅜ × 6¾. Binding, cloth. Type, Times Roman Monotype.

Minor Printing

The Carnegie Foundation for the Advancement of Teaching, Thirty-seventh Annual Report of the President and of the Treasurer, New York; *also* The Graduate Record Examination, A Descriptive Prospectus for College Students; The Graduate Record Examination, An Historical Minute, Reprinted from the Thirty-seventh Annual Report; *and* What's in a "Mark"?, Reprinted from the Thirty-seventh Annual Report.

The Month at Goodspeed's.

Athenæum Items.

Reports: John Carter Brown Library, Providence, Rhode Island, Report to the Corporation of Brown University, Providence; American Merchant Marine Library Association, Twentieth Annual Report of the Trustees; Emma Pendleton Bradley Home, Report for the Year 1941; Boston Athenæum, Reports of the Library Committee and Librarian for the Year 1941.

John Stanley Packer, Lieutenant R.N.V.R.

Books on Mathematics, Astronomy, Physics, Chemistry, Engineering from the Catalogue of Books Published by the Cambridge University Press (England).

The Frick Collection, Lecture Schedule, February 4–May 29, 1942.

Reprints from Proceedings of the Massachusetts Historical Society,

The Merrymount Press

Volume 66: The First Newspaper by Wilbur C. Abbott; The Military Telegraph in the Civil War by Roscoe Pound; Report of the Treasurer, April 14, 1938; A Marbleheader Meets the Last of the South Sea Pirates by Lawrence W. Jenkins; The Advancement of Learning during the Puritan Commonwealth by James B. Conant.

Thanksgiving, 1942, Consolidated Headquarters Detachment, First Service Command, Buckminster Hotel, Boston.

Christmas Day, 1942, Consolidated Headquarters Detachment, First Service Command, Buckminster Hotel, Boston.

1943

[937]

Publications | of | The Colonial Society of Massachusetts | Volume XXXIV | [*printer's ornaments*] | Transactions | 1937–1942 | [*seal*] | Boston | Published by the Society | 1943.

On reverse of title: D. B. Updike, The Merrymount Press, Boston, U.S.A. Collation: i–xvi, 1–645. Leaf, 6½ × 9⅜. Binding, cloth. With 12 collotype illustrations. Type, Caslon Monotype.

[938]

Remembering | Eleanor Widger | [*printer's ornament*] | Privately Printed. [n.d.]

On reverse of title: The Merrymount Press, Boston. Collation: [i–x], 1–45. Leaf, 5⅛ × 8⅛. Binding, cloth. With photogravure portrait. Type, Caslon Monotype and Janson.

[939]

Century | Memorials | 1942 | [*border*] | [*floret*] | [*border*] | New York | 1943.

On reverse of title: [*printer's ornament*] D. B. Updike, The Merrymount Press, Boston [*printer's ornament*]. Collation: [i–iv], 1–78. Leaf, 5½ × 8⅜. Binding, cloth. Type, Baskerville Monotype.

[940]

A Century of Scholars | Rhode Island Alpha of | Phi Beta Kappa | 1830–1930 | [*floret*] | Edited by William T. Hastings,

[318]

Bibliography

'03 | Chapter Secretary | (with supplement) | Providence | Rhode Island | 1943.

On reverse of title: D. B. Updike, The Merrymount Press, Boston. Collation: [i–viii], 1–255. Leaf, 6 × 9¼. Binding, cloth. Type, Janson.
Reissue of No. 750.

[941]
Winthrop | Papers | Volume III | 1631–1637 | [*seal*] | The Massachusetts Historical Society | 1943.

On reverse of title: The Merrymount Press, Boston, Mass., U.S.A. Collation: i–xl, [1–2], 1–544. Leaf, 7⅛ × 9¾. Binding, boards. With frontispiece in colour and collotype illustration. Type, Baskerville Monotype.

[942]
Recollections of | Daniel Berkeley Updike | By | Stanley Morison | and | Rudolph Ruzicka | With an Introduction by M. A. DeWolfe Howe | [*seal*] | Boston | The Club of Odd Volumes | 1943.

Colophon: Two hundred and one copies have been printed on hand-made paper for the Club of Odd Volumes at The Merrymount Press, Boston, Massachusetts, in October 1943. Cover paper designed and executed by Rosamond B. Loring. Collation: i–xiv, 1–29, [30]. Leaf, 4¼ × 6⅞. Binding, boards. With 4 illustrations. Type, Janson.

[943]
A Fiction on Facts | The Story of a Politician | Who Was Not Knifed | By Robert Washburn | [*cut*] | Privately Printed. [n.d.]

On reverse of title: The Merrymount Press, Boston. Collation: 1–20. Leaf, 5 × 7¼. Binding, paper. Type, Caslon Monotype and Janson.

[944]
The | Century Association | Year-Book | 1943 | [*border*] | [*floret*] | [*border*] | New York | 1943.

On reverse of title: [*printer's ornament*] D. B. Updike, The Merrymount Press, Boston [*printer's ornament*]. Collation: [i–vi], 1–148. Leaf, 5⅜ × 6¾. Binding, cloth. Type, Times Roman Monotype.

The Merrymount Press

Minor Printing

The Carnegie Foundation for the Advancement of Teaching, Thirty-eighth Annual Report of the President and of the Treasurer, New York; *also* The Graduate Record Examination, A Descriptive Prospectus for College Students; Publications of the Foundation; Priorities and the Colleges by Walter A. Jessup, Reprinted from the Thirty-seventh Annual Report; *and* Two Decades of Educational Enquiry by William S. Learned, Reprinted from the Thirty-eighth Annual Report.

The Month at Goodspeed's.

Athenæum Items.

Reports: John Carter Brown Library, Providence, Rhode Island, Report to the Corporation of Brown University, Providence; Providence Public Library, Sixty-fifth Annual Report; Boston Athenæum, Report of the Library Committee and Librarian for the Year 1942; One Hun-, dred & Sixth and Seventh Annual Reports, Providence Athenæum Providence; American Merchant Marine Library Association, Twenty-first Annual Report of the Trustees.

A Letter to Dean Donham.

American Notes and Queries, April, May, June, July, August, September, October, November.

American Bibliography 1639–1729 by Charles Evans Hughes, illustrated with Fifth-nine Original Leaves from Early American Books and an Historical Notice of the Author and His Work by Lawrence C. Wroth.

A Century of Scholars, Supplement, 1943.

War Creed for The United States (Broadside).

The Associates of the Harvard Business School.

Thanksgiving, 1943, Headquarters Detachment and Military Police Company, Headquarters, First Service Command, Buckminster Hotel, Boston.

Christmas Day, 1943, Headquarters Detachment and Military Police Company, Headquarters, First Service Command, Buckminster Hotel, Boston.

Reprints from Colonial Society of Massachusetts Transactions, Volume XXXIV: Quaker Relief during the Seige of Boston by Henry J. Cadbury; The Misfortunes of Dorcas Griffiths by Frank W. C. Hersey; Tar and Feathers: The Adventures of Captain John Malcolm by Frank

Bibliography

W. C. Hersey; Catholicism and the New England Mind by Rev. Arthur J. Riley; John Harvard's Library by Henry J. Cadbury; A War Refugee of 1800 by Robert E. Peabody; Gavelkind and the Charter of Massachusetts Bay by George L. Haskins; The American Merchant and the Constitution by Curtis P. Nettels; A Boston Heiress and Her Husbands, A True Story, by Edmund S. Morgan; John Wilkes and William Palfrey by George M. Elsey; More Hints from Joseph Hawley, January, 1776 by Paul Fullam and George M. Elsey; The Proposed Colony of Georgia in New England, 1713–1733 by Robert E. Moody; The Boston Theatre, 1800 by Peter Oliver; John Mein: Scourge of Patriots by John E. Alden; The Development of Frederick Jackson Turner as an Historical Thinker by Fulmer Mood; The Topical Verses of Edward Taylor by Thomas H. Johnson.

1944

[945]

The | Seamen's Handbook | for Shore Leave | By | Mrs. Henry Howard | [*cut*] | Eighth Edition | New York 6 | American Merchant Marine | Library Association | 45 Broadway. [n.d.]

On reverse of title: Printed in The United States of America by The Merrymount Press, Boston, Mass., U.S.A. Collation: i–xl, 1–350. Leaf, 3½ × 5¾. Binding, cloth. Type, Times Roman Monotype. *With folding map inside back cover. Reissue of No. 930.*

[946]

The Story of a Family | Through Eleven Centuries | Illustrated by Portraits and Pedigrees | Being a | History of the Family of Gorges | By | Raymond Gorges | Based on Material Prepared by the Rev. Frederick Brown, F.S.A. | [*arms*] | Boston | Privately Printed | 1944.

On reverse of title: D. B. Updike, The Merrymount Press, Boston. Collation: [i–ii], i–xxiv, 1–289. Leaf, 8⅝ × 11½. Binding, cloth. Title in 2 colours. With 52 illustrations and a folding chart. Type, Caslon Monotype and Janson.

[947]

Talavera Pottery | With a Catalogue of the Collection | of The Hispanic Society of America | By | Alice Wilson Frothingham |

The Merrymount Press

Corresponding Member | The Hispanic Society of America | [*seal*] | With 157 illustrations | Printed by Order of | The Trustees | New York | 1944.

Collation: i–xviii. 1–191. Leaf, 6⅛ × 9. Binding, paper. Type, Time Roman Monotype.

[948]
[*within rules*] The | Felicities of Sixty | By | I. H. Lionberger | [*printer's ornament*] | Privately Printed. [n.d.]

On reverse of title: The Merrymount Press, Boston. Collation: [i–vi], 1–34, [35]. Leaf, 5⅛ × 7¾. Binding, boards. With photogravure frontispiece. Type, Caslon Monotype and Janson.
Reissue of No. 550.

[949]
The Carnegie Foundation for the Advancement of Teaching | Studies in | American Graduate | Education | A Report to the Carnegie Foundation | By Marcia Edwards | Assistant Dean, School of Education, the University of Minnesota | With Introduction by | Walter A. Jessup | President of the Foundation | [*printer's ornament*] | New York City | 522 Fifth Avenue | 1944.

On reverse of title: D. B. Updike, The Merrymount Press, Boston. Collation: i–xvi, 1–71. Leaf, 6⅛ × 9¼. Binding, cloth. Type, Caslon Monotype.
Also issued in paper covers.

[950]
Sir Max Beerbohm | Bibliographical Notes | By | A. E. Gallatin | [*seal*] | Harvard University Press | Cambridge, Massachusetts | 1944.

Colophon: Four hundred copies printed by D. B. Updike, The Merrymount Press, Boston in April, 1944. Collation: i–xiv, 1–121, [122–127]. Leaf, 6 × 9¼. Binding, cloth. Type, Caslon Monotype.

[951]
A Century of Butler Hospital | 1844–1944 | [*seal*] | Providence, Rhode Island | 1944.

Colophon: [*cut*] Printed by authorization of The Board of Trustees under the direction of The Centennial Committee John S. Chafee, Charles M.

Bibliography

Smith, III, John Nicholas Brown, Chairman. The Merrymount Press, Boston. Collation: [i–iv], 1–49, [50]. Leaf, 8⅝ × 11½. Binding, boards. With 10 collotype illustrations. Type, Times Roman Monotype.

[952]
The | Century Association | Year-Book | 1944 | [*border*] | [*floret*] | [*border*] | New York | 1944.

On reverse of title: [*printer's ornament*] D. B. Updike, The Merrymount Press Boston [*printer's ornament*]. Collation: [i–vi], 1–150. Leaf, 5⅜ × 6¾. Binding, cloth. Type, Times Roman Monotype.

[953]
Winthrop | Papers | Volume IV | 1638–1644 | [*seal*] | The Massachusetts Historical Society | 1944.

On reverse of title: The Merrymount Press, Boston, Mass., U.S.A. Collation: i–xl, [1–2], 1–531. Leaf, 7⅛ × 9¾. Binding, boards. With frontispiece in colour and folding map in collotype. Type, Baskerville Monotype.

[954]
[*printer's ornament*] | The Prayer Book Office | Morning Prayer and Evening Prayer | According to the | American Book of Common Prayer | With Invitatories and Hymns | Antiphons to the Gospel Canticles | And other Enrichments | [*florets*] | 1944 | Morehouse-Gorham Co. | New York | [*printer's ornament*].

On reverse title: The Merrymount Press, Boston. Colophon: In the name of God, Amen. To the Praise and Glory of the Most Holy Trinity, To the Honour of the Blessed Virgin Mary and of all the Company of Heaven [*press mark*] this Divine Office Book was happily completed at The Merrymount Press, Boston on the Feast of Saint Dominic in the year of Our Lord MDCCCCXLIV. Collation: i–lxvi, 1–801, [802]. Leaf, 4¼ × 6⅜. Binding, cloth. Type, Times Roman Monotype.

[955]
Wilkie Collins | The Moonstone | with illustrations by William Sharp | [*cut*] | Doubleday, Doran & Company, Inc. | Garden City, New York | 1944.

At front: This edition is limited to one thousand numbered copies signed by the artist (Wm. Sharp). This is copy No. —. Colophon: Doubleday Doran Limited Editions illustrated by famous American artists [*cut*]. The type used for this edition is Bulmer Monotype cast from matrices imported from Eng-

The Merrymount Press

land. It was set and printed by The Merrymount Press, Boston, Mass. The illustrations, by William Sharp, were printed in gravure by the Photogravure & Color Co., New York, N.Y. The book was designed by A. P. Tedesco under whose direction it was produced. Collations: [i–vi], 1–444, [445]. Leaf, 6½ × 9½. Binding, cloth. Title in 2 colours. With 16 full-page illustrations in colour and numerous smaller illustrations in black. Type, Bulmer Monotype.

[956]

[*cut*] The Way | of All Flesh | By Samuel Butler | Illustrated by André Durenceau | Doubleday, Doran & Company, Inc. | Garden City, New York. 1944.

At front: This edition is limited to one thousand numbered copies signed by the artist (André Durenceau). This is copy No. —. Colophon: Doubleday Doran Limited Editions illustrated by famous American artists [*cut*]. The type used for this edition is English Monotype Baskerville. It was set and printed by The Merrymount Press, Boston, Mass. The illustrations, by André Durenceau, were printed by the gelatine process by the Ullman Co. The book was designed by A. P. Tedesco under whose direction it was produced. Collation: [i–viii], 1–429, [430]. Leaf, 6½ × 9½. Binding, cloth. Title in 2 colours. With 8 full-page illustrations in colour and numerous smaller illustrations in black. Type, Baskerville Monotype.

[957]

Century | Memorials | 1943 | [*border*] | [*floret*] | [*border*] | New York | 1944.

On reverse of title: [*printer's ornament*] D. B. Updike, The Merrymount Press, Boston [*printer's ornament*]. Collation: [i–iv], 1–93. Leaf, 5½ × 8⅜. Binding, cloth. Type, Baskerville Monotype.

[958]

Notes | Hispanic | [*seal*] | IV | Printed by Order of | The Trustees | New York | 1944.

Collation: [i–viii], 1–132, [133]. Leaf, 6 × 9. Binding, paper. With 173 illustrations. Type, Caslon Monotype.

[959]

Hispanic Silverwork | By | Ada Marshall Johnson | Corresponding Member | The Hispanic Society of America | [*seal*] | With 266 illustrations | Printed by Order of | The Trustees | New York | 1944.

Bibliography

Collation: i–xx, 1–308. Leaf, 6⅛ × 9. Binding, paper. Type, Times Roman Monotype.

Minor Printing

The Carnegie Foundation for the Advancement of Teaching, Thirty-ninth Annual Report of the President and of the Treasurer, New York; *also* A General Examination for Advanced College Students; The Graduate Record Examination and Returning Service Personnel, Reprinted from the Thirty-eighth Annual Report; *and* The Graduate Record Examination, A Measurement and Guidance Project in Engineering Education, Reprinted from the Thirty-eighth Annual Report.

The Month at Goodspeed's.

Athenæum Items.

Reports: John Carter Brown Library, Providence, Rhode Island, Report to the Corporation of Brown University, Providence; Boston Athenæum, Reports of the Library Committee and the Librarian for the Year 1943; Emma Pendleton Bradley Home, Report for the Year 1943.

Proposals with Reference to a Center for the Advanced Study of International Affairs under the Auspices of the Foreign Service Educational Foundation.

Vienna After Thirty-four Years by William Osler, M.D.

Willis Fisher, 1894–1944.

Pine Harbor, Pascoag, Rhode Island.

Edith Walcott Homans, 1892–1944.

Thanksgiving, 1944, Military Police Company and Headquarters Detachment, Headquarters, First Service Command, Hotel Buckminster, Boston.

1945

[960]

Robinson | Crusoe The Life and | Strange Surprising Adventures of Robinson Crusoe, | of York, Mariner: Who Lived Eight and Twenty Years | all Alone in an Uninhabited Island

The Merrymount Press

on the Coast of | America, Near the Mouth of the Great River of Orinoco; | Having Been Cast on Shore by Shipwreck,Wherein all | the Men Perished but Himself. With an Account How | He was at Last as Strangely Delivered by Pirates. By | Daniel Defoe. Illustrated by Fritz Kredel. | [*cut*] | Doubleday, Doran and Company, Inc. | Garden City, New Yok, 1945.

At front: This edition is limited to one thousand numbered copies signed by the artist (Fritz Kredel). This is copy No. —. Colophon: Doubleday Doran Limited Editions illustrated by famous American artists [*cut*]. The type used for this edition is Monotype Times Roman. It was set and printed by The Merrymount Press, Boston, Mass. The illustrations and decorative initials were drawn by Fritz Kredel. The book was designed by A. P. Tedesco under whose direction it was produced. Collation: [i–vi], 1–397, [398]. Leaf, 6½ × 9½. Binding, cloth. Title in 2 colours. With 16 full-page illustrations in colour. Type, Times Roman Monotype.

[961]
Poems | By | Sigourney Thayer | 1896–1944 | Boston | Privately Printed | 1945.

On reverse of title: The Merrymount Press, Boston. Collation: i–x, 1–37. Leaf, 4⅝ × 7¼. Binding, cloth. Type, Baskerville Monotype.

[962]
[*title within cut*] Pride | and | Prejudice | Garden City, New York | Doubleday, Doran & Company, Inc. | 1945.

At front: This edition is limited to one thousand numbered copies signed by the artist (Robert Ball). This is copy.No. —. Colophon: Doubleday Doran Limited Editions illustrated by famous American artists [*cut*]. The type used for this edition is Monotype Scotch Roman. It was set and printed by The Merrymount Press, Boston, Mass. The illustrations were drawn by Robert Ball. The book was designed by A. P. Tedesco under whose direction it was produced. Collation: [i–vi], 1–378, [379–380]. Leaf, 6½ × 9½. Binding, cloth. Rubricated title. With 13 illustrations in colour and numerous illustrations in black. Type, Scotch-face Monotype.

[963]
The | Century Association | Year-Book | 1945 | [*border*] | [*floret*] | [*border*] | New York | 1945.

On last page: The Merrymount Press, Boston. Collation, [i–vi], 1–154. Leaf, 5⅜ × 6¾. Binding, cloth. Type, Times Roman Monotype.

[326]

Bibliography

[964]

Catalogue Ten-Summer 1945 | Medical and Scientific Books | of | 16th and 17th Century England | Among the Many Noteworthy Items: | Robert Boyle Collection, Items 24-62 | William Harvey, Items 164-182 | Herball, 1526 Number 189 | Jones, 1579 No. 202 | Turner, Items | 299-301 | Willis, Items 318-327 | [cut] | Schuman's . . . New York 21 | 20 East 70th Street Telephone: REgent 7-4844.

On outside back cover: The Merrymount Press, Boston. Collation: 1-142, [143-144]. Leaf, 6⅝ × 9⅞. Binding, paper. With numerous illustrations. Type, Times Roman Monotype and Black Letter.

[965]

[within border] The | Inaugural Addresses | of | Franklin D. Roosevelt | President of the United States | Worcester: Achille J. St. Onge | 1945.

Colophon: [border] Two thousand copies of the Inaugural Addresses of Franklin D. Roosevelt have been printed from Times New Roman type on Ecusta Bible paper by The Merrymount Press, Boston, Mass., U.S.A. [border]. Collation: [i–vi], 1-88, [89]. Leaf, 2 × 3. Binding, cloth. With photogravure frontispiece. Type, Times Roman Monotype.

[966]

Architecture | A Profession and a Career | The American Institute of Architects | The Octagon, Washington, D. C. | 1945.

On last page: The Merrymount Press, Boston. Collation: [i–vi], 1-57, [58]. Leaf, 6⅛ × 9¼. Binding, boards. Type, Times Roman Monotype.
Also issued in paper covers.

[967]

Notes | Hispanic | [seal] | V | Printed by Order of | The Trustees | New York | 1945.

Collation: [i–vi], 1-132, [133-134]. Leaf, 6 × 9. Binding, paper. With 86 illustrations. Type, Caslon Monotype.

[968]

Proceedings | of the | Massachusetts Historical Society | Volume LXVII | October, 1941–May, 1944 | [seal] | Boston | Published by the Society | 1945.

The Merrymount Press

On reverse of title: The Merrymount Press, Boston, Mass., U.S.A. Collation: i–xiv, 1–686. Leaf, 6¼ × 9½. Binding, cloth. With photogravure frontispiece and 10 illustrations in collotype. Type, Caslon Monotype.

[969]
Thomas Bonaventure Lawler | 1864–1945. [n.d.]

On reverse of title: The Merrymount Press, Boston. Collation: [i–ii], 1–6. Leaf, 5½ × 8½. Binding, paper. With photogravure portrait. Type, Janson.

[970]
Groton School | [*seal*] | Groton, Massachusetts. [n.d.]

On last page: Produced by Vincent-Curtis, The Merrymount Press, and The Meriden Gravure Company. Collation: [i–iv], [1–46]. Leaf, 9 × 11¾. Binding, boards. With numerous illustrations. Type, Janson.
Composition only by the Press.

[971]
The Church | Serves | [*cut*] | A Guide to Churches | and Their Facilities in the Boston Area | for Students at the | Massachusetts Institute of Technology | Published Annually by | The Technology Christian Association | Religious Action Division | 1945 Edition.

On reverse of title: The Merrymount Press, Boston. Collation: i–x, 1–26. Leaf, 5 × 7¾. Binding, paper. Type, Times Roman Monotype.

[972]
National Security | Supported by | I. Scientific Research | II. Universal Military Training | By | Karl T. Compton | President, Massachusetts Institute of Technology | Cambridge | The Technology Press | Massachusetts Institute of Technology. [n.d.]

On reverse of title: The Merrymount Press, Boston. Collation: [i–ii], 1–19. Leaf, 6 × 9. Binding, paper. Type, Bulmer Monotype.

Minor Printing

The Carnegie Foundation for the Advancement of Teaching, Fortieth Annual Report of the President and of the Treasurer, New York; *also*

Bibliography

Publications of the Foundation *and* Measuring The Outcome of Higher Education, Reprinted from the Fortieth Annual Report.

The Month at Goodspeed's.

Athenæum Items.

Reports: John Carter Brown Library, Providence, Rhode Island, Report to the Corporation of Brown University, Providence; Boston Athenæum, Reports of the Library Committee and the Librarian for the Year 1944; Emma Pendleton Bradley Home, Report for the Year 1944; One Hundred & Eighth and Ninth Annual Reports, Providence Athenæum, Providence; Butler Hospital for the Treatment of Mental and Nervous Illness, Reports for the Year 1944 (101st Annual Report).

Catalogue of Saint Mark's School 1944–1945, Southborough, Massachusetts.

Catalogue Isabella Stewart Gardner Museum, Fenway Court.

An Office of Compline.

Reprints from Proceedings of the Massachusetts Historical Society, Volume 67: William Orne, A Distinguished but Forgotten Merchant by James Duncan Phillips; Bureaus and Bureau Methods in the Civil War Era by Roscoe Pound; False Faces, A Study of the Use and Misue of Portraits as Historical Documents by Henry Wilder Foote; Marches and Camp Sites of The French Army beyond New England during the Revolutionary War by Allan Forbes; Pretenders to the French Throne in Numismatics by Shepard Pond; The Setting for Dictatorship in Latin America by Clarence Henry Haring; The Man Who Murdered Garfield by Stewart Mitchell; The Last Half-Century of *Transcript* History by Robert Lincoln O'Brien.

1946

[973]

The First Century of the | John Carter Brown Library | A History with a Guide | to the Collections | By | Lawrence C. Wroth | [arms] | Providence, Rhode Island | The Associates of the John Carter Brown Library | MDCCCCXLVI.

On reverse of title: D. B. Updike, The Merrymount Press, Boston. Collation: i–vi, 1–88. Leaf, 6¼ × 9⅜. Binding, boards. Type, Bulmer Monotype. *Various patterns of marble paper were used on the binding.*

The Merrymount Press

[974]

A New Garland for | Word Lovers | [cut] | Privately Printed: G. & C. Merriam Co. | Publishers of Merriam-Webster Dictionaries | Springfield, Massachusetts: 1946.

On last leaf: The Merrymount Press, Boston. Collation: 1–53, [54–55]. Leaf, 3⅛ × 4½. Binding, boards. Rubricated title and opening text page. Type, Times Roman Monotype.

[975]

Fullness of Life | [rule] | A Memoir of | Elizabeth Shaw Morison | 1886-1945 | By | Samuel Eliot Morison | [printer's ornaments] | Privately Printed | 1945.

Colophon: Two hundred copies of this book bound in paper designed and executed by Rosamond B. Loring were printed by The Merrymount Press, Boston. This copy for —. Collation: [i–x], 1–63, [64–65]. Leaf, 5¼ × 8⅛. Binding, boards. With 5 collotype illustrations. Type, Caslon Monotype.

[976]

An Exhibition of | Paintings | Drawings and Prints | by | J. M. W. Turner | John Constable | R. P. Bonington | March 21 to April 28, 1946 | Museum of Fine Arts, Boston.

On reverse of title: The Merrymount Press, Boston. Collation: i–viii, 1–79. Leaf, 5⅝ × 9¼. Binding, paper. With 16 collotype illustrations. Type, Bulmer Monotype.
Various patterns of marble paper were used on the cover.

[977]

Getting Things Done | By | Percy R. Creed | [quotation] | Boston: 1946.

On last page: The Merrymount Press, Boston, U.S.A. Collation: i–xviii, [i–ii], 1–95, [96–98]. Leaf, 6⅛ × 9¼. Binding, paper. With collotype portrait. Type, Times Roman Monotype.

[978]

Dante Alighieri | The Divine | Comedy | Illustrated by Umberto Romano | Doubleday & Company, Inc. | Garden City New York 1946.

At front: This edition is limited to one thousand numbered copies signed by the artist. This is copy No. — (Umberto Romano). Colophon: Doubleday

Bibliography

Doran Limited Editions illustrated by famous American artists [*cut*]. The type used for this edition is Monotype Times Roman. It was set and printed by The Merrymount Press, Boston, Mass. The illustrations were drawn by Umberto Romano. The book was designed by A. P. Tedesco under whose direction it was produced. Collation; [i–viii], 1–475, [476]. Leaf, 6½ × 9½. Binding, cloth. Title-page in 2 colours. With 12 illustrations in colour and numerous illustrations in black. Type, Times Roman Monotype.

[979]
An Exhibition of Drawings | By | Francis Dahl | and | Gluyas Williams | May 29 to September 1, 1946 | Museum of Fine Arts, Boston.

On reverse of title: The Merrymount Press, Boston, U.S.A. Collation: 1–31. Leaf, 7⅞ × 6 (*oblong*). Binding, paper. With numerous illustrations. Type, Times Roman Monotype.

[980]
Harvard College | Class of 1926 | Twentieth Anniversary Report | [*seal*] | Cambridge | Printed for the Class | 1946.

On reverse of title: D. B. Updike, The Merrymount Press, Boston, U.S.A. Collation: i–xvi, 1–328, [329]. Leaf, 6 × 9. Binding, cloth. Type, Caslon Monotype.

[981]
[*within rules*] Keats' Reputation | in America | to 1848 | By | Hyder Edward Rollins | [*cut*] | 1946 | Cambridge, Massachusetts | Harvard University Press.

Colophon: This first edition consists of seven hundred and fifty copies printed by D. B. Updike, The Merrymount Press, Boston. Collation: [i–vi], 1–147, [148]. Leaf, 5½ × 8¼. Binding, cloth. Rubricated throughout. With 5 illustrations. Type, Bulmer Monotype.

[982]
[*seal*] | A Memorial Service | Commemorating | the Sons of Phillips Academy | who Gave their Lives for their Country | in the Second World War | Friday, June the Seventh | Nineteen Hundred and Forty-six | The Cochran Chapel | Andover, Massachusetts.

On last page: The Merrymount Press, Boston, U.S.A. Collation: [1–16]. Leaf, 6½ × 9¾. Binding, paper. Title in 2 colours. Type, Caslon Monotype.

[331]

The Merrymount Press

[983]
The | Century Association | Year-Book | 1946 | [*border*] |
[*floret*] | [*border*] | New York | 1946.

On last page: The Merrymount Press, Boston. Collation: [i–vi], 1–158.
Leaf, 5⅜ × 6¾. Binding, cloth. Type, Times Roman Monotype.

[984]
Spirit Level | and Other Poems | By | Christopher Morley |
[*seal*] | Harvard University Press | Cambridge, Massachusetts |
1946.

On reverse of title: The Merrymount Press, Boston. Collation: i–x, 1–52.
Leaf, 5 × 7⅜. Binding, cloth. Type, Times Roman Monotype.

[985]
[*within rules*] [*monogram*] | Letters of | Nelly | Macdonald |
Houston | 1905–1946 | Printed for the Family, Christmas, 1946.

On reverse of title: The Merrymount Press, Boston. Collation: [i–vi], 1–98.
Leaf, 5½ × 8⅜. Binding, cloth. With 37 illustrations consisting of photographic prints, 2 of which are in colour. Type, Baskerville Monotype.
30 copies printed.

[986]
[*printer's ornament*] | Hail Chant and | Water Chant | Recorded
by | Mary C. Wheelwright | Navajo Religion Series | Volume
II | Museum of Navajo Ceremonial Art | Sante Fe, New Mex-
ico | 1946 | [*printer's ornament*].

On reverse of title: The Merrymount Press, Boston, U.S.A. Collation:
[i–viii], 1–237. Leaf, 8 × 10. Binding, cloth. With 24 serigraphs of sand
paintings executed by Louie Ewing. Type, Times Roman Monotype.

[987]
Carnegie Institution of Washington | [*printer's ornament*] | War
Activities of the | Trustees and Staff | 1939–1946 | Washing-
ton, D.C. | December, 1946.

On reverse of title: The Merrymount Press, Boston. Collation: [i–ii], 1–56.
Leaf, 5 × 7½. Binding, paper. Type, Times Roman Monotype.

Bibliography

[988]

George Berkeley | in Apulia | By | Alice Brayton | Boston | The Merrymound Press | 1946.

On reverse of title: D. B. Updike, The Merrymount Press, Boston, U.S.A. Collation: [i–viii], 1–113. Leaf, 8⅜ × 10⅞. Binding, cloth. With 41 collotype illustrations. Type, Caslon Monotype.

[989]

Nathaniel Stevens | 1786–1865 | An Account of His Life and | The Business He Founded | By Horace Nathaniel Stevens | [*seal*] | North Andover, Massachusetts | 1946.

On reverse of title: D. B. Updike, The Merrymount Press, Boston. Collation: i–xvi, 1–266. Leaf, 6⅛ × 9¼. Binding, cloth. With 49 photogravure illustrations. Type, Caslon Monotype.

[990]

The Rediscovery | of a | Lost Orchid | By | Oakes Ames | [*floret*] | Boston: 1946.

On reverse of title: The Merrymount Press, Boston. Collation: [i–ii], 1–16. Leaf, 5 × 7½. Binding, paper. Type, Caslon Monotype.

[991]

Educational | Opportunities | at the Massachusetts | Institute of Technology | [*dash*] | [*cut*] | [*dash*] | Cambridge | Massachusetts Institute of Technology | 1946.

On reverse of title: The Merrymount Press, Boston. Collation: [i–viii], 1–48. Leaf, 6 × 9. Binding, paper. With 2 illustrations. Type, Times Roman Monotype.

Revised edition of No. 933.

[992]

The Middle East | Institute | [*cut*] | Washington, D. C. | 1906 Florida Avenue, N.W. [n.d.]

On reverse of title: The Merrymount Press, Boston. Collation: [i–ii], 1–8, [9–11]. Leaf, 6⅛ × 9¼. Binding, paper. With 2 illustrations. Type, Times Roman Monotype.

The Merrymount Press

Minor Printing

The Carnegie Foundation for the Advancement of Teaching, Forty-first Annual Report of the President and of the Treasurer, New York; *also* Amending the Court Order of November 18, 1939.

Reports: John Carter Brown Library, Providence, Rhode Island, Report to the Corporation of Brown University, Providence; Boston Athenæum, Reports of the Library Committee and the Librarian for the Year 1945; Emma Pendleton Bradley Home, Fifteenth Annual Report, 1945; Butler Hospital for the Treatment of Nervous and Mental Illness, Reports for the Year 1945 (102nd Annual Report).

The Month at Goodspeed's.

Athenæum Items.

A Memoir of Four Years, Frances Crosby Bartter, August 23, 1879–June 13, 1946.

Catalogue of Saint Mark's School 1945–1946, Southborough, Massachusetts.

A Mighty Moment.

1947

[993]
The Maypole of | Merrymount | From Twice-Told | Tales by Nathaniel | Hawthorne | [*cut*] | With Greetings for | The Year MDCCCCXLVII | To the Friends of | The Merrymount Press.

Colophon: [*press mark*] Printed by D. B. Updike, The Merrymount Press at the Sign of the Maypole, 712 Beacon Street, Boston, Mass., U.S.A. Collation: i–vi, 1–29, [30]. Leaf, 4 × 6. Binding, paper. Rubricated throughout. Type, Times Roman Monotype.

[994]
Beautiful on the Earth | By | Margaret Erwin Schevill | with Five Illustrations | Reproduced from the Author's Drawings in Serigraph by | Louie Ewing | Hazel Dreis Editions | Santa Fe, New Mexico. [n.d.]

Colophon: Five hundred copies of Beautiful on the Earth have been printed under the direction of Hazel Dreis at The Merrymount Press, Boston,

[334]

Bibliography

U.S.A. The text type is monotype Bulmer and the paper Beckett Tweed Text. Collation: i–xvi, 1–155, [156]. Leaf, 8 × 10. Binding, cloth. Type, Bulmer Monotype.

[995]
Heritage from My Father | An Autobiography | By Ira Nelson Morris | [*monogram*] | New York | Privately Printed | 1947.

On reverse of title: D. B. Updike, The Merrymount Press, Boston, U.S.A. Collation: i–viii, 1–263. Leaf, 7 × 9½. Binding, cloth. With 3 collotype illustrations. Type, Caslon Monotype.

[996]
Memorial Meeting | for | Simon Flexner | Speakers | Herbert S. Gasser | Learned Hand | Peyton Rous | Raymond B. Fosdick | John D. Rockefeller, Jr. | The Rockefeller Institute for Medical Research | June Twelfth | Nineteen Hundred Forty-Six.

On reverse of title: The Merrymount Press, Boston, U.S.A. Collation: [i–ii], 1–36. Leaf, 6⅛ × 9¼. Binding, paper. With frontispiece portrait in collotype. Type, Caslon Monotype.

[997]
The Carnegie Foundation for the Advancement of Teaching | The Colleges and | The Courts | 1941–45 | Recent Judicial Decisions Regarding | Higher Education in the United States | By M. M. Chambers | Assistant Director, Commission on Implications of | Armed Services Educational Programs, | American Council on Education | With a Foreword | By Edward C. Elliott | President-emeritus, Purdue University | [*florets*] | New York City | 522 Fifth Avenue | 1946.

On reverse of title: D. B. Updike, The Merrymount Press, Boston. Collation: i–xviii, 1–156. Leaf, 6 × 9. Binding, cloth. Type, Caslon Monotype. *Also issued in paper covers.*

[998]
[*printer's ornament*] | Book of Divine Service | Morning and Evening Prayer | According to the | American Book of Common Prayer | together with | The Collects throughout the Year | The Psalter | The Holy Bible | [*florets*] | 1947 | Morehouse-Gorham Co. | New York | [*printer's ornament*].

The Merrymount Press

On reverse of title: The Merrymount Press, Boston. Collation: i–lvi, 1–254, A1–A44, [A45–A50], [i–vi], 1–767, [768], 1–235. Leaf, 4¼ × 6¹⁄₁₆. Binding, cloth. Type, Times Roman Monotype.

The Holy Bible not the work of the Press.

[999]
Memories of Fifty Years │ In the Last Century │ Written for Her Grandchildren by │ Caroline Gardiner Curtis │ and │ A Sketch of Mrs. Louis Agassiz │ By Emma Forbes Cary │ [*cut*] │ Boston │ Privately Printed │ 1947.

On reverse of title: The Merrymount Press, Boston. Collation: [i–xii], 1–145. Leaf, 5⅜ × 8⅝. Binding, cloth. With 5 illustrations, 4 of which are collotype. Type, Caslon Monotype.

[1000]
Ante Altare Dei │ Preces Ante et Post Missam │ Arranged with an Introduction │ By │ Rev. Joseph B. Collins, S.S., D.D., Ph.D. │ and │ Rev. Raphael J. Collins, B.A. │ [*cut*] │ The Newman Bookshop │ Westminster, Maryland │ 1947.

On reverse of title: The Merrymount Press, Boston. Collation: i–xiv, 1–79. Leaf, 4½ × 6⅝. Binding, cloth. Type, Times Roman Monotype.

[1001]
The │ Wedding Journey │ Walter D. Edmonds │ [*cut*] │ Drawings by Alan Tompkins │ An Atlantic Monthly Press Book │ Little, Brown and Company, Boston │ 1947.

Collation: [i–viii], 1–118, [119]. Leaf, 5¼ × 7¾. Binding, cloth. With 17 illustrations and chapter initials in colour. Type, Scotch-face Monotype.
Composition and presswork only by the Press.

[1002]
The Oak Tree Coinage of │ Massachusetts │ By │ Sydney P. Noe │ [*seal*] │ The American Numismatic Society │ Broadway at 156th Street │ New York │ 1947.

On reverse of title: The Merrymount Press, Boston, U.S.A. Collation: i–viii, 1–23, [24–28]. Leaf, 6⅛ × 9. Binding, paper. With 10 collotype plates. Type, Caslon Monotype.
Numismatic Notes and Monographs No. 110.

Bibliography

[1003]

The | American Numismatic Society | Museum Notes | II | [*seal*] | The American Numismatic Society | Broadway at 156th Street | New York | 1947.

On reverse of title: The Merrymount Press, Boston, U.S.A. Collation: i–vi, 1–118. Leaf, 4½ × 6⅝. Binding, paper. With 19 collotype plates. Type, Caslon Monotype.

[1004]

The | United States Cents | of the Years | 1795, 1796, 1797 and 1800 | By George H. Clapp and Howard R. Newcomb | [*seal*] | The American Numismatic Society | New York | 1947.

On reverse of title: The Merrymount Press, Boston, U.S.A. Collation: i–vi, 1–74. Leaf, 9⅛ × 12. Binding, cloth. Rubricated title. With 4 illustrations. Type, Caslon Monotype.

[1005]

The | Century Association | Year-Book | 1947 | [*border*] | [*floret*] | [*border*] | New York | 1947.

On last page: The Merrymount Press, Boston. Collation: [i–vi], 1–158. Leaf, 5⅜ × 6¾. Binding, cloth. Type, Times Roman Monotype.

[1006]

[*within border*] Old Testament | Stories | in Woodcut | Text from the King James | Version of the Bible | Illustrated | with Reproductions from | Works of Fifteenth and | Sixteenth Century | Artists | Compiled by | Helen Slocum Estabrook | [*rule*] | Boston, Massachusetts | The Beacon Press | MDCCCCXLVII.

On reverse of title: The Merrymount Press, Boston. Collation: i–x, 1–158, Leaf, 8⅞ × 12½. Binding, cloth. Rubricated title. With 71 illustrations. Type, Poliphilus and Blado.

[1007]

[*within border*] Scenes from the Life of Jesus | in Woodcut | Text from the | King James Version of the Bible | Illustrated with Fifteenth and | Sixteenth Century Woodcuts | Compiled by | Susan Nichols Pulsifer | [*outside of cut*] Boston, Massachusetts, The Beacon Press, MDCCCCXLVII.

[337]

The Merrymount Press

On reverse of title: The Merrymount Press, Boston. Collation: i–xii, 1–168. Leaf, 8⅞ × 12½. Binding, cloth. Title in 2 colours. With 81 illustrations. Type, Poliphilus and Blado.

[1008]

Woodcuts U.S.A. | [*cut*] | By Helen West Heller | With an introduction by John Taylor Arms | Oxford University Press, New York, 1947.

Colophon: Woodcuts U.S.A. was designed by John Begg, printed by D. B. Updike, The Merrymount Press, Boston, and bound by J. F. Tapley Company, New York. This edition, limited to 750 copies, of which 150 are offered for sale, has been printed on Enfield Collotype paper from the original wood blocks cut by Helen West Heller. This copy, signed by the Artist is No. —. Collation: [i–vi], [1–41]. Leaf, 8⅞ × 12. Binding, cloth. With 20 illustrations. Type, Times Roman Monotype.

[1009]

Woodcuts | U.S.A. | By Helen West Heller | With an introduction by John Taylor Arms | [*seal*] | Oxford University Press, New York, 1947.

Colophon: Woodcuts U.S.A. was designed by John Begg and printed by D. B. Updike, The Merrymount Press, Boston. Collation: [i–viii], [1–33]. Leaf, 5⅞ × 4¼ oblong. Binding, paper. Type, Times Roman Monotype. *The regular edition of No. 1008.*

[1010]

Three Capitals | A Book About the | First Three Capitals of Alabama | St. Stephens, Huntsville & Cahawba | [*rule*] | Including Information About the Politics, Laws, and Men of | The Territory and State of Alabama | 1818 to 1826 | Also Significant Historical Documents and Records | [*rule*] | By William H. Brantley | [*cut*] | Privately Printed | 1947.

On reverse of title: The Merrymount Press, Boston, U.S.A. Collation: [i–xii], [1–2], 1–265. Leaf, 6 × 9. Binding, cloth. With 10 illustrations, 6 of which are in photogravure and 3 are maps in colour. Type, Baskerville Monotype.

[1011]

Winthrop | Papers | Volume V | 1645–1649 | [*seal*] | The Massachusetts Historical Society | 1947.

Bibliography

On reverse of title: The Merrymount Press, Boston, Mass., U.S.A. Collation: i–xxxviii, [1–2], 1–408. Leaf, 7⅛ × 9¾. Binding, boards. With frontispiece in colour. Type, Baskerville Monotype.

[1012]

[*printer's ornament*] | The Prayer Book Office | Morning Prayer and Evening Prayer | According to the | American Book of Common Prayer | With Invitatories and Hymns | Antiphons to the Gospel Canticles | And other Enrichments | [*florets*] | 1947 | Morehouse-Gorham Co. | New York | [*printer's ornament*].

On reverse of title: The Merrymount Press, Boston. Collation: i–lxvi, 1–254, [255–256], 377–801, [802], A1–A48, [A49–A50], [i–vi], 1–767, [768], 1–235. Leaf, 4¼ × 6¹⁄₁₆. Binding, cloth. Type, Times Roman Monotype.
Reissue of No. 954 with certain omissions and corrections, and with the addition of The Holy Bible which is not the work of the Press.

[1013]

Zion Research Library | [*cut*] | 120 Seaver Street | Brookline 46, Massachusetts. [n.d.]

On reverse of title: The Merrymount Press, Boston, U.S.A. Collation: [i–iv], [1–9]. Leaf, 6⅛ × 9¼. Binding, paper. Type, Baskerville Monotype.

[1014]

Humanities and | Social Sciences | at the Massachusetts | Institute of Technology | [*dash*] | [*cut*] | [*dash*] | Cambridge | Massachusetts Institute of Technology | 1947.

On reverse of title: The Merrymount Press, Boston. Collation: [i–viii], 1–38. Leaf, 6 × 9. Binding, paper. With illustration. Type, Times Roman Monotype.
2 different cuts were used on the cover, both by Samuel Chamberlain.

[1015]

Some American Contributions | to the | Art of Navigation | 1519–1802 | By Lawrence C. Wroth | [*cut*] | Providence | The Associates of the John Carter Brown Library | 1947.

On reverse of title: The Merrymount Press, Boston. Collation: [i–ii], 1–41. Leaf, 6¼ × 9½. Binding, paper. With 9 collotype illustrations. Type, Caslon Monotype.

The Merrymount Press

Pre-printed from Proceedings of the Massachusetts Historical Society, Volume LXVIII.

Minor Printing

The Carnegie Foundation for the Advancement of Teaching, Forty-second Annual Report of the President and of the Treasurer, New York; *also* Publications of the Foundation *and* The Carnegie Foundation for the Advancement of Teaching, Reprinted from the Thirty-second Annual Report.

The Month at Goodspeed's.

Athenæum Items.

Numismatic Literature, No. 1.

Catalogue of Saint Mark's School 1946–1947, Southborough, Massachusetts.

Henry H. Hilton, In Recognition of His Long and Valued Services with Ginn and Company.

O. J. Laylander, In Recognition of His Long and Notable Services with Ginn and Company.

Reports: John Carter Brown Library, Providence, Rhode Island, Report to the Corporation of Brown University, Providence; Emma Pendleton Bradley Home, Sixteenth Annual Report, 1946; One Hundred & Tenth and Eleventh Annual Reports, Providence Athenæum, Providence; Butler Hospital for the Treatment of Nervous and Mental Illness, Reports for the Year 1946 (103rd Annual Report); Boston Athenæum, Reports of the Library Committee and the Librarian for the Year 1946.

History of Spain, I Old Stone Age; II New Stone Age.

The Way of the Cross, Baguio, Mission of the Resurrection, 1947.

An Office of Compline, Reprinted from "The Prayer Book Office."

Preparation and Thanksgiving, Reprinted from "The Prayer Book Office."

Bibliography
1948

[1016]

Arthur Young | and | The Business He Founded | (Personal Reminiscences) | New York | Privately Printed | 1948.

On reverse of title: The Merrymount Press, Boston, U.S.A. Collation: i–xii, [1–2], 1–71. Leaf, 5⅜ × 8⅝. Binding, cloth. With 7 photogravure illustrations. Type, Caslon Monotype.

[1017]

Early Arabic | Glass Weights and Stamps | By George C. Miles | With a Study of the Manufacture of | Eighth-Century Egyptian Glass Weights and Stamps | By Frederick R. Matson | [seal] | The American Numismatic Society | Broadway at 156th Street | New York | 1948.

On reverse of title: The Merrymount Press, Boston, U.S.A. Collation: i–viii, 1–168, [169–172]. Leaf, 6⅛ × 9. Binding, paper. With 14 collotype plates. Type, Caslon Monotype.

[1018]

The Fox Club | Founded in 1898 | [cut] | Cambridge | Printed for the Club | 1948.

On reverse of title: The Merrymount Press, Boston. Collation: 1–56. Leaf, 5 × 7½. Binding, paper. Type, Times Roman Monotype.

[1019]

Porcellian Club | in | World War II | [cut] | Cambridge | Printed for the Club | 1948.

On reverse of title: The Merrymount Press, Boston. Collation: i–xii, 1–162, [163]. Leaf, 6 × 9¼. Binding, cloth. With 24 collotype illustrations. Type, Baskerville Monotype.

[1020]

Velazquez | By | Elizabeth Du Gué Trapier | Member of The Hispanic Society of America | [seal] | With 252 Illustrations | Printed by Order of | The Trustees | New York | 1948.

Collation: i–xxii, 1–434. Leaf, 9 × 12. Binding, cloth. Type, Times Roman Monotype.

[341]

The Merrymount Press

[1021]

The Log | of | Cleopatra's | Barge II | 1928-1942 | Boston, Privately Printed, 1948.

On reverse of title: D. B. Updike, The Merrymount Press, Boston. Collation: i–xviii, 1–280. Leaf, 9 × 11. Binding, half leather. Rubricated title. With 12 collotype illustrations. Type, Times Roman Monotype.

[1022]

The Walpole Society | [*within cut*] A | Tribute to | Its | Founders | Original Members | and Other | Walpoleans | of Their Time | [*outside of cut*] Boston, Privately Printed, 1948.

Colophon: Of The Walpole Society: A Tribute to Its Founders, Original Members and Other Walpoleans of Their Time, fifty-two copies have been printed on special Worthy Hand and Arrows by D. B. Updike, The Merrymount Press, Boston, U.S.A., in July 1948. Collation: i–viii, 1–68, [69]. Leaf, 4¾ × 7¾. Binding, boards. Title and opening page of Foreword in 2 colours. Type, Mountjoye.
Various patterns of Italian Block (Rizzi) paper used in the binding.

[1023]

Rena Van Slyke | In Memoriam | by | Aura E. Severinghaus | [*cut*] | January sixth, 1948.

On reverse of title: The Merrymount Press, Boston. Collation: 1–10. Leaf, 5¾ × 8⅜. Binding, paper. With photogravure portrait. Type, Janson.

[1024]

Charting My Life | By | Henry Howard | Boston | The Merry mount Press. [n.d.]

On reverse of title: D. B. Updike, The Merrymount Press, Boston. Collation: i–xxvi, 1–398. Leaf, 6 × 9¼. Binding, cloth. With 44 collotype illustrations. Type, Baskerville Monotype.

[1025]

The Carnegie Foundation for the Advancement of Teaching | Charters of | Philanthropies | A Study of Selected Trust Instruments, Charters, | By-Laws, and Court Decisions | By M. M. Chambers | Director, Foreign Universities | Project of the | American Council on Eduation | With a Foreword | By Edward C. Elliott | President-emeritus, Purdue University | [*florets*] | New York City | 522 Fifth Avenue | 1948.

Bibliography

On reverse of title: D. B. Updike, The Merrymount Press, Boston. Collation: i–viii, 1–247. Leaf, 6 × 9. Binding, cloth. Type, Caslon Monotype. *Also issued in paper covers.*

[1026]

[*within rules*] The Winthrop Family | in America | [*rule*] | By | Lawrence Shaw Mayo | [*rule*] | [*arms*] | [*rule*] | Boston | The Massachusetts Historical Society | 1948.

On reverse of title: The Merrymount Press, Boston, U.S.A. Collation: i–xii, 1–507. Leaf, 8¼ × 11⅛. Binding, cloth With 23 illustrations in photogravure, Confirmation of the Winthrop Grant of Arms in colour, and folding Genealogical Chart. Type, Caslon Monotype.

[1027]

The American Numismatic Society | Museum Notes | III | [*seal*] | The American Numismatic Society | Broadway at 156th Street | New York | 1948.

On reverse of title: The Merrymount Press, Boston, U.S.A. Collation: i–vi, 1–154. Leaf, 6⅛ × 9. Binding, paper. With 26 collotype plates. Type, Caslon Monotype.

[1028]

Three Essays | By | Lawrence Shaw Mayo | An Appreciation | With a Bibliography | Boston | Privately Printed | 1948.

On reverse of title: The Merrymount Press, Boston, U.S.A. Colophon: This Memorial Volume is limited to an edition of three hundred copies. Collation: i–x, 1–94, [95]. Leaf, 5⅜ × 8⅝. Binding, cloth. With photogravure portrait. Type, Caslon Monotype.

[1029]

The | Century Association | Year-Book | 1948 | [*border*] | [*floret*] | [*border*] | New York | 1948.

On last page: The Merrymount Press, Boston, Mass. Collation: i–vi, 1–121, [122]. Leaf, 5¼ × 6¾. Binding, cloth. Type, Times Roman Monotype.

[1030]

Humanities and | Social Sciences | at the Massachusetts | Institute of Technology | [*dash*] | [*cut*] | [*dash*] | Cambridge | Massachusetts Institute of Technology | 1948.

[343]

The Merrymount Press

On reverse of title: The Merrymount Press, Boston. Collation: [i–viii], 1–38. Leaf, 6 × 9. Binding, paper. With illustration. Type, Times Roman Monotype.

Reissue of No. 1014 with minor textual changes.

[1031]

The Middle East | Institute | [*cut*] | Washington, D.C. | 1906 Florida Avenue, N.W. [n.d.]

On reverse of title: The Merrymount Press, Boston. Collation: [i–ii], 1–13, [14–16]. Leaf, 6⅛ × 9¼. Binding, paper. With 1 illustration. Type, Times Roman Monotype.

Reissue of No. 992 with additional material.

[1032]

[*within border*] Henry | David | Thoreau | [*ornament*] | Quotations | from his Writings | Selected by | Amy W. Smith | [*ornament*] | Achille J. St. Onge | Worcester · 1948.

Colophon: [*border*] Seven hundred and fifty copies of Selected Quotations from the Writings of Henry David Thoreau were printed on Worthy Hand and Arrows paper by The Merrymount Press, Boston, Mass^tts. [*border*]. Collation: [i–x], 1–33, [34–35]. Leaf, 2 × 3. Binding, cloth. With half-tone portrait. Type, Monotype Scotch-face.

Minor Printing

The Carnegie Foundation for the Advancement of Teaching, Forty-third Annual Report of the President and of the Treasurer, New York.

The Month at Goodspeed's (January to June).

Athenæum Items.

Reports: Boston Athenæum, Reports of the Library Committee, the Director, and the Treasurer for the Year 1947; Emma Pendleton Bradley Home, Seventeenth Annual Report, 1947.

Catalogue of Saint Mark's School 1947–1948, Southborough, Massachusetts.

The Cambridge "Platform of Church Discipline" 1648. The Historical Narrative of the Platform by Frederick L. Fagley. The Significance and Influence of The Platform by Henry Wilder Foote.

Bibliography

The Pastel Portraits of Consuelo Cloos.

Members of the Middle East Institute, June 1, 1948.

Reef Point Gardens Bulletin Vol. I, No. 3.

The Ninth Annual Liturgical Week, Boston.

New York Academy of Sciences Publications: Current Trends in Clinical Psychology; Teleological Mechanisms; The Inhibition of Malarial Relapses by Toxoid of *Clostridium Tetani*; Recent Studies in the Mechanisms of Embryonic Development; Newer Synthetic Analgesics; The Mechanics of Development.

1949

[1033]

Morning and Night | Family Prayers for | Daily Use in Common | Compiled by | Benjamin Francis Musser | [*cut*] | The Newman Press | Westminster, Maryland | 1949.

On reverse of title: The Merrymount Press, Boston. Collation: i–x, 1–45, [46]. Leaf, 4½ × 6⅝. Binding, cloth. Type, Times Roman Monotype.

[1034]

"Barbarous Radiates" | Imitations of Third-Century Roman Coins | By Philip V. Hill | [*seal*] | The American Numismatic Society | Broadway at 156th Street | New York | 1949.

On reverse of title: The Merrymount Press, Boston. Collation: [i–viii], 1–44, [45–48]. Leaf, 6⅛ × 9. Binding, paper. With 4 collotype plates. Type, Caslon Monotype.
Numismatic Notes and Monographs No. 112.

[1035]

Notes on the Early | Coinage of Transoxiana | By Richard N. Frye | [*seal*] | The American Numismatic Society | Broadway at 156th Street | New York | 1949.

On reverse of title: The Merrymount Press, Boston. Collation: [i–vi], 1–49, [50–54]. Leaf, 6⅛ × 9. Binding, paper. With frontispiece in collotype. Type, Caslon Monotype.
Numismatic Notes and Monographs No. 113.

[345]

The Merrymount Press

Minor Printing

One Hundred & Twelfth and Thirteenth Annual Reports, Providence
Athenæum, Providence.

New York Academy of Sciences Publications: Thyroid Function as
disclosed by Newer Methods of Study.

Appendix

Annual Keepsakes

PRINTED FOR THE FRIENDS OF THE
MERRYMOUNT PRESS

1903. At the Sign of the May-Pole
Designed by Mary J. Newill

1910. Song: "Orpheus with his lute made trees"
Decoration from old Italian copper-plate

1910. A Keepsake printed for the Friends of The Merrymount Press
English eighteenth-century decorative design

1912. A View of the Old State House, Boston
This and all the following Keepsakes except that for 1925 were designed and engraved by Rudolph Ruzicka

1913. A View of Faneuil Hall, Boston

1914. A View of the Old West Church, Boston

1915. A Corner of Louisburg Square, Beacon Hill, Boston

1916. A View of Bunker Hill Monument, Charlestown

1917. A View of the First Church, Lancaster, Massachusetts

1918. A View of Camp Devens, near Ayer, Massachusetts

1919. Armistice Day Design

1920. The Custom-house Tower, Boston

1921. A View of Beacon Hill, Boston

1922. A View of Charles Street Church, Boston

1923. A View of the Granary Burying-ground, Boston

1924. A View of University Hall, Harvard University

1925. Decorative Design
Reproduced from engraving by Jean Pillement

1926. A View of the House of Seven Gables, Salem, Massachusetts

[349]

The Merrymount Press

Specimen

OF THE CHIEF TEXT TYPES USED AT
THE MERRYMOUNT PRESS

LETTRE BATARDE   *Acquired 1901*

The name of The Merrymount Press is derived from
the ancient estate of a certain Thomas Morton, a very
sturdy Englishman, who with a company of friends
emigrated to New England in 1628. Bradford, in the
second book of his History of Plymouth, says: "Aboute
some three or four years before this time, there came
over one Captaine Wollastone (a man of pretie parts),
& with him three or four more of some eminencie, who

LETTRE DE SOMME   *Acquired 1901*

brought with them a great many servants, with provisions & other impla//
ments for to begine a plantation; and pitched themselves in a place within
the Massachusets, which they called, after their Captaine's name, Mount//
Wollaston. Amongst whom was one Mr. Morton, who, it should seem, had
some small adventure (of his owne or other mens) amongst them." Morton,
with the others, settled at Wollaston, near Quincy, calling his house Ma//re
Mount, or Merrymount; a name still attaching to that locality. About the
character of Morton, opinions differ. By some he is described as a roystering,
worthless fellow, who made Merrymount the scene of carousal and the home
of the idle ne'er//do//well. Others have painted his picture as that of an easy//

PICA ENGLISH BLACK   *Acquired 1898*

going country gentleman, more Cavalier than
Roundhead in his tendencies, whose attachment
to the Church of England led to malignment by
his Puritan neighbours. Probably neither one
nor yet the other view is true. But it is true that
he made Merrymount the scene of old English
sports, and that he there set up a Maypole; per=
haps as a protest against the gloomy life of the

[351]

The Merrymount Press

JANSON   *Acquired 1903*

Puritans. Morton, in that odd old book, The New English Canaan, says that "the Inhabitants of Pasonagessit, (having translated the name of their habitation from that ancient Salvage name to Ma-re Mount, and being resolved to have the new name confirmed for a memorial to after ages,) did devise amongst themselves to have it performed in a solemne manner, with Revels and merriment after the old English custome; [they] prepared to sett up a

CASLON   *Acquired 1896*

Maypole upon the festivall day of Philip and Jacob, and therefore brewed a barrell of excellent beare and provided a case of bottles, to be spent, with other good cheare, for all comers of that day. And because they would have it in a compleat forme, they had prepared a song fitting to the time and present occasion. And upon Mayday they brought the Maypole to the place appointed, with drumes, gunnes, pistols and other fitting instruments, for that purpose; and there erected it with

MOUNTJOYE (BELL)   *Acquired 1903*

the help of Salvages, that came thither of purpose to see the manner of our Revels. A goodly pine tree of 80. foote longe was reared up, with a peare of buckshorns nayled one somewhat neare unto the top of it: where it stood, as a faire sea marke for directions how to finde out the way to mine Host of Ma-re Mount." As to the real Morton, the reader may suit his own prejudices, which, if adverse,

[352]

Specimen of Types

may be made more so by the biographical sketch prefixed to an edition of Morton's New English Canaan; or if more favourable, by Hawthorne's pretty web of romance spun around The Maypole of Merrymount in Twice-Told Tales. It is enough for the purpose of The Merrymount Press, if, in disregard of any analogies or paradoxes with which curious persons bewilder themselves, we regard the Maypole as a symbol of happiness found in workaday things; of a high aim and pleasure in trying to attain it,

an ideal to which The Merrymount Press has always endeavoured to be true. The name of The Merrymount Press is derived from the ancient estate of a certain Thomas Morton, which now gives title to a suburb of Quincy. He was a sturdy Englishman, who with a company of friends emigrated to New England in 1628. Bradford, in the second book of his History of Plymouth, says: "Aboute some three or four years before this time, there came over one Captaine Wollastone (a man of pretie parts), & with him three or four more of some eminen-

cie, who brought with them a great many servants, with provisions & other implaments for to begine a plantation; and pitched themselves in a place within the Massachusets, which they called, after their Captaine's name, Mount-Wollaston. Amongst whom was one Mr. Morton, who, it should seem, had some small adventure (of his owne or other mens) amongst them." Morton, with the others, settled at Wollaston,

[353]

The Merrymount Press

near Quincy, calling his house Ma-re Mount, or Merry-mount; a name still attaching to that locality. About the character of Morton, opinions differ. By some he is described as a roystering, worthless fellow, who made Merry-mount the scene of carousal and the home of the idle ne'er-do-well. Others have painted his picture as that of an easy-going country gentleman, more Cavalier than Round-head in his tendencies, whose attachment to the Church of England led to malignment by his Puritan neighbours.

Probably neither one nor yet the other view is true. But it is true that he made Merrymount a scene of old English sports, and that he there set up a Maypole; perhaps as a protest against the gloomy life of the Puritans. Morton, in that odd old book, The New English Canaan, says that "the Inhabitants of Pasonages-sit, (having translated the name of their habitation from that ancient Salvage name to Ma-re Mount, and being resolved to have the new name confirmed for a

memorial to after ages,) did devise amongst them-selves to have it performed in a solemne manner, with Revels and merriment after the old English custome; [they] prepared to sett up a Maypole upon the festivall day of Philip and Jacob, and therefore brewed a barrell of excellent beare and provided a case of bottles, to be spent, with other good cheare, for all comers of that day. And be-cause they would have it in a compleat forme,

Specimen of Types

they had prepared a song fitting to the time and present occasion. And upon Mayday they brought the Maypole to the place appointed, with drumes, gunnes, pistols and other fitting instruments, for that purpose; and there erected it with the help of Salvages, that came thither of purpose to see the manner of our Revels. A goodly pine tree of 80. foote longe was reared up, with a peare of buckshorns nayled one somewhat neare unto the top of it: where it stood, as a faire sea marke for directions how to find out the way to mine Host

SCOTCH–FACE ITALIC

of Ma-re Mount." As to the real Morton, the reader may suit his own prejudices, which, if adverse, may be made more so by the biographical sketch prefixed to an edition of Morton's New English Canaan; or if more favourable, by Hawthorne's pretty web of romance spun around The Maypole of Merrymount in Twice-Told Tales. It is enough for the purpose of The Merrymount Press, if, in disregard of any analogies or paradoxes with which curious persons bewilder themselves,

FRENCH SCRIPT   *Acquired 1910*

we regard the Maypole as a symbol of happiness found in workaday things; of a high aim and pleasure in trying to attain it, an ideal to which The Merrymount Press has always endeavoured to be true.

The name of The Merrymount Press is derived from the ancient estate of a certain Thomas Morton, which now gives title to a suburb of Quincy. He was a sturdy Englishman, who with a company of friends

[355]

The Merrymount Press

BODONI *Acquired 1930*
emigrated to New England in 1628. Bradford, in
the second book of his History of Plymouth, says:
"Aboute some three or four years before this time,
there came over one Captaine Wollastone (a man
of pretie parts), & with him three or four more of
some eminencie, who brought with them a great
many servants, with provisions & other implaments for to begine a plantation; and pitched themselves in a place within the Massachusets, which

POLIPHILUS *Acquired 1925*
they called, after their Captaine's name, Mount⁄Wollas⁄
ton. Amongst whom was one Mr. Morton, who, it should
seem, had some small adventure (of his owne or other
mens) amongst them." Morton, with the others, settled at
Wollaston, near Quincy, calling his house Ma⁄re Mount,
or Merrymount; a name still attaching to that locality.
About the character of Morton, opinions differ. By some
he is described as a roystering, worthless fellow, who
made Merrymount the scene of carousal and the home of

LUTETIA *Acquired 1927*
the idle ne'er-do-well. Others have painted his picture as
that of an easy-going country gentleman, more Cavalier
than Roundhead in his tendencies, whose attachment to
the Church of England led to malignment by his Puritan
neighbours. Probably neither one nor yet the other view
is true. But it is true that he made Merrymount the scene
of old English sports, and that he there set up a Maypole;
perhaps as a protest against the gloomy life of the Puritans. Morton, in that odd old book, The New English

Specimen of Types

Canaan, says that "the Inhabitants of Pasonages-sit, (having translated the name of their habitation from that ancient Salvage name to Ma-re Mount, and being resolved to have the new name confirmed for a memorial to after ages,) did devise amongst themselves to have it performed in a solemne manner, with Revels and merriment after the old English custome; [they] prepared to sett up a Maypole upon the festivall day of Philip and Jacob, and

therefore brewed a barrell of excellent beare and provided a case of bottles, to be spent, with other good cheare, for all comers of that day. And because they would have it in a compleat forme, they had prepared a song fitting to the time and present occasion. And upon Mayday they brought the Maypole to the place appointed, with drumes, gunnes, pistols and other fitting instruments, for that purpose; and there erected it with the help of Salvages, that came thither of purpose to see the manner of our Revels. A goodly pine tree of 80. foote longe was reared up, with a peare

of buckshorns nayled one somewhat neare unto the top of it: where it stood, as a faire sea marke for directions how to finde out the way to mine Host of Ma-re Mount." As to the real Morton, the reader may suit his own prejudices, which, if adverse, may be made more so by the biographical sketch prefixed to an edition of Morton's New English Canaan; or if more favourable, by Hawthorne's pretty web of romance spun around The Maypole of Merrymount in Twice-Told Tales. It is enough for the purpose of The Merrymount Press, if in disregard of any analogies or paradoxes with which

The Merrymount Press

MONTALLEGRO (NO ITALIC)   *Acquired 1904*
curious persons bewilder themselves, we regard
the Maypole as a symbol of happiness found in
workaday things; of a high aim and pleasure in
trying to attain it, an ideal to which The Merrymount Press has always endeavoured to be true.

MERRYMOUNT (NO ITALIC)   *Acquired 1894*
The name of the Merrymount Press
is derived from the ancient estate of a
certain Thomas Morton, a sturdy Eng'
lishman, who with a company of friends
emigrated to New England in 1628.

The above types were specially cut for the Press
Herbert Horne designing the Montallegro
and Bertram Grosvenor Goodhue
the Merrymount fount